CHILDREN'S DAILY PRAYER

for the School Year 2019–2020

Margaret Burk
and Vivian E. Williams

LTP

LITURGY
TRAINING
PUBLICATIONS

Nihil Obstat
Reverend Mr. Daniel G. Welter, JD
Chancellor
Archdiocese of Chicago
October 23, 2018

Imprimatur
Most Reverend Ronald A. Hicks
Vicar General
Archdiocese of Chicago
October 23, 2018

The *Nihil Obstat* and *Imprimatur* are official declarations that the material is free from doctrinal or moral error, and thus is granted permission to publish in accordance with c. 827. No legal responsibility is assumed by the grant of this permission. No implication is contained herein that those who have granted the *Nihil Obstat* and *Imprimatur* agree with the content, opinions, or statements expressed.

Many of the concepts and guidelines, as well as various prayer services offered in this book, were originally conceived and developed by Dr. Sofia Cavalletti, Ms. Gianna Gobbi, and their collaborators. Theological underpinnings and many elements of these prayer services were first documented in Cavalletti's foundational books including, *The Religious Potential of the Child* and *The Religious Potential of the Child, 6 to 12 Years Old*.

Liturgy Training Publications acknowledges the significant contribution made by Elizabeth McMahon Jeep to the development of *Children's Daily Prayer*. For more than fifteen years, Ms. Jeep worked tirelessly to cultivate this book into the essential prayer resource it is today for children and their parents, as well for teachers and catechists. We are indebted to her for her authorship and guidance.

CHILDREN'S DAILY PRAYER 2019–2020 © 2019 Archdiocese of Chicago: Liturgy Training Publications, 3949 South Racine Avenue, Chicago, IL 60609; 800-933-1800; orders@ltp.org; fax 800-933-7094. All rights reserved. See our website at www.LTP.org.

Closing prayers written by Margaret Brennan.

The cover art is by Mikela Prevost, and the interior art is by Paula Wiggins © LTP. Paper Clip image by Babich Alexander, used under license from Shutterstock.com. This book was compiled by Margaret Brennan and edited by Michaela I. Tudela; Lauren L. Murphy was the production editor; Juan Alberto Castillo was the designer and production artist.

Printed in the United States of America

ISBN 978-1-61671-459-8

CDP20

CONTENTS

CONTENTS

The editors appreciate your feedback.
Email: cdp@ltp.org.

UNDERSTANDING THE ORDER OF PRAYER

Children's Daily Prayer is a form of the Liturgy of the Hours, adapted for children. It is based on the Church's tradition of Morning Prayer. A selected psalm is prayed for several weeks at a time. The readings for the daily prayers have been chosen to help children become familiar with significant themes and major stories in Scripture. The Sunday reading is always the Gospel of the day. Reflection questions for silent meditation or group conversation follow the reading.

For schools and homeschooling families, this book provides an order of prayer for each day of the school year (Prayer for the Day). For religious education settings, it provides prayer services for once a week (Prayer for the Week). Not every prayer element in the order of prayer will be useful in every situation. From the elements listed below, you can choose the ones that will be most effective for your group, setting, and time available.

OPENING

This gives the context for the Scripture reading and, when space allows, introduces the saint to be remembered that day. It also indicates when a particular theme or focus will be followed for the week. Sometimes difficult words or concepts in the reading are explained.

SIGN OF THE CROSS

An essential ritual action Catholics use to begin and end prayer. By making the Sign of the Cross, we place ourselves in the presence of the Father, the Son, and the Holy Spirit. Young children may need to practice making the Sign of the Cross.

PSALM

Praying the psalm is central to Morning Prayer. You may use the short version on the prayer page or the longer version on the Reproducible Psalms pages.

READING OR GOSPEL

Daily Scripture texts have been carefully selected to help children "walk through the Bible" and become familiar with the great stories and themes of Salvation History. By following a story or exploring a theme for several days, the children experience how God has spoken to us through the words of Scripture and also through particular people and events in history. They begin to see how people have cooperated with God in bringing about God's Kingdom on earth and to realize their role in this great work. The Prayer for the Week always uses the Sunday Gospel.

FOR SILENT REFLECTION

This is designed to be a time of silence so the children can ponder the Scripture they have heard and experience the value of silence in prayer. You might prefer to use this question at another time when discussing the reading or for journal writing. You may want to substitute your own instruction and questions. Regardless, some silence should be kept after proclaiming the Scripture.

CLOSING PRAYER

This prayer element begins with intercessions and ends with a brief prayer related to the liturgical season. In preparing for daily prayer, children can write the intercessions for the day and include relevant events to school and classroom life, as well as the world. They can also be encouraged to offer their own intentions spontaneously. You may choose to end with the Our Father.

PRAYER SERVICES

Children need to learn that the Church's prayer forms are rich and varied. We have the celebration of the Eucharist and traditional prayers such as the Rosary. We also have a long tradition of other forms of prayer, such as the Liturgy of the Hours, which emphasizes the psalms, or the Liturgy of the Word, which focuses on Holy Scripture. Additional prayer services are offered in this book for specific liturgical times, memorials, feasts, or solemnities. (Check the table of contents.) You may prefer to use one of these instead of the Prayer for the Day. Consider using these prayer services when the whole school gathers to celebrate a season. You might add an entrance procession and children and adults can do the ministerial roles.

GRACE BEFORE MEALS AND PRAYER AT DAY'S END

In order to instill in children the habit of prayer, use these prayers before lunch or at the end of the day.

PSALMS AND CANTICLES

Additional psalms and canticles (liturgical songs from the Bible: e.g., the Magnificat) are provided at the end of the book, and you will find many more in your Bible. Substitute these for any of the psalm excerpts in the prayer services or pray these with the children at any time a different choice is better for what is happening in your classroom community.

HOME PRAYERS

Children enjoy connecting their classroom and home lives. The Home Prayers offer a wonderful catechetical tool and resource for family prayer. You may photocopy these pages to send home.

CREATING A SACRED SPACE AND TIME FOR PRAYER

Children and adults benefit from having a consistent time for prayer. Where possible, it is helpful to the formation of prayer life to have a "sacred space"—that is, a designated place or table with religious objects such as the Bible, a cross, a beautiful cloth that reflects the color of the liturgical season. The introductions to each liturgical season will offer specific ideas on how to do the following:

1. Use the language in the introduction to help the children understand the character of the time.

2. Look for practical suggestions for how to celebrate the liturgical time in a classroom setting:

- how to arrange a sacred space within the classroom
- what colors and objects to use in the sacred space
- what songs to sing in each liturgical time
- suggestions for special prayers for that liturgical time and how best to introduce them to children
- help with adapting ideas from this book to special circumstances, especially for catechists who meet with students once a week

HOW CHILDREN PRAY

THE YOUNGEST CHILDREN

Children are natural liturgists and theologians. Young children (up until age 6) will pray simple but profound acclamations when they are given a real opportunity to hear the Word of God or to experience the language of signs found in our liturgy. Their spontaneous prayers most often reflect their understanding of the Word of God, their thanksgiving for God's goodness, and the joy they receive in their relationship with Christ. Here are some examples of prayers collected by catechists: "Thank you, Lord, for the light!" (a 3-year-old); "Thank you

TIPS FOR GIVING CHILDREN A GREATER ROLE IN PRAYER

This book is intended to be used by children. It will help them become comfortable as leaders of prayer and will form them in the habit of daily prayer.

1. Ideally daily prayer takes place at the beginning of the day in individual classrooms. Consider inviting the children to work in groups to prepare and lead the prayer in your classroom. The group can take on the roles of leader, psalmist, lector, and perhaps music leader for the *Alleluia*. An intercessor might compose and lead a few petitions and then invite the class to add individual ones.

2. If it is necessary to begin the prayer over the public address system, consider doing only the opening and Sign of the Cross over the loud speaker. Then invite the individual classrooms to continue the prayer in their own setting.

3. If you wish to lead the whole prayer over the public address system, consider inviting children from the various grades to do the roles listed in the first paragraph.

4. To help the younger children learn to lead prayer consider inviting older children to lead in the lower grade classrooms as mentioned in item one.

5. Invite your older students to help orient the younger ones to the prayer service. The older ones can help the younger ones practice the readings and compose intercessions so that eventually the younger ones can lead prayer in their own classrooms.

for everything!" (a 4-year-old); "I love you!" (a 3-year-old); and "I want to take a bath in your light" (a 4-year-old). These prayers point to the young child's ability to appreciate the greatest of realities: life in relationship with God.

When praying with these "little ones," it is best to proclaim the Scripture (explaining difficult words in advance to help their understanding) and then to ask one or two open-ended questions to help them to reflect on what the passage is saying to them. If you then invite them to say something to Jesus about what they've heard, you may be surprised at what comes out of the mouths of those budding little theologians!

PRAYING WITH OLDER CHILDREN

Older children (ages 6–12) begin to appreciate the gift of prayer language. We should go slowly and use a light touch, though. When they're younger, give them one beautiful phrase ("Our Father, who art in heaven") that they can begin to appreciate and love. As they grow you can add a second phrase, then a third. But make sure that they understand the words they are using, and encourage them to pray slowly.

Older children also enjoy leading prayer and composing their own prayers. If you give them each a small prayer journal and give them time to write in it, they will produce meaningful prayers and little theological drawings (particularly if you give them time to write and draw right after reading Scripture together).

PSALMS

The psalms offer a treasure trove of prayer language. Consider praying with one or two verses at a time. You could write one or two verses onto an unlined index card and display it up on your prayer table. You can invite older children to copy them into their prayer journals. But remember to go over each word with the class, asking them to reflect on what the prayer wants to say to God. Children need time to explore the rich implications in their prayer. Also, psalms may be sung or chanted (after all, they were written as songs). Perhaps a parish cantor or choir member would lead a sung version of the psalm once in a while. At least the refrain might be sung on one note.

MUSIC IN PRAYER

It is a fact that the songs we sing in church are all prayers, so include singing in your classroom prayer life. What a wonderful difference it makes! Don't be shy, and don't worry about how well you sing. Even if you don't think you have a good voice, children will happily sing with you. So go ahead and make a joyful noise! Children enjoy the chance to lift their voices to God. You may even have a few gifted singers in the class who can help you lead the singing.

The best music to use in the classroom is what your parish sings during the Sunday liturgy. You might incorporate the Penitential Act ("Lord Have Mercy, Christ Have Mercy, Lord Have Mercy") in Lent, the refrain of the Gloria in Easter, the Gospel Acclamation (Alleluia), even a chanted Our Father. But any songs, hymns, or chants that your parish sings would be a good choice. Your parish music director or diocesan director of music can be good resources.

Also, in the introductions to each liturgical time, you will find a wealth of music suggestions.

ART AS PRAYER

Once in a while suggest the children draw a picture after having heard the Scripture reading. Their drawings often reveal their joy and love in ways that language can't always express. Some children are more visual than verbal. Drawing allows them to lengthen and deepen their enjoyment of prayer time.

Don't give the children assignments or themes for these "prayer" drawings, and don't offer a lot of fancy art supplies or media. The best, most reverent drawings come from children who are simply invited to draw something that has to do with what they have just heard in the Scripture reading, something to do with the Mass, or anything to do with God. These open-ended suggestions allow the Holy Spirit room to enter into the children's work.

PRAYER CANNOT BE EVALUATED

This book is most often used in school or religious education programs. In these settings, teachers are often required to give children a grade in religion. However, prayer is not class work and teachers and catechists who have any choice in the matter should make certain **not to give the children a grade for prayer!** Prayer expresses an inner, mysterious reality, for which teachers can provide the environment. Prayer is a person's conversation with God. Consider Jesus' teaching on prayer (Matthew 6:5–13) or take a close look at his parable of the Pharisee and the tax collector (Luke 18:9–14). We don't want the children to pray for the benefit of a grade or praise from the teacher; rather, we want them to pray from their feeling of relationship with a listening God.

JOY

In all you do with the children, feel free to communicate your joy to them, especially your joy in praying. Joy is a great sign of the presence of Christ. If you take pleasure in your students' company, they will understand that they are precious children of God. If you take pleasure in your work, they will understand that work is a beautiful gift. If you listen to them and take their words seriously, you will be incarnating Christ, who so valued children.

Perhaps you will be the initial prayer leader and model that role. Something to model is a relaxed attitude when things go wrong (e.g., someone begins the Scripture too early). Try to give simple, clear directions ahead of time and then correct the situation as gently as possible. While you must keep order in your classrooms and an atmosphere of dignity in prayer, don't be afraid of a little silliness at times. Both laughter and tears are signs of the presence of the Holy Spirit.

ABOUT THE AUTHORS

Vivian E. Williams holds a master of arts degree in pastoral studies, with a concentration in Word and Worship, from Catholic Theological Union, Chicago. She formerly served as liturgy director for the St. Giles Family Mass Community in Oak Park, Illinois; a Catholic school teacher; and a parish catechist. Vivian writes and speaks on topics related to liturgy, ministry, and catechesis. She is the author of *Classroom Prayer Basics* (Oregon Catholic Press), co-author of the *When Children Gather* series (GIA Publications, Inc.) and *Children's Liturgy of the Word 2016-2017* (Liturgy Training Publications), and a contributor to *Sourcebook for Sundays, Seasons and Weekdays* (Liturgy Training Publications) in 2012 and 2013.

Margaret Burk has a masters of arts degree in communication from Michigan State University and has done additional study at Catholic Theological Union. She completed three hundred hours of certification in the Catechesis of the Good Shepherd training and has been a catechist for over twenty years.

Theresa Marshall-Patterson wrote the Prayer Services. She is director of RCIA and liturgical ministries at St. Vincent de Paul Catholic Church in Wichita, Kansas.

ABOUT THE ARTISTS AND THE ART

The cover art is by illustrator Mikela Prevost, who received her BA in painting from the University of Redlands, California, and her MFA from California State Fullerton. Her artistic rendering of children leading prayer and praying together in the classroom captures the spirit and intent of this annual resource.

The interior art is by Paula Wiggins, who lives and works in Cincinnati. At the top of the page for each day's prayer, you will find a little picture that reflects on the liturgical time. During Ordinary Time in the autumn, a sturdy mustard tree with tiny seeds blowing from it reminds us of the parable of the mustard seed. For Advent we find the familiar Advent wreath. During the short season of Christmas Time, there is a manger scene with sheep and a dove. As we begin counting Ordinary Time, we find an oyster shell with pearls—an image for the parable of the pearl of great price. During Lent, bare branches remind us of this time of living simply, without decoration and distraction, so that we can feel God's presence. During Easter Time, we find the empty tomb in the early dawn of the first Easter. And as we return to Ordinary Time after Pentecost, a beautiful grape vine reminds us of Jesus' parable of the vine and the branches.

At the beginning of each new liturgical time, special art accompanies the Grace before Meals and Prayer at Day's End, and you will find appropriate scenes for the various prayer services throughout the year. Finally, notice the harps accompanying the psalms, reminding us that these prayers were originally sung. The incense on the pages of canticles pictures the way we want our prayers to rise to God.

A NOTE ABOUT COPIES

As a purchaser of this book, you have permission to duplicate only the Reproducible Psalms pages, the Grace before Meals and Prayer at Day's End pages, the Prayer Services, and the Home Prayer pages; these copies may be used only with your class or group. The Home Prayer pages may be used only in the students' households. You may not duplicate the psalms or prayers unless you are using them with this book. Other parts of this book may not be duplicated without the permission of Liturgy Training Publications or the copyright holders listed on the acknowledgments page.

INSTRUCTIONS FOR PRAYER FOR THE DAY AND WEEK

FOR THE WHOLE GROUP

All of us participate in the prayer each day by lifting our hearts and voices to God. When the leader begins a Scripture passage by saying, "A reading from the holy Gospel according to . . . ," we respond "Glory to you, O Lord." At the conclusion of the Gospel, we say, "Praise to you, Lord Jesus Christ." At the conclusion of other Scripture readings, we say, "Thanks be to God." We offer our prayers and our intentions to God. When we conclude a prayer we say, "Amen."

Amen means: "Yes! I believe it is true!" Let your "Amen" be heard by all.

FOR THE LEADER

1. Find the correct page and read it silently. Parts in bold black type are for everyone. All others are for you alone.

2. Practice reading your part aloud, and pronounce every syllable clearly. The parts marked with ◆ and ✚ are instructions for what to do. Follow the instructions but do not read them or the headings aloud. If you stumble over a word, repeat it until you can say it smoothly.

3. Pause after "A reading from the holy Gospel according to . . . " so the class can respond. Pause again after "The Gospel of the Lord." Remember to allow for silence when the instructions call for it, especially after the Gospel and after reading the questions "For Silent Reflection."

4. Pause after "Let us bring our hopes and needs to God . . . " so that individuals may offer their prayers aloud or in silence. After each petition, the group responds, "Lord, hear our prayer."

5. When you make the Sign of the Cross, use your right hand and do it slowly and reverently, first touching your forehead ("In the name of the Father"), next just below your chest ("and of the Son"), then your left shoulder ("and of the Holy Spirit"), and finally your right shoulder ("Amen").

6. At prayer time, stand in the front of the class straight and tall. Ask the students to use their reproducible sheet of psalms for reading their part. Read slowly and clearly.

IF THERE ARE TWO LEADERS

One leader reads the Reading or Gospel while the other reads all of the other parts. Practice reading your part(s). Both leaders should stand in front of the class during the entire prayer.

Remember to read very slowly, with a loud, clear voice.

REPRODUCIBLE PSALMS
ORDINARY TIME, AUTUMN

ORDINARY TIME, AUTUMN

Psalm for Sunday, August 11—Friday, September 27

Psalm 66:1–3a, 5, 8, 16–17

LEADER: Make a joyful noise to God, all the earth.

ALL: **Make a joyful noise to God, all the earth.**

LEADER: Make a joyful noise to God, all the earth;
sing the glory of his name;
give to him glorious praise.
Say to God, "How awesome are
your deeds!"

ALL: **Make a joyful noise to God, all the earth.**

Short version: use above only; Long version: use above and below.

SIDE A: Come and see what God has done:
he is awesome in his deeds
among mortals.
Bless our God, O peoples,
let the sound of his praise be heard.

SIDE B: Come and hear, all you who fear God,
and I will tell you what
he has done for me.
I cried aloud to him,
and he was extolled with my tongue.

ALL: **Make a joyful noise to God, all the earth.**

ORDINARY TIME, AUTUMN

Psalm for Sunday, September 29—Thursday, October 24

Psalm 145:2–3, 4–5, 10–11

LEADER: I will praise your name for ever, LORD.

ALL: **I will praise your name for ever, LORD.**

LEADER: Every day I will bless you,
and praise your name forever and ever.
Great is the LORD, and greatly
to be praised;
his greatness is unsearchable.

ALL: **I will praise your name for ever, LORD.**

Short version: use above only; Long version: use above and below.

SIDE A: One generation shall laud your works
to another, and shall declare your
mighty acts.
On the glorious splendor of your majesty,
and on your wondrous works,
I will meditate.

SIDE B: All your works shall give thanks to you,
O LORD, and all your faithful shall
bless you.
They shall speak of the glory of your
kingdom, and tell of your power.

ALL: **I will praise your name for ever, LORD.**

REPRODUCIBLE PSALMS
ORDINARY TIME, AUTUMN; ADVENT

ORDINARY TIME, AUTUMN

Psalm for Friday, October 25—Wednesday, November 27

Psalm 98:1, 2–3, 3–4

LEADER: The LORD has made known his victory.

ALL: **The LORD has made known his victory.**

LEADER: O sing to the LORD a new song,
for he has done marvelous things.
His right hand and his holy arm have
gotten him victory.

ALL: **The LORD has made known his victory.**

Short version: use above only; Long version: use above and below.

SIDE A: The LORD has made known his victory;
he has revealed his vindication in the
sight of the nations.
He has remembered his steadfast love
and faithfulness to the house of Israel.

SIDE B: All the ends of the earth have seen the
victory of our God.
Make a joyful noise to the LORD,
all the earth; break forth into joyous
song and sing praises.

ALL: **The LORD has made known his victory.**

ADVENT

Psalm for Sunday, December 1—Sunday, December 22

Psalm 85:4a, 8, 10–11, 12–13

LEADER: Restore us again,
O God of our salvation!

ALL: **Restore us again,
O God of our salvation!**

LEADER: Let me hear what God the LORD
will speak,
for he will speak peace to his people,
to his faithful, to those who turn to
him in their hearts.

ALL: **Restore us again, O God of our
salvation!**

Short version: use above only; Long version: use above and below.

SIDE A: Steadfast love and faithfulness will meet;
righteousness and peace will kiss
each other.
Faithfulness will spring up from
the ground,
and righteousness will look down
from the sky.

SIDE B: The LORD will give what is good,
and our land will yield its increase.
Righteousness will go before him,
and will make a path for his steps.

ALL: **Restore us again,
O God of our salvation!**

CHILDREN'S DAILY PRAYER 2019–2020 © 2019 Archdiocese of Chicago: Liturgy Training Publications, 3949 South Racine Avenue, Chicago, IL 60609. All rights reserved. Orders: 800-933-1800 or www.LTP.org. Scripture excerpts are taken from *The New Revised Standard Version Bible: Catholic Edition*, ©1989, Division of Christian Education of the National Council of the Churches of Christ in the United States of America. Used with permission. All rights reserved.

CHRISTMAS TIME; ORDINARY TIME, WINTER

CHRISTMAS TIME

Psalm for Thursday, January 2—Sunday, January 12

Psalm 96:1–2a, 2b–3, 5b–6, 11a

LEADER: Let the heavens be glad and the
earth rejoice!

ALL: **Let the heavens be glad and the
earth rejoice!**

LEADER: O sing to the Lord a new song;
sing to the Lord, all the earth.
Sing to the Lord; bless his name.

ALL: **Let the heavens be glad and the
earth rejoice!**

Short version: use above only; Long version: use above and below.

SIDE A: Tell of his salvation from day to day.

Declare his glory among the nations,
his marvelous works among all
the peoples.

SIDE B: The Lord made the heavens.
Honor and majesty are before him;
strength and beauty are in his sanctuary.

ALL: **Let the heavens be glad and the
earth rejoice!**

ORDINARY TIME, WINTER

Psalm for Monday, January 13—Tuesday, February 25

Psalm 23:1–3a, 3b–4, 5, 6

LEADER: I shall dwell in the house of the Lord my
whole life long.

ALL: **I shall dwell in the house of the Lord my
whole life long.**

LEADER: The Lord is my shepherd,
I shall not want.
He makes me lie down in
green pastures;
he leads me beside still waters;
he restores my soul.

ALL: **I shall dwell in the house of the Lord my
whole life long.**

Short version: use above only; Long version: use above and below.

SIDE A: He leads me in right paths
for his name's sake.
Even though I walk through the
darkest valley,
I fear no evil; for you are with me;
your rod and your staff—
they comfort me.

SIDE B: You prepare a table before me
in the presence of my enemies;
you anoint my head with oil;
my cup overflows.

ALL: **I shall dwell in the house of the Lord my
whole life long.**

LENT

Psalm for Wednesday, February 26—Wednesday, April 8

Psalm 34:4–5, 6–7, 16–17, 18–19

LEADER: The LORD saves the crushed in spirit.

ALL: **The LORD saves the crushed in spirit.**

LEADER: I sought the LORD, and he answered me,
  and delivered me from all my fears.
  Look to him, and be radiant;
   so your faces shall never be ashamed.

ALL: **The LORD saves the crushed in spirit.**

Short version: use above only; Long version: use above and below.

SIDE A: This poor soul cried, and was heard by
   the LORD,
   and was saved from every trouble.
  The angel of the LORD encamps
   around those who fear him, and
   delivers them.

SIDE B: The face of the LORD is against evildoers,
   to cut off the remembrance of them
   from the earth.
  When the righteous cry for help,
   the LORD hears,
   and rescues them from all
   their troubles.

ALL: **The LORD saves the crushed in spirit.**

LEADER: The LORD is near to the brokenhearted,
   and saves the crushed in spirit.
  Many are the afflictions of the righteous,
   but the LORD rescues them from
   them all.

ALL: **The LORD saves the crushed in spirit.**

EASTER TIME

Psalm for Monday, April 13—Friday, May 1

Psalm 105:1–2, 3–4, 6–7

LEADER: Let the hearts of those who seek the
   LORD rejoice.

ALL: **Let the hearts of those who seek the
   LORD rejoice.**

LEADER: O give thanks to the LORD, call on
   his name,
   make known his deeds among
   the peoples.
  Sing to him, sing praises to him;
   tell of all his wonderful works.

ALL: **Let the hearts of those who seek
   the LORD rejoice.**

Short version: use above only; Long version: use above and below.

SIDE A: Glory in his holy name;
   let the hearts of those who seek the
   LORD rejoice.
  Seek the LORD and his strength;
   seek his presence continually.

SIDE B: O offspring of his servant Abraham,
   children of Jacob, his chosen ones.
  He is the LORD our God;
   his judgments are in all the earth.

ALL: **Let the hearts of those who seek
   the LORD rejoice.**

EASTER TIME

Psalm for Sunday, May 3—Sunday, May 31

Psalm 118:1–2, 4, 22–24, 25–27a

LEADER: The stone that the builders rejected
has become the chief cornerstone.

ALL: **The stone that the builders rejected
has become the chief cornerstone.**

LEADER: O give thanks to the LORD, for he is good;
his steadfast love endures forever!
Let Israel say,
"His steadfast love endures forever."
Let those who fear the LORD say,
"His steadfast love endures forever."

ALL: **The stone that the builders rejected
has become the chief cornerstone.**

Short version: use above only; Long version: use above and below.

SIDE A: The stone that the builders rejected
has become the chief cornerstone.
This is the LORD's doing;
it is marvelous in our eyes.
This is the day that the LORD has made;
let us rejoice and be glad in it.

SIDE B: Save us, we beseech you, O LORD!
O LORD, we beseech you,
give us success!
Blessed is the one who comes in the name
of the LORD.
We bless you from the house
of the LORD.
The LORD is God,
and he has given us light.

ALL: **The stone that the builders rejected
has become the chief cornerstone.**

ORDINARY TIME, SUMMER

Psalm for Monday, June 1—Friday, June 26

Psalm 85:8–9, 10–11, 12–13

LEADER: The LORD speaks of peace to his people.

ALL: **The LORD speaks of peace to his people.**

LEADER: Let me hear what God the LORD
will speak,
for he will speak peace to his people,
to his faithful, to those who turn to
him in their hearts.
Surely his salvation is at hand for those
who fear him,
that his glory may dwell in our land.

ALL: **The LORD speaks of peace to his people.**

Short version: use above only; Long version: use above and below.

SIDE A: Steadfast love and faithfulness will meet;
righteousness and peace will kiss
each other.
Faithfulness will spring up from
the ground,
and righteousness will look down
from the sky.

SIDE B: The LORD will give what is good,
and our land will yield its increase.
Righteousness will go before him,
and will make a path for his steps.

ALL: **The LORD speaks of peace to his people.**

ORDINARY TIME AUTUMN

SUNDAY, AUGUST 11 — WEDNESDAY, NOVEMBER 27

AUTUMN ORDINARY TIME

THE MEANING OF ORDINARY TIME

Times and seasons on our liturgical calendar, in contrast to the secular calendar, are valued in a different, altogether new way. Our Christian calendar even has a different shape! Instead of a rectangle, we draw all the days of a year in a circle. Instead of marking off times according to the weather, we celebrate those great moments when God reveals a great love for us in marvelous and mysterious ways.

Our liturgical calendar has four primary seasons. Advent (the four weeks before Christmas); Christmas; Lent (the six weeks before Easter); Easter (which extends for fifty days after Easter through Pentecost) but, the longest part of the calendar is called Ordinary Time.

Ordinary Time is thirty-three or thirty-four weeks a year. It is called "Ordinary Time" because the weeks are numbered. The Latin word *ordinalis*, which refers to numbers in a series and stems from the Latin word *ordo*, from which we get the English word *order*. Ordinary time is therefore "ordered time." Calling it "Ordered Time" reminds us of God's great plan for creation. There was a specific time for the creation of light, planets, water, earth, plants, animals, and humankind. Ordinary Time begins after Christmas, continues until Ash Wednesday when it stops for Lent and Easter, then picks up again after Pentecost Sunday and runs through the summer and autumn until the beginning of Advent. Each Sunday in Ordinary Time has a number and the numbers increase each week.

During autumn Ordinary Time, there are weekly themes for the Scripture readings. Some of the themes help us to understand qualities of our faith: importance of community, friendship, keeping the Sabbath holy, prayer, service and the great commandment to love God and love one another. In these weeks, the readings cover a historical spectrum of Scripture.

From the New Testament, we will read parables or stories that Jesus told. With moral parables in week twenty-one, like the sower, the wicked tenants, and the barren fig tree, Jesus teaches us about the consequences of our behavior.

From the Old Testament we will read beautiful passages about Wisdom in the Book of Sirach. We will read from the Book of Genesis and wonder at the marvelous story of Creation. We will spend three weeks on the story of Moses who was one of the greatest heroes in the Old Testament. God chose Moses to lead the Hebrew people out of slavery in Egypt. During their escape and on their long journey through the deserts, the people met many challenges: the Egyptian army, lack of food and water, hostile tribes. But God was always with them and taking care of them. One of the greatest gifts God gave to the Hebrew people and to people of all time is the Gift of the Law: the Ten Commandments, which give clear instructions on how people can live together in peace.

As we come to the end of Ordinary Time and prepare for Advent in the thirty-third and thirty fourth weeks, the theme is, "Who is Jesus?" Jesus is Messiah, Savior of Israel, Son of Man, Lord of the Sabbath, Teacher and Healer, Good Shepherd, and Christ the King!

PREPARING TO CELEBRATE ORDINARY TIME IN THE CLASSROOM

SACRED SPACE

You want the prayer table or space to be in a place where the children will see it often and perhaps go to it in their free moments. If you can have a separate prayer table it should not be too small, perhaps a coffee-table size. You may wish to buy one or two inexpensive cushions to place before your prayer table so that children will feel invited to sit or kneel there. The essential things for the prayer table are a cross or crucifix (unless one is on the wall), a Bible, a substantial candle and a cloth of liturgical color. Cover the prayer table with a plain green cloth or one that mixes green with other Autumn colors. Large table napkins or placemats work, or remnants from a sewing store. Green, the color of hope and life, is the color of Ordinary Time. If you can, set the Bible on a bookstand. Point out the candle beside the Bible, and remind them that Jesus said, "I am the Light of the world" (John 8:12). You might light the candle, open the Bible, and read that verse to the class. Other objects you might want to include are a simple statue of Mary (September 8), images of angels (Archangels, September 29 and Guardian, October 2), an image of St. Francis or the children's pets (October 4), a rosary (October 7). Use natural objects, too, such as flowers, dried leaves or small gourds. If there is the space, pictures of loved ones who have died would be appropriate in November.

MOVEMENT AND GESTURE

Consider reverencing the Word of God in the Bible by carrying it in procession. Place a candle ahead of it and perhaps carry wind chimes as it moves through the room. At the prayer space the processors turn and the Bible is raised. The class reverences with a profound bow (a bow from the waist) then the Bible and candle are placed, and the chimes' are silenced. Also consider reverencing the Crucifix or the Cross near September 14, the Triumph of the Cross. Take the crucifix from the wall (or use another one) and carry it in procession at the beginning of prayer in a similar manner or take the cross to each child and let them kiss it or hold it or make a head bow before it.

FESTIVITY IN SCHOOL AND HOME

For Ordinary Time in autumn, *Children's Daily Prayer* provides several special prayer services to use in the classroom—or with larger groups such as the whole school—to celebrate the beginning of the school year, to pray for peace (on September 11), and to honor Our Lady of the Rosary (October 7). The Home Prayer pages can be duplicated for the students to take home and share with their families: Morning Prayer for Families Departing for the Day; Home Prayer for Remembering the Dead; and a Meal Prayer for Thanksgiving.

SACRED MUSIC

One of the best ways to help the children enter into the special qualities of this or any liturgical time is by teaching them the Sunday music of their parish. Teach the children (or invite the school music teacher, parish music director or a choir member/cantor to do it) how your church sings her "Alleluia!" See what songs and hymns the children know and love. For example, in Ordinary Time, consider "For the Beauty of the Earth" and "Make Me a Channel of Your Peace." Learn and sing just a good refrain. Singing is an integral part of how we pray.

PRAYERS FOR ORDINARY TIME

During this season, take some time to discuss the meaning of the various intercessions of the Our Father with the children in your class. In particular, discuss the Kingdom of God—that time of peace and justice proclaimed by and fulfilled in Jesus. Ask what it means for God's Kingdom to come. Go through the prayer one intercession at a time asking what each means. Explore with them what Jesus is teaching us about how we should pray: We ask for God's name to be treated as blessed and holy, for the coming of the Kingdom of God, for God's will to be accomplished on earth, for our "daily bread," for forgiveness, and for strength in the face of temptation.

A NOTE TO CATECHISTS

Because you meet with your students once a week, you may wish to use the Prayer for the Week pages. These weekly prayer pages contain an excerpt from the Sunday Gospel and will help to prepare the children for Mass. Sometimes, though, you may wish to substitute the Prayer for the Day if it falls on an important solemnity, feast, or memorial of the Church (Our Lady of the Rosary, October 7, for example). In this introduction, you will see the suggestions for your prayer space. You may have to set up a prayer space each time you meet with your group. Think in advance about where to place it, have all your materials in one box, and always set it up in the same place.

GRACE BEFORE MEALS

FOR ORDINARY TIME • AUTUMN

LEADER:

Lord, you gift us with your love in so many ways.

ALL: We praise you and thank you!

✚ All make the Sign of the Cross.

In the name of the Father, and of the Son, and of the Holy Spirit. Amen.

LEADER:

Father, Son, and Spirit,
you bring us joy
through your abundant grace.
As we gather to share this meal,
may we be grateful for the
loving people who prepared it
every step of the way.
We thank all those in lands far from us
and those nearby who
helped grow, nurture, package,
transport, store, and cook our food.
We bless these brothers and sisters
as we bless each other here,
for you created all of us in
your image of goodness and love.
May this meal nourish our bodies
to give you glory and to build your Kingdom.
We ask this through Jesus Christ, our Lord.

ALL: Amen.

✚ All make the Sign of the Cross.

In the name of the Father, and of the Son, and of the Holy Spirit. Amen.

PRAYER AT DAY'S END
FOR ORDINARY TIME • AUTUMN

LEADER:
God of all wisdom,
we offer back to you
all that we have done today
through the gift of your gentle Spirit.

ALL: For your love is in our hearts!

✚ All make the Sign of the Cross.

In the name of the Father, and of the Son, and of the Holy Spirit. Amen.

LEADER:
We are grateful for
the signs and wonders of this day,
for the ordinary events and its surprises,
big and small.
We thank you for the
loving people who surround us.
May we continue to reflect your goodness
to others in your name.
We ask this through your beloved Son, Jesus.

ALL: Amen.

✚ All make the Sign of the Cross.

In the name of the Father, and of the Son, and of the Holy Spirit. Amen.

PRAYER SERVICE
BEGINNING OF THE YEAR FOR SCHOOL STAFF

Seek volunteers to lead this prayer service. You may involve up to seven leaders (as marked below). The fourth leader will need a Bible for the Scripture passage. Choose hymns for the beginning and ending if you wish.

FIRST LEADER:
We gather in Christ's name
to celebrate all of God's children.
Let us ask the Holy Spirit for guidance
as we begin our journey again with them.

◆ Gesture for all to stand.

Together we enter this time of prayer as we make the Sign of the Cross.

✚ All make the Sign of the Cross.

In the name of the Father, and of the Son, and of the Holy Spirit. Amen.

SECOND LEADER:
Spirit of God,
enlighten our minds
as we begin another school year, for
these children are gifts of new life.
Draw us closer to all
that is good and true
so that through us
all that they see
is you.
We ask this through Christ our Lord.

Amen.

THIRD LEADER:
Spirit of your Son Jesus,
grant us your wisdom and
integrity each and every day,
for you are the breath of all
that is holy.

Refresh us with ideas that
inspire our youth with your energy
and enthusiasm.
We ask this in Christ's name.

Amen.

◆ Gesture for all to sit.

FOURTH LEADER: Romans 8:31b–35, 37–39
A reading from the Letter of Paul to Romans.

◆ Read the Scripture passage from the Bible.

The Word of the Lord.

◆ All observe silence.

FIFTH LEADER:

◆ Gesture for all to stand.

Let us bring our hopes and needs to God as we pray from the Opening Prayer of our Church leadership as they embarked on the Second Vatican Council. Our response will be: **Guide us with your love.**

For light and strength to know your will,
to make it our own,
and to live it in our lives,
we pray to the Lord.

ALL: Guide us with your love.

For justice for all;
enable us to uphold the rights of others;
do not allow us to be misled by ignorance
or corrupted by fear or favor,
we pray to the Lord.

ALL: Guide us with your love.

Unite us to yourself in the bond of love
and keep us faithful to all that is true,
we pray to the Lord.

ALL: Guide us with your love.

May we temper justice with love,
so that all our discussions and reflections
may be pleasing to you, and earn the reward
promised to good and faithful servants,
we pray to the Lord.

ALL: Guide us with your love.

SIXTH LEADER:
Let us pray as Jesus taught us:
Our Father . . . Amen.

◆ Pause and then say:
Let us offer one another the sign of
Christ's peace.

◆ All offer one another a sign of peace.

SEVENTH LEADER:
Let us pray:
God, our Creator,
your presence through the
Holy Spirit strengthens us
for the days ahead.
Guide us with your patience
and compassion as we
mentor our future leaders in Christ.

Amen.

✠ All make the Sign of the Cross.

In the name of the Father, and of the Son, and of the Holy Spirit. Amen.

PRAYER SERVICE
BEGINNING OF THE YEAR FOR STUDENTS

This prayer service may be led by the eighth grade students or by older students. The third and fifth leaders will need a Bible for the passages from Matthew and Luke. Take time to help the third and fifth leaders practice the readings. You may wish to sing "This Little Light of Mine" as the opening and closing songs. If the group will sing, prepare someone to lead the songs.

FIRST LEADER:

We are embarking on a journey together
in this brand new school year.
As we look ahead at all that this year
might reveal,
let us remember Jesus,
who will walk beside us every step of the way.

SONG LEADER:

Let us begin by singing the first few verses of
our song.

◆ Gesture for all to stand, and lead the first few
   verses of the song.

SECOND LEADER:

✛ All make the Sign of the Cross.

**In the name of the Father, and of the
Son, and of the Holy Spirit. Amen.**

Let us pray:
God our Creator,
we were made in
your image and likeness.
Help us to be gentle with
ourselves and each other
as we mature this year with your grace.

Guide us in our studies and help us develop with knowledge and maturity.
We ask this through Christ our Lord.

Amen.

◆ Remain standing and sing Alleluia.

THIRD LEADER: Matthew 5:14–16
A reading from the holy Gospel according to Matthew.

◆ Read the Gospel passage from the Bible.

The Gospel of the Lord.

◆ All sit and observe silence.

FOURTH LEADER:

◆ Gesture for all to stand.

Let us bring our hopes and needs to God as we pray, Let your light shine through us.

ALL: Let your light shine through us.

Help us to show honor and respect to all those who teach and coach us,
we pray to the Lord.

ALL: Let your light shine through us.

Guide us with your counsel, Lord,
when we are frustrated with our studies,
we pray to the Lord.

ALL: Let your light shine through us.

Help us to take care of our minds and bodies
so that we give you glory in
everything we do,
we pray to the Lord.

ALL: Let your light shine through us.

Help us to remember all that we learn so that we can apply it to our lives in the months and years ahead,
we pray to the Lord.

ALL: Let your light shine through us.

FIFTH LEADER: Luke 6:31–36
Let us listen to what Jesus teaches to his disciples:

A reading from the holy Gospel according to Luke.

◆ Read the Gospel passage from the Bible.

The Gospel of the Lord.

SIXTH LEADER:
Let us pray:
O God,
we know you are with us on this journey.
Help us to love one another
as you love us.
Guide us with your light of mercy and justice.
May we be considerate with our friends
and respectful of all who lead us.
Help us to learn and grow in your
wisdom throughout this year.
We ask this through Christ our Lord.

Amen.

✚ All make the Sign of the Cross.

In the name of the Father, and of the Son, and of the Holy Spirit. Amen.

SONG LEADER:
Please join in singing the final verses of our closing song.

HOME PRAYER
MORNING PRAYER FOR FAMILIES DEPARTING FOR THE DAY

The Catechism of the Catholic Church *calls the family the "domestic church" where children are first introduced to the faith (CCC, 2204 and 2225). A blessing is a prayer that acknowledges and thanks God for the good things in our lives and asks God to be with us. When the household gathers in the morning, perhaps at breakfast, a parent, grandparent, or other adult may lead this blessing.*

The longer prayer can be used on one of the first days of school and other special occasions. At other times, you may just want to bless the child with the Sign of the Cross on the forehead and a "God bless you" as he or she leaves for school.

✚ All make the Sign of the Cross.

In the name of the Father, and of the Son, and of the Holy Spirit. Amen.

LEADER:

We each have important things
to do today, and so we ask God's blessing.
We go to school and to work.
We learn and play.
We praise and thank God for each other
and for the love we share.
We ask God to be with those
who are lonely or sick
or without basic needs.
We ask this in Jesus' name.

All: Amen.

LEADER:

Holy God,
giver of all good gifts,
walk with us today,
guide our words and our actions,
and keep us on the path of truth.
Bring us back together in peace
at the end of this day.
We ask this through Christ our Lord.

✚ The Leader makes the Sign of the Cross on one person's forehead saying:

"God bless you and keep you today."

ALL: Amen.

CHILDREN'S DAILY PRAYER 2019–2020 © 2019 Archdiocese of Chicago: Liturgy Training Publications, 3949 South Racine Avenue, Chicago, IL 60609. All rights reserved. Orders: 800-933-1800 or www.LTP.org. Scripture excerpts are taken from *The New Revised Standard Version Bible: Catholic Edition*, copyright © 1989, Division of Christian Education of the National Council of the Churches of Christ in the United States of America. Used with permission. All rights reserved.

OPENING

In today's Gospel, Jesus tells people to be prepared and to have their lamps lit. As we begin a new school year, let us think about how we can prepare ourselves to see Jesus in one another and in our studies. Like the servants in the Gospel, we must be alert to greet Jesus, our true master, and to see him in the people we meet.

✚ All make the Sign of the Cross.

In the name of the Father, and of the Son, and of the Holy Spirit. Amen.

PSALM

(For a longer psalm, see page xi.)
Psalm 66:1–3a, 5, 8, 16–17

Make a joyful noise to God, all the earth.

Make a joyful noise to God, all the earth.

Make a joyful noise to God, all the earth;
 sing praise to the glory of his name;
 give to him glorious praise.
Say to God, "How awesome are your deeds!"

Make a joyful noise to God, all the earth.

◆ All stand and sing **Alleluia.**

GOSPEL

Luke 12:35–40

A reading from the holy Gospel according to Luke.

Jesus said, "Be dressed for action and have your lamps lit; be like those who are waiting for their master to return from the wedding banquet, so that they may open the door for him as soon as he comes and knocks. Blessed are those slaves whom the master finds alert when he comes; truly I tell you, he will fasten his belt and have them sit down to eat, and he will come and serve them. If he comes during the middle of the night, or near dawn, and finds them so, blessed are those slaves. But know this: if the owner of the house had known at what hour the thief was coming, he would not have let his house be broken into. You also must be ready, for the Son of Man is coming at an unexpected hour."

The Gospel of the Lord.

◆ All sit and observe silence.

FOR SILENT REFLECTION

Think about this silently in your heart. Do you ever see Jesus in the face of someone in need?

CLOSING PRAYER

Let us pray to God for our needs and the needs of others: our family, neighborhood, and the world. For each need we say, "Lord, hear our prayer."

◆ All may add their own prayers here.

Let us pray: **Our Father . . . Amen.**

Help us to be alert
to your presence, O Lord.
Help us to recognize you in one another and
to treat others as we would treat you.
We ask this through Christ our Lord.

Amen.

✚ All make the Sign of the Cross.

OPENING

This week our Scripture readings are about hope. The prophet Jeremiah [jayr-uh-MI- uh] lived at the time when Jerusalem was invaded by the Babylonians. He helped people to have hope by telling them of God's promises of love. Today is the feast of St. Jane Frances de Chantal. She is the patron saint of parents who have been separated from their children.

✚ All make the Sign of the Cross.

In the name of the Father, and of the Son, and of the Holy Spirit. Amen.

PSALM
(For a longer psalm, see page xi.)
Psalm 66:1–3a, 5, 8, 16–17

Make a joyful noise to God, all the earth.

Make a joyful noise to God, all the earth.

Make a joyful noise to God, all the earth;
   sing praise to the glory of his name;
   give to him glorious praise.
Say to God, "How awesome are your deeds!"

Make a joyful noise to God, all the earth.

READING
Jeremiah 31:1–2a, 3b–5ac, 8, 16a, 17a

A reading from the Book of prophet Jeremiah.

At that time, says the LORD, I will be the God of all the families of Israel, and they shall be my people. Thus says the LORD: I have loved you with an everlasting love; therefore I have continued my faithfulness to you. Again I will build you, and you shall be built, O virgin Israel! Again you shall take your tambourines, and go forth in the dance of the merrymakers. Again you shall plant vineyards on the mountains of Samaria, and shall enjoy the fruit.

See, I am going to bring them from the land of the north, and gather them from the farthest parts of the earth, among them the blind and the lame, those with child and those in labor, together; a great company, they shall return here. Thus says the LORD: Keep your voice from weeping; there is hope for your future, says the LORD.

The Word of the Lord.

◆ All observe silence.

FOR SILENT REFLECTION

Think about this silently in your heart. What do you hope for today?

CLOSING PRAYER

Let us pray to God for our needs and the needs of others: our family, neighborhood, and the world. For each need we say, "Lord, hear our prayer."

◆ All may add their own prayers here.

Let us pray: **Our Father . . . Amen.**

Because you are faithful to your promise
to be with us, O God,
we can hope for a world
of peace and joy for all.
We give you thanks
for the gift of your everlasting love.
We ask this through Christ our Lord.

Amen.

✚ All make the Sign of the Cross.

OPENING

The prophet Baruch [buh-ROOK] wrote at the same time as the prophet Jeremiah [jayr-uh-MI-uh], when Jerusalem was invaded by the Babylonians. It was a hard, dark time for the Hebrew people. Baruch tells people that life is difficult because they have forgotten to follow the Law that was given to Moses. These laws are words of wisdom that teach people how to live in peace. Baruch says to not lose hope and to ask for help. God will not forsake them.

✛ All make the Sign of the Cross.

In the name of the Father, and of the Son, and of the Holy Spirit. Amen.

PSALM

(For a longer psalm, see page xi.)
Psalm 66:1–3a, 5, 8, 16–17

Make a joyful noise to God, all the earth.

Make a joyful noise to God, all the earth.

Make a joyful noise to God, all the earth;
  sing praise to the glory of his name;
  give to him glorious praise.
Say to God, "How awesome are your deeds!"

Make a joyful noise to God, all the earth.

READING

Baruch 3:10a, 12–13; 4:5, 8a, 17, 21–22

A reading from the Book of prophet Baruch.

Why is it, O Israel, that you are in the land of your enemies? You have forsaken the fountain of wisdom. If you had walked in the way of God, you would be living in peace forever. Take courage my people, who perpetuate Israel's name! You forgot the everlasting God, who brought you up. But I, how can I help you? Take courage my children, cry to God, and he will deliver you from the power and hand of the enemy. For I have put my hope in the Everlasting to save you, and joy has come to me from the Holy One, because of the mercy that will soon come to you from your everlasting savior.

The Word of the Lord.

◆ All observe silence.

FOR SILENT REFLECTION

Think about this silently in your heart. When do you need courage to follow God's commands and turn to him?

CLOSING PRAYER

Let us pray to God for our needs and the needs of others: our family, neighborhood, and the world. For each need we say, "Lord, hear our prayer."

◆ All may add their own prayers here.

Let us pray: **Our Father . . . Amen.**

Faithful, loving God,
give us the courage
to follow your commands.
Help us to trust in you and to turn to you when we are in need.
We pray in Christ's name.

Amen.

✛ All make the Sign of the Cross.

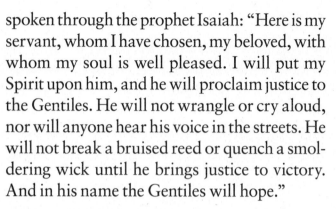

OPENING

Our reading today says Jesus will proclaim justice and bring hope to the Gentiles [JEN-tĭls]. Gentiles were people of the nations around Judah [JOO-duh] who were not of the house of Israel. Jews and Gentiles did not get along, but Jesus, who was a Jew, did not exclude anyone. He wanted all people to see that peace could come about if they worked for justice and did not hurt one another. Today we celebrate the Memorial of St. Maximilian Kolbe, who was martyred at Auschwitz when he volunteered his own life in place of another prisoner sentenced to die.

✠ All make the Sign of the Cross.

In the name of the Father, and of the Son, and of the Holy Spirit. Amen.

PSALM

(For a longer psalm, see page xi.)
Psalm 66:1–3a, 5, 8, 16–17

Make a joyful noise to God, all the earth.

Make a joyful noise to God, all the earth.

Make a joyful noise to God, all the earth;
   sing praise to the glory of his name;
   give to him glorious praise.
Say to God, "How awesome are your deeds!"

Make a joyful noise to God, all the earth.

◆ All stand and sing **Alleluia.**

GOSPEL

Matthew 12:15b–21

A reading from the holy Gospel according to Matthew.

Many crowds followed Jesus, and he cured all of them, and Jesus ordered them not to make him known. This was to fulfill what had been spoken through the prophet Isaiah: "Here is my servant, whom I have chosen, my beloved, with whom my soul is well pleased. I will put my Spirit upon him, and he will proclaim justice to the Gentiles. He will not wrangle or cry aloud, nor will anyone hear his voice in the streets. He will not break a bruised reed or quench a smoldering wick until he brings justice to victory. And in his name the Gentiles will hope."

The Gospel of the Lord.

◆ All sit and observe silence.

FOR SILENT REFLECTION

Think about this silently in your heart. God has also chosen us and puts his Spirit on us. How does it feel to be God's beloved son or daughter?

CLOSING PRAYER

Let us pray to God for our needs and the needs of others: our family, neighborhood, and the world. For each need we say, "Lord, hear our prayer."

◆ All may add their own prayers here.

Let us pray: **Our Father . . . Amen.**

O God, help us to be like Jesus.
He trusted in your love for him,
and he shared that love with others.
We thank you for loving us.
For this we pray
through Christ our Lord.

Amen.

✠ All make the Sign of the Cross.

OPENING

Today we celebrate the Assumption of the Blessed Virgin Mary into heaven. Our Gospel reading tells the story of Mary's visit to her cousin Elizabeth. Elizabeth recognized that Mary had been chosen by God to be the mother of his Son, Jesus.

✛ All make the Sign of the Cross.

In the name of the Father, and of the Son, and of the Holy Spirit. Amen.

PSALM

(For a longer psalm, see page xi.)
Psalm 66:1–3a, 5, 8, 16–17

Make a joyful noise to God, all the earth.

Make a joyful noise to God, all the earth.

Make a joyful noise to God, all the earth;
   sing praise to the glory of his name;
   give to him glorious praise.
Say to God, "How awesome are your deeds!"

Make a joyful noise to God, all the earth.

◆ All stand and sing **Alleluia.**

GOSPEL

Luke 1:41–47

A reading from the holy Gospel according to Luke.

When Elizabeth heard Mary's greeting, the child leaped in her womb. And Elizabeth was filled with the Holy Spirit and exclaimed with a loud cry, "Blessed are you among women, and blessed is the fruit of your womb. And why has this happened to me, that the mother of my Lord comes to me? For as soon as I heard the sound of your greeting, the child in my womb leaped for joy. And blessed is she who believed that there would be a fulfillment of what was spoken to her by the Lord."

And Mary said: "My soul magnifies the Lord, and my spirit rejoices in God my Savior."

The Gospel of the Lord.

◆ All sit and observe silence.

FOR SILENT REFLECTION

Think about this silently in your heart. How can Mary be a model for you?

CLOSING PRAYER

Let us pray to God for our needs and the needs of others: our family, neighborhood, and the world. For each need we say, "Lord, hear our prayer."

◆ All may add their own prayers here.

Let us pray: **Our Father . . . Amen.**

O Mary, Mother of God,
today we honor you.
Please pray for us, that we may
hear God's word and follow it,
as you did.
We pray in the name of your Son
Jesus Christ, our Lord.

Amen.

✛ All make the Sign of the Cross.

OPENING

In today's reading St. Paul speaks of putting on the "breastplate of faith and love" and the "helmet of hope." Faith, hope, and love are primary virtues for a Christian. A breastplate and helmet are for protection. These virtues help us to meet the challenges we face each day. We celebrate the Memorial of St. Stephen of Hungary today. He is the patron saint of that country, as well as of kings, masons, and children who are dying.

✚ All make the Sign of the Cross.

In the name of the Father, and of the Son, and of the Holy Spirit. Amen.

PSALM

(For a longer psalm, see page xi.)
Psalm 66:1–3a, 5, 8, 16–17

Make a joyful noise to God, all the earth.

Make a joyful noise to God, all the earth.

Make a joyful noise to God, all the earth;
   sing praise to the glory of his name;
   give to him glorious praise.
Say to God, "How awesome are your deeds!"

Make a joyful noise to God, all the earth.

READING

1 Thessalonians 5:1–2, 4, 6, 8–10

A reading from the Letter of Paul to the Thessalonians.

Now concerning the times and the seasons, brothers and sisters, you do not need to have anything written to you. For you yourselves know very well that the day of the Lord will come like a thief in the night. But you, beloved, are not in darkness, for that day to surprise you like a thief. So then let us not fall asleep as others do, but let us keep awake and be sober. But since we belong to the day, let us be sober, and put on the breastplate of faith and love, and for a helmet the hope of salvation. For God has destined us not for wrath but for obtaining salvation through our Lord Jesus Christ, who died for us, so that whether we are awake or asleep we may live with him.

The Word of the Lord.

✚ All observe silence.

FOR SILENT REFLECTION

Think about this silently in your heart. Can you imagine how strong you would feel with a "breastplate of love" and a "helmet of hope"?

CLOSING PRAYER

Let us pray to God for our needs and the needs of others: our family, neighborhood, and the world. For each need we say, "Lord, hear our prayer."

◆ All may add their own prayers here.

Let us pray: **Our Father . . . Amen.**

Faithful God,
we thank you for the gifts of faith,
hope, and love.
These virtues give us strength and courage and help us to live good and holy lives.
We pray in Christ's name.

Amen.

✚ All make the Sign of the Cross.

OPENING

When the Kingdom of God comes, it will be like a fire that purifies and unites everything in God. Before that happens people will argue and even fight about what is right and what is wrong. Today some people fight about who has the right beliefs. Jesus came to earth to show us what the Kingdom of God is like by his actions and teachings.

✝ All make the Sign of the Cross.

In the name of the Father, and of the Son, and of the Holy Spirit. Amen.

PSALM

(For a longer psalm, see page xi.)
Psalm 66:1–3a, 5, 8, 16–17

Make a joyful noise to God, all the earth.

Make a joyful noise to God, all the earth.

Make a joyful noise to God, all the earth;
   sing praise to the glory of his name;
   give to him glorious praise.
Say to God, "How awesome are your deeds!"

Make a joyful noise to God, all the earth.

◆ All stand and sing **Alleluia.**

GOSPEL

Luke 12:49–53

A reading from the holy Gospel according to Luke.

Jesus said, "I came to bring fire to the earth, and how I wish it were already kindled! I have a baptism with which to be baptized, and what stress I am under until it is completed! Do you think that I have come to bring peace to the earth? No, I tell you, but rather division! From now on five in one household will be divided, three against two and two against three; they will be divided: father against son and son against father, mother against daughter and daughter against mother, mother-in-law against her daughter-in-law and daughter-in-law against mother-in-law."

The Gospel of the Lord.

✝ All sit and observe silence.

FOR SILENT REFLECTION

Think about this silently in your heart. Are there disagreements between you and your family or friends? How can you bring peace?

CLOSING PRAYER

Let us pray to God for our needs and the needs of others: our family, neighborhood, and the world. For each need we say, "Lord, hear our prayer."

✝ All may add their own prayers here.

Let us pray: **Our Father . . . Amen.**

God of peace,
we pray for a world where
divisions are healed and your
peace reigns.
Help us to do our part
to bring your Kingdom to earth.
We ask this through Christ our Lord.

Amen.

✝ All make the Sign of the Cross.

OPENING

The next few days we will explore what happens when people are visited by angels. God often works through ordinary people. In today's reading, we hear of the angel Raphael's visit to Tobit and Tobias. Angels almost always say, "Do not be afraid," since their presence can be scary. Raphael was sent to help cure Tobit of blindness and help Sarah marry Tobias. Today we remember St. John Eudes, a French priest who founded religious communities for priests and for women.

✚ All make the Sign of the Cross.

In the name of the Father, and of the Son, and of the Holy Spirit. Amen.

PSALM
(For a longer psalm, see page xi.)
Psalm 66:1–3a, 5, 8, 16–17

Make a joyful noise to God, all the earth.

Make a joyful noise to God, all the earth.

Make a joyful noise to God, all the earth;
   sing praise to the glory of his name;
   give to him glorious praise.
Say to God, "How awesome are your deeds!"

Make a joyful noise to God, all the earth.

READING
Tobit 12:6ab, 11a, 14–17ab, 18ab

A reading from the Book of Tobit.

Then Raphael called Tobit and his son Tobias privately and said to them, "Bless God and acknowledge him in the presence of all the living for the good things he has done for you. I will now declare the whole truth to you and will conceal nothing from you. I was sent to you to test you. And at the same time God sent me to heal you and Sarah your daughter-in-law. I am Raphael, one of the seven angels who stand ready and enter before the glory of the Lord." The two of them were shaken; they fell face down, for they were afraid. But he said to them, "Do not be afraid; peace be with you. As for me, when I was with you, I was not acting on my own will, but by the will of God."

The Word of the Lord.

◆ All observe silence.

FOR SILENT REFLECTION

Think about this silently in your heart. How might we recognize an angel?

CLOSING PRAYER

Let us pray to God for our needs and the needs of others: our family, neighborhood, and the world. For each need we say, "Lord, hear our prayer."

◆ All may add their own prayers here.

Let us pray: **Our Father . . . Amen.**

Heavenly Father,
help us to be open to your messengers.
May we learn to listen to your word
and to follow your will.
Through Christ our Lord.

Amen.

✚ All make the Sign of the Cross.

OPENING

For the next two days we will hear the story of Gideon from the Book of Judges. Gideon was a young man from a very small tribe, yet he is called to lead Israel in battle against Midian. An angel of the Lord appears to Gideon. Although Gideon wonders if he will be strong enough to lead, the angel blesses him. We remember a Doctor of the Church today, St. Bernard.

✚ All make the Sign of the Cross.

In the name of the Father, and of the Son, and of the Holy Spirit. Amen.

PSALM

(For a longer psalm, see page xi.)
Psalm 66:1–3a, 5, 8, 16–17

Make a joyful noise to God, all the earth.

Make a joyful noise to God, all the earth.

Make a joyful noise to God, all the earth;
    sing praise to the glory of his name;
    give to him glorious praise.
Say to God, "How awesome are your deeds!"

Make a joyful noise to God, all the earth.

READING

Judges 6:11acd–13d, 14–16b

A reading from the Book of Judges.

Now the angel of the Lord came and sat under the oak at Ophrah [OF-ruh], as Joash's son Gideon was beating out wheat in the wine press, to hide it from the Midianites [MID-ee-uh-nites]. The angel of the Lord appeared to Gideon and said to him, "The Lord is with you, you mighty warrior." Gideon answered him, "But sir, if the Lord is with us, why then has all this happened to us? And where are all his wonderful deeds that our ancestors recounted to us?" Then the Lord turned to him and said, "Go in this might of yours and deliver Israel from the hand of Midian; I hereby commission you." He responded, "But sir, how can I deliver Israel? My clan is the weakest in Manasseh [muh-NAS-uh], and I am the least in my family." The Lord said to him, "But I will be with you."

The Word of the Lord.

◆ All observe silence.

FOR SILENT REFLECTION

Think about this silently in your heart. Even when you feel weak, God is with you. Ask God for what you need.

CLOSING PRAYER

Let us pray to God for our needs and the needs of others: our family, neighborhood, and the world. For each need we say, "Lord, hear our prayer."

◆ All may add their own prayers here.

Let us pray: **Our Father . . . Amen.**

Ever-present God,
help us to trust that you
are always with us.
Help us to believe in you
even when life is difficult and challenging.
We ask this in Christ's name.

Amen.

✚ All make the Sign of the Cross.

OPENING

Gideon asks for a sign that the angel is from God. The angel responds by creating a flame of fire on the rock that holds Gideon's offerings. The "kid" that Gideon prepares is a young goat. Because of St. Pius X, whose memorial we celebrate today, children as young as seven may receive First Communion.

✦ All make the Sign of the Cross.

In the name of the Father, and of the Son, and of the Holy Spirit. Amen.

PSALM

(For a longer psalm, see page xi.)
Psalm 66:1–3a, 5, 8, 16–17

Make a joyful noise to God, all the earth.

Make a joyful noise to God, all the earth.

Make a joyful noise to God, all the earth;
    sing praise to the glory of his name;
    give to him glorious praise.
Say to God, "How awesome are your deeds!"

Make a joyful noise to God, all the earth.

READING

Judges 6:17ac, 19abd–20ac, 21, 22bc, 23acd

A reading from the Book of Judges.

Then Gideon said to the angel, "Then show me a sign that it is you who speak with me." So Gideon went into his house and prepared a kid, and unleavened cakes from an ephah [EE-fuh] of flour; and brought them to the angel under the oak and presented them. The angel of God said to him, "Put them on this rock." Then the angel of the LORD reached out the tip of the staff that was in his hand, and touched the meat and the unleavened cakes; and fire sprang up from the rock and consumed the meat and the unleavened cakes; and the angel of the LORD vanished from Gideon's sight. And Gideon said, "Help me, Lord GOD! For I have seen the angel of the LORD face to face." But the LORD said to him, "Do not fear, you shall not die."

The Word of the Lord.

✦ All observe silence.

FOR SILENT REFLECTION

Think about this silently in your heart. How does God speak to us or send messages to us today?

CLOSING PRAYER

Let us pray to God for our needs and the needs of others: our family, neighborhood, and the world. For each need we say, "Lord, hear our prayer."

✦ All may add their own prayers here.

Let us pray: **Our Father . . . Amen.**

O God,
Open our eyes,
our ears,
and our hearts
to your presence.
Thank you for guiding us.
We trust in you
through Christ our Lord.

Amen.

✦ All make the Sign of the Cross.

OPENING

A common message from God's messengers, the angels, is to not be afraid. Today we hear about a time an angel appeared to St. Paul and reassured him that he would be safe in a storm. We also celebrate the Queenship of Mary today. As the mother of our Lord Jesus, Mary is honored with many special titles.

✚ All make the Sign of the Cross.

In the name of the Father, and of the Son, and of the Holy Spirit. Amen.

PSALM

(For a longer psalm, see page xi.)
Psalm 66:1–3a, 5, 8, 16–17

Make a joyful noise to God, all the earth.

Make a joyful noise to God, all the earth.

Make a joyful noise to God, all the earth;
  sing praise to the glory of his name;
  give to him glorious praise.
Say to God, "How awesome are your deeds!"

Make a joyful noise to God, all the earth.

READING

Acts 27:13c, 14ac, 18, 21bc, 23–24ac, 25

A reading from the Acts of the Apostles.

So the sailors weighed anchor and began to sail past Crete. But soon a violent wind rushed down from Crete. We were being pounded by the storm so violently that on the next day they began to throw the cargo overboard. Paul then stood up among them and said, "Men, you should have listened to me and not have set sail from Crete and thereby avoided this damage and loss. For last night there stood by me an angel of the God to whom I belong and whom I worship, and he said, 'Do not be afraid, Paul;

God has granted safety to all those who are sailing with you.' So keep up your courage, men, for I have faith in God that it will be exactly as I have been told."

The Word of the Lord.

✚ All observe silence.

FOR SILENT REFLECTION

Think about this silently in your heart. Is there anything you fear? Pray to God to calm those fears.

CLOSING PRAYER

Let us pray to God for our needs and the needs of others: our family, neighborhood, and the world. For each need we say, "Lord, hear our prayer."

✚ All may add their own prayers here.

Let us pray: **Our Father . . . Amen.**

Holy and mighty God,
be with us when we experience
storms and struggles in our lives.
Help us to trust in your constant care and
guide us safely on the path of life.
Through Christ our Lord.

Amen.

✚ All make the Sign of the Cross.

OPENING

Today's story is from the last book of the Bible, Revelation. We hear how St. Michael the Archangel and the good angels defeat a dragon, which is actually Satan. Satan was thrown out of heaven, but the battle between good and evil is still happening on earth. Today we remember St. Rose of Lima, who dedicated her life to God.

✚ All make the Sign of the Cross.

In the name of the Father, and of the Son, and of the Holy Spirit. Amen.

PSALM
(For a longer psalm, see page xi.)
Psalm 66:1–3a, 5, 8, 16–17

Make a joyful noise to God, all the earth.

Make a joyful noise to God, all the earth.

Make a joyful noise to God, all the earth;
sing praise to the glory of his name;
give to him glorious praise.
Say to God, "How awesome are your deeds!"

Make a joyful noise to God, all the earth.

READING
Revelation 12:7–10ab, 12a

A reading from the Book of Revelation.

And war broke out in heaven; Michael and his angels fought against the dragon. The dragon and his angels fought back, but they were defeated, and there was no longer any place for them in heaven. The great dragon was thrown down, that ancient serpent, who is called the Devil and Satan, the deceiver of the whole world—he was thrown down to the earth, and his angels were thrown down with him. Then I heard a loud voice in heaven, proclaiming, "Now have come the salvation and the power and the kingdom of our God and the authority of his Messiah. Rejoice then, you heavens and those who dwell in them!"

The Word of the Lord.

◆ All observe silence.

FOR SILENT REFLECTION

Think about this silently in your heart. What can we do to fight against evil so that the goodness of the Kingdom of God will come?

CLOSING PRAYER

Let us pray to God for our needs and the needs of others: our family, neighborhood, and the world. For each need we say, "Lord, hear our prayer."

◆ All may add their own prayers here.

Let us pray: **Our Father . . . Amen.**

O God, give us your Spirit's gifts
of right judgment and courage
so we may truly be the hands, feet,
and voice of Jesus for everyone we meet.
We ask this in Christ's name.

Amen.

✚ All make the Sign of the Cross.

PRAYER FOR THE WEEK

WITH A READING FROM THE GOSPEL FOR **SUNDAY, AUGUST 25, 2019**

OPENING

We cannot always tell from appearances who is following Jesus, and we may be surprised. Today's Gospel reminds us of this as Jesus cautions that those who are first may be last and the last may be first!

✚ All make the Sign of the Cross.

In the name of the Father, and of the Son, and of the Holy Spirit. Amen.

PSALM

(For a longer psalm, see page xi.)
Psalm 66:1–3a, 5, 8, 16–17

Make a joyful noise to God, all the earth.

Make a joyful noise to God, all the earth.

Make a joyful noise to God, all the earth;
   sing praise to the glory of his name;
   give to him glorious praise.
Say to God, "How awesome are your deeds!"

Make a joyful noise to God, all the earth.

◆ All stand and sing **Alleluia.**

GOSPEL

Luke 13:22–25, 29–30

A reading from the holy Gospel according to Luke.

Jesus went through one town and village after another, teaching as he made his way to Jerusalem. Someone asked him, "Lord, will only a few be saved?" He said to them, "Strive to enter through the narrow door; for many, I tell you, will try to enter and will not be able. When once the owner of the house has got up and shut the door, and you begin to stand outside and to knock at the door, saying, 'Lord, open to us,' then in reply he will say to you, 'I do not know where you come from.' Then people will come from east and west, from north and south, and will eat in the kingdom of God. Indeed, some are last who will be first, and some are first who will be last."

The Gospel of the Lord.

◆ All sit and observe silence.

FOR SILENT REFLECTION

Think about this silently in your heart. Why might the last be first and the first be last in the Kingdom of God?

CLOSING PRAYER

Let us pray to God for our needs and the needs of others: our family, neighborhood, and the world. For each need we say, "Lord, hear our prayer."

◆ All may add their own prayers here.

Let us pray: **Our Father . . . Amen.**

Loving and merciful God,
you desire that all people
find their way to you.
Help us to listen to the words
of your Son Jesus
and to follow his example.
In his name we pray.

Amen.

✚ All make the Sign of the Cross.

PRAYER FOR
MONDAY, AUGUST 26, 2019

OPENING

In our readings this week we will reflect on some of Jesus' parables. Jesus used parables to teach important truths about God's Kingdom and about how we should live our lives.

✛ All make the Sign of the Cross.

In the name of the Father, and of the Son, and of the Holy Spirit. Amen.

PSALM

(For a longer psalm, see page xi.)
Psalm 66:1–3a, 5, 8, 16–17

Make a joyful noise to God, all the earth.

Make a joyful noise to God, all the earth.

Make a joyful noise to God, all the earth;
    sing praise to the glory of his name;
    give to him glorious praise.
Say to God, "How awesome are your deeds!"

Make a joyful noise to God, all the earth.

◆ All stand and sing **Alleluia.**

GOSPEL

Luke 6:39–42

A reading from the holy Gospel according to Luke.

Jesus told his disciples a parable: "Can a blind person guide a blind person? Will not both fall into a pit? A disciple is not above the teacher, but everyone who is fully qualified will be like the teacher. Why do you see the speck in your neighbor's eye, but do not notice the log in your own eye? Or how can you say to your neighbor, 'Friend, let me take out the speck in your eye,' when you yourself do not see the log in your own eye? You hypocrite, first take the log out of your own eye, and then you will see clearly to take the speck out of your neighbor's eye."

The Gospel of the Lord.

◆ All sit and observe silence.

FOR SILENT REFLECTION

Think about this silently in your heart. Why does Jesus tell us to correct our own faults or mistakes before we try to change someone else's?

CLOSING PRAYER

Let us pray to God for our needs and the needs of others: our family, neighborhood, and the world. For each need we say, "Lord, hear our prayer."

◆ All may add their own prayers here.

Let us pray: **Our Father . . . Amen.**

Heavenly Father,
you desire that the human family
live together in peace.
You sent your Son Jesus
to show us how we should act.
Help us to be good followers
of his word.
In his name we pray.

Amen.

✛ All make the Sign of the Cross.

OPENING

In today's parable, Jesus uses the image of trees that bear fruit. The parable asks us to think of ourselves as a tree. What kind of fruit do we bear? Is it fruit that nourishes people or harms them? Today we celebrate St. Monica, the mother of St. Augustine. Because of her constant prayers, her son turned away from sin and became a Christian leader and teacher.

✚ All make the Sign of the Cross.

In the name of the Father, and of the Son, and of the Holy Spirit. Amen.

PSALM
(For a longer psalm, see page xi.)
Psalm 66:1–3a, 5, 8, 16–17

Make a joyful noise to God, all the earth.

Make a joyful noise to God, all the earth.

Make a joyful noise to God, all the earth;
    sing praise to the glory of his name;
    give to him glorious praise.
Say to God, "How awesome are your deeds!"

Make a joyful noise to God, all the earth.

◆ All stand and sing **Alleluia.**

GOSPEL
Luke 6:43–45

A reading from the holy Gospel according to Luke.

Jesus said to his disciples, "No good tree bears bad fruit, nor again does a bad tree bear good fruit; for each tree is known by its own fruit. Figs are not gathered from thorns, nor are grapes picked from a bramble bush. The good person out of the good treasure of the heart produces good, and the evil person out of evil treasure produces evil; for it is out of the abundance of the heart that the mouth speaks."

The Gospel of the Lord.

◆ All sit and observe silence.

FOR SILENT REFLECTION

Think about this silently in your heart. Do your words and actions come from a kind and loving heart?

CLOSING PRAYER

Let us pray to God for our needs and the needs of others: our family, neighborhood, and the world. For each need we say, "Lord, hear our prayer."

◆ All may add their own prayers here.

Let us pray: **Our Father . . . Amen.**

Loving and generous God,
give us loving hearts so that
our actions will be good and right.
We ask this in the name of Christ our Lord.

Amen.

✚ All make the Sign of the Cross.

OPENING

In the parable we hear today, Jesus uses the image of building a house. If the foundation is strong like rock or steel, the house will stand even when there are strong storms. He says that when we listen to his words and follow him, we are building a strong foundation for our lives. Today is the feast of St. Augustine, the son of St. Monica. He is considered one of the most important early Church writers, and his books continue to inspire Christians today.

◆ All make the Sign of the Cross.

In the name of the Father, and of the Son, and of the Holy Spirit. Amen.

PSALM

(For a longer psalm, see page xi.)
Psalm 66:1–3a, 5, 8, 16–17

Make a joyful noise to God, all the earth.

Make a joyful noise to God, all the earth.

Make a joyful noise to God, all the earth;
    sing praise to the glory of his name;
    give to him glorious praise.
Say to God, "How awesome are your deeds!"

Make a joyful noise to God, all the earth.

◆ All stand and sing **Alleluia.**

GOSPEL

Luke 6:46–49

A reading from the holy Gospel according to Luke.

Jesus said to his disciples, "Why do you call me 'Lord, Lord', and do not do what I tell you? I will show you what someone is like who comes to me, hears my words, and acts on them. That one is like a man building a house, who dug deeply and laid the foundation on rock; when a flood arose, the river burst against that house but could not shake it, because it had been well built. But the one who hears and does not act is like a man who built a house on the ground without a foundation. When the river burst against it, immediately it fell, and great was the ruin of that house."

The Gospel of the Lord.

◆ All sit and observe silence.

FOR SILENT REFLECTION

Think about this silently in your heart. In your life, what people or groups have given you a strong spiritual foundation?

CLOSING PRAYER

Let us pray to God for our needs and the needs of others: our family, neighborhood, and the world. For each need we say, "Lord, hear our prayer."

◆ All may add their own prayers here.

Let us pray: **Our Father . . . Amen.**

We long to listen to your words,
O Lord, and to act on them.
Help us to build our lives
on the firm foundation
of the Gospel.
Hear our prayer
through Christ our Lord.

Amen.

◆ All make the Sign of the Cross.

OPENING

Today we observe the memorial of the Passion of St. John the Baptist. He prepared the way for Jesus and preached the good news throughout his life. He was martyred by King Herod. The parable today reminds us that we are saved by God, not earthly riches.

✚ All make the Sign of the Cross.

In the name of the Father, and of the Son, and of the Holy Spirit. Amen.

PSALM

(For a longer psalm, see page xi.)
Psalm 66:1–3a, 5, 8, 16–17

Make a joyful noise to God, all the earth.

Make a joyful noise to God, all the earth.

Make a joyful noise to God, all the earth;
   sing praise to the glory of his name;
   give to him glorious praise.
Say to God, "How awesome are your deeds!"

Make a joyful noise to God, all the earth.

◆ All stand and sing **Alleluia.**

GOSPEL

Luke 12:15–21

A reading from the holy Gospel according to Luke.

Jesus said to his disciples, "Take care! Be on your guard against all kinds of greed; for one's life does not consist in the abundance of possessions." Then he told them a parable: "The land of a rich man produced abundantly. And he thought to himself, 'What should I do, for I have no place to store my crops?' Then he said, 'I will do this: I will pull down my barns and build larger ones, and there I will store all my grain and my goods. And I will say to my soul, Soul, you have ample goods laid up for many years; relax, eat, drink, be merry.' But God said to him, 'You fool! This very night your life is being demanded of you. And the things you have prepared, whose will they be?' So it is with those who store up treasures for themselves but are not rich toward God."

The Gospel of the Lord.

◆ All sit and observe silence.

FOR SILENT REFLECTION

Think about this silently in your heart. What kinds of actions make you rich in God's eyes?

CLOSING PRAYER

Let us pray to God for our needs and the needs of others: our family, neighborhood, and the world. For each need we say, "Lord, hear our prayer."

◆ All may add their own prayers here.

Let us pray: **Our Father . . . Amen.**

O God,
help us to know what is truly important
in life.
Help us to be rich in kindness
and respect others.
We ask this in the name of Jesus Christ
our Lord.

Amen.

✚ All make the Sign of the Cross.

OPENING

In today's parable a host invites his friends to a grand banquet. When his friends all give excuses why they can't come, the host is upset. But he finds others to enjoy his feast. Parables teach us about how God works.

✛ All make the Sign of the Cross.

In the name of the Father, and of the Son, and of the Holy Spirit. Amen.

PSALM

(For a longer psalm, see page xi.)
Psalm 66:1–3a, 5, 8, 16–17

Make a joyful noise to God, all the earth.

Make a joyful noise to God, all the earth.

Make a joyful noise to God, all the earth;
  sing praise to the glory of his name;
  give to him glorious praise.
Say to God, "How awesome are your deeds!"

Make a joyful noise to God, all the earth.

◆ All stand and sing **Alleluia.**

GOSPEL

Luke 14:16–20, 21b, 23b–24

A reading from the holy Gospel according to Luke.

Jesus told this parable, "Someone gave a great dinner and invited many. At the time for the dinner he sent his slave to say to those who had been invited, 'Come; for everything is ready now.' But they all alike began to make excuses. The first said to him, 'I have bought a piece of land, and I must go out and see it; please accept my regrets.' Another said, 'I have bought five yoke of oxen, and I am going to try them out; please accept my regrets.' Another said, 'I have just been married, and therefore I cannot come.' Then the owner of the house became angry and said to his slave, 'Go out at once into the streets and lanes of the town and bring in the poor, the crippled, the blind, and the lame. Go out into the roads and lanes, and compel people to come in, so that my house may be filled. For I tell you, none of those who were invited will taste my dinner.'"

The Gospel of the Lord.

◆ All sit and observe silence.

FOR SILENT REFLECTION

Think about this silently in your heart. How do you respond to God's invitation to spend time with him?

CLOSING PRAYER

Let us pray to God for our needs and the needs of others: our family, neighborhood, and the world. For each need we say, "Lord, hear our prayer."

◆ All may add their own prayers here.

Let us pray: **Our Father . . . Amen.**

Generous and loving God,
we pray that we
are always ready to do your will.
May we always be open
to your call.
Through Christ our Lord.

Amen.

✛ All make the Sign of the Cross.

PRAYER FOR THE WEEK

OPENING

In today's Gospel, Jesus reminds us of the importance of reaching out to those in need. It is easy to be kind and generous to our friends and family. As followers of Jesus, we also need to be kind and generous to people who cannot repay us. Today is the Day of Prayer for All Creation.

✛ All make the Sign of the Cross.

In the name of the Father, and of the Son, and of the Holy Spirit. Amen.

PSALM

(For a longer psalm, see page xi.)
Psalm 66:1–3a, 5, 8, 16–17

Make a joyful noise to God, all the earth.

Make a joyful noise to God, all the earth.

Make a joyful noise to God, all the earth;
   sing praise to the glory of his name;
   give to him glorious praise.
Say to God, "How awesome are your deeds!"

Make a joyful noise to God, all the earth.

◆ All stand and sing **Alleluia.**

GOSPEL

Luke 14:1, 12–14

A reading from the holy Gospel according to Luke.

On one occasion when Jesus was going to the house of a leader of the Pharisees to eat a meal on the sabbath, they were watching him closely. He said also to the one who had invited him, "When you give a luncheon or a dinner, do not invite your friends or your brothers or your relatives or rich neighbors, in case they may invite you in return, and you would be repaid.

But when you give a banquet, invite the poor, the crippled, the lame, and the blind. And you will be blessed, because they cannot repay you, for you will be repaid at the resurrection of the righteous."

The Gospel of the Lord.

◆ All sit and observe silence.

FOR SILENT REFLECTION

Think about this silently in your heart. Why do you think it is important to give without expecting anything in return?

CLOSING PRAYER

Let us pray to God for our needs and the needs of others: our family, neighborhood, and the world. For each need we say, "Lord, hear our prayer."

◆ All may add their own prayers here.

Let us pray: **Our Father . . . Amen.**

Loving and generous God,
Jesus reached out to everyone.
Help us to be more like him and
to be kind to all we meet.
For this we pray
through Christ our Lord.

Amen.

✛ All make the Sign of the Cross.

OPENING

This week we will hear the story of Jonah, a prophet who lived in the fifth century BC, and the conflict between him and God. God commands Jonah to go to Nineveh and tell the people to repent. Jonah resists because Nineveh is the capital of the Assyrian empire, the traditional enemy of Israel. It was unthinkable to Jonah, an Israelite, to believe that a nation as wicked as Assyria could be forgiven. Jonah tries to flee, but God has a plan.

✦ All make the Sign of the Cross.

In the name of the Father, and of the Son, and of the Holy Spirit. Amen.

PSALM
(For a longer psalm, see page xi.)
Psalm 66:1–3a, 5, 8, 16–17

Make a joyful noise to God, all the earth.

Make a joyful noise to God, all the earth.

Make a joyful noise to God, all the earth;
 sing praise to the glory of his name;
 give to him glorious praise.
Say to God, "How awesome are your deeds!"

Make a joyful noise to God, all the earth.

READING
Jonah 1:1–2a, 2c–3b, 4–5ace, 6acd

A reading from the Book of prophet Jonah.

Now the word of the LORD came to Jonah son of Amittai [uh-MIT-ahy], saying, "Go at once to Nineveh, and cry out against it; for their wickedness has come up before me." But Jonah set out to flee to Tarshish from the presence of the LORD. He went down to Joppa and found a ship going to Tarshish. But the LORD hurled a great wind upon the sea, and such a mighty storm came upon the sea that the ship threatened to break up. Then the mariners were afraid. They threw the cargo that was in the ship into the sea, to lighten it for them. Jonah, meanwhile, was fast asleep. The captain came and said to him, "Get up, call on your god! Perhaps the god will spare us a thought so that we do not perish."

The Word of the Lord.

◆ All observe silence.

FOR SILENT REFLECTION

Think about this silently in your heart. Why do you think God caused the wind to create a storm when Jonah tried to flee?

CLOSING PRAYER

Let us pray to God for our needs and the needs of others: our family, neighborhood, and the world. For each need we say, "Lord, hear our prayer."

◆ All may add their own prayers here.

Let us pray: **Our Father . . . Amen.**

Holy and faithful God,
no one can hide from you.
Help us to listen for your voice and to respond to your call.
We pray in the name of
Christ our Lord.

Amen.

✦ All make the Sign of the Cross.

OPENING

As we heard previously, God creates a storm at sea so that the boat that Jonah is trying to escape on is in danger of capsizing. The men on the boat blame Jonah and ask him what they should do to calm the sea. Jonah makes an interesting suggestion, which we will hear today.

✚ All make the Sign of the Cross.

In the name of the Father, and of the Son, and of the Holy Spirit. Amen.

PSALM

(For a longer psalm, see page xi.)
Psalm 66:1–3a, 5, 8, 16–17

Make a joyful noise to God, all the earth.

Make a joyful noise to God, all the earth.

Make a joyful noise to God, all the earth;
    sing praise to the glory of his name;
    give to him glorious praise.
Say to God, "How awesome are your deeds!"

Make a joyful noise to God, all the earth.

READING

Jonah 1:10–12, 15, 17

A reading from the Book of prophet Jonah.

Then the men were even more afraid, and said to Jonah, "What is this that you have done!" For the men knew that he was fleeing from the presence of the LORD, because he had told them so. Then they said to him, "What shall we do to you, that the sea may quiet down for us?" For the sea was growing more and more tempestuous. He said to them, "Pick me up and throw me into the sea; then the sea will quiet down for you; for I know it is because of me that this great storm has come upon you."

So they picked Jonah up and threw him into the sea; and the sea ceased from its raging. But the LORD provided a large fish to swallow up Jonah; and Jonah was in the belly of the fish three days and three nights.

The Word of the Lord.

◆ All observe silence.

FOR SILENT REFLECTION

Think about this silently in your heart. What is God calling you to do that you are avoiding or don't want to do?

CLOSING PRAYER

Let us pray to God for our needs and the needs of others: our family, neighborhood, and the world. For each need we say, "Lord, hear our prayer."

◆ All may add their own prayers here.

Let us pray: **Our Father . . . Amen.**

O God,
be with us in the storms of life.
Just as you protected Jonah,
keep us safe from all harm.
We ask this in Christ's name.

Amen.

✚ All make the Sign of the Cross.

OPENING

In the belly of a great fish, Jonah is desperate. He is in darkness and despair for three days, and when he sees no hope for his life he prays for mercy. God has not forgotten Jonah but hears his cries. We can look at Jonah's story as a metaphor for our own lives.

✚ All make the Sign of the Cross.

In the name of the Father, and of the Son, and of the Holy Spirit. Amen.

PSALM

(For a longer psalm, see page xi.)
Psalm 66:1–3a, 5, 8, 16–17

Make a joyful noise to God, all the earth.

Make a joyful noise to God, all the earth.

Make a joyful noise to God, all the earth;
   sing praise to the glory of his name;
   give to him glorious praise.
Say to God, "How awesome are your deeds!"

Make a joyful noise to God, all the earth.

READING

Jonah 2:1, 3–5a, 6b–7, 9–10

A reading from the Book of prophet Jonah.

Then Jonah prayed to the LORD his God from the belly of the fish, saying, "You cast me into the deep, into the heart of the seas, and the flood surrounded me; all your waves and your billows passed over me. Then I said, 'I am driven away from your sight; how shall I look again upon your holy temple?' The waters closed in over me; the deep surrounded me; yet you brought up my life from the Pit, O LORD my God. As my life was ebbing away, I remembered the LORD; and my prayer came to you, into your holy temple. But I with the voice of thanksgiving will sacrifice to you; what I have vowed I will pay. Deliverance belongs to the LORD!" Then the LORD spoke to the fish, and it spewed Jonah out upon the dry land.

The Word of the Lord.

◆ All observe silence.

FOR SILENT REFLECTION

Think about this silently in your heart. God was merciful to Jonah. Have people forgiven you when you have apologized? Have you forgiven anyone who said sorry to you?

CLOSING PRAYER

Let us pray to God for our needs and the needs of others: our family, neighborhood, and the world. For each need we say, "Lord, hear our prayer."

◆ All may add their own prayers here.

Let us pray: **Our Father . . . Amen.**

O God,
when we do something wrong
help us to ask for forgiveness.
We trust in your mercy and
your loving care.
We pray in the name of Jesus Christ, your Son.

Amen.

✚ All make the Sign of the Cross.

OPENING

God gives Jonah a second chance, and this time Jonah obeys God. Jonah goes to Nineveh [NIN-uh-vuh] and proclaims God's message. Jonah learns a valuable lesson about the Lord's mercy and forgiveness, which extends beyond Jonah and Israel to all people who repent and believe.

✚ All make the Sign of the Cross.

In the name of the Father, and of the Son, and of the Holy Spirit. Amen.

PSALM

(For a longer psalm, see page xi.)
Psalm 66:1–3a, 5, 8, 16–17

Make a joyful noise to God, all the earth.

Make a joyful noise to God, all the earth.

Make a joyful noise to God, all the earth;
  sing praise to the glory of his name;
  give to him glorious praise.
Say to God, "How awesome are your deeds!"

Make a joyful noise to God, all the earth.

READING

Jonah 3:1–2ac, 4–7a, 8b, 10

A reading from the Book of prophet Jonah.

The word of the LORD came to Jonah a second time, saying, "Get up, go to Nineveh, and proclaim to it the message that I tell you." Jonah began to go into the city, going a day's walk. And he cried out, "Forty days more, and Nineveh shall be overthrown!" And the people of Nineveh believed God; they proclaimed a fast, and everyone, great and small, put on sackcloth. When the news reached the king of Nineveh, he rose from his throne, removed his robe, covered himself with sackcloth, and sat in ashes. Then he had a proclamation made in Nineveh: "All shall turn from their evil ways and from the violence that is in their hands." When God saw what they did, God changed his mind about the calamity that he had said he would bring upon them; and he did not do it.

The Word of the Lord.

◆ All observe silence.

FOR SILENT REFLECTION

Think about this silently in your heart. When have you experienced a change of heart and changed how you act toward someone?

CLOSING PRAYER

Let us pray to God for our needs and the needs of others: our family, neighborhood, and the world. For each need we say, "Lord, hear our prayer."

◆ All may add their own prayers here.

Let us pray: **Our Father . . . Amen.**

We thank you, O God,
for your love and mercy,
which you give us even when we fail.
May we turn away from evil and violence
and truly live as your people.
We ask this in Christ's name.

Amen.

✚ All make the Sign of the Cross.

OPENING

Today's Gospel reading has some strong words. It is addressed to adults more than to children. Jesus uses the example of what is needed to build a tower to teach his disciples that following him will not be easy and will require sacrifices.

✚ All make the Sign of the Cross.

In the name of the Father, and of the Son, and of the Holy Spirit. Amen.

PSALM

(For a longer psalm, see page xi.)
Psalm 66:1–3a, 5, 8, 16–17

Make a joyful noise to God, all the earth.

Make a joyful noise to God, all the earth.

Make a joyful noise to God, all the earth;
    sing praise to the glory of his name;
    give to him glorious praise.
Say to God, "How awesome are your deeds!"

Make a joyful noise to God, all the earth.

◆ All stand and sing **Alleluia.**

GOSPEL

Luke 14:25–30, 33

A reading from the holy Gospel according to Luke.

Now large crowds were traveling with Jesus; and he turned and said to them, "Whoever comes to me and does not hate father and mother, wife and children, brothers and sisters, yes, and even life itself, cannot be my disciple. Whoever does not carry the cross and follow me cannot be my disciple. For which of you, intending to build a tower, does not first sit down and estimate the cost, to see whether he has enough to complete it? Otherwise, when he has laid a foundation and is not able to finish, all who see it will begin to ridicule him, saying, 'This fellow began to build and was not able to finish.' So therefore, none of you can become my disciple if you do not give up all your possessions."

The Gospel of the Lord.

◆ All sit and observe silence.

FOR SILENT REFLECTION

Think about this silently in your heart. Do you ever feel that following Jesus' teachings is hard?

CLOSING PRAYER

Let us pray to God for our needs and the needs of others: our family, neighborhood, and the world. For each need we say, "Lord, hear our prayer."

◆ All may add their own prayers here.

Let us pray: **Our Father . . . Amen.**

O God, give us your Spirit's gifts
of right judgment and courage
so we may truly be the hands, feet,
and voice of Jesus for everyone we meet.
We ask this in Christ's name.

Amen.

✚ All make the Sign of the Cross.

OPENING

The prophet Jeremiah [jayr-uh-MI-uh] lived during a difficult time when Israel was attacked by hostile nations again and again. It was hard for the people to remain hopeful. Jeremiah reminds people to listen to God's voice and to remember God's covenant of love and protection with Israel. Listening to God helps the people remain hopeful. Today we remember St. Peter Claver, who spent his life offering hope to the African slaves in Colombia and tending to their physical and spiritual needs.

✚ All make the Sign of the Cross.

In the name of the Father, and of the Son, and of the Holy Spirit. Amen.

PSALM

(For a longer psalm, see page xi.)
Psalm 66:1–3a, 5, 8, 16–17

Make a joyful noise to God, all the earth.

Make a joyful noise to God, all the earth.

Make a joyful noise to God, all the earth;
  sing praise to the glory of his name;
  give to him glorious praise.
Say to God, "How awesome are your deeds!"

Make a joyful noise to God, all the earth.

READING

Jeremiah 11:1–3ab, 4cd–6

A reading from the Book of the prophet Jeremiah.

The word that came to Jeremiah from the LORD: Hear the words of this covenant, and speak to the people of Judah and the inhabitants of Jerusalem. You shall say to them, Thus says the LORD, the God of Israel, Listen to my voice, and do all that I command you. So shall you be my people, and I will be your God, that I may perform the oath that I swore to your ancestors, to give them a land flowing with milk and honey, as at this day. Then I answered, "So be it, LORD." And the LORD said to me: Proclaim all these words in the cities of Judah, and in the streets of Jerusalem: Hear the words of this covenant and do them.

The Word of the Lord.

◆ All observe silence.

FOR SILENT REFLECTION

Think about this silently in your heart. Does praying, which is talking and listening to God, make you feel hopeful when you are troubled?

CLOSING PRAYER

Let us pray to God for our needs and the needs of others: our family, neighborhood, and the world. For each need we say, "Lord, hear our prayer."

◆ All may add their own prayers here.

Let us pray: **Our Father . . . Amen.**

Help us to listen to your voice, O God.
Like the prophet Jeremiah,
may we hear your words
and proclaim your covenant.
This we ask through Christ our Lord.

Amen.

✚ All make the Sign of the Cross.

OPENING

In today's reading, Samuel, who became a great leader and prophet of the Hebrew people, is praying in the temple when God calls him. At first, Samuel thinks it is a person nearby who is calling him. He needs help to realize that it is the Lord who is calling his name. Sometimes God's voice is very quiet; sometimes it is loud and clear.

✚ All make the Sign of the Cross.

In the name of the Father, and of the Son, and of the Holy Spirit. Amen.

PSALM

(For a longer psalm, see page xi.)
Psalm 66:1–3a, 5, 8, 16–17

Make a joyful noise to God, all the earth.

Make a joyful noise to God, all the earth.

Make a joyful noise to God, all the earth;
  sing praise to the glory of his name;
  give to him glorious praise.
Say to God, "How awesome are your deeds!"

Make a joyful noise to God, all the earth.

READING

1 Samuel 3:2ac, 3b, 4–6ac, 8ac–9ab, 10

A reading from the First Book of Samuel.

At that time Eli was lying down in his room; and Samuel was lying down in the temple of the LORD. Then the LORD called, "Samuel! Samuel!" and he said, "Here I am!" and ran to Eli, and said, "Here I am, for you called me." But Eli said, "I did not call; lie down again." So Samuel went and lay down. The LORD called again, "Samuel!" Samuel got up and went to Eli. But he said, "I did not call." The LORD called Samuel again. Then Eli perceived that the LORD was calling the boy. Therefore Eli said to Samuel, "Go, lie down; and if he calls you, you shall say, 'Speak, LORD, for your servant is listening.'" Now the LORD came and stood there, calling as before, "Samuel! Samuel!" And Samuel said, "Speak, for your servant is listening."

The Word of the Lord.

◆ All observe silence.

FOR SILENT REFLECTION

Think about this silently in your heart. Can you pray like Samuel and say, "Speak, Lord, for your servant is listening"?

CLOSING PRAYER

Let us pray to God for our needs and the needs of others: our family, neighborhood, and the world. For each need we say, "Lord, hear our prayer."

◆ All may add their own prayers here.

Let us pray: **Our Father . . . Amen.**

O God, give us your Spirit's gifts
of right judgment and courage
so we may truly be the hands, feet,
and voice of Jesus for everyone we meet.
We ask this in Christ's name.

Amen.

✚ All make the Sign of the Cross.

OPENING

Often we are so busy with school, sports, homework, chores, and friends that it is difficult to find time to quietly pray and listen to God. Today's Gospel reading is about two sisters, Martha and Mary. One takes the time to listen to Jesus. Today we remember all of the people who died on September 11, 2001. We honor them by praying for peace in our world.

✦ All make the Sign of the Cross.

In the name of the Father, and of the Son, and of the Holy Spirit. Amen.

PSALM

(For a longer psalm, see page xi.)
Psalm 66:1–3a, 5, 8, 16–17

Make a joyful noise to God, all the earth.

Make a joyful noise to God, all the earth.

Make a joyful noise to God, all the earth;
  sing praise to the glory of his name;
  give to him glorious praise.
Say to God, "How awesome are your deeds!"

Make a joyful noise to God, all the earth.

◆ All stand and sing **Alleluia.**

GOSPEL

Luke 10:38–42

A reading from the holy Gospel according to Luke.

Now as they went on their way, Jesus entered a certain village, where a woman named Martha welcomed him into her home. She had a sister named Mary, who sat at the Lord's feet and listened to what he was saying. But Martha was distracted by her many tasks; so she came to him and asked, "Lord, do you not care that my sister has left me to do all the work by myself? Tell her then to help me." But the Lord answered her, "Martha, Martha, you are worried and distracted by many things; there is need of only one thing. Mary has chosen the better part, which will not be taken away from her."

The Gospel of the Lord.

◆ All sit and observe silence.

FOR SILENT REFLECTION

Think about this silently in your heart. Can you make some quiet time today to talk and listen to God?

CLOSING PRAYER

Let us pray to God for our needs and the needs of others: our family, neighborhood, and the world. For each need we say, "Lord, hear our prayer."

◆ All may add their own prayers here.

Let us pray: **Our Father . . . Amen.**

Holy God, Father of all,
you desire that we all live in peace.
Help us to be peacemakers in our families,
our classrooms,
and our neighborhoods.
We ask this through Jesus Christ, our Lord.

Amen.

✦ All make the Sign of the Cross.

PRAYER SERVICE
NATIONAL DAY OF SERVICE AND REMEMBRANCE ON SEPTEMBER 11

Prepare six leaders for this service. The second leader will need a Bible for the Scripture and may need help practicing for the reading. You may begin by singing "Healer of Our Every Ill," "Song of the Body of Christ," or "This Is My Song," or perhaps begin in silence with a simple tolling of a hand bell.

FIRST LEADER:
May the grace and peace of our Lord Jesus Christ be with us, now and for ever.

Amen.

Let us pray:
Lord Jesus Christ,
we remember all those who died
on that September day in 2001,
people of different faiths and
backgrounds and ways of life.
We turn to you now, Lord of all,
to give us the courage to be peacemakers
and servants to all people in the world.

Amen.

◆ All stand and sing **Alleluia.**

SECOND LEADER: Luke 6:36–37
A reading from the holy Gospel according
to Luke.

◆ Read the Gospel passage from the Bible.

The Gospel of the Lord.

THIRD LEADER:
Let us pause and pray in silence for all those who have died in wars and other conflicts around the world.

◆ Allow a minute of silence.

FOURTH LEADER:
We recall the beautiful prayer of peace of St. Francis of Assisi:

Lord, make me an instrument of your peace;
where there is hatred, let me sow love;
where there is injury, pardon;
where there is doubt, faith;
where there is despair, hope;
where there is darkness, light;
and where there is sadness, joy.
Grant that I may not so much seek
to be consoled as to console;
to be understood as to understand;
to be loved as to love;
for it is in giving that we receive,
it is in pardoning that we are pardoned,
and it is in dying that we are born to
eternal life.

Amen.

FIFTH LEADER:
Now let us offer to one another a sign of Christ's peace:

◆ All offer one another a sign of peace.

SIXTH LEADER:
And may the Lord bless us,

✠ All make the Sign of the Cross.

protect us from all evil,
and bring us to everlasting life.

Amen.

CHILDREN'S DAILY PRAYER 2019–2020 © 2019 Archdiocese of Chicago: Liturgy Training Publications. All rights reserved. Orders: 800-933-1800 or www.LTP.org.

OPENING

Today we honor the Most Holy Name of Mary. There are many devotions to Mary, the Mother of God, because of her special place in salvation history. Mary said yes to God's invitation to be the mother of Jesus, and when we hear her name, we are reminded that we are also called to say yes to God's invitation.

✦ All make the Sign of the Cross.

In the name of the Father, and of the Son, and of the Holy Spirit. Amen.

PSALM

(For a longer psalm, see page xi.)
Psalm 66:1–3a, 5, 8, 16–17

Make a joyful noise to God, all the earth.

Make a joyful noise to God, all the earth.

Make a joyful noise to God, all the earth;
   sing praise to the glory of his name;
   give to him glorious praise.
Say to God, "How awesome are your deeds!"

Make a joyful noise to God, all the earth.

READING

Colossians 3:12–16

A reading from the Letter of Paul to the Colossians.

As God's chosen ones, holy and beloved, clothe yourselves with compassion, kindness, humility, meekness, and patience. Bear with one another and, if anyone has a complaint against another, forgive each other; just as the Lord has forgiven you, so you must also forgive. Above all, clothe yourself with love, which binds everything together in perfect harmony. And let the peace of Christ rule in your hearts, to which indeed you were called in the one body. And be thankful. Let the word of Christ dwell in you richly; teach and admonish one another in all wisdom; and with gratitude in your hearts sing psalms, hymns, and spiritual songs to God.

The Word of the Lord.

◆ All observe silence.

FOR SILENT REFLECTION

Think about this silently in your heart. You are also chosen by God. How might you clothe yourself in compassion and kindness?

CLOSING PRAYER

Let us pray to God for our needs and the needs of others: our family, neighborhood, and the world. For each need we say, "Lord, hear our prayer."

◆ All may add their own prayers here.

Let us pray: **Our Father . . . Amen.**

Grant to us, O Lord,
the desire to follow your will.
May we see in Mary, the mother of your Son Jesus,
a good example to live by.
We ask this through Christ our Lord.

Amen.

✦ All make the Sign of the Cross.

OPENING

Today we remember St. John Chrysostom. He was a bishop and Doctor of the Church. The name Chrysostom means "golden mouth," and he became a great teacher. Our reading tells about Lydia, a woman who listened to the Apostles preaching about Jesus and then she followed them.

✦ All make the Sign of the Cross.

In the name of the Father, and of the Son, and of the Holy Spirit. Amen.

PSALM

(For a longer psalm, see page xi.)
Psalm 66:1–3a, 5, 8, 16–17

Make a joyful noise to God, all the earth.

Make a joyful noise to God, all the earth.

Make a joyful noise to God, all the earth;
  sing praise to the glory of his name;
  give to him glorious praise.
Say to God, "How awesome are your deeds!"

Make a joyful noise to God, all the earth.

READING

Acts 16:11a, 12ac, 13–15

A reading from the Acts of the Apostles.

We set sail from Troas [TROH-az] and took a straight course to Samothrace, and from there to Philippi [fih-LIP-ī]. We remained in this city for some days. On the sabbath day we went outside the gate by the river, where we supposed there was a place of prayer; and we sat down and spoke to the women who had gathered there. A certain woman named Lydia, a worshiper of God, was listening to us; she was from the city of Thyatira [thī-uh-TĪ-ruh] and a dealer in purple cloth. The Lord opened her heart to listen eagerly to what was said by Paul. When she and her household were baptized, she urged us saying, "If you have judged me to be faithful to the Lord, come and stay at my home." And she prevailed upon us.

The Word of the Lord.

◆ All observe silence.

FOR SILENT REFLECTION

Think about this silently in your heart. What do you want to know about God? What Scripture stories help you know more about God?

CLOSING PRAYER

Let us pray to God for our needs and the needs of others: our family, neighborhood, and the world. For each need we say, "Lord, hear our prayer."

◆ All may add their own prayers here.

Let us pray: **Our Father . . . Amen.**

Loving God, we give you thanks
for the people in our lives who help
us to hear your word
and to know more about you.
May we listen with open minds and hearts.
We ask this through Christ our Lord.

Amen.

✦ All make the Sign of the Cross.

OPENING

Today's Gospel tells the parable of the shepherd who goes in search of the lost sheep. Jesus is revealing how God cares for each and every person.

✚ All make the Sign of the Cross.

In the name of the Father, and of the Son, and of the Holy Spirit. Amen.

PSALM

(For a longer psalm, see page xi.)
Psalm 66:1–3a, 5, 8, 16–17

Make a joyful noise to God, all the earth.

Make a joyful noise to God, all the earth.

Make a joyful noise to God, all the earth;
  sing praise to the glory of his name;
  give to him glorious praise.
Say to God, "How awesome are your deeds!"

Make a joyful noise to God, all the earth.

◆ All stand and sing **Alleluia.**

GOSPEL

Luke 15:1–7

A reading from the holy Gospel according to Luke.

Now all the tax collectors and sinners were coming near to listen to him. And the Pharisees and the scribes were grumbling and saying, "This fellow welcomes sinners and eats with them." So he told them this parable: "Which one of you, having a hundred sheep and losing one of them, does not leave the ninety-nine in the wilderness and go after the one that is lost until he finds it? When he has found it, he lays it on his shoulders and rejoices. And when he comes home, he calls together his friends and neighbors, saying to them, 'Rejoice with me, for I have found my sheep that was lost.' Just so, I tell you, there will be more joy in heaven over one sinner who repents than over ninety-nine righteous persons who need no repentance."

The Gospel of the Lord.

◆ All sit and observe silence.

FOR SILENT REFLECTION

Think about this silently in your heart. Did you notice how happy the shepherd is when he finds the lost sheep? What makes him so joyful?

CLOSING PRAYER

Let us pray to God for our needs and the needs of others: our family, neighborhood, and the world. For each need we say, "Lord, hear our prayer."

◆ All may add their own prayers here.

Let us pray: **Our Father . . . Amen.**

We praise and thank you,
O Father,
for your great love and care.
Help us to follow you always.
We pray this in the name of Jesus Christ,
our Good Shepherd.

Amen.

✚ All make the Sign of the Cross.

OPENING

In Scripture, God tells us repeatedly how he wants us to live. This message is in both the Old Testament and the New Testament and is called the Great Commandment. In today's reading, Moses tells the Hebrews how important this commandment is. Today is the Memorial of Sts. Cornelius and Cyprian, who both helped and welcomed back Christians who were persecuted.

✦ All make the Sign of the Cross.

In the name of the Father, and of the Son, and of the Holy Spirit. Amen.

PSALM
(For a longer psalm, see page xi.)
Psalm 66:1–3a, 5, 8, 16–17

Make a joyful noise to God, all the earth.

Make a joyful noise to God, all the earth.

Make a joyful noise to God, all the earth;
    sing praise to the glory of his name;
    give to him glorious praise.
Say to God, "How awesome are your deeds!"

Make a joyful noise to God, all the earth.

READING
Deuteronomy 5:1a; 6:1, 3a, 5–9

A reading from the Book of Deuteronomy.

Moses convened all Israel, and said to them: Now this is the commandment—the statutes and the ordinances—that the LORD your God charged me to teach you to observe in the land that you are about to cross into and occupy. Hear therefore, O Israel, and observe them diligently, so that it may go well with you. You shall love the LORD your God with all your heart, and with all your soul, and with all your might. Keep these words that I am commanding you today in your heart. Recite them to your children and talk about them when you are at home and when you are away, when you lie down and when you rise. Bind them as a sign on your hand, fix them as an emblem on your forehead, and write them on the doorposts of your house and on your gates.

The Word of the Lord.

◆ All observe silence.

FOR SILENT REFLECTION

Think about this silently in your heart. How do you show that you love the Lord your God with all your heart?

CLOSING PRAYER

Let us pray to God for our needs and the needs of others: our family, neighborhood, and the world. For each need we say, "Lord, hear our prayer."

◆ All may add their own prayers here.

Let us pray: **Our Father . . . Amen.**

Holy God,
help us to love you with our whole heart, and soul, and might.
We know that if we love you,
we will do your will.
We ask this in Christ's name.

Amen.

✦ All make the Sign of the Cross.

OPENING

Today's reading from the New Testament repeats the Great Commandment we heard yesterday, and adds a new command. This double commandment reflects the two tablets of the Ten Commandments. The first three command that we love God, and the last seven command that we love our neighbor. Today is the feast of St. Robert Bellarmine (1542–1621). He was known for his good preaching and leadership.

✦ All make the Sign of the Cross.

In the name of the Father, and of the Son, and of the Holy Spirit. Amen.

PSALM

(For a longer psalm, see page xi.)
Psalm 66:1–3a, 5, 8, 16–17

Make a joyful noise to God, all the earth.

Make a joyful noise to God, all the earth.

Make a joyful noise to God, all the earth;
   sing praise to the glory of his name;
   give to him glorious praise.
Say to God, "How awesome are your deeds!"

Make a joyful noise to God, all the earth.

◆ All stand and sing **Alleluia.**

GOSPEL

Luke 10:25–28

A reading from the holy Gospel according to Luke.

Just then a lawyer stood up to test Jesus. "Teacher," he said, "what must I do to inherit eternal life?" He said to him, "What is written in the law? What do you read there?" He answered, "You shall love the Lord your God with all your heart, and with all your soul, and with all your strength, and with all your mind; and your neighbor as yourself." And Jesus said to him, "You have given the right answer; do this, and you will live."

The Gospel of the Lord.

◆ All sit and observe silence.

FOR SILENT REFLECTION

Think about this silently in your heart. Jesus tells us it is important to love ourselves. Why?

CLOSING PRAYER

Let us pray to God for our needs and the needs of others: our family, neighborhood, and the world. For each need we say, "Lord, hear our prayer."

◆ All may add their own prayers here.

Let us pray: **Our Father . . . Amen.**

God of love and mercy,
your law is a law of love.
You desire that all people
live together in peace and goodwill.
Help us to follow your Great Commandment.
For this we pray
through Jesus Christ, our Lord.

Amen.

✦ All make the Sign of the Cross.

OPENING

The Great Commandment says, "Love your neighbor as yourself." In our readings today and tomorrow, Jesus challenges the religious law of his time. Religious leaders were forbidden from touching people considered unclean. If they did touch them, they would become unclean themselves and suffer shame. So Jesus tells a story about a wounded person and the people who do and do not act like a neighbor. Levites assisted the priests in the Temple.

✚ All make the Sign of the Cross.

In the name of the Father, and of the Son, and of the Holy Spirit. Amen.

PSALM

(For a longer psalm, see page xi.)
Psalm 66:1–3a, 5, 8, 16–17

Make a joyful noise to God, all the earth.

Make a joyful noise to God, all the earth.

Make a joyful noise to God, all the earth;
    sing praise to the glory of his name;
    give to him glorious praise.
Say to God, "How awesome are your deeds!"

Make a joyful noise to God, all the earth.

◆ All stand and sing **Alleluia.**

GOSPEL

Luke 10:29–32

A reading from the holy Gospel according to Luke.

But wanting to justify himself, the lawyer asked Jesus, "And who is my neighbor?" Jesus replied, "A man was going down from Jerusalem to Jericho, and fell into the hands of robbers, who stripped him, beat him, and went away, leaving him half dead. Now by chance a priest was going down that road; and when he saw him, he passed by on the other side. So likewise a Levite, when he came to the place and saw him, passed by on the other side."

The Gospel of the Lord.

◆ All sit and observe silence.

FOR SILENT REFLECTION

Think about this silently in your heart. What do you think of how the priest and the Levite acted?

CLOSING PRAYER

Let us pray to God for our needs and the needs of others: our family, neighborhood, and the world. For each need we say, "Lord, hear our prayer."

◆ All may add their own prayers here.

Let us pray: **Our Father . . . Amen.**

Good and generous God,
no one is beyond your care.
We pray that we will be good neighors
and friends,
especially to those in need.
We pray this in Christ's name.

Amen.

✚ All make the Sign of the Cross.

OPENING

Today we continue the parable from yesterday. Jews and Samaritans [suh-MAYR-uh-tuhns] hated one another because of centuries of war between their peoples. Despite the hostility, the Samaritan is the one in Jesus' story who is able to set aside prejudice and show compassion for the injured man after the religious leaders pass him by!

✛ All make the Sign of the Cross.

In the name of the Father, and of the Son, and of the Holy Spirit. Amen.

PSALM

(For a longer psalm, see page xi.)
Psalm 66:1–3a, 5, 8, 16–17

Make a joyful noise to God, all the earth.

Make a joyful noise to God, all the earth.

Make a joyful noise to God, all the earth;
   sing praise to the glory of his name;
   give to him glorious praise.
Say to God, "How awesome are your deeds!"

Make a joyful noise to God, all the earth.

◆ All stand and sing **Alleluia.**

GOSPEL

Luke 10:33–37

A reading from the holy Gospel according to Luke.

"But a Samaritan while traveling came near the half-dead man; and when he saw him, he was moved with pity. The Samaritan went to him and bandaged his wounds, having poured oil and wine on them. Then he put him on his own animal, brought him to an inn, and took care of him. The next day he took out two denarii, gave them to the innkeeper, and said, 'Take care of him; and when I come back, I will repay you whatever more you spend.' Which of these three, do you think, was a neighbor to the man who fell into the hands of the robbers?" The lawyer said, "The one who showed him mercy." Jesus said to him, "Go and do likewise."

The Gospel of the Lord.

◆ All sit and observe silence.

FOR SILENT REFLECTION

Think about this silently in your heart. Who is your neighbor?

CLOSING PRAYER

Let us pray to God for our needs and the needs of others: our family, neighborhood, and the world. For each need we say, "Lord, hear our prayer."

◆ All may add their own prayers here.

Let us pray: **Our Father . . . Amen.**

Good and gracious God,
help us to follow the example
of the Samaritan.
May we show care and kindness
to those in need.
We pray this in Christ's name.

Amen.

✛ All make the Sign of the Cross.

PRAYER FOR
FRIDAY, SEPTEMBER 20, 2019

OPENING

In today's reading, St. Paul is writing to the early Christians at Ephesus [EF-uh-suhs]. He tells them how to be good neighbors to one another. His advice is a guide to how we should treat our family, our friends and classmates, and our neighbors. He tells us how to live the Great Commandment. Like St. Paul, who did much to establish the young Church, Sts. Andrew Kim Tae-gŏn, Paul Chŏng Ha-sang, and Companions gave their lives to spread the Catholic Church in Korea. We remember them today.

✦ All make the Sign of the Cross.

In the name of the Father, and of the Son, and of the Holy Spirit. Amen.

PSALM
(For a longer psalm, see page xi.)
Psalm 66:1–3a, 5, 8, 16–17

Make a joyful noise to God, all the earth.

Make a joyful noise to God, all the earth.

Make a joyful noise to God, all the earth;
   sing praise to the glory of his name;
   give to him glorious praise.
Say to God, "How awesome are your deeds!"

Make a joyful noise to God, all the earth.

READING
Ephesians 4:25–26, 29, 31—5:2

A reading from the Letter of Paul to the Ephesians [ee-FEE-zhuhnz].

So then, putting away falsehood, let all of us speak the truth to our neighbors, for we are members of one another. Be angry but do not sin; do not let the sun go down on your anger. Let no evil talk come out of your mouths, but only what is useful for building up, as there is need, so that your words may give grace to those who hear. Put away from you all bitterness and wrath and anger and wrangling and slander, together with all malice, and be kind to one another, tenderhearted, forgiving one another, as God in Christ has forgiven you. Therefore be imitators of God, as beloved children, and live in love, as Christ loved us and gave himself up for us, a fragrant offering and sacrifice to God.

The Word of the Lord.

✦ All observe silence.

FOR SILENT REFLECTION

Think about this silently in your heart. St. Paul says that words can give grace. Think of how your words may be grace for others today.

CLOSING PRAYER

Let us pray to God for our needs and the needs of others: our family, neighborhood, and the world. For each need we say, "Lord, hear our prayer."

✦ All may add their own prayers here.

Let us pray: **Our Father . . . Amen.**

God of grace and mercy,
may we use the gift of speech
to show kindness, forgiveness,
and love.
May we follow your Son, Jesus,
in whose name we pray.

Amen.

✦ All make the Sign of the Cross.

OPENING

In today's Gospel Jesus tells a puzzling parable. It appears that the manager is cheating his master, yet the master praises him. It is a moral parable, which means it gives a message for how we should live our lives.

✛ All make the Sign of the Cross.

In the name of the Father, and of the Son, and of the Holy Spirit. Amen.

PSALM
(For a longer psalm, see page xi.)
Psalm 66:1–3a, 5, 8, 16–17

Make a joyful noise to God, all the earth.

Make a joyful noise to God, all the earth.

Make a joyful noise to God, all the earth;
  sing praise to the glory of his name;
  give to him glorious praise.
Say to God, "How awesome are your deeds!"

Make a joyful noise to God, all the earth.

◆ All stand and sing **Alleluia.**

GOSPEL
Luke 16:1–3a, 4–6, 8a

A reading from the holy Gospel according to Luke.

Then Jesus said to the disciples, "There was a rich man who had a manager, and charges were brought to him that this man was squandering his property. So he summoned him and said to him, 'What is this that I hear about you? Give me an accounting of your management, because you cannot be my manager any longer.' Then the manager said to himself, 'I have decided what to do so that, when I am dismissed as manager, people may welcome me into their homes.' So, summoning his master's debtors one by one, he asked the first, 'How much do you owe my master?' He answered, 'A hundred jugs of olive oil.' He said to him, 'Take your bill, sit down quickly, and make it fifty.' And his master commended the dishonest manager because he had acted shrewdly."

The Gospel of the Lord.

◆ All sit and observe silence.

FOR SILENT REFLECTION

Think about this silently in your heart. What do you think about the manager's forgiving part of the people's debt?

CLOSING PRAYER

Let us pray to God for our needs and the needs of others: our family, neighborhood, and the world. For each need we say, "Lord, hear our prayer."

◆ All may add their own prayers here.

Let us pray: **Our Father . . . Amen.**

Holy and loving God,
you see what is in our hearts.
Judge us kindly, O God,
and help us to be
your faithful servants.
For this we pray
through Christ our Lord.

Amen.

✛ All make the Sign of the Cross.

OPENING

For the next two weeks, we will read the story of the creation of the world. Each day something new and wonderful comes into being. In the beginning there was nothing, and little by little God created our marvelous universe. As you listen, imagine that you are there. Each day you witness the creation of an essential and marvelous element of the universe take shape.

✚ All make the Sign of the Cross.

In the name of the Father, and of the Son, and of the Holy Spirit. Amen.

PSALM

(For a longer psalm, see page xi.)
Psalm 66:1–3a, 5, 8, 16–17

Make a joyful noise to God, all the earth.

Make a joyful noise to God, all the earth.

Make a joyful noise to God, all the earth;
    sing praise to the glory of his name;
    give to him glorious praise.
Say to God, "How awesome are your deeds!"

Make a joyful noise to God, all the earth.

READING

Genesis 1:1–8

A reading from the Book of Genesis.

In the beginning when God created the heavens and the earth, the earth was a formless void and darkness covered the face of the deep, while a wind from God swept over the face of the waters. Then God said, "Let there be light"; and there was light. And God saw that the light was good; and God separated the light from the darkness. God called the light Day, and the darkness he called Night. And there was evening and there was morning, the first day. And

God said, "Let there be a dome in the midst of the waters, and let it separate the waters from the waters." So God made the dome and separated the waters that were under the dome from the waters that were above the dome. And it was so. God called the dome Sky. And there was evening and there was morning, the second day.

The Word of the Lord.

◆ All observe silence.

FOR SILENT REFLECTION

Think about this silently in your heart. How do you imagine light and dark, day and night coming into being?

CLOSING PRAYER

Let us pray to God for our needs and the needs of others: our family, neighborhood, and the world. For each need we say, "Lord, hear our prayer."

◆ All may add their own prayers here.

Let us pray: **Our Father . . . Amen.**

Holy God, you are the Creator of all life.
We thank you for the beauty
of the earth, the skies, and the seas.
Help us to care for the gift of life
in all its forms.
We ask this in Christ's name.

Amen.

✚ All make the Sign of the Cross.

OPENING

Today we hear about the third day of creation when the earth began to bloom with flowers and plants. The earth was becoming more beautiful and also capable of sustaining life. Much of what is needed for animal and human life is being prepared on this day. As you listen, think of what types of flowers and plants grow where you live.

✛ All make the Sign of the Cross.

In the name of the Father, and of the Son, and of the Holy Spirit. Amen.

PSALM

(For a longer psalm, see page xi.)
Psalm 66:1–3a, 5, 8, 16–17

Make a joyful noise to God, all the earth.

Make a joyful noise to God, all the earth.

Make a joyful noise to God, all the earth;
   sing praise to the glory of his name;
   give to him glorious praise.
Say to God, "How awesome are your deeds!"

Make a joyful noise to God, all the earth.

READING

Genesis 1:9–13

A reading from the Book of Genesis.

And God said, "Let the waters under the sky be gathered together into one place, and let the dry land appear." And it was so. God called the dry land Earth, and the waters that were gathered together he called Seas. And God saw that it was good. Then God said, "Let the earth put forth vegetation: plants yielding seed, and fruit trees of every kind on earth that bear fruit with the seed in it." And it was so. The earth brought forth vegetation: plants yielding seed of every kind, and trees of every kind bearing fruit with the seed in it. And God saw that it was good. And there was evening and there was morning, the third day.

The Word of the Lord.

◆ All observe silence.

FOR SILENT REFLECTION

Think about this silently in your heart. Imagine what the earth looked like as plants began to grow, and give thanks for the flowers, plants, and trees.

CLOSING PRAYER

Let us pray to God for our needs and the needs of others: our family, neighborhood, and the world. For each need we say, "Lord, hear our prayer."

◆ All may add their own prayers here.

Let us pray: **Our Father . . . Amen.**

Holy God, you are the Creator of all life.
We thank you for the beauty
and bounty of flowers, plants, and trees.
Help us to care for the gift of life
in all its forms.
We ask this in Christ's name.

Amen.

✛ All make the Sign of the Cross.

PRAYER FOR
WEDNESDAY, SEPTEMBER 25, 2019

OPENING

On the fourth day of creation, God makes the day and night skies different from each other. He creates the sun and the moon, stars, and planets. In this way, God creates the possibility for different seasons and times of the year. In creating night and day, God provides time for activity and for quiet, for growth and for rest.

✝ All make the Sign of the Cross.

In the name of the Father, and of the Son, and of the Holy Spirit. Amen.

PSALM

(For a longer psalm, see page xi.)
Psalm 66:1–3a, 5, 8, 16–17

Make a joyful noise to God, all the earth.

Make a joyful noise to God, all the earth.

Make a joyful noise to God, all the earth;
    sing praise to the glory of his name;
    give to him glorious praise.
Say to God, "How awesome are your deeds!"

Make a joyful noise to God, all the earth.

READING

Genesis 1:14–19

A reading from the Book of Genesis.

And God said, "Let there be lights in the dome of the sky to separate the day from the night; and let them be for signs and for seasons and for days and years, and let them be lights in the dome of the sky to give light upon the earth." And it was so. God made the two great lights—the greater light to rule the day and the lesser light to rule the night—and the stars. God set them in the dome of the sky to give light upon the earth, to rule over the day and over the night, and to separate the light from the darkness. And God

saw that it was good. And there was evening and there was morning, the fourth day.

The Word of the Lord.

◆ All observe silence.

FOR SILENT REFLECTION

Think about this silently in your heart. How can we thank God for the marvels of moon, stars, and sun?

CLOSING PRAYER

Let us pray to God for our needs and the needs of others: our family, neighborhood, and the world. For each need we say, "Lord, hear our prayer."

◆ All may add their own prayers here.

Let us pray: **Our Father . . . Amen.**

Holy God, Creator of all life,
we thank you for the light
of the sun, stars, and moon, and
for the seasons that help us mark the year.
Help us to care for the gift of life
in all its forms.
We ask this in Christ's name.

Amen.

✝ All make the Sign of the Cross.

OPENING

On the fifth day of the Creation story, God begins to fill the earth and seas and skies with living creatures. We know that it took a lot longer than a day for all of these marvelous creatures to inhabit the earth. But the writers of the Creation story use the measure of a day to show us how the earth developed over time. Today we remember the brothers Sts. Cosmas and Damian, who are mentioned in Eucharistic Prayer I. Listen for their names at Mass.

✝ All make the Sign of the Cross.

In the name of the Father, and of the Son, and of the Holy Spirit. Amen.

PSALM

(For a longer psalm, see page xi.)
Psalm 66:1–3a, 5, 8, 16–17

Make a joyful noise to God, all the earth.

Make a joyful noise to God, all the earth.

Make a joyful noise to God, all the earth;
  sing praise to the glory of his name;
  give to him glorious praise.
Say to God, "How awesome are your deeds!"

Make a joyful noise to God, all the earth.

READING

Genesis 1:20–25abd

A reading from the Book of Genesis.

And God said, "Let the waters bring forth swarms of living creatures, and let birds fly above the earth across the dome of the sky." So God created the great sea monsters and every living creature that moves, of every kind, with which the waters swarm, and every winged bird of every kind. And God saw that it was good. God blessed them, saying, "Be fruitful and multiply and fill the waters in the seas, and let birds multiply on the earth." And there was evening and there was morning, the fifth day. And God said, "Let the earth bring forth living creatures of every kind: cattle and creeping things and wild animals of the earth of every kind." And it was so. God made the wild animals of the earth of every kind, and the cattle of every kind. And God saw that it was good.

The Word of the Lord.

◆ All observe silence.

FOR SILENT REFLECTION

Think about this silently in your heart. Notice how all that God creates, God calls "good." What does that tell you about creation?

CLOSING PRAYER

Let us pray to God for our needs and the needs of others: our family, neighborhood, and the world. For each need we say, "Lord, hear our prayer."

◆ All may add their own prayers here.

Let us pray: **Our Father . . . Amen.**

Holy God, all of creation
reflects your goodness.
Help us to enjoy and to care for
the birds in the air, the fish in
the sea, and the animals that
live on earth.
We ask this in Christ's name.

Amen.

✝ All make the Sign of the Cross.

OPENING

On the sixth day, God creates human beings. As humans, we are made in God's very image. Humans are given dominion over other living things. We have learned that this means that we must respect the natural world and be caregivers of it. This is a great trust from God. Pope Francis wrote about this in his 2015 encyclical, *Praised Be*. Today is the feast of St. Vincent de Paul, who dedicated his life to serving those in need.

✛ All make the Sign of the Cross.

In the name of the Father, and of the Son, and of the Holy Spirit. Amen.

PSALM

(For a longer psalm, see page xi.)
Psalm 66:1–3a, 5, 8, 16–17

Make a joyful noise to God, all the earth.

Make a joyful noise to God, all the earth.

Make a joyful noise to God, all the earth;
 sing praise to the glory of his name;
 give to him glorious praise.
Say to God, "How awesome are your deeds!"

Make a joyful noise to God, all the earth.

READING

Genesis 1:26–28

A reading from the Book of Genesis.

Then God said, "Let us make humankind in our image, according to our likeness; and let them have dominion over the fish of the sea, and over the birds of the air, and over the cattle, and over all the wild animals of the earth, and over every creeping thing that creeps upon the earth." So God created humankind in his image, in the image of God he created them;

male and female he created them. God blessed them, and God said to them, "Be fruitful and multiply, and fill the earth and subdue it; and have dominion over the fish of the sea and over the birds of the air and over every living thing that moves upon the earth."

The Word of the Lord.

◆ All observe silence.

FOR SILENT REFLECTION

Think about this silently in your heart. What does it mean to you to be made in the image of God?

CLOSING PRAYER

Let us pray to God for our needs and the needs of others: our family, neighborhood, and the world. For each need we say, "Lord, hear our prayer."

◆ All may add their own prayers here.

Let us pray: **Our Father . . . Amen.**

Holy God, you created us
in your image so that we can
cooperate with you.
Help us to tend your creation
and give you glory.
We ask this in Christ's name.

Amen.

✛ All make the Sign of the Cross.

PRAYER FOR THE WEEK

OPENING

In the time of Jesus, riches were seen as a sign of God's blessing and poverty and sickness as signs of God's displeasure. Jesus challenges this way of thinking. Today's Gospel teaches that earthly riches are to be shared by all people. The story of Lazarus shows us how much God cares for and loves those who suffer.

✚ All make the Sign of the Cross.

In the name of the Father, and of the Son, and of the Holy Spirit. Amen.

PSALM

(For a longer psalm, see page xi.)
Psalm 145:2–3, 4–5, 10–11

I will praise your name for ever, LORD.

I will praise your name for ever, LORD.

Every day I will bless you,
  and praise your name forever and ever.
Great is the LORD, and greatly to be praised;
  his greatness is unsearchable.

I will praise your name for ever, LORD.

◆ All stand and sing **Alleluia.**

GOSPEL

Luke 16:19–21a, 22–23ac, 24–25

A reading from the holy Gospel according to Luke.

There was a rich man who was dressed in purple and fine linen and who feasted sumptuously every day. And at his gate lay a poor man named Lazarus, covered with sores, who longed to satisfy his hunger with what fell from the rich man's table. The poor man died and was carried away by the angels to be with Abraham. The rich man also died and was buried. In Hades, he looked up and saw Abraham far away with Lazarus by his side. He called out, "Father Abraham, have mercy on me, and send Lazarus to dip the tip of his finger in water and cool my tongue; for I am in agony in these flames." But Abraham said, "Child, remember that during your lifetime you received your good things, and Lazarus in like manner evil things; but now he is comforted here, and you are in agony."

The Gospel of the Lord.

◆ All sit and observe silence.

FOR SILENT REFLECTION

Think about this silently in your heart. How might you share with people who have less than you have?

CLOSING PRAYER

Let us pray to God for our needs and the needs of others: our family, neighborhood, and the world. For each need we say, "Lord, hear our prayer."

◆ All may add their own prayers here.

Let us pray: **Our Father . . . Amen.**

God of justice and mercy,
help us to notice those who need our care.
Help us to be generous and share
what we have with others.
We ask this through Christ our Lord.

Amen.

✚ All make the Sign of the Cross.

OPENING

This week we continue to hear about the creation of the world and the great care God took to provide for all of our needs. On the sixth day of creation God provides food for humans and animals in the form of plants that have seeds. Because they have seeds, the plants will continue to grow and be a source of nourishment. Today is the memorial of St. Jerome. He is the patron saint of students and librarians.

✛ All make the Sign of the Cross.

In the name of the Father, and of the Son, and of the Holy Spirit. Amen.

PSALM

(For a longer psalm, see page xi.)
Psalm 145:2–3, 4–5, 10–11

I will praise your name for ever, LORD.

I will praise your name for ever, LORD.

Every day I will bless you,
   and praise your name forever and ever.
Great is the LORD, and greatly to be praised;
   his greatness is unsearchable.
I will praise your name for ever, LORD.

READING

Genesis 1:29–31

A reading from the Book of Genesis.

God said, "See, I have given you every plant yielding seed that is upon the face of all the earth, and every tree with seed in its fruit; you shall have them for food. And to every beast of the earth, and to every bird of the air, and to everything that creeps on the earth, everything that has the breath of life, I have given every green plant for food." And it was so. God saw everything that he had made, and indeed, it was very good. And there was evening and there was morning, the sixth day.

The Word of the Lord.

◆ All observe silence.

FOR SILENT REFLECTION

Think about this silently in your heart. How do you give thanks for the food that nourishes you and gives you the energy you need to live?

CLOSING PRAYER

Let us pray to God for our needs and the needs of others: our family, neighborhood, and the world. For each need we say, "Lord, hear our prayer."

◆ All may add their own prayers here.

Let us pray: **Our Father . . . Amen.**

Holy God, you are the creator of all life.
We thank you for the gift
of plants that feed us and flowers
that make our world
colorful and joyful.
Help us to appreciate these gifts.
We ask this in Christ's name.

Amen.

✛ All make the Sign of the Cross.

OPENING

Today we will finish our reading of the story of creation from the Book of Genesis. On the seventh day, creation was finished. God rested and hallowed that day. To "hallow" means to make holy. Today we remember the young saint St. Thérèse of the Child Jesus. She believed that small acts of great love were just as important as heroic deeds.

✦ All make the Sign of the Cross.

In the name of the Father, and of the Son, and of the Holy Spirit. Amen.

PSALM

(For a longer psalm, see page xi.)
Psalm 145:2–3, 4–5, 10–11

I will praise your name for ever, LORD.

I will praise your name for ever, LORD.

Every day I will bless you,
  and praise your name forever and ever.
Great is the LORD, and greatly to be praised;
  his greatness is unsearchable.

I will praise your name for ever, LORD.

READING

Genesis 2:1–4a

A reading from the Book of Genesis.

Thus the heavens and the earth were finished, and all their multitude. And on the seventh day God finished the work that he had done, and he rested on the seventh day from all the work that he had done. So God blessed the seventh day and hallowed it, because on it God rested from all the work that he had done in creation.

These are the generations of the heavens and the earth when they were created.

The Word of the Lord.

✦ All observe silence.

FOR SILENT REFLECTION

Think about this silently in your heart. Imagine the beauty of the earth, and give thanks for what you most enjoy in creation.

CLOSING PRAYER

Let us pray to God for our needs and the needs of others: our family, neighborhood, and the world. For each need we say, "Lord, hear our prayer."

✦ All may add their own prayers here.

Let us pray: **Our Father . . . Amen.**

Holy God, creator of the universe,
we praise you!
We thank you for the many gifts
of creation.
We ask you to bless all that lives.
Help us to care for creation
as you have cared for us.
We ask this in Christ's name.

Amen.

✦ All make the Sign of the Cross.

PRAYER FOR
WEDNESDAY, OCTOBER 2, 2019

OPENING

We know that God rested after completing the work of creation. In today's reading, we hear how the Lord gives Moses the command to have the people work for six days and then rest on the seventh day. God knows people need rest to stay well physically and spiritually, so it is important to take a break or to slow down. Today we honor the memorial of the Holy Guardian Angels, who guard and guide us in all we do.

✚ All make the Sign of the Cross.

In the name of the Father, and of the Son, and of the Holy Spirit. Amen.

PSALM

(For a longer psalm, see page xi.)
Psalm 145:2–3, 4–5, 10–11

I will praise your name for ever, Lord.

I will praise your name for ever, Lord.

Every day I will bless you,
    and praise your name forever and ever.
Great is the Lord, and greatly to be praised;
    his greatness is unsearchable.

I will praise your name for ever, Lord.

READING

Exodus 34:1a, 21, 26a, 27; 35:1–2ab, 3

A reading from the Book of Exodus.

The Lord said to Moses: Six days you shall work, but on the seventh day you shall rest; even in plowing time and in harvest time you shall rest. The best of the first fruits of your ground you shall bring to the house of the Lord your God. The Lord said to Moses: Write these words; in accordance with these words I have made a covenant with you and with Israel. Moses assembled all the congregation of the Israelites and said to them: These are the things that the Lord has commanded you to do: Six days shall work be done, but on the seventh day you shall have a holy sabbath of solemn rest to the Lord. You shall kindle no fire in all your dwellings on the sabbath day.

The Word of the Lord.

◆ All observe silence.

FOR SILENT REFLECTION

Think about this silently in your heart. How do you rest on Sunday?

CLOSING PRAYER

Let us pray to God for our needs and the needs of others: our family, neighborhood, and the world. For each need we say, "Lord, hear our prayer."

◆ All may add their own prayers here.

Let us pray: **Our Father . . . Amen.**

Angel of God, my guardian dear,
to whom God's love commits me here,
ever this day be at my side
to light and guard, to rule and guide.

Amen.

✚ All make the Sign of the Cross.

OPENING

In our reading, Isaiah speaks of how God's word is like the rain and the snow that waters the earth and makes it fruitful. Listening to God's word helps us to bear good fruit in our lives.

✝ All make the Sign of the Cross.

In the name of the Father, and of the Son, and of the Holy Spirit. Amen.

PSALM
(For a longer psalm, see page xi.)
Psalm 145:2–3, 4–5, 10–11

I will praise your name for ever, LORD.

I will praise your name for ever, LORD.

Every day I will bless you,
  and praise your name forever and ever.
Great is the LORD, and greatly to be praised;
  his greatness is unsearchable.

I will praise your name for ever, LORD.

READING
Isaiah 55:10–12

A reading from the Book of the prophet Isaiah.

For as the rain and the snow come down from heaven, and do not return there until they have watered the earth, making it bring forth and sprout, giving seed to the sower and bread to the eater, so shall my word be that goes out from my mouth; it shall not return to me empty, but it shall accomplish that which I purpose, and succeed in the thing for which I sent it. For you shall go out in joy, and be led back in peace; the mountains and the hills before you shall burst into song, and all the trees of the field shall clap their hands.

The Word of the Lord.

◆ All observe silence.

FOR SILENT REFLECTION

Think about this silently in your heart. God created a beautiful and healthy earth. How can you care for the part of earth where you live?

CLOSING PRAYER

Let us pray to God for our needs and the needs of others: our family, neighborhood, and the world. For each need we say, "Lord, hear our prayer."

◆ All may add their own prayers here.

Let us pray: **Our Father . . . Amen.**

Creator God,
May we accomplish the purpose
for which you created us.
May we be joyful and bring peace.
We ask this in Christ's name.

Amen.

✝ All make the Sign of the Cross.

OPENING

Judith, a Jewish heroine who saved her people from the Assyrian army, wrote a joyful hymn thanking God for his help. In the reading today, we hear her praise God as the Lord of all creation. We also celebrate St. Francis of Assisi today. He also wrote songs in praise of creation and is remembered for his love of animals and people.

✛ All make the Sign of the Cross.

In the name of the Father, and of the Son, and of the Holy Spirit. Amen.

PSALM

(For a longer psalm, see page xi.)
Psalm 145:2–3, 4–5, 10–11

I will praise your name for ever, LORD.

I will praise your name for ever, LORD.

Every day I will bless you,
   and praise your name forever and ever.
Great is the LORD, and greatly to be praised;
   his greatness is unsearchable.

I will praise your name for ever, LORD.

READING

Judith 15:14—16:1, 13–15

A reading from the Book of Judith.

Judith began this thanksgiving before all Israel, and all the people loudly sang this song of praise. And Judith said, Begin a song to my God with tambourines, sing to my Lord with cymbals. Raise to him a new psalm; exalt him, and call upon his name. I will sing to my God a new song: O Lord you are great and glorious, wonderful in strength, invincible. Let all your creatures serve you, for you spoke, and they were made. You sent forth your spirit, and it formed them; there is none that can resist your voice. For the mountains shall be shaken to their foundations with the waters; before your glance the rocks shall melt like wax. But to those who fear you, you show mercy.

The Word of the Lord.

◆ All observe silence.

FOR SILENT REFLECTION

Think about this silently in your heart. How do you praise God? How do you think all creation praises God?

CLOSING PRAYER

Let us pray to God for our needs and the needs of others: our family, neighborhood, and the world. For each need we say, "Lord, hear our prayer."

◆ All may add their own prayers here.

Let us pray: **Our Father . . . Amen.**

God of all creation,
help us to learn from the example of
your servant, St. Francis of Assisi.
May we be good, faithful stewards
of all of creation.
This we ask through Christ our Lord.

Amen.

✛ All make the Sign of the Cross.

PRAYER FOR THE WEEK

WITH A READING FROM THE GOSPEL FOR **SUNDAY, OCTOBER 6, 2019**

OPENING

Today's reading reminds us how powerful faith in God is. Even faith as small as a mustard seed can bring about great changes in our lives. When we have faith, we gladly respond to God's call.

✛ All make the Sign of the Cross.

In the name of the Father, and of the Son, and of the Holy Spirit. Amen.

PSALM

(For a longer psalm, see page xi.)
Psalm 145:2–3, 4–5, 10–11

I will praise your name for ever, LORD.

I will praise your name for ever, LORD.

Every day I will bless you,
 and praise your name forever and ever.
Great is the LORD, and greatly to be praised;
 his greatness is unsearchable.

I will praise your name for ever, LORD.

◆ All stand and sing **Alleluia.**

GOSPEL

Luke 17:5–10

A reading from the holy Gospel according to Luke.

The apostles said to the Lord, "Increase our faith!" The Lord replied, "If you had faith the size of a mustard seed, you could say to this mulberry tree, 'Be uprooted and planted in the sea,' and it would obey you. Who among you would say to your slave who has just come in from plowing or tending sheep in the field, 'Come here at once and take your place at the table'? Would you not rather say to him, 'Prepare supper for me, put on your apron and serve me while I eat and drink; later you may eat and drink'? Do you thank the slave for doing what was commanded? So you also, when you have done all that you were ordered to do, say, 'We are worthless slaves; we have done only what we ought to have done!'"

The Gospel of the Lord.

◆ All sit and observe silence.

FOR SILENT REFLECTION

Think about this silently in your heart. Can you imagine yourself as God's servant? What do you think that would mean?

CLOSING PRAYER

Let us pray to God for our needs and the needs of others: our family, neighborhood, and the world. For each need we say, "Lord, hear our prayer."

◆ All may add their own prayers here.

Let us pray: **Our Father . . . Amen.**

Increase our faith, O God.
When we are in need,
help us to have faith in you.
Let our faith grow deep roots
and flourish like strong trees.
We ask this through Christ our Lord.

Amen.

✛ All make the Sign of the Cross.

PRAYER SERVICE
MEMORIAL OF OUR LADY OF THE ROSARY

Prepare eight leaders for this service. The third and fourth leaders will need Bibles for the Scripture passages and may need help practicing the readings. You may wish to begin by singing "The Servant Song" and end with "We Have Been Told." If the group will sing, prepare a song leader.

FIRST LEADER:

✝ All make the Sign of the Cross.

May the grace and peace of our Lord Jesus Christ be with us, now and forever.

Amen.

SECOND LEADER:

Today we celebrate Mary,
the Mother of our Lord Jesus,
whose life of holiness always pointed
toward Christ our Savior.
And today we honor her with this feast
in thanksgiving for the Rosary
that highlights the mysteries of
the life and Death of our Messiah.
May we say "yes" to God
as she did throughout her life.
We ask this through Christ our Lord.

Amen.

◆ All stand and sing Alleluia.

THIRD LEADER: Luke 1:39–45

A reading from the holy Gospel according to Luke.

◆ Read the passage from a Bible.

The Gospel of the Lord.

Response: **Praise to you, Lord Jesus Christ.**

FOURTH LEADER: Luke 1:46–56

A reading from the holy Gospel according to Luke.

◆ Read the passage from a Bible.

The Gospel of the Lord.

Response: Praise to you, Lord Jesus Christ.

◆ All sit and observe silence.

FIFTH LEADER:

Lord Jesus,
your Mother's life
was centered around you.
Through the gift of the Rosary,
we can reflect on the key events
in your life filled with
joy, sorrow, and glory.
Guide us toward living as fully
as Mary did as we meditate on
your mysteries.
In your name we pray.

Amen.

SIXTH LEADER:

Together let us pray one decade of
the Rosary in honor of this
feast of our Mother Mary:

Hail Mary, full of grace
the Lord is with you,
blessed are you among women
and blessed is the fruit of your womb, Jesus.
Holy Mary, Mother of God,
pray for us sinners,
now and at the hour of our death.

Amen.

Glory be to the Father,
and to the Son,
and to the Holy Spirit.
As it was in the beginning,
is now and ever shall be
world without end.

Amen.

SEVENTH LEADER:

Loving Jesus,
fill our hearts with the same
loving response as Mary had
when the angel Gabriel asked her
to be the Mother of our Lord.
May we be mindful of how you
also remained faithful to God's will
through the tragedies and joys
of your life.
Help us to be vessels of your grace.
In your name we pray.

Amen.

EIGHTH LEADER:

May the love of God,

✛ All make the Sign of the Cross.

Father, Son, and Holy Spirit,
keep us connected with the help of
our Mother Mary,
now and forever.

Amen.

PRAYER FOR
MONDAY, OCTOBER 7, 2019

OPENING

Today we celebrate Mary, Our Lady of the Rosary. The Rosary, one of the most beloved devotions in the Catholic Church, dates to the Middle Ages when a practice developed of praying the Hail Mary on a set of beads. The Rosary honors Mary, who praised God for looking with favor upon her. She served God and all humanity when she said yes to be the mother of Jesus.

✦ All make the Sign of the Cross.

In the name of the Father, and of the Son, and of the Holy Spirit. Amen.

PSALM
(For a longer psalm, see page xi.)
Psalm 145:2–3, 4–5, 10–11

I will praise your name for ever, LORD.

I will praise your name for ever, LORD.

Every day I will bless you,
and praise your name forever and ever.
Great is the LORD, and greatly to be praised;
his greatness is unsearchable.

I will praise your name for ever, LORD.

◆ All stand and sing **Alleluia.**

GOSPEL
Luke 22:14–15, 24–25a, 26–27

A reading from the holy Gospel according to Luke.

When the hour came, Jesus took his place at the table, and the apostles with him. He said to them, "I have eagerly desired to eat this Passover with you before I suffer." A dispute also arose among them as to which one of them was to be regarded as the greatest. But Jesus said to them, "The kings of the Gentiles lord it over them. But not so with you; rather the greatest among you must become like the youngest, and the leader like one who serves. For who is greater, the one who is at the table or the one who serves? Is it not the one at the table? But I am among you as one who serves."

The Gospel of the Lord.

◆ All sit and observe silence.

FOR SILENT REFLECTION

Think about this silently in your heart. To follow Jesus, we must learn how to be of service to others. How can you serve others?

CLOSING PRAYER

Let us pray to God for our needs and the needs of others: our family, neighborhood, and the world. For each need we say, "Lord, hear our prayer."

◆ All may add their own prayers here.

Let us pray: **Our Father . . . Amen.**

Holy God,
may we learn from the example
of Mary, who called herself your lowly
servant, and from your Son Jesus,
who showed us how to serve others.
We ask this through your Son,
our Lord Jesus Christ.

Amen.

✦ All make the Sign of the Cross.

OPENING

In today's reading, St. Paul says that we serve one another when we do not let differences between us become obstacles to friendship and love. He uses the example of eating certain foods, which Jews were forbidden to eat. Yet, he says, we should not let rules and beliefs be the cause of tension. Rather, we should seek the spirit of peace and joy.

✦ All make the Sign of the Cross.

In the name of the Father, and of the Son, and of the Holy Spirit. Amen.

PSALM

(For a longer psalm, see page xi.)
Psalm 145:2–3, 4–5, 10–11

I will praise your name for ever, LORD.

I will praise your name for ever, LORD.

Every day I will bless you,
and praise your name forever and ever.
Great is the LORD, and greatly to be praised;
his greatness is unsearchable.

I will praise your name for ever, LORD.

READING

Romans 14:13–18

A reading from the Letter of Paul to the Romans.

Let us therefore no longer pass judgment on one another, but resolve instead never to put a stumbling block or hindrance in the way of another. I know and am persuaded in the Lord Jesus that nothing is unclean in itself; but it is unclean for anyone who thinks it unclean. If your brother or sister is being injured by what you eat, you are no longer walking in love. Do not let what you eat cause the ruin of one for whom Christ died. So do not let your good be spoken of as evil. For the kingdom of God is not food and drink but righteousness and peace and joy in the Holy Spirit. The one who thus serves Christ is acceptable to God and has human approval.

The Word of the Lord.

◆ All observe silence.

FOR SILENT REFLECTION

Think about this silently in your heart. Why do you think it is important not to judge others?

CLOSING PRAYER

Let us pray to God for our needs and the needs of others: our family, neighborhood, and the world. For each need we say, "Lord, hear our prayer."

◆ All may add their own prayers here.

Let us pray: **Our Father . . . Amen.**

God of love and mercy,
please give us a generous spirit.
Help us to live in peace and truth
with one another.
We know this is your will for us,
and we pray in Christ's name.

Amen.

✦ All make the Sign of the Cross.

PRAYER FOR
WEDNESDAY, OCTOBER 9, 2019

OPENING

This week we have been listening to readings about how we can serve others and live peacefully together. Today's reading gives us some very specific ways to live as Christians. Each of us is called to share our gifts with others.

✦ All make the Sign of the Cross.

In the name of the Father, and of the Son, and of the Holy Spirit. Amen.

PSALM

(For a longer psalm, see page xi.)
Psalm 145:2–3, 4–5, 10–11

I will praise your name for ever, Lord.

I will praise your name for ever, Lord.

Every day I will bless you,
  and praise your name forever and ever.
Great is the Lord, and greatly to be praised;
  his greatness is unsearchable.

I will praise your name for ever, Lord.

READING

1 Peter 4:7–11

A reading from the First Letter of Peter.

The end of all things is near; therefore be serious and discipline yourselves for the sake of your prayers. Above all, maintain constant love for one another, for love covers a multitude of sins. Be hospitable to one another without complaining. Like good stewards of the manifold grace of God, serve one another with whatever gift each of you has received. Whoever speaks must do so as one speaking the very words of God; whoever serves must do so with the strength that God supplies, so that God may be glorified in all things through Jesus Christ. To him belong the glory and the power forever and ever. Amen.

The Word of the Lord.

✦ All observe silence.

FOR SILENT REFLECTION

Think about this silently in your heart. St. Paul says that we must serve one another with the gifts we each received from God. What are some of your gifts?

CLOSING PRAYER

Let us pray to God for our needs and the needs of others: our family, neighborhood, and the world. For each need we say, "Lord, hear our prayer."

✦ All may add their own prayers here.

Let us pray: **Our Father . . . Amen.**

God our Creator,
you made each one of us unique.
You gave each of us gifts to share.
We thank you and praise you for the
diversity of gifts and talents in our world.
May we use them to glorify you.
In Jesus Christ's name we pray.

Amen.

✦ All make the Sign of the Cross.

OPENING

One way that we serve others is to be generous with our gifts, talents, and possessions. In today's reading, we hear that God wants us to give with a cheerful spirit.

✚ All make the Sign of the Cross.

In the name of the Father, and of the Son, and of the Holy Spirit. Amen.

PSALM

(For a longer psalm, see page xi.)
Psalm 145:2–3, 4–5, 10–11

I will praise your name for ever, Lord.

I will praise your name for ever, Lord.

Every day I will bless you,
and praise your name forever and ever.
Great is the Lord, and greatly to be praised;
his greatness is unsearchable.

I will praise your name for ever, Lord.

READING

2 Corinthians 9:7–8a, 10–11

A reading from the Second Letter of Paul to the Corinthians.

Each of you must give as you have made up your mind, not reluctantly or under compulsion, for God loves a cheerful giver. And God is able to provide you with every blessing in abundance. He who supplies seed to the sower and bread for food will supply and multiply your seed for sowing and increase the harvest of your righteousness. You will be enriched in every way for your great generosity, which will produce thanksgiving to God through us.

The Word of the Lord.

◆ All observe silence.

FOR SILENT REFLECTION

Think about this silently in your heart. God gives us gifts to share with others. What gift can you share? Is it kindness or humor or help?

CLOSING PRAYER

Let us pray to God for our needs and the needs of others: our family, neighborhood, and the world. For each need we say, "Lord, hear our prayer."

◆ All may add their own prayers here.

Let us pray: **Our Father . . . Amen.**

God of all good gifts,
help us to give cheerfully to others.
Help us to be grateful for all of the gifts
you have given to us.
We ask this in Christ's name.

Amen.

✚ All make the Sign of the Cross.

PRAYER FOR
FRIDAY, OCTOBER 11, 2019

OPENING

Today we remember St. John XXIII [the twenty-third], a pope and great leader of our Church. He called for the Second Vatican Council during the 1960s and opened new interfaith dialogues with Protestants, Jews, and Muslims. In our reading today, we hear about the importance of living together in unity.

✚ All make the Sign of the Cross.

In the name of the Father, and of the Son, and of the Holy Spirit. Amen.

PSALM

(For a longer psalm, see page xi.)
Psalm 145:2–3, 4–5, 10–11

I will praise your name for ever, Lord.

I will praise your name for ever, Lord.

Every day I will bless you,
    and praise your name forever and ever.
Great is the Lord, and greatly to be praised;
    his greatness is unsearchable.

I will praise your name for ever, Lord.

READING

Ephesians 2:14, 19–22

A reading from the Letter of Paul to the Ephesians [ee-FEE-zhuhnz]

Christ is our peace; in his flesh he has made both groups into one and has broken down the dividing wall, that is, the hostility between us. So then you are no longer strangers and aliens, but you are citizens with the saints and also members of the household of God, built upon the foundation of the apostles and prophets, with Christ Jesus himself as the cornerstone. In him the whole structure is joined together and grows into a holy temple in the Lord; in whom you also are built together spiritually into a dwelling place for God.

The Word of the Lord.

◆ All observe silence.

FOR SILENT REFLECTION

Think about this silently in your heart. Is there anything you need to do to get along better with people who are different from you?

CLOSING PRAYER

Let us pray to God for our needs and the needs of others: our family, neighborhood, and the world. For each need we say, "Lord, hear our prayer."

◆ All may add their own prayers here.

Let us pray: **Our Father . . . Amen.**

Holy God, Creator of all peoples,
we pray that we may learn
to live together in peace.
Help us to see you in each person we meet.
This we ask through your Son, Jesus Christ our Lord.

Amen.

✚ All make the Sign of the Cross.

PRAYER FOR THE WEEK

WITH A READING FROM THE GOSPEL FOR **SUNDAY, OCTOBER 13, 2019**

OPENING

Today's Gospel challenges us to think about the importance of gratitude. Although Jesus heals ten lepers, only one says thank you.

✚ All make the Sign of the Cross.

In the name of the Father, and of the Son, and of the Holy Spirit. Amen.

PSALM

(For a longer psalm, see page xi.)
Psalm 145:2–3, 4–5, 10–11

I will praise your name for ever, LORD.

I will praise your name for ever, LORD.

Every day I will bless you,
 and praise your name forever and ever.
Great is the LORD, and greatly to be praised;
 his greatness is unsearchable.

I will praise your name for ever, LORD.

◆ All stand and sing **Alleluia.**

GOSPEL

Luke 17:11–19

A reading from the holy Gospel according to Luke.

On the way to Jerusalem Jesus was going through the region between Samaria and Galilee. As he entered a village, ten lepers approached him. Keeping their distance, they called out, saying, "Jesus, Master, have mercy on us!" When he saw them, he said to them, "Go and show yourselves to the priests." And as they went, they were made clean. Then one of them, when he saw that he was healed, turned back, praising God with a loud voice. He prostrated himself at Jesus' feet and thanked him. And he was a Samaritan. Then Jesus asked, "Were not ten made clean? But the other nine, where are they? Was none of them found to return and give praise to God except this foreigner?" Then he said to him, "Get up and go on your way; your faith has made you well."

The Gospel of the Lord.

◆ All sit and observe silence.

FOR SILENT REFLECTION

Think about this silently in your heart. Why do you think it is important to say thank you and show appreciation?

CLOSING PRAYER

Let us pray to God for our needs and the needs of others: our family, neighborhood, and the world. For each need we say, "Lord, hear our prayer."

◆ All may add their own prayers here.

Let us pray: **Our Father . . . Amen.**

Grant us grateful hearts, O God.
Help us to show appreciation
to others and, most of all,
to give you thanks for
your many great gifts to us.
We ask this in the name of Jesus Christ,
our Lord.

Amen.

✚ All make the Sign of the Cross.

PRAYER FOR
MONDAY, OCTOBER 14, 2019

OPENING

A covenant is an agreement between two parties to respect and honor one another. God established a covenant with humankind. God gave the first man and woman guidance about how to live. Today we read the first part of this story that we will continue throughout the week.

✚ All make the Sign of the Cross.

In the name of the Father, and of the Son, and of the Holy Spirit. Amen.

PSALM

(For a longer psalm, see page xi.)
Psalm 145:2–3, 4–5, 10–11

I will praise your name for ever, LORD.

I will praise your name for ever, LORD.

Every day I will bless you,
    and praise your name forever and ever.
Great is the LORD, and greatly to be praised;
    his greatness is unsearchable.

I will praise your name for ever, LORD.

READING

Genesis 2:15–18, 21–23, 25

A reading from the Book of Genesis.

The LORD God took the man and put him in the garden of Eden to till it and keep it. And the LORD God commanded the man, "You may freely eat of every tree of the garden; but of the tree of the knowledge of good and evil you shall not eat, for in the day that you eat of it you shall die." Then the LORD God said, "It is not good that the man should be alone; I will make him a helper as his partner." So the LORD God caused a deep sleep to fall upon the man, and he slept; then he took one of his ribs and closed up its place with flesh. And the rib that the LORD God had taken from the man he made into a woman and brought her to the man. Then the man said, "This at last is bone of my bones and flesh of my flesh; this one shall be called Woman, for out of Man this one was taken." And the man and his wife were both naked, and were not ashamed.

The Word of the Lord.

◆ All observe silence.

FOR SILENT REFLECTION

Think about this silently in your heart. Why would God ask the man not to eat from the tree of knowledge of good and evil?

CLOSING PRAYER

Let us pray to God for our needs and the needs of others: our family, neighborhood, and the world. For each need we say, "Lord, hear our prayer."

◆ All may add their own prayers here.

Let us pray: **Our Father . . . Amen.**

O God,
help us to keep our promise to be faithful
and to honor you.
We ask this through Christ our Lord.

Amen.

✚ All make the Sign of the Cross.

OPENING

Today we hear how the serpent tempts the man and woman to eat from the tree of knowledge. Today we celebrate St. Teresa of Avila. She was a strong, wise, and capable woman who wrote many important books about God and the spiritual life.

✚ All make the Sign of the Cross.

In the name of the Father, and of the Son, and of the Holy Spirit. Amen.

PSALM

(For a longer psalm, see page xi.)
Psalm 66:1–3a, 5 and 8, 16–17

I will praise your name for ever, LORD.

I will praise your name for ever, LORD.

Every day I will bless you,
   and praise your name forever and ever.
Great is the LORD, and greatly to be praised;
   his greatness is unsearchable.

I will praise your name for ever, LORD.

READING

Genesis 3:1–6acd, 7a

A reading from the Book of Genesis.

Now the serpent was more crafty than any other wild animal that the LORD God had made. He said to the woman, "Did God say, 'You shall not eat from any tree in the garden'?" The woman said to the serpent, "We may eat of the fruit of the trees in the garden; but God said, 'You shall not eat of the fruit of the tree that is in the middle of the garden, nor shall you touch it, or you shall die.'" But the serpent said to the woman, "You will not die; for God knows that when you eat of it your eyes will be opened, and you will be like God, knowing good and evil." So when the woman saw that the tree was good for food, she took of its fruit and ate; and she also gave some to her husband, and he ate. Then the eyes of both were opened, and they knew that they were naked.

The Word of the Lord.

◆ All observe silence.

FOR SILENT REFLECTION

Think about this silently in your heart. Are you sometimes tempted to do things you shouldn't? Is it hard to say no?

CLOSING PRAYER

Let us pray to God for our needs and the needs of others: our family, neighborhood, and the world. For each need we say, "Lord, hear our prayer."

◆ All may add their own prayers here.

Let us pray: **Our Father . . . Amen.**

Loving God,
forgive us when we fail
to do what is right.
Help us to live as your
obedient sons and daughters.
We ask this in Christ's name.

Amen.

✚ All make the Sign of the Cross.

WEDNESDAY, OCTOBER 16, 2019

OPENING

Tempted by the serpent, the man and the woman disobeyed God and ate the fruit of the tree he forbade them to eat. Now they are ashamed and try to hide from God. Whereas before they were happy, now they experience fear and blame. Today we remember St. Margaret Mary Alacoque, who promoted the devotion of God's great love for us in the Most Sacred Heart of Jesus.

✛ All make the Sign of the Cross.

In the name of the Father, and of the Son, and of the Holy Spirit. Amen.

PSALM

(For a longer psalm, see page xi.)
Psalm 145:2–3, 4–5, 10–11

I will praise your name for ever, LORD.

I will praise your name for ever, LORD.

Every day I will bless you,
  and praise your name forever and ever.
Great is the LORD, and greatly to be praised;
  his greatness is unsearchable.

I will praise your name for ever, LORD.

READING

Genesis 3:8–13

A reading from the Book of Genesis.

The man and the woman heard the sound of the LORD God walking in the garden at the time of the evening breeze, and the man and his wife hid themselves from the presence of the LORD God among the trees of the garden. But the LORD God called to the man, and said to him, "Where are you?" He said, "I heard the sound of you in the garden, and I was afraid, because I was naked; and I hid myself."

The LORD God said, "Who told you that you were naked? Have you eaten from the tree of which I commanded you not to eat?" The man said, "The woman whom you gave to be with me, she gave me fruit from the tree, and I ate." Then the LORD God said to the woman, "What is this that you have done?" The woman said, "The serpent tricked me, and I ate."

The Word of the Lord.

◆ All observe silence.

FOR SILENT REFLECTION

Think about this silently in your heart. What made the man blame the woman, and the woman blame the serpent? How do you think they were feeling when God questioned them?

CLOSING PRAYER

Let us pray to God for our needs and the needs of others: our family, neighborhood, and the world. For each need we say, "Lord, hear our prayer."

◆ All may add their own prayers here.

Let us pray: **Our Father . . . Amen.**

God of love and mercy,
we trust that you will forgive us
when we admit our wrongdoing.
We trust in your love and forgiveness.
In Christ's name we pray.

Amen.

✛ All make the Sign of the Cross.

OPENING

Today we hear how God responds to the man and woman who ate from the forbidden tree. There are consequences for their actions. These great stories in the Book of Genesis were told to help people understand the world and their experience. They realize that when they disobey God's commands, there is sin, which causes suffering and pain. Today we remember St. Ignatius of Antioch, a bishop and martyr who wrote about Christ's humanity and divinity and the importance of the Eucharist.

✚ All make the Sign of the Cross.

In the name of the Father, and of the Son, and of the Holy Spirit. Amen.

PSALM

(For a longer psalm, see page xi.)
Psalm 145:2–3, 4–5, 10–11

I will praise your name for ever, LORD.

I will praise your name for ever, LORD.

Every day I will bless you,
   and praise your name forever and ever.
Great is the LORD, and greatly to be praised;
   his greatness is unsearchable.

I will praise your name for ever, LORD.

READING

Genesis 3:14, 16ab, 17ad–19

A reading from the Book of Genesis.

The LORD God said to the serpent, "Because you have done this, cursed are you among all animals and among all wild creatures; upon your belly you shall go, and dust you shall eat all the days of your life." To the woman he said, "I will greatly increase your pangs in childbearing; in pain you shall bring forth chil-dren." And to the man he said, "Cursed is the ground because of you; in toil you shall eat of it all the days of your life; thorns and thistles it shall bring forth for you; and you shall eat the plants of the field. By the sweat of your face you shall eat bread until you return to the ground, for out of it you were taken; you are dust, and to dust you shall return."

The Word of the Lord.

◆ All observe silence.

FOR SILENT REFLECTION

Think about this silently in your heart. Have you ever experienced a difficult consequence for an action you have taken?

CLOSING PRAYER

Let us pray to God for our needs and the needs of others: our family, neighborhood, and the world. For each need we say, "Lord, hear our prayer."

◆ All may add their own prayers here.

Let us pray: **Our Father . . . Amen.**

Holy and loving God,
may we always stay in good
and right relationship to you.
When we sin, help us to ask for forgiveness.
We trust in your mercy.
For this we pray through Christ our Lord.

Amen.

✚ All make the Sign of the Cross.

PRAYER FOR
FRIDAY, OCTOBER 18, 2019

OPENING

The first man is called Adam because he came from the earth (*adamah*). Adam names his wife Eve, which in Hebrew means "to breathe" or "living one." We have heard how Adam and Eve were punished, but the story does not end with punishment. God sends the man and woman out to work the earth but not without an expression of divine care. Today is the feast of St. Luke, the Evangelist. We have been hearing his Gospel on most Sundays this past year.

✝ All make the Sign of the Cross.

In the name of the Father, and of the Son, and of the Holy Spirit. Amen.

PSALM

(For a longer psalm, see page xi.)
Psalm 145:2–3, 4–5, 10–11

I will praise your name for ever, LORD.

I will praise your name for ever, LORD.

Every day I will bless you,
   and praise your name forever and ever.
Great is the LORD, and greatly to be praised;
   his greatness is unsearchable.

I will praise your name for ever, LORD.

READING

Genesis 3:20–21, 23–24

A reading from the Book of Genesis.

The man named his wife Eve, because she was the mother of all living. And the LORD God made garments of skins for the man and for his wife, and clothed them.

The LORD God sent them forth from the garden of Eden, to till the ground from which he was taken. He drove out the man; and at the east of the garden of Eden he placed the cherubim, and a sword flaming and turning to guard the way to the tree of life.

The Word of the Lord.

◆ All observe silence.

FOR SILENT REFLECTION

Think about this silently in your heart. God set angels and a flaming sword to guard the tree of life. Why was that necessary?

CLOSING PRAYER

Let us pray to God for our needs and the needs of others: our family, neighborhood, and the world. For each need we say, "Lord, hear our prayer."

◆ All may add their own prayers here.

Let us pray: **Our Father . . . Amen.**

God, our Creator,
even when we sin, you care for us.
We thank you for the many ways
you show us your love.
Help us to live by your Word.
We ask this in Christ's name.

Amen.

✝ All make the Sign of the Cross.

OPENING

Today's Gospel is a parable about a woman who persists, or does not give up, in asking the judge for what she needs.

✚ All make the Sign of the Cross.

In the name of the Father, and of the Son, and of the Holy Spirit. Amen.

PSALM

(For a longer psalm, see page xi.)
Psalm 145:2–3, 4–5, 10–11

I will praise your name for ever, LORD.

I will praise your name for ever, LORD.

Every day I will bless you,
 and praise your name forever and ever.
Great is the LORD, and greatly to be praised;
 his greatness is unsearchable.

I will praise your name for ever, LORD.

◆ All stand and sing **Alleluia.**

GOSPEL

Luke 18:1–8a

A reading from the holy Gospel according to Luke.

Then Jesus told them a parable about their need to pray always and not to lose heart. He said, "In a certain city there was a judge who neither feared God nor had respect for people. In that city there was a widow who kept coming to him and saying, 'Grant me justice against my opponent.' For a while the judge refused; but later he said to himself, 'Though I have no fear of God and no respect for anyone, yet because this widow keeps bothering me, I will grant her justice, so that she may not wear me out by continually coming.'" And the Lord said, "Listen to what the unjust judge says. And will not God grant justice to his chosen ones who cry to him day and night? Will he delay long in helping them? I tell you, he will quickly grant justice to them."

The Gospel of the Lord.

◆ All sit and observe silence.

FOR SILENT REFLECTION

Think about this silently in your heart. Have you given up on something too easily? Might you try again?

CLOSING PRAYER

Let us pray to God for our needs and the needs of others: our family, neighborhood, and the world. For each need we say, "Lord, hear our prayer."

◆ All may add their own prayers here.

Let us pray: **Our Father . . . Amen.**

Faithful God,
you never tire of hearing our prayers.
Help us to trust that you want us to come to you with all of our needs.
Help us to trust that you hear us.
In Christ's name we pray.

Amen.

✚ All make the Sign of the Cross.

OPENING

This week our readings remind us of the importance of prayer. Today we will hear about King Solomon [SOL-uh-muhn] who built the first Temple in Jerusalem. Solomon, who is considered great in wisdom, wealth, and power, speaks of prayer as "inclining"— that is, "opening"—our hearts to God.

✚ All make the Sign of the Cross.

In the name of the Father, and of the Son, and of the Holy Spirit. Amen.

PSALM

(For a longer psalm, see page xi.)
Psalm 145:2–3, 4–5, 10–11

I will praise your name for ever, LORD.

I will praise your name for ever, LORD.

Every day I will bless you,
   and praise your name forever and ever.
Great is the LORD, and greatly to be praised;
   his greatness is unsearchable.

I will praise your name for ever, LORD.

READING

1 Kings 8:22–23ab, 27, 30a, 56ab, 57–58a

A reading from the First Book of Kings.

Then Solomon stood before the altar of the LORD in the presence of all the assembly of Israel, and spread out his hands to heaven. He said, "O LORD, God of Israel, there is no God like you in heaven above or on earth beneath. But will God indeed dwell on the earth? Even heaven and the highest heaven cannot contain you, much less this house that I have built! Hear the plea of your servant and of your people Israel when they pray toward this place. Blessed be the LORD, who has given rest to his people Israel according to all that he promised; not one word has failed of all his good promise. The LORD our God be with us, as he was with our ancestors; may he not leave us or abandon us, but incline our hearts to him, to walk in all his ways."

The Word of the Lord.

◆ All observe silence.

FOR SILENT REFLECTION

Think about this silently in your heart. Can you say a prayer of praise and thanksgiving to God?

CLOSING PRAYER

Let us pray to God for our needs and the needs of others: our family, neighborhood, and the world. For each need we say, "Lord, hear our prayer."

◆ All may add their own prayers here.

Let us pray: **Our Father . . . Amen.**

Incline our hearts to you, O God.
May we be like Solomon and recognize you in all that you have created.
May we trust in your promises always.
This we ask through Christ our Lord.

Amen.

✚ All make the Sign of the Cross.

OPENING

Today we remember Pope St. John Paul II, who died in 2005. He was the first pope to visit a Jewish synagogue since St. Peter. He observed a Jewish tradition and left a written prayer in the Western Wall in Israel. The reading today is St. Luke's account of how Jesus taught his disciples to pray.

✚ All make the Sign of the Cross.

In the name of the Father, and of the Son, and of the Holy Spirit. Amen.

PSALM

(For a longer psalm, see page xi.)
Psalm 145:2–3, 4–5, 10–11

I will praise your name for ever, LORD.

I will praise your name for ever, LORD.

Every day I will bless you,
    and praise your name forever and ever.
Great is the LORD, and greatly to be praised;
    his greatness is unsearchable.

I will praise your name for ever, LORD.

◆ All stand and sing **Alleluia.**

GOSPEL

Luke 11:1–4, 9–10

A reading from the holy Gospel according to Luke.

Jesus was praying in a certain place, and after he had finished, one of his disciples said to him, "Lord, teach us to pray, as John taught his disciples." He said to them, "When you pray, say: Father, hallowed be your name. Your kingdom come. Give us each day our daily bread. And forgive us our sins, for we ourselves forgive everyone indebted to us. And do not bring us to the time of trial. So I say to you, Ask, and it will be given you; search, and you will find; knock, and the door will be opened for you. For everyone who asks receives, and everyone who searches finds, and for everyone who knocks, the door will be opened."

The Gospel of the Lord.

◆ All sit and observe silence.

FOR SILENT REFLECTION

Think about this silently in your heart. Pray the Our Father silently in your heart before we pray it aloud together.

CLOSING PRAYER

Let us pray to God for our needs and the needs of others: our family, neighborhood, and the world. For each need we say, "Lord, hear our prayer."

◆ All may add their own prayers here.

Let us pray: **Our Father . . . Amen.**

God, our Father, your Son Jesus
taught us to come to you with our needs.
We thank you and praise you
for hearing our prayers.
We pray in Christ's name.

Amen.

✚ All make the Sign of the Cross.

OPENING

Today we remember St. John Capistrano (1386–1456). He preached so powerfully that many people turned to God. Today's reading is another parable about prayer; Jesus teaches us about the right attitude for prayer.

✝ All make the Sign of the Cross.

In the name of the Father, and of the Son, and of the Holy Spirit. Amen.

PSALM

(For a longer psalm, see page xi.)
Psalm 145:2–3, 4–5, 10–11

I will praise your name for ever, LORD.

I will praise your name for ever, LORD.

Every day I will bless you,
   and praise your name forever and ever.
Great is the LORD, and greatly to be praised;
   his greatness is unsearchable.

I will praise your name for ever, LORD.

◆ All stand and sing **Alleluia.**

GOSPEL

Luke 18:9–14

A reading from the holy Gospel according to Luke.

Jesus also told this parable to some who trusted in themselves that they were righteous and regarded others with contempt: "Two men went up to the temple to pray, one a Pharisee and the other a tax collector. The Pharisee, standing by himself, was praying thus, 'God, I thank you that I am not like other people: thieves, rogues, adulterers, or even like this tax collector. I fast twice a week; I give a tenth of all my income.' But the tax collector, standing far off, would not even look up to heaven, but was beating his breast and saying, 'God, be merciful to me, a sinner!' I tell you, this man went down to his home justified rather than the other; for all who exalt themselves will be humbled, but all who humble themselves will be exalted."

The Gospel of the Lord.

◆ All sit and observe silence.

FOR SILENT REFLECTION

Think about this silently in your heart. Why do you think Jesus praises the tax collector and not the Pharisee?

CLOSING PRAYER

Let us pray to God for our needs and the needs of others: our family, neighborhood, and the world. For each need we say, "Lord, hear our prayer."

◆ All may add their own prayers here.

Let us pray: **Our Father . . . Amen.**

Holy and loving God,
you desire that we pray to you in our weakness.
Help us to be honest and true
in our prayer to you.
We pray in the name of your Son,
Jesus Christ, our Lord.

Amen.

✝ All make the Sign of the Cross.

OPENING

In today's reading from the Acts of the Apostles, St. Luke tells a story that illustrates how prayer can fill us with a spirit that helps us feel stronger, especially in times of trouble. Today we remember St. Anthony Mary Claret, the founder of the Claretians. These missionaries have a long history of evangelizing people to the faith, especially Latinos.

✝ All make the Sign of the Cross.

In the name of the Father, and of the Son, and of the Holy Spirit. Amen.

PSALM

(For a longer psalm, see page xi.)
Psalm 145:2–3, 4–5, 10–11

I will praise your name for ever, Lord.

I will praise your name for ever, Lord.

Every day I will bless you,
 and praise your name forever and ever.
Great is the Lord, and greatly to be praised;
 his greatness is unsearchable.

I will praise your name for ever, Lord.

READING

Acts 4:1–2, 18, 23b–24a, 29, 31

A reading from the Acts of the Apostles.

While Peter and John were speaking to the people, the priests, the captain of the temple, and the Sadducees came to them, much annoyed because they were teaching the people and proclaiming that in Jesus there is the resurrection of the dead. So they called the apostles and ordered them not to speak or teach at all in the name of Jesus. Peter and John went to their friends and reported what the chief priests and the elders had said to them. When they heard it, they raised their voices together to God and said, "And now, Lord, look at their threats, and grant to your servants to speak your word with all boldness." When they had prayed, the place in which they were gathered together was shaken; and they were all filled with the Holy Spirit and spoke the word of God with boldness.

The Word of the Lord.

◆ All observe silence.

FOR SILENT REFLECTION

Think about this silently in your heart. Does praying ever help you feel stronger and more confident?

CLOSING PRAYER

Let us pray to God for our needs and the needs of others: our family, neighborhood, and the world. For each need we say, "Lord, hear our prayer."

◆ All may add their own prayers here.

Let us pray: **Our Father . . . Amen.**

Gracious and generous God,
help us to listen for your voice
and to be open to your Spirit.
Like the Claretians and St. Anthony Mary Claret, let us be bold
in telling others about you.
We pray in Christ's name.

Amen.

✝ All make the Sign of the Cross.

OPENING

In today's reading we hear St. Paul's prayer for the people of Ephesus [EF-uh-suhs]. At Mass, in the Prayers of Intercession, we pray for church and world leaders; we pray for people who are sick or in crisis; we pray for those who have died; we pray in thanksgiving for people we love. We pray individually, with family, and in community. What a blessing our prayers are to one another.

✚ All make the Sign of the Cross.

In the name of the Father, and of the Son, and of the Holy Spirit. Amen.

PSALM

(For a longer psalm, see page xii.)
Psalm 98:1, 2–3, 3–4

The LORD has made known his victory.

The LORD has made known his victory.

O sing to the LORD a new song,
   for he has done marvelous things.
His right hand and his holy arm
   have gotten him victory.

The LORD has made known his victory.

READING

Ephesians 3:14–19, 21

A reading from the Letter of Paul to the Ephesians [ee-FEE-zhuhnz].

For this reason I bow my knees before the Father, from whom every family in heaven and on earth takes its name. I pray that, according to the riches of God's glory, he may grant that you may be strengthened in your inner being with power through his Spirit, and that Christ may dwell in your hearts through faith, as you are being rooted and grounded in love. I pray

that you may have the power to comprehend, with all the saints, what is the breadth and length and height and depth, and to know the love of Christ that surpasses knowledge, so that you may be filled with all the fullness of God. To God be glory in the church and in Christ Jesus to all generations, forever and ever. Amen.

The Word of the Lord.

◆ All observe silence.

FOR SILENT REFLECTION

Think about this silently in your heart. Who prays for you? Say a prayer of thanks and blessing for them.

CLOSING PRAYER

Let us pray to God for our needs and the needs of others: our family, neighborhood, and the world. For each need we say, "Lord, hear our prayer."

◆ All may add their own prayers here.

Let us pray: **Our Father . . . Amen.**

Loving God,
we know that to love you and to love others
are the greatest commandments.
May our prayers root us
and ground us in love.
For this we pray through Christ our Lord.

Amen.

✚ All make the Sign of the Cross.

PRAYER FOR THE WEEK

WITH A READING FROM THE GOSPEL FOR **SUNDAY, OCTOBER 27, 2019**

OPENING

Jesus offers us another parable about prayer. He contrasts the Pharisee, a religious leader, with a tax collector, who was considered an outsider.

✝ All make the Sign of the Cross.

In the name of the Father, and of the Son, and of the Holy Spirit. Amen.

PSALM

(For a longer psalm, see page xii.)
Psalm 98:1, 2–3, 3–4

The LORD has made known his victory.

The LORD has made known his victory.

O sing to the LORD a new song,
   for he has done marvelous things.
His right hand and his holy arm
   have gotten him victory.

The LORD has made known his victory.

◆ All stand and sing **Alleluia.**

GOSPEL

Luke 18:9–14

A reading from the holy Gospel according to Luke.

Jesus also told this parable to some who trusted in themselves that they were righteous and regarded others with contempt: "Two men went up to the temple to pray, one a Pharisee and the other a tax collector. The Pharisee, standing by himself, was praying thus, 'God, I thank you that I am not like other people: thieves, rogues, adulterers, or even like this tax collector. I fast twice a week; I give a tenth of all my income.' But the tax collector, standing far off, would not even look up to heaven, but was beating his breast and saying, 'God, be merciful to me, a sinner!' I tell you, this man went down to his home justified rather than the other; for all who exalt themselves will be humbled, but all who humble themselves will be exalted."

The Gospel of the Lord.

◆ All sit and observe silence.

FOR SILENT REFLECTION

Think about this silently in your heart. What do you learn from Jesus about how to approach God in prayer?

CLOSING PRAYER

Let us pray to God for our needs and the needs of others: our family, neighborhood, and the world. For each need we say, "Lord, hear our prayer."

◆ All may add their own prayers here.

Let us pray: **Our Father . . . Amen.**

Loving and merciful God,
help us to know ourselves
and to be humble before you.
We ask this in Christ's name.

Amen.

✝ All make the Sign of the Cross.

PRAYER FOR
MONDAY, OCTOBER 28, 2019

OPENING

Today is the Feast of Sts. Simon and Jude, two Apostles who spread the Good News. Over the next two weeks we will read the story of Noah and the Flood. The tradition of a "universal flood" that almost destroyed all life on earth is widespread among many Mesopotamian [mes-uh-poh-TAY-mee-uhn] people's traditions. In the Book of Genesis, this story reveals the nature of God and what human behavior is acceptable.

✛ All make the Sign of the Cross.

In the name of the Father, and of the Son, and of the Holy Spirit. Amen.

PSALM   (For a longer psalm, see page xii.) Psalm 98:1, 2–3, 3–4

The LORD has made known his victory.

The LORD has made known his victory.

O sing to the LORD a new song,
   for he has done marvelous things.
His right hand and his holy arm
   have gotten him victory.

The LORD has made known his victory.

READING   Genesis 6:9bc, 11, 13ab, 14–17

A reading from the Book of Genesis.

Noah was a righteous man, blameless in his generation; Noah walked with God. Now the earth was corrupt in God's sight, and the earth was filled with violence. And God said to Noah, "I have determined to make an end of all flesh, for the earth is filled with violence because of them. Make yourself an ark of cypress wood; make rooms in the ark, and cover it inside and out with pitch. This is how

you are to make it: the length of the ark three hundred cubits, its width fifty cubits, and its height thirty cubits. Make a roof for the ark, and finish it to a cubit above; and put the door of the ark in its side; make it with lower, second, and third decks. For my part, I am going to bring a flood of waters on the earth, to destroy from under heaven all flesh in which is the breath of life; everything that is on the earth shall die."

The Word of the Lord.

◆ All observe silence.

FOR SILENT REFLECTION

Think about this silently in your heart. The reading says, "Noah walked with God." What do you think that means?

CLOSING PRAYER

Let us pray to God for our needs and the needs of others: our family, neighborhood, and the world. For each need we say, "Lord, hear our prayer."

◆ All may add their own prayers here.

Let us pray: **Our Father . . . Amen.**

Let the earth and all that is in it
give you praise and glory, O God.
May we learn to be good stewards
of creation
and care for all that you have made.
For this we pray through Christ our Lord.

Amen.

✛ All make the Sign of the Cross.

OPENING

A covenant is a holy relationship—an agreement to honor and respect one another. God desires to be in a covenant relationship with humankind. We previously heard that Adam and Eve did not honor this relationship with God. God makes a covenant with Noah, and Noah responds by following God's commands.

✛ All make the Sign of the Cross.

In the name of the Father, and of the Son, and of the Holy Spirit. Amen.

PSALM　(For a longer psalm, see page xii.) Psalm 98:1, 2–3, 3–4

The LORD has made known his victory.

The LORD has made known his victory.

O sing to the LORD a new song,
  for he has done marvelous things.
His right hand and his holy arm
  have gotten him victory.

The LORD has made known his victory.

READING　　Genesis 6:18–22

A reading from the Book of Genesis.

God said to Noah, "I will establish my covenant with you; and you shall come into the ark, you, your sons, your wife, and your sons' wives with you. And of every living thing, of all flesh, you shall bring two of every kind into the ark, to keep them alive with you; they shall be male and female. Of the birds according to their kinds, and of the animals according to their kinds, of every creeping thing of the ground according to its kind, two of every kind shall come in to you, to keep them alive. Also take with you every kind of food that is eaten, and store it up; and it shall serve as food for you and for them." Noah did this; he did all that God commanded him.

The Word of the Lord.

◆ All observe silence.

FOR SILENT REFLECTION

Think about this silently in your heart. Noah trusted God and obeyed him. What helps you be able to trust in God?

CLOSING PRAYER

Let us pray to God for our needs and the needs of others: our family, neighborhood, and the world. For each need we say, "Lord, hear our prayer."

◆ All may add their own prayers here.

Let us pray: **Our Father . . . Amen.**

Holy and loving God,
in establishing a covenant with Noah
you showed your love for all of life.
Let all of creation praise your holy name.
We pray in Christ's name.

Amen.

✛ All make the Sign of the Cross.

OPENING

Numbers in the Bible are largely symbolic. Noah is not really six hundred years old, but he is very old and wise. The number forty indicates a time of preparation that precedes significant events (such as forty days of Lent). The Hebrew word for the number seven means fullness, completion, perfection. In using these numbers, the writer tells the Hebrew people that this is a story of hope.

✛ All make the Sign of the Cross.

In the name of the Father, and of the Son, and of the Holy Spirit. Amen.

PSALM   (For a longer psalm, see page xii.) Psalm 98:1, 2–3, 3–4

The LORD has made known his victory.

The LORD has made known his victory.

O sing to the LORD a new song,
  for he has done marvelous things.
His right hand and his holy arm
  have gotten him victory.

The LORD has made known his victory.

READING   Genesis 7:1–5, 11–12

A reading from the Book of Genesis.

Then the LORD said to Noah, "Go into the ark, you and all your household, for I have seen that you alone are righteous before me in this generation. Take with you seven pairs of all clean animals, the male and its mate; and a pair of the animals that are not clean, the male and its mate; and seven pairs of the birds of the air also, male and female, to keep their kind alive on the face of all the earth. For in seven days I will send rain on the earth for forty days and forty nights; and every living thing that I have made I will blot out from the face of the ground." And Noah did all that the LORD had commanded him. In the six hundredth year of Noah's life, in the second month, on the seventeenth day of the month, on that day all the fountains of the great deep burst forth, and the windows of the heavens were opened. The rain fell on the earth forty days and forty nights.

The Word of the Lord.

◆ All observe silence.

FOR SILENT REFLECTION

Think about this silently in your heart. How does trusting in God's goodness help us have hope even when life feels very difficult?

CLOSING PRAYER

Let us pray to God for our needs and the needs of others: our family, neighborhood, and the world. For each need we say, "Lord, hear our prayer."

◆ All may add their own prayers here.

Let us pray: **Our Father . . . Amen.**

Almighty and loving God,
in your goodness you protected Noah
and his household.
Please protect us from all danger.
We ask this in Christ's name.

Amen.

✛ All make the Sign of the Cross.

OPENING

Remember that numbers are used symbolically in the Bible. The number fifty (which occurs in the account of the flood in the number 150, fifty times three) means a new era or time is beginning. The word *subside* means to go down to a normal level. *Abate* means to get less intense.

✚ All make the Sign of the Cross.

In the name of the Father, and of the Son, and of the Holy Spirit. Amen.

PSALM   (For a longer psalm, see page xii.) Psalm 98:1, 2–3, 3–4

The LORD has made known his victory.

The LORD has made known his victory.

O sing to the LORD a new song,
for he has done marvelous things.
His right hand and his holy arm
have gotten him victory.

The LORD has made known his victory.

READING   Genesis 8:1–5

A reading from the Book of Genesis.

But God remembered Noah and all the wild animals and all the domestic animals that were with him in the ark. And God made a wind blow over the earth, and the waters subsided; the fountains of the deep and the windows of the heavens were closed, the rain from the heavens was restrained, and the waters gradually receded from the earth. At the end of one hundred fifty days the waters had abated; and in the seventh month, on the seventeenth day of the month, the ark came to rest on the mountains of Ararat. The waters con-tinued to abate until the tenth month; in the tenth month, on the first day of the month, the tops of the mountains appeared.

The Word of the Lord.

◆ All observe silence.

FOR SILENT REFLECTION

Think about this silently in your heart. Does the story today help you feel hopeful? What are you hopeful for?

CLOSING PRAYER

Let us pray to God for our needs and the needs of others: our family, neighborhood, and the world. For each need we say, "Lord, hear our prayer."

◆ All may add their own prayers here.

Let us pray: **Our Father . . . Amen.**

We thank you and praise you, O God,
for your eternal covenant with us.
On this All Hallows' Eve,
we give thanks for the example of Noah.
He listened to your command
and joined you in a covenant
that preserved all life.
For this we pray through Christ our Lord.

Amen.

✚ All make the Sign of the Cross.

OPENING

To know if it would be safe to leave the ark, Noah sends out a dove. When the dove finally returns with an olive branch, he knows that the waters had dried up and new life was growing. Traditionally, the olive branch represents peace, an end to destruction. The dove is also a sign of a messenger of peace. Today is the Solemnity of All Saints. We honor all the holy men and women before us and now who are friends of God.

✚ All make the Sign of the Cross.

In the name of the Father, and of the Son, and of the Holy Spirit. Amen.

PSALM (For a longer psalm, see page xii.) Psalm 98:1, 2–3, 3–4

The LORD has made known his victory.

The LORD has made known his victory.

O sing to the LORD a new song,
    for he has done marvelous things.
His right hand and his holy arm
    have gotten him victory.

The LORD has made known his victory.

READING Genesis 8:6–12

A reading from the Book of Genesis.

At the end of forty days Noah opened the window of the ark that he had made and sent out the raven; and it went to and fro until the waters were dried up from the earth. Then he sent out the dove from him, to see if the waters had subsided from the face of the ground; but the dove found no place to set its foot, and it returned to him to the ark, for the waters were still on the face of the whole earth. So he put out his hand and took it and brought it into the ark with him. He waited another seven days, and again he sent out the dove from the ark; and the dove came back to him in the evening, and there in its beak was a freshly plucked olive leaf; so Noah knew that the waters had subsided from the earth. Then he waited another seven days, and sent out the dove; and it did not return to him any more.

The Word of the Lord.

◆ All observe silence.

FOR SILENT REFLECTION

Think about this silently in your heart. How do you think Noah felt as he waited for the dove's return and then when it brought the green branch?

CLOSING PRAYER

Let us pray to God for our needs and the needs of others: our family, neighborhood, and the world. For each need we say, "Lord, hear our prayer."

◆ All may add their own prayers here.

Let us pray: **Our Father . . . Amen.**

On this holy day when we honor all of the saints, we praise and thank you, O Lord.
By their example we learn
how to live and to love you.
To you be glory and praise.
Through Christ our Lord.

Amen.

✚ All make the Sign of the Cross.

CELEBRATING THE SAINTS, REMEMBERING THE DEAD

Find the reading (1 Thessalonians 4:13–18) in your Bible, ask for a volunteer to read it, and encourage the reader to practice reading it a few times. Then gather the household in one room. You may want to light a candle to create an even more prayerful environment.

LEADER:
Saints live among us today as well as with Christ in heaven. These heroes of our faith persevere in troubled times as they follow the path of Jesus. Their unselfish actions, as well as their talents, skills, and virtuous living inspire us as they pray for us.

✚ All make the Sign of the Cross.

ALL: In the name of the Father, and of the Son, and of the Holy Spirit. Amen.

LEADER: Psalm 112: 1–6
Let us pray the psalm response:
Happy are those who fear the LORD.

ALL: Happy are those who fear the LORD.

LEADER:
Praise the LORD!
    Happy are those who fear the LORD,
    who greatly delight in his commandments.
Their descendants will be mighty in the land;
    the generation of the upright will
        be blessed.

ALL: Happy are those who fear the LORD.

LEADER:
Wealth and riches are in their houses,
    and their righteousness endures forever.
They rise in the darkness as a light for the
        upright;
    they are gracious, merciful, and righteous.

ALL: Happy are those who fear the LORD.

LEADER: 1 Thessalonians 4:13–18
A reading from the First Letter of Paul to the Thessalonians.

◆ Read the Scripture passage from the Bible.

The Word of the Lord.

◆ All observe a brief silence.

LEADER:
And now let us remember family members and friends who have died:

◆ The leader begins, then pauses so others may add names too.

LEADER:
Lord God,
we ask you to bring these and all
those who have gone before us
into your beloved presence.

◆ Leader pauses, then continues.

Jesus, our Savior,
you are the Source of all life.
We are grateful for our leaders in faith,
as well as our family members and friends
who are with you now in heaven.
Their goodness reveals your holy truth.
Help us to honor your Spirit within us in
everything we do.
We ask this in your name.

ALL: Amen.

✚ All make the Sign of the Cross.

PRAYER FOR THE WEEK
WITH A READING FROM THE GOSPEL FOR **SUNDAY, NOVEMBER 3, 2019**

OPENING

Today's Gospel tells us about Jesus' interaction with a tax collector whose true spirit is noticed by Jesus. The Pharisees, however, see the tax collector as a sinner.

✛ All make the Sign of the Cross.

In the name of the Father, and of the Son, and of the Holy Spirit. Amen.

PSALM   (For a longer psalm, see page xii.) Psalm 98:1, 2–3, 3–4

The LORD has made known his victory.

The LORD has made known his victory.

O sing to the LORD a new song,
   for he has done marvelous things.
His right hand and his holy arm
   have gotten him victory.

The LORD has made known his victory.

◆ All stand and sing **Alleluia.**

GOSPEL   Luke 19:2–3ab, 4a, 5, 7–9ab

A reading from the holy Gospel according to Luke.

A man was there named Zacchaeus (zuh-KEE-uhs); he was a chief tax collector and was rich. He was trying to see who Jesus was, but on account of the crowd he could not. So he ran ahead and climbed a sycamore tree to see him. When Jesus came to the place, he looked up and said to him, "Zacchaeus, hurry and come down; for I must stay at your house today." All who saw it began to grumble and said, "He has gone to be the guest of one who is a sinner." Zacchaeus stood there and said to the Lord, "Look, half of my possessions, Lord, I will give to the poor; and if I have defrauded anyone of anything, I will pay back four times as much." Then Jesus said to him, "Today salvation has come to this house."

The Gospel of the Lord.

◆ All sit and observe silence.

FOR SILENT REFLECTION

Think about this silently in your heart. Jesus asks to stay at Zacchaeus' home. How does Jesus ask to stay or to be with us?

CLOSING PRAYER

Let us pray to God for our needs and the needs of others: our family, neighborhood, and the world. For each need we say, "Lord, hear our prayer."

◆ All may add their own prayers here.

Let us pray: **Our Father . . . Amen.**

Good and gracious God,
grant us a generous spirit.
May we be like Zacchaeus
and open our hearts and our homes to you.
We ask this in the name of the one who
wants to be with us,
Jesus Christ.

Amen.

✛ All make the Sign of the Cross.

OPENING

After a very, very long time, Noah, his family, and all the animals left the ark and were able to touch the ground again. As you listen to today's reading, think about how it must have felt for them to realize they had been given the opportunity and responsibility to build a new life that would be pleasing to God.

✦ All make the Sign of the Cross.

In the name of the Father, and of the Son, and of the Holy Spirit. Amen.

PSALM   (For a longer psalm, see page xii.) Psalm 98:1, 2–3, 3–4

The Lord has made known his victory.

The Lord has made known his victory.

O sing to the Lord a new song,
for he has done marvelous things.
His right hand and his holy arm
have gotten him victory.

The Lord has made known his victory.

READING   Genesis 8:13–19

A reading from the Book of Genesis.

In the six hundred and first year, in the first month, on the first day of the month, the waters were dried up from the earth; and Noah removed the covering of the ark, and looked, and saw that the face of the ground was drying. In the second month, on the twenty-seventh day of the month, the earth was dry. Then God said to Noah, "Go out of the ark, you and your wife, and your sons and your sons' wives with you. Bring out with you every living thing that is with you of all flesh—birds and animals and every creeping thing that creeps on the earth—

so that they may abound on the earth, and be fruitful and multiply on the earth." So Noah went out with his sons and his wife and his sons' wives. And every animal, every creeping thing, and every bird, everything that moves on the earth, went out of the ark by families.

The Word of the Lord.

◆ All observe silence.

FOR SILENT REFLECTION

Think about this silently in your heart. Can you imagine what it felt like to leave the ark and be able to start to live on the land again?

CLOSING PRAYER

Let us pray to God for our needs and the needs of others: our family, neighborhood, and the world. For each need we say, "Lord, hear our prayer."

◆ All may add their own prayers here.

Let us pray: **Our Father . . . Amen.**

We praise and thank you, O God,
for all that you have made.
In your care for Noah, his family, and the creatures of the earth, you reveal your love for all of creation.
Help us to care for your creation as well.
This we ask through Christ our Lord.

Amen.

✦ All make the Sign of the Cross.

OPENING

We are almost finished listening to the story of God's covenant with Noah. Today we hear the special words that God says to Noah. Because he was faithful, God assures him that his family and all of the animals, birds, and creatures that were in the ark will continue to live. In this we see how much God loves the earth and all that is in it.

✜ All make the Sign of the Cross.

In the name of the Father, and of the Son, and of the Holy Spirit. Amen.

PSALM
(For a longer psalm, see page xii.) Psalm 98:1, 2–3, 3–4

The LORD has made known his victory.

The LORD has made known his victory.

O sing to the LORD a new song,
for he has done marvelous things.
His right hand and his holy arm
have gotten him victory.

The LORD has made known his victory.

READING
Genesis 8:20a; 9:1, 8–11

A reading from the Book of Genesis.

Then Noah built an altar to the LORD. God blessed Noah and his sons, and said to them, "Be fruitful and multiply, and fill the earth." Then God said to Noah and to his sons with him, "As for me, I am establishing my covenant with you and your descendants after you, and with every living creature that is with you, the birds, the domestic animals, and every animal of the earth with you, as many as came out of the ark. I establish my covenant with you, that never again shall all flesh be cut off by the waters of a flood, and never again shall there be a flood to destroy the earth."

The Word of the Lord.

◆ All observe silence.

FOR SILENT REFLECTION

Think about this silently in your heart. God promises he will never destroy the earth again. How should we hold up our end of that covenant?

CLOSING PRAYER

Let us pray to God for our needs and the needs of others: our family, neighborhood, and the world. For each need we say, "Lord, hear our prayer."

◆ All may add their own prayers here.

Let us pray: **Our Father . . . Amen.**

Thank you, gracious God,
for your promise to Noah.
In listening to this story, we are reminded
of your endless love for us.
We offer you praise
through Christ our Lord.

Amen.

✜ All make the Sign of the Cross.

OPENING

Today we conclude the story of Noah. In our reading, we hear about the rainbow. A rainbow symbolizes God's promise to never again destroy the earth, and all that lives on the earth, by water. With the rainbow, God offers a sign of love and compassion.

✛ All make the Sign of the Cross.

In the name of the Father, and of the Son, and of the Holy Spirit. Amen.

PSALM

(For a longer psalm, see page xii.) Psalm 98:1, 2–3, 3–4

The LORD has made known his victory.

The LORD has made known his victory.

O sing to the LORD a new song,
 for he has done marvelous things.
His right hand and his holy arm
 have gotten him victory.

The LORD has made known his victory.

READING

Genesis 9:12–15, 17

A reading from the Book of Genesis.

God said to Noah, "This is the sign of the covenant that I make between me and you and every living creature that is with you, for all future generations: I have set my bow in the clouds, and it shall be a sign of the covenant between me and the earth. When I bring clouds over the earth and the bow is seen in the clouds, I will remember my covenant that is between me and you and every living creature of all flesh; and the waters shall never again become a flood to destroy all flesh." God said to Noah, "This is the sign of the covenant that I have established between me and all flesh that is on the earth."

The Word of the Lord.

◆ All observe silence.

FOR SILENT REFLECTION

Think about this silently in your heart. Imagine a rainbow. Remember God's love for you and all of God's creatures on earth and in heaven.

CLOSING PRAYER

Let us pray to God for our needs and the needs of others: our family, neighborhood, and the world. For each need we say, "Lord, hear our prayer."

◆ All may add their own prayers here.

Let us pray: **Our Father . . . Amen.**

In the beauty of the colors of the rainbow,
your love and care shine forth, O God.
May we be faithful to our part of the
covenant you have made with us.
May we appreciate and celebrate the gift of
life in all its many forms.
We ask this in Christ's name.

Amen.

✛ All make the Sign of the Cross.

OPENING

As we heard in the story of Noah, the Hebrew people understood that sin destroyed all creation, not just human beings. But the biblical message is always a message of hope. In the outbreak of evil there is always a seed that is stronger than destruction, a seed from which life can be restored. Noah is such a seed in the Old Testament. In the New Testament, Jesus Christ is that seed of new life.

✚ All make the Sign of the Cross.

In the name of the Father, and of the Son, and of the Holy Spirit. Amen.

PSALM   (For a longer psalm, see page xii.) Psalm 98:1, 2–3, 3–4

The LORD has made known his victory.

The LORD has made known his victory.

O sing to the LORD a new song,
   for he has done marvelous things.
His right hand and his holy arm
   have gotten him victory.

The LORD has made known his victory.

READING   Isaiah 54:9–10

A reading from the Book of prophet Isaiah.

This is like the days of Noah to me: Just as I swore that the waters of Noah would never again go over the earth, so I have sworn that I will not be angry with you and will not rebuke you. For the mountains may depart and the hills be removed, but my steadfast love shall not depart from you, and my covenant of peace shall not be removed, says the LORD, who has compassion on you.

The Word of the Lord.

◆ All observe silence.

FOR SILENT REFLECTION

Think about this silently in your heart. How does Jesus Christ give us hope for a new peace-filled world?

CLOSING PRAYER

Let us pray to God for our needs and the needs of others: our family, neighborhood, and the world. For each need we say, "Lord, hear our prayer."

◆ All may add their own prayers here.

Let us pray: **Our Father . . . Amen.**

We give you thanks for your great compassion, O Lord.
You know our weakness,
and yet you promise your steadfast love.
Your promise brings us peace.
In Christ's name we pray.

Amen.

✚ All make the Sign of the Cross.

OPENING

Today's reading is from the Book of Sirach [SEER-ak] in the Old Testament. Sirach lived in Jerusalem in the first century before Jesus was born. He wrote to help people maintain their faith through study of the holy books and tradition. In today's reading, Sirach reminds the people to be grateful for their ancestors, the people who have gone before them in faith.

✚ All make the Sign of the Cross.

In the name of the Father, and of the Son, and of the Holy Spirit. Amen.

PSALM   (For a longer psalm, see page xii.) Psalm 98:1, 2–3, 3–4

The LORD has made known his victory.

The LORD has made known his victory.

O sing to the LORD a new song,
   for he has done marvelous things.
His right hand and his holy arm
   have gotten him victory.

The LORD has made known his victory.

READING   Sirach 44:1, 10–13, 17

A reading from the Book of Sirach.

Let us now sing the praises of famous men, our ancestors in their generations. These also were godly men, whose righteous deeds have not been forgotten; their wealth will remain with their descendants, and their inheritance with their children's children. Their descendants stand by the covenants; their children also, for their sake. Their offspring will continue forever, and their glory will never be blotted out. Noah was found perfect and righteous; in the time of wrath he kept the race alive; therefore a remnant was left on the earth when the flood came.

The Word of the Lord.

◆ All observe silence.

FOR SILENT REFLECTION

Think about this silently in your heart. Who has helped you to have faith?

CLOSING PRAYER

Let us pray to God for our needs and the needs of others: our family, neighborhood, and the world. For each need we say, "Lord, hear our prayer."

◆ All may add their own prayers here.

Let us pray: **Our Father . . . Amen.**

This month we remember the saints and all who have gone before us
marked with the sign of faith.
We are grateful for all who have helped us to grow in faith: our parents and grandparents,
our priests and teachers,
our families and friends.
Thank you, holy God,
for bringing them into our lives.
This we pray through Christ our Lord.

Amen.

✚ All make the Sign of the Cross.

OPENING

During the month of November, we continue to remember those whom we have loved and who have died. Today Jesus speaks about the time after death—when our earthly concerns are transformed by new life with God for all eternity.

✝ All make the Sign of the Cross.

In the name of the Father, and of the Son, and of the Holy Spirit. Amen.

PSALM   (For a longer psalm, see page xii.) Psalm 98:1, 2–3, 3–4

The LORD has made known his victory.

The LORD has made known his victory.

O sing to the LORD a new song,
   for he has done marvelous things.
His right hand and his holy arm
   have gotten him victory.

The LORD has made known his victory.

◆ All stand and sing **Alleluia.**

GOSPEL   Luke 20:27–28ac, 29–30ac, 33–36

A reading from the holy Gospel according to Luke.

Some Sadducees, [SAD-yoo-seez] those who say there is no resurrection, came to Jesus and asked him a question, "Teacher, Moses wrote for us that if a man's brother dies, the man shall marry the widow and raise up children for his brother. Now there were seven brothers; the first married, and died childless; then the second, and so in the same way all seven died childless. In the resurrection, therefore, whose wife will the woman be? For the seven had married her." Jesus said to them, "Those who belong to this age marry and are given in marriage; but those who are considered worthy of a place in that age and in the resurrection from the dead neither marry nor are given in marriage. Indeed they cannot die anymore, because they are like angels and are children of God, being children of the resurrection."

The Gospel of the Lord.

◆ All sit and observe silence.

FOR SILENT REFLECTION

Think about this silently in your heart. Say a prayer for someone you know who has died.

CLOSING PRAYER

Let us pray to God for our needs and the needs of others: our family, neighborhood, and the world. For each need we say, "Lord, hear our prayer."

◆ All may add their own prayers here.

Let us pray: **Our Father . . . Amen.**

We thank you, almighty God,
for the gift of eternal life.
We rejoice that those we have loved and have gone before us now live with you in heaven.
In your mercy may we enjoy the same.
This we ask through Christ our Lord.

Amen.

✝ All make the Sign of the Cross.

OPENING

Today is the memorial of St. Martin of Tours, a Roman soldier who lived in the fourth century. When he saw a beggar who was cold, Martin cut his cloak in half and shared it with him. After this, he had a vision of Christ wrapped in a cloak. He then became a faithful follower of Jesus. This week, we will hear many more stories about faithfulness.

✛ All make the Sign of the Cross.

In the name of the Father, and of the Son, and of the Holy Spirit. Amen.

PSALM   (For a longer psalm, see page xii.) Psalm 98:1, 2–3, 3–4

The Lord has made known his victory.

The Lord has made known his victory.

O sing to the Lord a new song,
    for he has done marvelous things.
His right hand and his holy arm
    have gotten him victory.

The Lord has made known his victory.

READING   Deuteronomy 5:1ab; 7:7–9, 11

A reading from the Book of Deuteronomy.

Moses convened all Israel, and said to them: Hear, O Israel, the statutes and ordinances that I am addressing to you today. It was not because you were more numerous than any other people that the Lord set his heart on you and chose you—for you were the fewest of all peoples. It was because the Lord loved you and kept the oath that he swore to your ancestors, that the Lord has brought you out with a mighty hand, and redeemed you from the house of slavery, from the hand of Pharaoh king of Egypt. Know therefore that the Lord your God is God, the faithful God who maintains covenant loyalty with those who love him and keep his commandments, to a thousand generations. Therefore, observe diligently the commandment—the statutes and the ordinances—that I am commanding you today.

The Word of the Lord.

◆ All observe silence.

FOR SILENT REFLECTION

Think of this silently in your heart. God is faithful to a thousand generations. Try to imagine how long that is.

CLOSING PRAYER

Let us pray to God for our needs and the needs of others: our family, neighborhood, and the world. For each need we say, "Lord, hear our prayer."

◆ All may add their own prayers here.

Let us pray: **Our Father . . . Amen.**

O God,
we are strengthened by your covenant with the Israelites and with us.
May we, like St. Martin of Tours, practice mercy and always be faithful to you.
This we ask through Christ our Lord.

Amen.

✛ All make the Sign of the Cross.

OPENING

Today's reading tells of two Hebrew kings, Ahaz [AY-haz] and Hezekiah [hehz-eh-KĪ-uh]. King Ahaz glorifies himself, but his son, King Hezekiah, focuses on serving God and repairing the places of worship. Today we remember St. Josaphat [JOS-uh-fat], a bishop in Ukraine in the sixteenth century. He wanted all Christians to be united.

✦ All make the Sign of the Cross.

In the name of the Father, and of the Son, and of the Holy Spirit. Amen.

PSALM   (For a longer psalm, see page xii.) Psalm 98:1, 2–3, 3–4

The Lord has made known his victory.

The Lord has made known his victory.

O sing to the Lord a new song,
    for he has done marvelous things.
His right hand and his holy arm
    have gotten him victory.

The Lord has made known his victory.

READING   2 Chronicles 28:24c–25, 27c; 29:3; 31:20–21

A reading from the Second Book of Chronicles.

King Ahaz [AY-haz] shut up the doors of the house of the Lord and made himself altars in every corner of Jerusalem. In every city of Judah he made high places to make offerings to other gods, provoking to anger the Lord, the God of his ancestors. His son Hezekiah [hehz-eh-KĪ-uh] succeeded him. In the first year of his reign, in the first month, he opened the doors of the house of the Lord and repaired them. Hezekiah did this throughout all Judah;

he did what was good and right and faithful before the Lord his God. And every work that he undertook in the service of the house of God, and in accordance with the law and the commandments, to seek his God, he did with all his heart; and he prospered.

The Word of the Lord.

◆ All observe silence.

FOR SILENT REFLECTION

Think about this silently in your heart. King Hezekiah served God with all his heart. What does it mean to serve God with all your heart?

CLOSING PRAYER

Let us pray to God for our needs and the needs of others: our family, neighborhood, and the world. For each need we say, "Lord, hear our prayer."

◆ All may add their own prayers here.

Let us pray: **Our Father . . . Amen.**

Help us to be like King Hezekiah, O Lord, and serve you with all our heart and soul. Help us also to be like St. Josaphat and promote unity.
We ask this in Christ's name.

Amen.

✦ All make the Sign of the Cross.

OPENING

Today is the feast of St. Frances Xavier Cabrini, also known as Mother Cabrini. She is the patron saint of immigrants because she came to the United States to minister to Italian immigrants. Our Scripture reading tells of the disciple Barnabas, who, like Mother Cabrini, traveled to spread the Good News of Christ.

✝ All make the Sign of the Cross.

In the name of the Father, and of the Son, and of the Holy Spirit. Amen.

PSALM

(For a longer psalm, see page xii.) Psalm 98:1, 2–3, 3–4

The LORD has made known his victory.

The LORD has made known his victory.

O sing to the LORD a new song,
   for he has done marvelous things.
His right hand and his holy arm
   have gotten him victory.

The LORD has made known his victory.

READING

Acts 11:19–24

A reading from the Acts of the Apostles.

Now those who were scattered because of the persecution that took place over Stephen traveled as far as Phoenicia [fuh-NEE-shuh], Cyprus [SIGH-pruhs], and Antioch [AN-tee-ahk], and they spoke the word to no one except Jews. But among them were some men of Cyprus and Cyrene [sigh-REEN] who, on coming to Antioch, spoke to the Hellenists also, proclaiming the Lord Jesus. The hand of the Lord was with them, and a great number became believers and turned to the Lord. News of this came to the ears of the church in Jerusalem, and they sent Barnabas to Antioch. When he came and saw the grace of God, he rejoiced, and he exhorted them all to remain faithful to the Lord with steadfast devotion; for he was a good man, full of the Holy Spirit and of faith. And a great many people were brought to the Lord.

The Word of the Lord.

◆ All observe silence.

FOR SILENT REFLECTION

Think about this silently in your heart. Why are people attacked because of their faith? Pray for all who suffer for their beliefs.

CLOSING PRAYER

Let us pray to God for our needs and the needs of others: our family, neighborhood, and the world. For each need we say, "Lord, hear our prayer."

◆ All may add their own prayers here.

Let us pray: **Our Father . . . Amen.**

O Loving God,
may we care for one another
as Mother Cabrini did.
We ask this in Christ's name.

Amen.

✝ All make the Sign of the Cross.

OPENING

In today's reading, St. Paul, preaching to the people of Galatia [guh-LAY-shuh], reminds them that love is the greatest commandment. If we love one another, we will live in peace and with joy.

✚ All make the Sign of the Cross.

In the name of the Father, and of the Son, and of the Holy Spirit. Amen.

PSALM   (For a longer psalm, see page xii.) Psalm 98:1, 2–3, 3–4

The LORD has made known his victory.

The LORD has made known his victory.

O sing to the LORD a new song,
   for he has done marvelous things.
His right hand and his holy arm
   have gotten him victory.

The LORD has made known his victory.

READING   Galatians 5:13–14, 16–17ab, 22–23a, 25–26

A reading from the Letter of Paul to the Galatians.

For you were called to freedom, brothers and sisters; only do not use your freedom as an opportunity for self-indulgence, but through love become slaves to one another. For the whole law is summed up in a single commandment, "You shall love your neighbor as yourself." Live by the Spirit, I say, and do not gratify the desires of the flesh. For what the flesh desires is opposed to the Spirit, and what the Spirit desires is opposed to the flesh. By contrast, the fruit of the Spirit is love, joy, peace, patience, kindness, generosity, faithfulness, gentleness, and self-control. If we live by the Spirit, let us also be guided by the Spirit. Let us not become conceited, competing against one another, envying one another.

The Word of the Lord.

◆ All observe silence.

FOR SILENT REFLECTION

Think about this silently in your heart. Which gift of the Spirit do you need? Pray to the Holy Spirit for this gift.

CLOSING PRAYER

Let us pray to God for our needs and the needs of others: our family, neighborhood, and the world. For each need we say, "Lord, hear our prayer."

◆ All may add their own prayers here.

Let us pray: **Our Father . . . Amen.**

Just as you are faithful to us, O God,
you ask that we be faithful to you
and to one another.
We pray for the Spirit's gifts of love and joy,
peace and patience, kindness and generosity.
We ask this through Christ our Lord.

Amen.

✚ All make the Sign of the Cross.

OPENING

Today we celebrate St. Albert the Great. He loved learning and teaching about God. Like Gaius [Guy-is], about whom we will hear today, St. Albert was a coworker in the vineyard for truth. In today's reading, John praises the disciple Gaius for his faithfulness.

✚ All make the Sign of the Cross.

In the name of the Father, and of the Son, and of the Holy Spirit. Amen.

PSALM   (For a longer psalm, see page xii.) Psalm 98:1, 2–3, 3–4

The Lord has made known his victory.

The Lord has made known his victory.

O sing to the Lord a new song,
   for he has done marvelous things.
His right hand and his holy arm
   have gotten him victory.

The Lord has made known his victory.

READING   3 John 1:1–7a, 8

A reading from the Third Letter of John.

The elder to the beloved Gaius, whom I love in truth. Beloved, I pray that all may go well with you and that you may be in good health, just as it is well with your soul. I was overjoyed when some of the friends arrived and testified to your faithfulness to the truth, namely how you walk in the truth. I have no greater joy than this, to hear that my children are walking in the truth. Beloved, you do faithfully whatever you do for the friends, even though they are strangers to you; they have testified to your love before the church. You will do well to send them on in a manner worthy of God; for they began their journey for the sake of Christ. Therefore we ought to support such people, so that we may become co-workers with the truth.

The Word of the Lord.

◆ All observe silence.

FOR SILENT REFLECTION

Think about this silently in your heart. What do you think "walking in the truth" means?

CLOSING PRAYER

Let us pray to God for our needs and the needs of others: our family, neighborhood, and the world. For each need we say, "Lord, hear our prayer."

◆ All may add their own prayers here.

Let us pray: **Our Father . . . Amen.**

Faithful God,
help us always to walk in the truth.
When we struggle, give us strength.
When we doubt, give us faith.
Let us be your faithful and true servants.
We ask this through Christ our Lord.

Amen.

✚ All make the Sign of the Cross.

PRAYER FOR THE WEEK
WITH A READING FROM THE GOSPEL FOR **SUNDAY, NOVEMBER 17, 2019**

OPENING

Jesus warns the disciples that they could be persecuted for following him. But he also reassures them that he will be with them and will give them words of wisdom to speak to the persecutors.

✝ All make the Sign of the Cross.

In the name of the Father, and of the Son, and of the Holy Spirit. Amen.

PSALM   (For a longer psalm, see page xii.) Psalm 98:1, 2–3, 3–4

The LORD has made known his victory.

The LORD has made known his victory.

O sing to the LORD a new song,
  for he has done marvelous things.
His right hand and his holy arm
  have gotten him victory.

The LORD has made known his victory.

◆ All stand and sing **Alleluia**.

GOSPEL   Luke 21:5–6ab, 9–10a, 12a, 13, 15, 18

A reading from the holy Gospel according to Luke.

When some were speaking about the temple, how it was adorned with beautiful stones and gifts dedicated to God, Jesus said, "As for these things that you see, the days will come when not one stone will be left upon another. When you hear of wars and insurrections, do not be terrified; for these things must take place first, but the end will not follow immediately." Then he said to them, "Nation will rise against nation. But before all this occurs, they will arrest you and persecute you. This will give you an opportunity to testify. For I will give you words and a wisdom that none of your opponents will be able to withstand or contradict. But not a hair of your head will perish."

The Gospel of the Lord.

◆ All sit and observe silence.

FOR SILENT REFLECTION

Think about this silently in your heart. How can our words and actions testify that we follow Jesus?

CLOSING PRAYER

Let us pray to God for our needs and the needs of others: our family, neighborhood, and the world. For each need we say, "Lord, hear our prayer."

◆ All may add their own prayers here.

Let us pray: **Our Father . . . Amen.**

You, O God, are worthy of praise.
May our lives testify to our faith in you.
May our actions show that we love
and follow your Son Jesus,
in whose name we pray.

Amen.

✝ All make the Sign of the Cross.

OPENING

In the Scriptures, Jesus is given many names or titles, which help us to learn more about who God is. This week, we will hear some of these. Today's reading, about the angel Gabriel's annunciation to Mary, speaks of Jesus as the "Son of God." We also celebrate the Dedication of the Basilicas of Sts. Peter and Paul today. These two churches in Rome, Italy, symbolize our unity as a Church.

✛ All make the Sign of the Cross.

In the name of the Father, and of the Son, and of the Holy Spirit. Amen.

PSALM   (For a longer psalm, see page xii.) Psalm 98:1, 2–3, 3–4

The LORD has made known his victory.

The LORD has made known his victory.

O sing to the LORD a new song,
for he has done marvelous things.
His right hand and his holy arm
have gotten him victory.

The LORD has made known his victory.

◆ All stand and sing **Alleluia.**

GOSPEL   Luke 1:26–31, 35

A reading from the holy Gospel according to Luke.

The angel Gabriel was sent by God to a town in Galilee called Nazareth, to a virgin engaged to a man whose name was Joseph, of the house of David. The virgin's name was Mary. And he came to her and said, "Greetings, favored one! The Lord is with you." But she was much perplexed by his words and pondered what sort of greeting this might be. The angel said to her, "Do not be afraid, Mary, for you have found favor with God. And now, you will conceive in your womb and bear a son, and you will name him Jesus. The Holy Spirit will come upon you, and the power of the Most High will overshadow you; therefore the child to be born will be holy; he will be called Son of God."

The Gospel of the Lord.

◆ All sit and observe silence.

FOR SILENT REFLECTION

Think about this silently in your heart. We are also God's sons and daughters. How are we called to be holy?

CLOSING PRAYER

Let us pray to God for our needs and the needs of others: our family, neighborhood, and the world. For each need we say, "Lord, hear our prayer."

◆ All may add their own prayers here.

Let us pray: **Our Father . . . Amen.**

Thank you, loving God,
for sending us your Son Jesus.
We too are your beloved daughters and sons.
Bless us as one family of faith.
Through Christ our Lord.

Amen.

✛ All make the Sign of the Cross.

PRAYER FOR
TUESDAY, NOVEMBER 19, 2019

OPENING

In today's reading we hear Jesus remind the disciples that they have called him their "Lord and Teacher." In school, we learn from our teachers. As a teacher, Jesus shows us how to live as his followers.

✝ All make the Sign of the Cross.

In the name of the Father, and of the Son, and of the Holy Spirit. Amen.

PSALM (For a longer psalm, see page xii.) Psalm 98:1, 2–3, 3–4

The Lord has made known his victory.

The Lord has made known his victory.

O sing to the Lord a new song,
 for he has done marvelous things.
His right hand and his holy arm
 have gotten him victory.

The Lord has made known his victory.

◆ All stand and sing **Alleluia.**

GOSPEL   John 13:12–15

A reading from the holy Gospel according to John.

After he had washed their feet, had put on his robe, and returned to the table, Jesus said to his disciples, "Do you know what I have done to you? You call me Teacher and Lord—and you are right, for that is what I am. So if I, your Lord and Teacher, have washed your feet, you also ought to wash one another's feet. For I have set you an example, that you also should do as I have done to you."

The Gospel of the Lord.

◆ All sit and observe silence.

FOR SILENT REFLECTION

Think about this silently in your heart. What is Jesus teaching the disciples when he washes their feet?

CLOSING PRAYER

Let us pray to God for our needs and the needs of others: our family, neighborhood, and the world. For each need we say, "Lord, hear our prayer."

◆ All may add their own prayers here.

Let us pray: **Our Father . . . Amen.**

Holy and loving Father,
we praise you and we thank you.
Help us to follow the example of Jesus,
our Master Teacher,
in whose name we pray.

Amen.

✝ All make the Sign of the Cross.

OPENING

Today we hear Jesus refer to himself as the "Son of Man." In using this title, Jesus reveals his humility, and also his willingness to suffer, as he does the will of his Father in heaven.

✦ All make the Sign of the Cross.

In the name of the Father, and of the Son, and of the Holy Spirit. Amen.

PSALM
(For a longer psalm, see page xii.) Psalm 98:1, 2–3, 3–4

The Lord has made known his victory.

The Lord has made known his victory.

O sing to the Lord a new song,
for he has done marvelous things.
His right hand and his holy arm
have gotten him victory.

The Lord has made known his victory.

◆ All stand and sing **Alleluia.**

GOSPEL
Luke 5:17ab, 18a, 20–22ab, 23–25

A reading from the holy Gospel according to Luke.

One day, while Jesus was teaching, Pharisees and teachers of the law were sitting nearby. Just then some men came, carrying a paralyzed man on a bed. When Jesus saw their faith, he said, "Friend, your sins are forgiven you." Then the scribes and the Pharisees began to question, "Who is this who is speaking blasphemies? Who can forgive sins but God alone?" When Jesus perceived their questionings, he answered them, "Which is easier, to say, 'Your sins are forgiven you,' or to say, 'Stand up and walk'? But so that you may know that the Son of Man has authority on earth to forgive sins"—he said to the one who was paralyzed—"I say to you, stand up and take your bed and go to your home." Immediately he stood up before them, took what he had been lying on, and went to his home, glorifying God.

The Gospel of the Lord.

◆ All sit and observe silence.

FOR SILENT REFLECTION

Think about this silently in your heart. In what ways does Jesus, who is divine and human, reveal God's love?

CLOSING PRAYER

Let us pray to God for our needs and the needs of others: our family, neighborhood, and the world. For each need we say, "Lord, hear our prayer."

◆ All may add their own prayers here.

Let us pray: **Our Father . . . Amen.**

In becoming human, Jesus, the Son of God,
also became the Son of Man.
We thank you, Father, for Jesus,
who understands our weakness
and knows what we need.
May we learn from him always.
Through Christ our Lord.

Amen.

✦ All make the Sign of the Cross.

PRAYER FOR
THURSDAY, NOVEMBER 21, 2019

OPENING

Today we celebrate the Presentation of the Blessed Virgin Mary in the Temple. This is an ancient feast that honors Mary as the Mother of God. Her body was the Temple for the Child Jesus. In today's reading, we hear another title for Jesus: "the way, the truth, and the life."

✝ All make the Sign of the Cross.

In the name of the Father, and of the Son, and of the Holy Spirit. Amen.

PSALM   (For a longer psalm, see page xii.) Psalm 98:1, 2–3, 3–4

The Lord has made known his victory.

The Lord has made known his victory.

O sing to the Lord a new song,
   for he has done marvelous things.
His right hand and his holy arm
   have gotten him victory.

The Lord has made known his victory.

◆ All stand and sing **Alleluia.**

GOSPEL   John 14:1–7

A reading from the holy Gospel according to John.

"Do not let your hearts be troubled. Believe in God, believe also in me. In my Father's house thre are many dwelling places. If it were not so, would I have told you that I go to prepare a place for you? And if I go and prepare a place for you, I will come again and will take you to myself, so that where I am, there you may be also. And you know the way to the place where I am going." Thomas said to him, "Lord, we do not know where you are going. How can we know the way?" Jesus said to him, "I am the way, the truth, and the life. No come comes to the Father except through me. If you know me, you will know my Father also. From now on you do know him and have seen him."

The Gospel of the Lord.

◆ All sit and observe silence.

FOR SILENT REFLECTION

Think about this silently in your heart. How is Jesus the way to the Father for you?

CLOSING PRAYER

Let us pray to God for our needs and the needs of others: our family, neighborhood, and the world. For each need we say, "Lord, hear our prayer."

◆ All may add their own prayers here.

Let us pray: **Our Father . . . Amen.**

Loving God,
in Jesus we find the way to you.
In Jesus we learn the truth about you.
In Jesus we come to know life with you.
Thank you for sending Jesus to us
through the Virgin Mary.
We pray in Christ's name.

Amen.

✝ All make the Sign of the Cross.

OPENING

This week we have heard only a few of the names given to Jesus in Scripture, and these help us to realize how extraordinary he was. He was called teacher, healer, Son of God, and Son of Man, and also the way, the truth, and the life. Today we hear another familiar title for Jesus, the "light of the world." Today we honor St. Cecilia, the patron saint of musicians, singers, and poets.

✤ All make the Sign of the Cross.

In the name of the Father, and of the Son, and of the Holy Spirit. Amen.

PSALM   (For a longer psalm, see page xii.) Psalm 98:1, 2–3, 3–4

The LORD has made known his victory.

The LORD has made known his victory.

O sing to the LORD a new song,
    for he has done marvelous things.
His right hand and his holy arm
    have gotten him victory.

The LORD has made known his victory.

◆ All stand and sing **Alleluia.**

GOSPEL   John 8:12–15

A reading from the holy Gospel according to John.

Again Jesus spoke to them, saying, "I am the light of the world. Whoever follows me will never walk in darkness but will have the light of life." Then the Pharisees said to him, "You are testifying on your own behalf; your testimony is not valid." Jesus answered, "Even if I testify on my own behalf, my testimony is valid because I know where I have come from and where I am going, but you do not know where I come from or where I am going. You judge by human standards; I judge no one."

The Gospel of the Lord.

◆ All sit and observe silence.

FOR SILENT REFLECTION

Think about this silently in your heart. How is Jesus a light for you? What darkness does he dispel?

CLOSING PRAYER

Let us pray to God for our needs and the needs of others: our family, neighborhood, and the world. For each need we say, "Lord, hear our prayer."

◆ All may add their own prayers here.

Let us pray: **Our Father . . . Amen.**

Holy and loving God,
at Baptism we received the light of Christ.
We pray that we will keep
this light burning brightly.
We pray that the light of Christ
will shine in our world.
This we ask in his name.

Amen.

✤ All make the Sign of the Cross.

PRAYER FOR THE WEEK
WITH A READING FROM THE GOSPEL FOR **SUNDAY, NOVEMBER 24, 2019**

OPENING

On the Solemnity of Our Lord Jesus Christ, King of the Universe we hear two important titles for Jesus: Messiah and King of the Jews. Now we know that Jesus Christ is the Messiah and ruler of our hearts.

✝ All make the Sign of the Cross.

In the name of the Father, and of the Son, and of the Holy Spirit. Amen.

PSALM (For a longer psalm, see page xii.) Psalm 98:1, 2–3, 3–4

The LORD has made known his victory.

The LORD has made known his victory.

O sing to the LORD a new song,
for he has done marvelous things.
His right hand and his holy arm
have gotten him victory.

The LORD has made known his victory.

◆ All stand and sing **Alleluia.**

GOSPEL Luke 23:35–40a, 41bc

A reading from the holy Gospel according to Luke.

And the people stood by, watching; but the leaders scoffed at Jesus, saying, "He saved others; let him save himself if he is the Messiah of God, God's chosen one!" The soldiers also mocked him, coming up and offering him sour wine, and saying, "If you are the King of the Jews, save yourself!" There was also an inscription over him, "This is the King of the Jews." One of the criminals who were hanged there kept deriding him and saying, "Are you not the Messiah? Save yourself and us!" But the other rebuked him, saying, "Do you not fear God? For we are getting what we deserve for our deeds, but this man has done nothing wrong."

The Gospel of the Lord.

◆ All sit and observe silence.

FOR SILENT REFLECTION

Think about this silently in your heart. Why do you think Jesus is King of the Universe? What type of king is he?

CLOSING PRAYER

Let us pray to God for our needs and the needs of others: our family, neighborhood, and the world. For each need we say, "Lord, hear our prayer."

◆ All may add their own prayers here.

Let us pray: **Our Father . . . Amen.**

Christ our Lord,
in you we see God's Kingdom revealed.
May you have eternal glory and power.
Who live and reign with the Father in the unity of the Holy Spirit,
one God,
for ever and ever.

Amen.

✝ All make the Sign of the Cross.

OPENING

Yesterday we celebrated Jesus Christ as King of the Universe. This week we'll see what the Bible says about how a king should rule and care for his people. The prophet Isaiah says a king is just and seeks peace for his people.

✚ All make the Sign of the Cross.

In the name of the Father, and of the Son, and of the Holy Spirit. Amen.

PSALM   (For a longer psalm, see page xii.) Psalm 98:1, 2–3, 3–4

The Lord has made known his victory.

The Lord has made known his victory.

O sing to the Lord a new song,
   for he has done marvelous things.
His right hand and his holy arm
   have gotten him victory.

The Lord has made known his victory.

READING   Isaiah 31:4a; 32:1–2acd, 3, 16–18

A reading from the Book of the prophet Isaiah.

For thus the Lord said to me: See, a king will reign in righteousness, and princes will rule with justice. Each will be like a hiding place from the wind, like streams of water in a dry place, like the shade of a great rock in a weary land. Then the eyes of those who have sight will not be closed, and the ears of those who have hearing will listen. Then justice will dwell in the wilderness, and righteousness abide in the fruitful field. The effect of righteousness will be peace, and the result of righteousness, quietness and trust forever. My people will abide in a peaceful habitation, in secure dwellings, and in quiet resting places.

The Word of the Lord.

◆ All sit and observe silence.

FOR SILENT REFLECTION

Think about this silently in your heart. Is someone you know being treated unjustly? Is there anything you can do about it?

CLOSING PRAYER

Let us pray to God for our needs and the needs of others: our family, neighborhood, and the world. For each need we say, "Lord, hear our prayer."

◆ All may add their own prayers here.

Let us pray: **Our Father . . . Amen.**

It is your will, O God,
that people live happily and peacefully.
We ask that you guide our leaders
to make decisions that are wise and just.
Help us to be honest and fair
in all that we do.
We ask this through Christ our Lord.

Amen.

✚ All make the Sign of the Cross.

PRAYER FOR
TUESDAY, NOVEMBER 26, 2019

OPENING

The prophet Jeremiah says a good leader is like a shepherd who takes good care of the sheep. God gave us Jesus, the Good Shepherd.

✚ All make the Sign of the Cross.

In the name of the Father, and of the Son, and of the Holy Spirit. Amen.

PSALM   (For a longer psalm, see page xii.) Psalm 98:1, 2–3, 3–4

The LORD has made known his victory.

The LORD has made known his victory.

O sing to the LORD a new song,
  for he has done marvelous things.
His right hand and his holy arm
  have gotten him victory.

The LORD has made known his victory.

READING   Jeremiah 23:1–4

A reading from the Book of the prophet Jeremiah.

Woe to the shepherds who destroy and scatter the sheep of my pasture! says the LORD. Therefore thus says the LORD, the God of Israel, concerning the shepherds who shepherd my people: It is you who have scattered my flock, and have driven them away, and you have not attended to them. So I will attend to you for your evil doings, says the LORD. Then I myself will gather the remnant of my flock out of all the lands where I have driven them, and I will bring them back to their fold, and they shall be fruitful and multiply. I will raise up shepherds over them who will shepherd them, and they shall not fear any longer, or be dismayed, nor shall any be missing, says the LORD.

The Word of the Lord.

◆ All observe silence.

FOR SILENT REFLECTION

Think about this silently in your heart. Who takes good care of you? Say a prayer of thanksgiving for them.

CLOSING PRAYER

Let us pray to God for our needs and the needs of others: our family, neighborhood, and the world. For each need we say, "Lord, hear our prayer."

◆ All may add their own prayers here.

Let us pray: **Our Father . . . Amen.**

We thank you, O God,
for all who love and care for us.
We thank you for Jesus, our Good Shepherd,
who knows each one of us by name.
We thank you, O God,
for all of the ways you provide for us.
We praise you for your goodness
in Christ's name.

Amen.

✚ All make the Sign of the Cross.

OPENING

The prophet Zechariah insists a king needs to be a humble peacemaker. Jesus is this kind of king. Tomorrow is Thanksgiving, when we give thanks for the many gifts we have received, including our faith, our country, our family, and our freedom.

✚ All make the Sign of the Cross.

In the name of the Father, and of the Son, and of the Holy Spirit. Amen.

PSALM   (For a longer psalm, see page xii.) Psalm 98:1, 2–3, 3–4

The LORD has made known his victory.

The LORD has made known his victory.

O sing to the LORD a new song,
   for he has done marvelous things.
His right hand and his holy arm
   have gotten him victory.

The LORD has made known his victory.

READING   Zechariah 9:9–10, 16–17a

A reading from the Book of the prophet Zechariah.

Rejoice greatly, O daughter Zion! Shout aloud, O daughter Jerusalem! Lo, your king comes to you; triumphant and victorious is he, humble and riding on a donkey, on a colt, the foal of a donkey. He will cut off the chariot from Ephraim [E-fray-ihm] and the war-horse from Jerusalem; and the battle bow shall be cut off, and he shall command peace to the nations; his dominion shall be from sea to sea, and from the River to the ends of the earth. On that day the LORD their God will save them for they are the flock of his people; for like the jewels of a crown they shall shine on his land. For what goodness and beauty are his!

The Word of the Lord.

◆ All observe silence.

FOR SILENT REFLECTION

Think about this silently in your heart. For what are you most grateful?

CLOSING PRAYER

Let us pray to God for our needs and the needs of others: our family, neighborhood, and the world. For each need we say, "Lord, hear our prayer."

◆ All may add their own prayers here.

Let us pray: **Our Father . . . Amen.**

At this time of thanksgiving, may we learn to be grateful for the many gifts
you have given us, O Lord.
Please bless and care for all who need food or shelter or safety.
We ask you, gracious God, to bless us through Christ our Lord.

Amen.

✚ All make the Sign of the Cross.

PRAYER SERVICE
FOR THANKSGIVING

Prepare seven leaders for this service. The fourth leader will need a Bible to read the Gospel passage and may need help finding and practicing the reading. You may want to begin by singing "One Bread, One Body," and end with "Table of Plenty." If the group will sing, prepare a song leader.

FIRST LEADER:

✦ All make the Sign of the Cross.

In the name of the Father, and of the Son, and of the Holy Spirit. Amen.

Let us pray:

Almighty God,
you bless us every day with the
signs and wonders of your creation.
We thank you for the fresh air,
trees, stars, and planets, as well as
all the animals and creatures that live on
      land and in the sea.
We are grateful that you have entrusted us
with care of your environment.

SECOND LEADER: Psalm 136:1–9
Our refrain is: For his steadfast love
endures forever.

ALL: For his steadfast love endures forever.

LEADER: O give thanks to the Lord,
for he is good,

ALL: For his steadfast love endures forever;

LEADER: Who alone does great wonders,

ALL: For his steadfast love endures forever;

LEADER: Who by understanding made
the heavens,

ALL: For his steadfast love endures forever;

LEADER: Who spread out the earth on the waters,

ALL: For his steadfast love endures forever;

LEADER: Who made the great lights,

ALL: For his steadfast love endures forever;

LEADER: The sun to rule over the day,

ALL: For his steadfast love endures forever;

LEADER: The moon and stars to rule over the night,

ALL: For his steadfast love endures forever.

THIRD LEADER:
Creator God,
your presence is with us
today and always.
We are grateful for the
gift of your Son Jesus,
who lived and walked among us,
and whose Spirit fills our hearts
with gratitude and joy.

ALL: Amen.

FOURTH LEADER: 1 John 4:7–16
A reading from the first Letter of John.

◆ Read the Scripture passage from the Bible.

The Word of the Lord.

FIFTH LEADER: Psalm 100:1–5
Our refrain is: Make a joyful noise to the Lord.

ALL: Make a joyful noise to the Lord.

LEADER: Make a joyful noise to the Lord,
all the earth,
Worship the Lord with gladness;
Come into his presence with singing.

ALL: Make a joyful noise to the Lord.

LEADER: Know that the Lord is God.
It is he that made us, and we are his;
We are his people, and the sheep of
his pasture.

ALL: Make a joyful noise to the Lord.

LEADER: Enter his gates with thanksgiving,
and his courts with praise.
Give thanks to him, bless his name.

ALL: Make a joyful noise to the Lord.

SIXTH LEADER:
Loving God,
we thank you for all that you
provide for us.
We are grateful for all the loved ones
in our lives now,
and those who have gone before us.
You nurture us in so many ways.
May we always remember to praise you
and love others as you love us.
We ask this through Christ our Lord.

SEVENTH LEADER:
May the love of God,

✛ All make the Sign of the Cross.

Father, Son, and Holy Spirit,

always surround us in faith,
now and forever.

ALL: Amen.

HOME PRAYER
MEAL PRAYER FOR THANKSGIVING

Find the reading (John 15:12–17) in your Bible, ask for a volunteer to read the Scripture passage, and encourage the reader to practice reading it a few times. If practical, light candles for your Thanksgiving table. You may wish to begin with a simple song of thanksgiving or a favorite "Alleluia." Then an older child or an adult reads the leader parts.

LEADER:
Almighty God,
look at the abundance here before us!
It fills us with joy and gratitude.
Let us begin our prayer with the
     Sign of the Cross.

✚ All make the Sign of the Cross.

In the name of the Father, and of the Son, and of the Holy Spirit. Amen.

◆ All stand and sing **Alleluia.**

READER: John 15:12–17
A reading from the holy Gospel according
to John.

◆ Read the Gospel passage from the Bible.

The Gospel of the Lord.

◆ All sit and observe silence.

LEADER:
We come to this table,
grateful for the delicious meal we're about
to share,
as well as the family and friends who
surround us here.
Let us pray:
Heavenly Father,
we thank you for the love and friendship
that envelops us today.
Help us to nurture one another
with your peace and serenity in the
midst of our busy lives.
We thank all those who helped prepare
     this meal.
We are mindful of people in our
     community and
in other regions who may not have enough to
     eat today.
May we appreciate all that you provide for us
     now, and
we look forward to our heavenly banquet
     with you.
We ask this through our Lord Jesus Christ,
your Son, who lives and reigns with you
in the unity of the Holy Spirit, one God,
     for ever and ever.

ALL: Amen.

✚ All make the Sign of the Cross.

CHILDREN'S DAILY PRAYER 2019–2020 © 2019 Archdiocese of Chicago: Liturgy Training Publications, 3949 South Racine Avenue, Chicago, IL 60609. All rights reserved. Orders: 800-933-1800 or www.LTP.org. Scripture excerpts are taken from *The New Revised Standard Version Bible: Catholic Edition* © 1989, Division of Christian Education of the National Council of the Churches of Christ in the United States of America. Used with permission. All rights reserved.

ADVENT

SUNDAY, DECEMBER 1 — TUESDAY, DECEMBER 24

ADVENT

THE MEANING OF ADVENT

"A shoot shall come out from the stump of Jesse, and a branch shall grow out of his roots" (Isaiah 11:1).

Jesse was the father of King David, a great leader of the Jewish people. But then Jesse's descendants became weak and scattered. The Jewish people no longer had a strong ruler and they suffered many periods of darkness, misery, and despair. The people of Israel had become like a great tree cut down to its stump. Yet God did not forsake the people. God, Israel's faithful protector, promised to make a new plant sprout. The people waited and prayed and hoped for many years, knowing God would keep this promise. We too are a people to whom God has made a solemn promise.

Advent is our time of waiting in "devout and joyful expectation" (*General Norms for the Liturgical Year*, 39) for the celebration of Christ's Incarnation and also for his Second Coming. We prepare as we wait by giving a little more to the poor and taking stock of our souls, as well as baking cookies and thinking about gifts for those we love. We wait, as did our spiritual ancestors, to celebrate the nativity of the Messiah. The first Sunday of Advent is also when the Church begins her new calendar year.

We begin our Advent with a week of Scriptures called the Messianic Prophecies. The prophets foretell where Jesus will be born and who his mother will be. They also predict Jesus' triumphant entry into Jerusalem on a donkey, his title of Good Shepherd, and that he will suffer. In the second and third week of our waiting we hear encouraging words that the Messiah will be the Light that breaks the darkness of injustice and brings peace. We'll hear the call of John the Baptist to "Prepare the Way of the Lord" (Luke 3:4). Our final week tells the great Infancy Narrative stories of the angel's announcement to Mary and reassurance to Joseph, and Mary's visit to Elizabeth with her joyful hymn of praise for God's wonderful work, the *Magnificat*.

PREPARING TO CELEBRATE ADVENT IN THE CLASSROOM

SACRED SPACE

During Advent create a mood of anticipation in the classroom. Use purples and violets on the bulletin boards instead of red and green since we are an Advent people. You can place the empty manger from a Christmas Nativity scene on your classroom prayer table. Slowly add elements like straw and animals and, in the last week, the Holy Family and shepherds. You might wait to add the star and the Magi after Christmas vacation, but it is not necessary.

You can also use an Advent wreath, which has a circular candleholder usually decorated with pine branches. It has four candles: three violet and one rose-colored (but you can use all violet or even white). When you first introduce the wreath to your class, wonder together with the children about why it's circular, why use pine boughs, why four candles. Children will often come up with beautiful answers to these questions: the wreath is round because God's love has no beginning and no end; the pine branches never lose their leaves or color just as God's love for us can never die; and the four candles represent the four Sundays of Advent, the four points of the compass, the four branches of the cross, the four Gospels, and so on. Explain that each day you will light one candle for each week in Advent; when all the candles are lit, then Christmas will be right around the corner! The children may be curious about the rose-colored candle. Explain that it is the third one that we light, for the third Sunday in Advent, which is called Gaudete [gow-DAY-tay] (Latin for "rejoice") because our wait is almost over!

MOVEMENT AND GESTURE

Children of all ages love solemn processions. Consider organizing an Advent procession. After sharing some of the material in "The Meaning of Advent" with them, explain that Advent has a new color, violet. Suggest to the children that you have a procession to change the color of your prayer tablecloth. You will want to speak with the children about processions they have participated in or have seen in church. Explain that a procession is a prayerful way to walk, and stress the importance of silence (or singing along if you plan to sing). You'll need children to place the Bible, Advent wreath, and other elements after the cloth is laid and, finally, someone to light the first candle. If you are not singing the procession could be accompanied by a wind chime.

FESTIVITY IN SCHOOL AND HOME

There are two wonderful feasts to celebrate in Advent, St. Nicholas (you may wish to hand out candy canes or "gold" chocolate coins) on December 6, and on December 13, St. Lucy (you may wish hand out cookies and hot chocolate). You might celebrate them in the week even if their day comes on a Saturday or Sunday. Please consider saving your celebration of Christmas until true Christmas time *after* December 25. The time of Advent is a great spiritual gift that helps us grow in the beautiful theological virtue of hope. Also, if you wait until you return from Christmas break to celebrate the great Christmas feast of Epiphany, the children will have settled down and may be more able to listen to the glad tidings of great joy.

In this book you will find special prayer services that may be used in the classroom or with a larger group. One is a service for Advent, pages 116–117, which could be used at any time; the other is for the Solemnity of the Immaculate Conception of the Blessed Virgin Mary on December 9, pages 126–127.

SACRED MUSIC

Discover which songs your parish will be singing during Advent. Sometimes the setting for the sung parts of the Mass will change with the liturgical time. Other Advent songs that children love include "The King of Glory Comes," "People Look East," and "O Come, O Come, Emmanuel."

PRAYERS FOR ADVENT

A wonderful prayer to become acquainted with during Advent is the Mary's prayer of praise, the *Magnificat* (Luke 1:46–55). All those who pray the Liturgy of the Hours recite this beautiful prayer each evening to remember Mary's joy as she prayed to God, the Mighty One. It has been set to various tunes and may be sung. Two lovely sung versions are the Taizé "Magnificat" (canon) and "Holy Is Your Name."

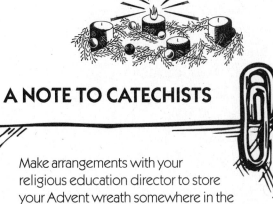

A NOTE TO CATECHISTS

Make arrangements with your religious education director to store your Advent wreath somewhere in the classroom during the week so that you don't need to carry it back and forth between school and home. Read the Festivity in School and Home section of the Introduction for ways to celebrate the saints that help us anticipate the celebration of Christmas.

GRACE BEFORE MEALS

ADVENT

LEADER:
Let the clouds rain down the Just One,
and the earth bring forth a Savior.

✚ All make the Sign of the Cross.

**In the name of the Father, and of the
Son, and of the Holy Spirit. Amen.**

LEADER:
Lord God,
you provide for us in so many ways.
You have given us the earth,
full of so much goodness.
You have blessed us with water to drink
and food to nourish our bodies.
As we look forward to your gift of the
Christ child,
we also think about the day
when we will be with you in heaven,
where everyone is filled with the joy
of your glorious presence.
We ask this through Jesus Christ our Lord.

ALL: Amen.

✚ All make the Sign of the Cross.

**In the name of the Father, and of the
Son, and of the Holy Spirit. Amen.**

PRAYER AT DAY'S END

LEADER:

O Wisdom of our God Most High,
guiding creation with power and love,
come to teach us the path of knowledge!

✚ All make the Sign of the Cross.

In the name of the Father, and of the Son, and of the Holy Spirit. Amen.

LEADER:

Holy God,
we thank you for this day
with all of its adventures, big and small.
May our days continue to be filled
with the light of your Son, our Lord,
your gift to us,
who shows us the way of
patience and forgiveness and love.
We ask this in his name.

ALL: Amen.

✚ All make the Sign of the Cross.

In the name of the Father, and of the Son, and of the Holy Spirit. Amen.

PRAYER SERVICE
ADVENT

Prepare a leader, reader, intercessor, and (if possible) a music leader for the service. Go over the intercessions with the class, and mention they are based on some Old Testament titles for Jesus we call the O Antiphons. Practice singing the refrain to "O Come, O Come Emmanuel" as the response, if possible. Place an Advent wreath on the table with a Bible and a purple cloth. Place the reading into the Bible and mark it with a ribbon or book mark. Review the reading with the reader and note that some verses are omitted. Decide who will light and extinguish the candles on the wreath. You might sing "Soon and Very Soon" at the end of the service.

LEADER:

◆ Gesture for all to stand.

✚ All make the sign of the Cross.

In the name of the Father, and of the Son, and of the Holy Spirit. Amen.

LEADER:
Let us pray:
O God of wonder,
as we are busy preparing for Christmas
help us prepare our hearts for Jesus.
We are grateful for your simple words
    of hope
and the gift of new life in the Christ child.
May we follow the true light of Jesus
that shines for all people
through the darkness of sin and sorrow.
We ask this through Christ our Lord.

ALL: Amen.

◆ Gesture for all to sit. An adult lights the appropriate number of candles on the Advent wreath. Allow a moment of silence to enjoy the beauty of the lit wreath. (For a discussion of the significance of the Advent wreath and a prayer for blessing it, see Preparing to Celebrate Advent in the Classroom, the section on Sacred Space on page 112.)

LEADER: Isaiah 40:5a, 11

Let us pray the Psalm Response:

The glory of the Lord shall be revealed.

ALL: The glory of the Lord shall be revealed.

LEADER:

He will feed his flock like a shepherd;
   he will gather the lambs in his arms,
and carry them in his bosom,
   and gently lead the mother sheep.

ALL: The glory of the Lord shall be revealed.

READER: Isaiah 11:1–10

A reading from the Book of the prophet Isaiah.

◆ Read the Scripture passage from a Bible.

The Word of the Lord.

◆ All observe silence.

INTERCESSOR:

O come, Emmanuel, free people who are held captive by racism, prejudice, and bullying. We sing:

ALL: "Rejoice! Rejoice! Emmanuel shall come to you, O Israel."

O come, Wisdom. Teach us how to be good to one another. We sing (say):

O come, Lord. Rule our hearts and minds in goodness. We sing (say):

O come, Shoot of Jesse's Stem. Forgive us our sins. We sing (say):

O come, Key of David. Open heaven for us. We sing (say):

O come, Dayspring. Replace the darkness of sin. We sing (say):

O come, Desire of Nations. Unite all the world's people. We sing (say):

LEADER:

Come quickly, Lord Jesus,
and guide us in God's way
of peace and justice.
Fill us with your gentle love
as we look forward to celebrating Christmas
with our family and friends.
You are our light and joy!

✚ All make the Sign of the Cross.

In the name of the Father, and of the Son and of the Holy Spirit.

◆ After the service someone extinguishes the candles on the Advent wreath.

PRAYER FOR THE WEEK

OPENING

Advent is the season of preparing and waiting. We prepare our hearts to remember Jesus' birth in Bethlehem over two thousand years ago and for his coming again in his glorified body. We do not know when Jesus will come again, but when he does, all of creation will be drawn into God.

✛ All make the Sign of the Cross.

In the name of the Father, and of the Son, and of the Holy Spirit. Amen.

PSALM

(For a longer psalm, see page xii.)
Psalm 85:4a, 8, 10–11, 12–13

Restore us again, O God of our salvation!

Restore us again, O God of our salvation!

Let me hear what God the LORD will speak,
for he will speak peace to his people,
to his faithful, to those who turn to him in
their hearts.

Restore us again, O God of our salvation!

◆ All stand and sing **Alleluia.**

GOSPEL

Matthew 24:37–38ac, 39–40, 42–44

A reading from the holy Gospel according to Matthew.

For as the days of Noah were, so will be the coming of the Son of Man. For as in those days before the flood they were eating and drinking, until the day Noah entered the ark, and they knew nothing until the flood came and swept them all away, so too will be the coming of the Son of Man. Then two will be in the field; one will be taken and one will be left. Keep awake therefore, for you do not know on what day your Lord is coming. But understand this: if the owner of the house had known in what part of the night the thief was coming, he would have stayed awake and would not have let his house be broken into. Therefore you also must be ready, for the Son of Man is coming at an unexpected hour.

The Gospel of the Lord.

◆ All sit and observe silence.

FOR SILENT REFLECTION

Think about this silently in your heart. How can you prepare your heart for Jesus?

CLOSING PRAYER

Let us pray to God for our needs and the needs of others: our family, neighborhood, and the world. For each need we say, "Lord, hear our prayer."

◆ All may add their own prayers here.

Let us pray: **Our Father . . . Amen.**

As we wait for the celebration
of Jesus' birth, O God,
show us how to use this time
to make our hearts ready.
Come, Jesus, Come!
We pray in the name of your Son Jesus Christ.

Amen.

✛ All make the Sign of the Cross.

OPENING

The Jewish people longed for the Messiah. The prophets of Israel gave hope to the Jewish people by telling what the Messiah would be like. These prophecies seem to describe the coming of Jesus. Today Micah predicts the Messiah will come from Bethlehem.

✣ All make the Sign of the Cross.

In the name of the Father, and of the Son, and of the Holy Spirit. Amen.

PSALM

(For a longer psalm, see page xii.)
Psalm 85:4a, 8, 10–11, 12–13

Restore us again, O God of our salvation!

Restore us again, O God of our salvation!

Let me hear what God the LORD will speak, for he will speak peace to his people,
to his faithful, to those who turn to him in their hearts.

Restore us again, O God of our salvation!

READING

Micah 1:2a; 5:1–2, 4–5a

A reading from the Book of the prophet Micah.

Hear, you peoples, all of you. Now you are walled around with a wall; siege is laid against us; with a rod they strike the ruler of Israel upon the cheek. But you, O Bethlehem [BETH-luh-hehm] of Ephrathah [EF-ruh-thuh], who are one of the little clans of Judah, from you shall come forth for me one who is to rule in Israel, whose origin is from of old, from ancient days. And he shall stand and feed his flock in the strength of the LORD, in the majesty of the name of the LORD his God. And they shall live secure, for now he shall be great to the ends of the earth; and he shall be the one of peace.

The Word of the Lord.

◆ All observe silence.

FOR SILENT REFLECTION

Think about this silently in your heart. Bethlehem was a small, insignificant town, yet it is where Jesus, the Savior of the world, is born. Why do you think he was born there?

CLOSING PRAYER

Let us pray to God for our needs and the needs of others: our family, neighborhood, and the world. For each need we say, "Lord, hear our prayer."

◆ All may add their own prayers here.

Let us pray: **Our Father . . . Amen.**

Bless us, O God,
as we begin this Advent season.
Help us to remember that even our small deeds prepare the way for the coming of your Son, Jesus,
in whose name we pray.

Amen.

✣ All make the Sign of the Cross.

PRAYER FOR
TUESDAY, DECEMBER 3, 2019

OPENING

Isaiah is impatient with King Ahaz [AY-haz], who doesn't trust God enough to ask for a sign that things will be OK. Isaiah gives this prophecy about the young, pregnant woman whose child is called Immanuel [ihm-MAN-yoo-el], which means "God-with-us." Today is the memorial of St. Francis Xavier, a Jesuit priest and missionary who taught people in Asia about Jesus.

✚ All make the Sign of the Cross.

In the name of the Father, and of the Son, and of the Holy Spirit. Amen.

PSALM

(For a longer psalm, see page xii.)
Psalm 85:4a, 8, 10–11, 12–13

Restore us again, O God of our salvation!

Restore us again, O God of our salvation!

Let me hear what God the LORD will speak,
    for he will speak peace to his people,
to his faithful, to those who turn to him in
    their hearts.

Restore us again, O God of our salvation!

READING

Isaiah 7:10–14

A reading from the Book of the prophet Isaiah.

The LORD spoke to Ahaz, saying, Ask a sign of the LORD your God; let it be deep as Sheol [SHAY-ohl] or high as heaven. But Ahaz said, I will not ask, and I will not put the LORD to the test. Then Isaiah said: "Hear then, O house of David! Is it too little for you to weary mortals, that you weary my God also? Therefore the Lord himself will give you a sign. Look, the young woman is with child and shall bear a son, and shall name him Immanuel."

The Word of the Lord.

◆ All observe silence.

FOR SILENT REFLECTION

Think about this silently in your heart. What does it mean to you that God is with us?

CLOSING PRAYER

Let us pray to God for our needs and the needs of others: our family, neighborhood, and the world. For each need we say, "Lord, hear our prayer."

◆ All may add their own prayers here.

Let us pray: **Our Father . . . Amen.**

As we wait for the celebration
of Jesus' birth, O God,
show us how to use this time
to make our hearts ready.
We await the coming of your Son,
our Lord Jesus Christ,
in whose name we pray.

Amen.

✚ All make the Sign of the Cross.

OPENING

Today we hear the prophet Ezekiel [ee-ZEE-kee-uhl] say that God is like a shepherd. As you listen to the reading, notice all of the ways that the shepherd will care for the sheep. We know that Jesus is the Good Shepherd who cares for us. Today we also remember St. John Damascene, who wrote many hymns and prayers.

✦ All make the Sign of the Cross.

In the name of the Father, and of the Son, and of the Holy Spirit. Amen.

PSALM

(For a longer psalm, see page xii.)
Psalm 85:4a, 8, 10–11, 12–13

Restore us again, O God of our salvation!

Restore us again, O God of our salvation!

Let me hear what God the LORD will speak,
     for he will speak peace to his people,
to his faithful, to those who turn to him in
     their hearts.

Restore us again, O God of our salvation!

READING

Ezekiel 34:11, 12c, 14–16

A reading from the Book of the prophet Ezekiel.

For thus says the Lord GOD: I myself will search for my sheep, and will seek them out. I will rescue them from all the places to which they have been scattered on a day of clouds and thick darkness. I will feed them with good pasture, and the mountain heights of Israel shall be their pasture; there they shall lie down in good grazing land, and they shall feed on rich pasture on the mountains of Israel. I myself will be the shepherd of my sheep, and I will make them lie down, says the Lord GOD. I will seek the lost, and I will bring back the strayed, and I will bind up the injured, and I will strengthen the weak, but the fat and the strong I will destroy. I will feed them with justice.

The Word of the Lord.

✦ All observe silence.

FOR SILENT REFLECTION

Think about this silently in your heart. What is injured in us or weak in us for which we need the Good Shepherd's help?

CLOSING PRAYER

Let us pray to God for our needs and the needs of others: our family, neighborhood, and the world. For each need we say, "Lord, hear our prayer."

◆ All may add their own prayers here.

Let us pray: **Our Father . . . Amen.**

Loving God,
you care for us as a good shepherd cares
for each of the sheep.
During Advent, we pray especially for those
who are suffering.
Please hold them in your care.
We ask this through Christ our Lord.

Amen.

✦ All make the Sign of the Cross.

PRAYER FOR
THURSDAY, DECEMBER 5, 2019

OPENING

The prophet Zechariah [zek-uh-RI-uh] tells of a king who will humbly ride a colt, a young male donkey, in triumph! Before his death Jesus entered Jerusalem on a colt, and everyone cheered and waved palm branches.

✚ All make the Sign of the Cross.

In the name of the Father, and of the Son, and of the Holy Spirit. Amen.

PSALM

(For a longer psalm, see page xii.)
Psalm 85:4a, 8, 10–11, 12–13

Restore us again, O God of our salvation!

Restore us again, O God of our salvation!

Let me hear what God the LORD will speak,
    for he will speak peace to his people,
to his faithful, to those who turn to him in
    their hearts.

Restore us again, O God of our salvation!

READING

Zechariah 9:9–11, 16–17a

A reading from the Book of the
prophet Zechariah.

Rejoice greatly, O daughter Zion! Shout aloud, O daughter Jerusalem! Lo, your king comes to you; triumphant and victorious is he, humble and riding on a donkey, on a colt, the foal of a donkey. He will cut off the chariot from Ephraim [EE-fray-ihm] and the war-horse from Jerusalem; and the battle-bow shall be cut off, and he shall command peace to the nations; his dominion shall be from sea to sea, and from the River to the ends of the earth. As for you also, because of the blood of my covenant with you, I will set your prisoners free from the waterless pit. On that day the LORD their God will save them for they are the flock of his people; for like the jewels of a crown they shall shine on his land. For what goodness and beauty are his!

The Word of the Lord.

◆ All observe silence.

FOR SILENT REFLECTION

Think about this silently in your heart. What message does a king give the people when he rides on a donkey and not in a fancy carriage?

CLOSING PRAYER

Let us pray to God for our needs and the needs of others: our family, neighborhood, and the world. For each need we say, "Lord, hear our prayer."

◆ All may add their own prayers here.

Let us pray: **Our Father . . . Amen.**

Loving God,
may we follow the example
of your Son Jesus.
Help us to be humble of heart as we
prepare for his coming at Christmas.
We ask this in his name.

Amen.

✚ All make the Sign of the Cross.

OPENING

Isaiah foretells of the "suffering servant," who, like Jesus, suffers so that others can be free. Isaiah even mentions a "tomb of the rich." Joseph of Arimathea [ayr-ih-muh-THEE-uh], a wealthy Jewish leader, gave his tomb to Jesus. Today we celebrate St. Nicholas, a fourth-century bishop. A traditional story about St. Nicholas is that he had heard that a poor man could not care for his three daughters. So one night, he tossed three bags of gold coins through the window of that poor man.

✛ All make the Sign of the Cross.

In the name of the Father, and of the Son, and of the Holy Spirit. Amen.

PSALM

(For a longer psalm, see page xii.)
Psalm 85:4a, 8, 10–11, 12–13

Restore us again, O God of our salvation!

Restore us again, O God of our salvation!

Let me hear what God the LORD will speak,
  for he will speak peace to his people,
to his faithful, to those who turn to him in
  their hearts.

Restore us again, O God of our salvation!

READING

Isaiah 53:3ac, 4–5, 7, 9

A reading from the Book of the prophet Isaiah.

He was despised and rejected by others; a man of suffering and acquainted with infirmity; and we held him of no account. Surely he has borne our infirmities and carried our diseases; yet we accounted him stricken, struck down by God, and afflicted. But he was wounded for our transgressions, crushed for our iniquities; upon him was the punishment that made us whole, and by his bruises we are healed. He was oppressed, and he was afflicted, yet he did not open his mouth; like a lamb that is led to the slaughter, and like a sheep that before its shearers is silent, so he did not open his mouth. They made his grave with the wicked and his tomb with the rich, although he had done no violence, and there was no deceit in his mouth.

The Word of the Lord.

◆ All observe silence.

FOR SILENT REFLECTION

Think about this silently in your heart. How do you think Jesus' wounds and suffering heal us?

CLOSING PRAYER

Let us pray to God for our needs and the needs of others: our family, neighborhood, and the world. For each need we say, "Lord, hear our prayer."

◆ All may add their own prayers here.

Let us pray: **Our Father . . . Amen.**

In the example of St. Nicholas, O God,
we see your love.
During this Advent, help us to be attentive
to those who need our care.
Help us to be generous
as St. Nicholas was generous.
For this we pray through Christ our Lord.

Amen.

✛ All make the Sign of the Cross.

OPENING

In our reading for this second week of Advent, John the Baptist proclaims that the Kingdom of heaven is near. He tells us that we must repent and prepare ourselves for the coming of the Lord.

✚ All make the Sign of the Cross.

In the name of the Father, and of the Son, and of the Holy Spirit. Amen.

PSALM

(For a longer psalm, see page xii.)
Psalm 85:4a, 8, 10–11, 12–13

Restore us again, O God of our salvation!

Restore us again, O God of our salvation!

Let me hear what God the LORD will speak,
  for he will speak peace to his people,
to his faithful, to those who turn to him in
  their hearts.

Restore us again, O God of our salvation!

◆ All stand and sing **Alleluia.**

GOSPEL

Matthew 3:1–6

A reading from the holy Gospel according to Matthew.

In those days John the Baptist appeared in the wilderness of Judea, proclaiming, "Repent, for the kingdom of heaven has come near." This is the one of whom the prophet Isaiah spoke when he said, "The voice of one crying out in the wilderness: 'Prepare the way of the Lord, make his paths straight.'" Now John wore cloting of camel's hair with a leather belt around his waist, and his food was locusts and wild honey. Then the people of Jerusalem and all Judea were going out to him, and all the region along the Jordan, and they were baptized by him in the river Jordan, confessing their sins.

The Gospel of the Lord.

◆ All sit and observe silence.

FOR SILENT REFLECTION

Think about this silently in your heart. How will you prepare yourself for the Lord's coming?

CLOSING PRAYER

Let us pray to God for our needs and the needs of others: our family, neighborhood, and the world. For each need we say, "Lord, hear our prayer."

◆ All may add their own prayers here.

Let us pray: **Our Father . . . Amen.**

As we wait for the celebration
of Jesus' birth, O God,
show us how to use this time
to make our hearts ready,
so that we might welcome Jesus
into our hearts and our homes.
We ask this in his name.

Amen.

✚ All make the Sign of the Cross.

OPENING

Today we celebrate the Solemnity of the Immaculate Conception of the Blessed Virgin Mary, the Patronal Feastday of the United States of America. Mary was without sin from the beginning of her life in her mother's womb. Although today is about Mary's conception, the reading is about how Jesus will be conceived in her. The reading also reminds us that Jesus is of the house of David.

✚ All make the Sign of the Cross.

In the name of the Father, and of the Son, and of the Holy Spirit. Amen.

PSALM

(For a longer psalm, see page xii.)
Psalm 85:4a, 8, 10–11, 12–13

Restore us again, O God of our salvation!

Restore us again, O God of our salvation!

Let me hear what God the LORD will speak,
    for he will speak peace to his people,
to his faithful, to those who turn to him in
    their hearts.

Restore us again, O God of our salvation!

◆ All stand and sing **Alleluia.**

GOSPEL

Luke 1:26–33

A reading from the holy Gospel according to Luke.

In the sixth month the angel Gabriel was sent by God to a town in Galilee called Nazareth, to a virgin engaged to a man whose name was Joseph, of the house of David. The virgin's name was Mary. And he came to her and said, "Greetings, favored one! The Lord is with you." But she was much perplexed by his words and pondered what sort of greeting this might be. The angel said to her, "Do not be afraid, Mary, for you have found favor with God. And now, you will conceive in your womb and bear a son, and you will name him Jesus. He will be great, and will be called the Son of the Most High, and the Lord God will give to him the throne of his ancestor David. He will reign over the house of Jacob forever, and of his kingdom there will be no end."

The Gospel of the Lord.

◆ All observe silence.

FOR SILENT REFLECTION

Think about this silently in your heart. Why did the angel tell Mary to not be afraid?

CLOSING PRAYER

Let us pray to God for our needs and the needs of others: our family, neighborhood, and the world. For each need we say, "Lord, hear our prayer."

◆ All may add their own prayers here.

Let us pray: **Our Father . . . Amen.**

Lord, our God,
open our hearts to receive you as Mary did,
with trust and faith.
Open our ears to hear your words
of assurance when we are afraid.
May we have the grace to do your will.
Through Christ our Lord.

Amen.

✚ All make the Sign of the Cross.

PRAYER SERVICE
SOLEMNITY OF THE IMMACULATE CONCEPTION OF MARY

Prepare six leaders for this service. The third leader will need a Bible for the passages from Luke. Help the third leader practice the readings. You may wish to sing "Sing of Mary" as the opening song. If the group will sing, prepare someone to lead it.

FIRST LEADER:

We remember Mary, the Mother of Jesus, on this special day. We celebrate her Immaculate Conception and believe she was conceived with God's special grace in her mother's womb so that one day she would bear Jesus, her Son, our Lord and Savior. She was filled with God's grace and the guidance of the Holy Spirit as she continually followed God's will. She nurtured Jesus in her womb, guided her Son in his youth, and stood by him in his ministry, even through his death and Resurrection. She is the patroness of the United States because of her constant courage. Let us begin our prayer service in her honor by singing the opening song.

SONG LEADER:

◆ Gesture for all to stand, and lead the first few verses of the song.

SECOND LEADER:

✚ All make the Sign of the Cross.

In the name of the Father, and of the Son, and of the Holy Spirit. Amen.

Let us pray:
Almighty Father,
you gave Mary special grace
when she was conceived
in her mother's womb.
You chose for her a unique role
to bring salvation to the world.
She is a sign of hope

because of her courage to say yes to you,
every moment of her life.
We pray with her to your Son Jesus,
our Lord and Savior,
in union with the Holy Spirit.

Amen.

◆ Remain standing and sing **Alleluia.**

THIRD LEADER: Luke 1:26–38
A reading from the holy Gospel according
to Luke.

◆ Read the Gospel passage from the Bible.

The Gospel of the Lord.

◆ All sit and observe silence.

FOURTH LEADER:

◆ Gesture for all to stand.

Let us bring our hopes and needs to God as
we pray, "Lord, hear our prayer."

For the courage to say, "yes" to God
as Mary did throughout her life,
we pray to the Lord.

For all who are struggling with
tough decisions in life,
may they look to Mary as
a true friend on their journey,
we pray to the Lord.

For all married people,
may they continue to be an example
of the love and devotion that
Mary and Joseph shared,
we pray to the Lord.

For all mothers
and those who nurture others,

help us to respect and protect life
from conception until natural death,
we pray to the Lord.

For those throughout the world
who are suffering from
hunger, lack of shelter, or disease,
and for those who have died,
may we have the compassion of Mary
to give us hope and the promise
of new life through Jesus,
we pray to the Lord.

FIFTH LEADER:
Let us pray the Hail Mary:

ALL: Hail Mary, full of grace . . .

◆ Pause, and then say:

Let us offer one another the sign of
Christ's peace.

◆ All offer one another a sign of peace.

SIXTH LEADER:
Let us pray Mary's special prayer,
the *Magnificat*:
"My soul magnifies the Lord,
    and my spirit rejoices in God my Savior,
for he has looked with favor on the lowliness
        of his servant.
    Surely, from now on all generations will
        call me blessed;
for the Mighty One has done great things
        for me,
    and holy is his name."

✢ All make the Sign of the Cross.

**In the name of the Father, and of the
Son, and of the Holy Spirit. Amen.**

OPENING

We are aware that the darkness of sin still exists in the world, but Isaiah calls us to wait in hope. During Advent, we begin to notice the little lights shining through the darkness. These lights give us hope.

✛ *All make the Sign of the Cross.*

In the name of the Father, and of the Son, and of the Holy Spirit. Amen.

PSALM
(For a longer psalm, see page xii.)
Psalm 85:4a, 8, 10–11, 12–13

Restore us again, O God of our salvation!

Restore us again, O God of our salvation!

Let me hear what God the LORD will speak,
    for he will speak peace to his people,
to his faithful, to those who turn to him in
    their hearts.

Restore us again, O God of our salvation!

READING
Isaiah 60:1–4ac, 5a

A reading from the Book of the prophet Isaiah.

Arise, shine; for your light has come, and the glory of the LORD has risen upon you. For darkness shall cover the earth, and thick darkness the peoples; but the LORD will arise upon you, and his glory will appear over you. Nations shall come to your light, and kings to the brightness of your dawn. Lift up your eyes and look around; your sons shall come from far away, and your daughters shall be carried on their nurses' arms. Then you shall see and be radiant; your heart shall thrill and rejoice.

The Word of the Lord.

◆ *All observe silence.*

FOR SILENT REFLECTION

Think about this silently in your heart. Where does the light of Jesus need to shine in your world?

CLOSING PRAYER

Let us pray to God for our needs and the needs of others: our family, neighborhood, and the world. For each need we say, "Lord, hear our prayer."

◆ *All may add their own prayers here.*

Let us pray: **Our Father . . . Amen.**

We give you thanks, O God,
for the lights that shine in the darkness.
They remind us of your Son Jesus,
the Light of World, which the darkness
cannot overcome.
We pray in his name.

Amen.

✛ *All make the Sign of the Cross.*

OPENING

The Jewish people waited a very long time for the Messiah. Isaiah talks about a "shoot" from a tree of Jesse, who was the father of King David. We know that Jesus came from the house of David. Some people make a Jesse Tree to show the ancestors of Jesus. Today is the Memorial of St. Damasus, who authorized the translation of the Bible from Hebrew and organized the books of Scripture.

✛ All make the Sign of the Cross.

In the name of the Father, and of the Son, and of the Holy Spirit. Amen.

PSALM

(For a longer psalm, see page xii.)
Psalm 85:4a, 8, 10–11, 12–13

Restore us again, O God of our salvation!

Restore us again, O God of our salvation!

Let me hear what God the LORD will speak,
   for he will speak peace to his people,
to his faithful, to those who turn to him in
   their hearts.

Restore us again, O God of our salvation!

READING

Isaiah 11:1–3a, 5, 10

A reading from the Book of the prophet Isaiah.

A shoot shall come out from the stump of Jesse, and a branch shall grow out of his roots. The spirit of the LORD shall rest on him, the spirit of wisdom and understanding, the spirit of counsel and might, the spirit of knowledge and the fear of the LORD. His delight shall be in the fear of the LORD. Righteousness shall be the belt around his waist, and faithfulness the belt

around his loins. On that day the root of Jesse shall stand as a signal to the peoples; the nations shall inquire of him, and his dwelling shall be glorious.

The Word of the Lord.

◆ All observe silence.

FOR SILENT REFLECTION

Think about this silently in your heart. Does Isaiah's description remind you of Jesus? How?

CLOSING PRAYER

Let us pray to God for our needs and the needs of others: our family, neighborhood, and the world. For each need we say, "Lord, hear our prayer."

◆ All may add their own prayers here.

Let us pray: **Our Father . . . Amen.**

We wait in joyful hope, O God,
for the coming of your Son Jesus.
As Isaiah promised,
your Spirit will rest upon him,
and he will show us the way to you.
We pray in Christ's name.

Amen.

✛ All make the Sign of the Cross.

PRAYER FOR
THURSDAY, DECEMBER 12, 2019

OPENING

Today we celebrate the Feast of Our Lady of Guadalupe, the Patroness of the Americas. The Blessed Virgin Mary appeared to Juan Diego Cuauhtlatoatzin, an Indian who had recently converted to Christianity, instructing him to ask the bishop to build a church in her honor. Juan Diego, fearing that the bishop would not believe him, asked for a sign for the bishop. Following the Lady's instruction, he found *rosas de Castilla* blooming in a barren area of a hilltop during the winter. He brought the roses back to the Lady, who arranged them in his tilma. When Juan Diego presented the roses to the bishop, there was imprinted on his cloak an image of the Virgin Mary, dressed like a young Aztec woman.

✚ All make the Sign of the Cross.

In the name of the Father, and of the Son, and of the Holy Spirit. Amen.

PSALM
(For a longer psalm, see page xii.)
Psalm 85:4a, 8, 10–11, 12–13

Restore us again, O God of our salvation!

Restore us again, O God of our salvation!

Let me hear what God the LORD will speak,
    for he will speak peace to his people,
to his faithful, to those who turn to him in
    their hearts.

Restore us again, O God of our salvation!

READING
Isaiah 60:1–4a, 5a

A reading from the Book of the prophet Isaiah. Arise, shine; for your light has come, and the glory of the LORD has risen upon you. For darkness shall cover the earth, and thick darkness the peoples; but the LORD will arise upon you, and his glory will appear over you. Nations shall come to your light, and kings to the brightness of your dawn. Lift up your eyes and look around. Then you shall see and be radiant; your heart shall thrill and rejoice.

The Word of the Lord.

◆ All observe silence.

FOR SILENT REFLECTION

Think about this silently in your heart. Light shines hope into darkness. How can you shine light today?

CLOSING PRAYER

Let us pray to God for our needs and the needs of others: our family, neighborhood, and the world. For each need we say, "Lord, hear our prayer."

◆ All may add their own prayers here.

Let us pray: **Our Father . . . Amen.**

Holy Mary, Our Lady of Guadalupe,
we ask you intercede
for the people of the Americas.
Watch over all of us,
especially those who are poor,
sick, or in need.
We ask this in Jesus Christ's name.

Amen.

✚ All make the Sign of the Cross.

OPENING

Today we celebrate St. Lucy. The name Lucy means "light." It is fitting that we celebrate St. Lucy during this dark time of the year, when we await the birth of the Light of the World. We continue to hear from the prophet Isaiah, who promises that the Messiah will bring peace and righteousness.

✣ All make the Sign of the Cross.

In the name of the Father, and of the Son, and of the Holy Spirit. Amen.

PSALM

(For a longer psalm, see page xii.)
Psalm 85:4a, 8, 10–11, 12–13

Restore us again, O God of our salvation!

Restore us again, O God of our salvation!

Let me hear what God the LORD will speak,
for he will speak peace to his people,
to his faithful, to those who turn to him in their hearts.

Restore us again, O God of our salvation!

READING

Isaiah 32:1, 16–18, 20

A reading from the Book of the prophet Isaiah.

See, a king will reign in righteousness, and princes will rule with justice. Then justice will dwell in the wilderness, and righteousness abide in the fruitful field. The effect of righteousness will be peace, and the result of righteousness, quietness and trust forever. My people will abide in a peaceful habitation, in secure dwellings, and in quiet resting places. Happy will you be who sow beside every stream, who let the ox and the donkey range freely.

The Word of the Lord.

◆ All observe silence.

FOR SILENT REFLECTION

Think about this silently in your heart. Can you take time during Advent to be quiet and peaceful? Why is having some quiet time important?

CLOSING PRAYER

Let us pray to God for our needs and the needs of others: our family, neighborhood, and the world. For each need we say, "Lord, hear our prayer."

◆ All may add their own prayers here.

Let us pray: **Our Father . . . Amen.**

As we wait for the celebration
of Jesus' birth, O God,
show us how to use this time
to make our hearts ready.
As we also remember the Memorial of
St. Lucy, Virgin and Martyr,
may we be a light for others today.
We ask this in Christ's name.

Amen.

✣ All make the Sign of the Cross.

PRAYER FOR THE WEEK

WITH A READING FROM THE GOSPEL FOR **SUNDAY, DECEMBER 15, 2019**

OPENING

We begin our third week of Advent by hearing Jesus' response to John the Baptist, who is in prison and has asked if Jesus is the long-awaited Messiah. Jesus, using the words of Isaiah's prophecy, assures John that he, Jesus, is the Messiah. Today is Gaudete [Gow-DAY-tay] Sunday. Gaudete comes from a Latin word that means "rejoice."

✚ All make the Sign of the Cross.

In the name of the Father, and of the Son, and of the Holy Spirit. Amen.

PSALM

(For a longer psalm, see page xii.)
Psalm 85:4a, 8, 10–11, 12–13

Restore us again, O God of our salvation!

Restore us again, O God of our salvation!

Let me hear what God the LORD will speak,
for he will speak peace to his people,
to his faithful, to those who turn to him in
their hearts.

Restore us again, O God of our salvation!

◆ All stand and sing **Alleluia.**

GOSPEL

Matthew 11:2–7a, 10–11

A reading from the holy Gospel according to Matthew.

When John heard in prison what the Messiah was doing, he sent word by his disciples and said to him, "Are you the one who is to come, or are we to wait for another?" Jesus answered them, "Go and tell John what you hear and see: the blind receive their sight, the lame walk, the lepers are cleansed, the deaf hear, the dead are raised, and the poor have good news brought to them. And blessed is anyone who takes no offense at me." As they went away, Jesus began to speak to the crowds about John: "This is the one about whom it is written, 'See, I am sending my messenger ahead of you, who will prepare your way before you.' Truly I tell you, among those born of women no one has arisen greater than John the Baptist; yet the least in the kingdom of heaven is greater than he."

The Gospel of the Lord.

◆ All sit and observe silence.

FOR SILENT REFLECTION

Think about this silently in your heart. Who do you think the "least in the kingdom of heaven" might be?

CLOSING PRAYER

Let us pray to God for our needs and the needs of others: our family, neighborhood, and the world. For each need we say, "Lord, hear our prayer."

◆ All may add their own prayers here.

Let us pray: **Our Father . . . Amen.**

May our hearts be open to signs of your presence among us, O Lord.
May we, like John the Baptist, be faithful witnesses to your good works.
We pray in Christ's name.

Amen.

✚ All make the Sign of the Cross.

OPENING

Our third week of Advent waiting began with the word, "Gaudete" or "Rejoice." We rejoice because our waiting will soon be over. With Isaiah, whose words we hear, we can be strong.

✛ All make the Sign of the Cross.

In the name of the Father, and of the Son, and of the Holy Spirit. Amen.

PSALM

(For a longer psalm, see page xii.)
Psalm 85:4a, 8, 10–11, 12–13

Restore us again, O God of our salvation!

Restore us again, O God of our salvation!

Let me hear what God the LORD will speak,
  for he will speak peace to his people,
to his faithful, to those who turn to him in
  their hearts.

Restore us again, O God of our salvation!

READING

Isaiah 35:1, 3–6

A reading from the Book of the prophet Isaiah.

The wilderness and the dry land shall be glad, the desert shall rejoice and blossom. Strengthen the weak hands, and make firm the feeble knees. Say to those who are of a fearful heart, "Be strong, do not fear! Here is your God. He will come with vengeance, with terrible recompense. He will come and save you." Then the eyes of the blind shall be opened, and the ears of the deaf unstopped; then the lame shall leap like a deer, and the tongue of the speech-less sing for joy. For waters shall break forth in the wilderness, and streams in the desert.

The Word of the Lord.

◆ All observe silence.

FOR SILENT REFLECTION

Think about this silently in your heart. What do you imagine it will be like when Isaiah's prophecy is fulfilled?

CLOSING PRAYER

Let us pray to God for our needs and the needs of others: our family, neighborhood, and the world. For each need we say, "Lord, hear our prayer."

◆ All may add their own prayers here.

Let us pray: **Our Father . . . Amen.**

We long for the day, O Lord,
when the dry land shall be glad and the
desert shall rejoice and blossom.
Keep us faithful to you as we await the
celebration of your Son, Jesus.
We ask this in his name.

Amen.

✛ All make the Sign of the Cross.

OPENING

We continue to hear from the prophet Isaiah, who speaks words of encouragement as we wait for the celebration of Jesus' birth.

✚ All make the Sign of the Cross.

In the name of the Father, and of the Son, and of the Holy Spirit. Amen.

PSALM

(For a longer psalm, see page xii.)

Psalm 85:4a, 8, 10–11, 12–13

Restore us again, O God of our salvation!

Restore us again, O God of our salvation!

Let me hear what God the LORD will speak,
　　for he will speak peace to his people,
to his faithful, to those who turn to him in
　　their hearts.

Restore us again, O God of our salvation!

READING

Isaiah 40:9–11

A reading from the Book of the prophet Isaiah.

Get you up to a high mountain, O Zion, herald of good tidings; lift up your voice with strength, O Jerusalem, herald of good tidings, lift it up, do not fear; say to the cities of Judah, "Here is your God!" See, the Lord GOD comes with might, and his arm rules for him; his reward is with him, and his recompense before him. He will feed his flock like a shepherd; he will gather the lambs in his arms, and carry them in his bosom, and gently lead the mother sheep.

The Word of the Lord.

◆ All observe silence.

FOR SILENT REFLECTION

Think about this silently in your heart. What signs of God's light do you notice among us?

CLOSING PRAYER

Let us pray to God for our needs and the needs of others: our family, neighborhood, and the world. For each need we say, "Lord, hear our prayer."

◆ All may add their own prayers here.

Let us pray: **Our Father . . . Amen.**

As we wait for the celebration
of Jesus' birth, O God,
show us how to use this time
to make our hearts ready.
May we open our eyes and ears to notice
God's presence in our world.
We ask this through Christ our Lord.

Amen.

✚ All make the Sign of the Cross.

OPENING

Isaiah reminds the Israelites that God helped them cross the Red Sea and will bring them joy once again. As Christians, we are also called to remember God's goodness and to be people of joy. Remember that we began this week with Gaudete Sunday. We rejoice that we will soon celebrate Christ's coming into the world. Like the Israelites, we too will sing with gladness.

✦ All make the Sign of the Cross.

In the name of the Father, and of the Son, and of the Holy Spirit. Amen.

PSALM

(For a longer psalm, see page xii.)
Psalm 85:4a, 8, 10–11, 12–13

Restore us again, O God of our salvation!

Restore us again, O God of our salvation!

Let me hear what God the Lord will speak,
for he will speak peace to his people,
to his faithful, to those who turn to him in their hearts.

Restore us again, O God of our salvation!

READING

Isaiah 51:9ab, 10–11

A reading from the Book of the prophet Isaiah.

Awake, awake, put on strength, O arm of the Lord! Awake, as in days of old, the generations of long ago! Was it not you who dried up the sea, the waters of the great deep; who made the depths of the sea a way for the redeemed to cross over? So the ransomed of the Lord shall return, and come to Zion with singing; everlasting joy shall be upon their heads; they shall obtain joy and gladness, and sorrow and sighing shall flee away.

The Word of the Lord.

✦ All observe silence.

FOR SILENT REFLECTION

Think about this silently in your heart. Have you experienced joy during Advent? How have you shared that joy with others?

CLOSING PRAYER

Let us pray to God for our needs and the needs of others: our family, neighborhood, and the world. For each need we say, "Lord, hear our prayer."

✦ All may add their own prayers here.

Let us pray: **Our Father . . . Amen.**

Holy God,
with increasing joy we await the birth
of your Son Jesus.
You led the Israelites to freedom.
Jesus will show us the path to salvation.
We pray in Christ's name.

Amen.

✦ All make the Sign of the Cross.

PRAYER FOR
THURSDAY, DECEMBER 19, 2019

OPENING

Our reading from the prophet Isaiah reminds us of the words of John the Baptist, who cried out for the way to be prepared for the Messiah. We rejoice that Jesus is coming. He will reveal God's great glory and love.

✚ All make the Sign of the Cross.

In the name of the Father, and of the Son, and of the Holy Spirit. Amen.

PSALM

(For a longer psalm, see page xii.)
Psalm 85:4a, 8, 10–11, 12–13

Restore us again, O God of our salvation!

Restore us again, O God of our salvation!

Let me hear what God the Lord will speak,
    for he will speak peace to his people,
to his faithful, to those who turn to him in
    their hearts.

Restore us again, O God of our salvation!

READING

Isaiah 40:3–5

A reading from the Book of the prophet Isaiah.

A voice cries out: "In the wilderness prepare the way of the Lord, make straight in the desert a highway for our God. Every valley shall be lifted up, and every mountain and hill be made low; the uneven ground shall become level, and the rough places a plain. Then the glory of the Lord shall be revealed, and all people shall see it together, for the mouth of the Lord has spoken."

The Word of the Lord.

◆ All observe silence.

FOR SILENT REFLECTION

Think about this silently in your heart. Can you imagine mountains being made low and rough places smooth? What do you think Isaiah means by these words?

CLOSING PRAYER

Let us pray to God for our needs and the needs of others: our family, neighborhood, and the world. For each need we say, "Lord, hear our prayer."

◆ All may add their own prayers here.

Let us pray: **Our Father . . . Amen.**

We have been preparing our hearts,
O God, to welcome Jesus.
In these last days of Advent,
we look forward with joy to his birth.
May we be ready for his coming.
We pray in Christ's name.

Amen.

✚ All make the Sign of the Cross.

OPENING

Our Advent waiting is coming to an end. John the Baptist echoes Isaiah urging us to prepare. We have been preparing our hearts to welcome Jesus. Baking cookies, wrapping presents, and cleaning the house are all also part of preparing for Christmas.

✛ All make the Sign of the Cross.

In the name of the Father, and of the Son, and of the Holy Spirit. Amen.

PSALM

(For a longer psalm, see page xii.)
Psalm 85:4a, 8, 10–11, 12–13

Restore us again, O God of our salvation!

Restore us again, O God of our salvation!

Let me hear what God the LORD will speak, for he will speak peace to his people, to his faithful, to those who turn to him in their hearts.

Restore us again, O God of our salvation!

◆ All stand and sing **Alleluia.**

GOSPEL

Mark 1:1–4

A reading from the holy Gospel according to Mark.

The beginning of the good news of Jesus Christ, the Son of God. As it is written in the prophet Isaiah, "See, I am sending my messenger ahead of you, who will prepare your way; the voice of one crying out in the wilderness: 'Prepare the way of the Lord, make his paths straight,'" John the baptizer appeared in the wilderness, proclaiming a baptism of repentance for the forgiveness of sins.

The Gospel of the Lord.

◆ All sit and observe silence.

FOR SILENT REFLECTION

Think about this silently in your heart. What one or two things can you do to prepare your heart to celebrate God coming to us?

CLOSING PRAYER

Let us pray to God for our needs and the needs of others: our family, neighborhood, and the world. For each need we say, "Lord, hear our prayer."

◆ All may add their own prayers here.

Let us pray: **Our Father . . . Amen.**

Holy God,
as the days of Advent draw to a close,
help us to know that you are with us.
Be our light in the darkness
now and forever.
We ask this through Christ our Lord.

Amen.

✛ All make the Sign of the Cross.

PRAYER FOR THE WEEK

WITH A READING FROM THE GOSPEL FOR **SUNDAY, DECEMBER 22, 2019**

OPENING

We are almost ready to celebrate God coming to us as a human being. We call this the Incarnation [in-car-NAY-shun]. It is awesome! We call Jesus *Immanuel*, which means "God-with-us."

✚ *All make the Sign of the Cross.*

In the name of the Father, and of the Son, and of the Holy Spirit. Amen.

PSALM

(For a longer psalm, see page xii.)
Psalm 85:4a, 8, 10–11, 12–13

Restore us again, O God of our salvation!

Restore us again, O God of our salvation!

Let me hear what God the LORD will speak,
  for he will speak peace to his people,
to his faithful, to those who turn to him in
  their hearts.

Restore us again, O God of our salvation!

◆ *All stand and sing* **Alleluia.**

GOSPEL

Matthew 1:18, 20b–24

A reading from the holy Gospel according to Matthew.

Now the birth of Jesus the Messiah took place in this way. When his mother Mary had been engaged to Joseph, but before they lived together, she was found to be with child from the Holy Spirit. An angel of the Lord appeared to Joseph in a dream and said, "Joseph, son of David, do not be afraid to take Mary as your wife, for the child conceived in her is from the Holy Spirit. She will bear a son, and you are to name him Jesus, for he will save his people from their sins." All this took place to fulfill what had been spoken by the Lord through the prophet: "Look, the virgin shall conceive and bear a son, and they shall name him Emmanuel," which means, "God is with us." When Joseph awoke from sleep, he did as the angel of the Lord commanded him; he took her as his wife.

The Gospel of the Lord.

◆ *All sit and observe silence.*

FOR SILENT REFLECTION

Think about this silently in your heart. Is it hard to trust in God sometimes? What helps you trust God?

CLOSING PRAYER

Let us pray to God for our needs and the needs of others: our family, neighborhood, and the world. For each need we say, "Lord, hear our prayer."

◆ *All may add their own prayers here.*

Let us pray: **Our Father . . . Amen.**

Lord Jesus,
may we, like Joseph and Mary,
trust in your saving power
and welcome you as they did.
You live and reign with God the Father
in the unity of the Holy Spirit,
one God,
for ever and ever.

Amen.

✚ *All make the Sign of the Cross.*

OPENING

Our Advent waiting is almost finished. The Gospel reminds us that Mary was "perplexed," or filled with uncertainty, about what the angel said to her.

✦ All make the Sign of the Cross.

In the name of the Father, and of the Son, and of the Holy Spirit. Amen.

PSALM

(For a longer psalm, see page xii.)
Psalm 85:4a, 8, 10–11, 12–13

Restore us again, O God of our salvation!

Restore us again, O God of our salvation!

Let me hear what God the LORD will speak,
  for he will speak peace to his people,
to his faithful, to those who turn to him in
  their hearts.

Restore us again, O God of our salvation!

◆ All stand and sing **Alleluia.**

GOSPEL

Luke 1:26–32

A reading from the holy Gospel according to Luke.

In the sixth month the angel Gabriel was sent by God to a town in Galilee called Nazareth, to a virgin engaged to a man whose name was Joseph, of the house of David. The virgin's name was Mary. And he came to her and said, "Greetings, favored one! The Lord is with you." But she was much perplexed by his words and pondered what sort of greeting this might be. The angel said to her, "Do not be afraid, Mary, for you have found favor with God. And now, you will conceive in your womb and bear a son, and you will name him Jesus. He will be great, and will be called the Son of the Most High, and the Lord God will give to him the throne of his ancestor David."

The Gospel of the Lord.

◆ All sit and observe silence.

FOR SILENT REFLECTION

Think about this silently in your heart. Have you ever been perplexed, or filled with uncertainty, about what God wanted you to do? How did you respond?

CLOSING PRAYER

Let us pray to God for our needs and the needs of others: our family, neighborhood, and the world. For each need we say, "Lord, hear our prayer."

◆ All may add their own prayers here.

Let us pray: **Our Father . . . Amen.**

Holy Mary,
you were asked to bring the light of Jesus
into the world.
Give us the courage to follow you and to
bring the light of Jesus into the world today.
We ask you to pray for us
in Christ's name.

Amen.

✦ All make the Sign of the Cross.

PRAYER FOR
TUESDAY, DECEMBER 24, 2019

OPENING

In today's Gospel we hear Mary's response to the angel. She's still perplexed. The angel reminds her that nothing is impossible with God. That is one way of saying we should trust in God, and Mary does so.

✚ All make the Sign of the Cross.

In the name of the Father, and of the Son, and of the Holy Spirit. Amen.

PSALM

(For a longer psalm, see page xii.)
Psalm 85:4a, 8, 10–11, 12–13

Restore us again, O God of our salvation!

Restore us again, O God of our salvation!

Let me hear what God the LORD will speak,
for he will speak peace to his people,
to his faithful, to those who turn to him in
their hearts.

Restore us again, O God of our salvation!

◆ All stand and sing **Alleluia**.

GOSPEL

Luke 1:34–38

A reading from the holy Gospel according to Luke.

Mary said to the angel, "How can this be, since I am a virgin?" The angel said to her, "The Holy Spirit will come upon you, and the power of the Most High will overshadow you; therefore the child to be born will be holy; he will be called Son of God. And now, your relative Elizabeth in her old age has also conceived a son; and this is the sixth month for her who was said to be barren. For nothing will be impossible with God." Then Mary said, "Here am I, the servant of the Lord; let it be with me according to your word." Then the angel departed from her.

The Gospel of the Lord.

◆ All sit and observe silence.

FOR SILENT REFLECTION

Think about this silently in your heart. God is always with you. Do you trust God to help you to know the right thing to do when you're perplexed?

CLOSING PRAYER

Let us pray to God for our needs and the needs of others: our family, neighborhood, and the world. For each need we say, "Lord, hear our prayer."

◆ All may add their own prayers here.

Let us pray: **Our Father . . . Amen.**

We give you thanks, O God,
for this season of Advent.
We have prepared our hearts and are ready
to welcome the gift of your Son, Jesus.
We pray in his name.

Amen.

✚ All make the Sign of the Cros

CHRISTMAS TIME

THURSDAY, JANUARY 2 — SUNDAY, JANUARY 12

THE MEANING OF CHRISTMAS

"For a child has been born for us,
    a son given to us;
authority rests upon his shoulders;
    and he is named
Wonderful Counselor, Mighty God,
    Everlasting Father, Prince of Peace."

(Isaiah 9:6)

God keeps the great promise of the gift of Jesus! Of course, God amazes us with other gifts we never could have imagined or asked for. The earth is filled with God's gifts. Think of the solid ground that supports us, gravity that keeps us from floating away, the atmosphere that provides oxygen for breathing and a shield to protect us from the heat of the sun, and water that keeps our cells healthy. We need so many things just to stay alive. And yet the earth contains much more than is necessary to keep us going. Within the earth, precious metals and gems delight us with their shine. Seashells and spider webs amaze us with their geometry. Roses and lilacs fill the air with perfume. Peacocks and pinecones and pecans add to the world's great fascination. And every day our friends and family share new ways to love. What a world we have been given!

But God wants to give us something even more precious: a share in God's very own life. So Immanuel, God-with-us, came to us in Bethlehem. God, who was there before the universe, who was the Word that spoke the world into existence, gave himself to us as an infant who could do nothing for itself. This gift has changed everything. God's heart is opened for us. Out of the tree stump of despair, God has brought a flowering branch.

Our Scriptures are full of epiphanies or manifestations; that is, events that clearly show people that this baby, Jesus, is the promised Messiah. We will stand in front of the manger in Bethlehem this week and gaze in wonder with Mary, Joseph, the angels, the shepherds, and the Magi as we realize this holy child, Jesus, is our God.

PREPARING TO CELEBRATE CHRISTMAS IN THE CLASSROOM

SACRED SPACE

Replace the Advent wreath with a new, white pillar candle and change the purple cloth to a white one. You might add some gold tinsel or a gold cloth. Place the star and the Magi in the Nativity scene.

MOVEMENT AND GESTURE

If you have older students, they light and hold congregational candles (thin tapers) during the Epiphany Prayer Service.

FESTIVITY IN SCHOOL AND HOME

The prayer service for Epiphany on pages 146–147 provides a beautiful and prayerful way to celebrate the arrival of the Magi in Bethlehem.

SACRED MUSIC

Christmas Time is a time of music! Many beautiful carols, including "Joy to the World," "Angels We Have Heard on High," "O Come, All Ye Faithful," and "We Three Kings" can be sung with the children. You may even wish to organize a caroling party and go door to door through your school.

PRAYERS FOR CHRISTMAS

The opening verses of the Gospel according to St. John contain some of the most beautiful poetry in the world: "In the beginning was the Word, and the Word was with God, and the Word was God. He was in the beginning with God. All things came into being through him, and without him not one thing came into being. What has come into being in him was life, and the life was the light of all people. The light shines in the darkness, and the darkness did not overcome it" (John 1:1–5).

These verses beautifully express the mystery of the Incarnation, the mystery of God becoming a human being to be close to us. You might want to spend some time during religion class reading this beautiful hymn line by line. Ask the children whom St. John means when he speaks about the "Word of God." See what they say when you ask them how "all things came into being" through Christ when we know Jesus was born after the creation of the world. How can one person be the "light of all people"? What kind of light do people need? What do the children think St. John means when he says, "the darkness did not overcome" the Light of the World?

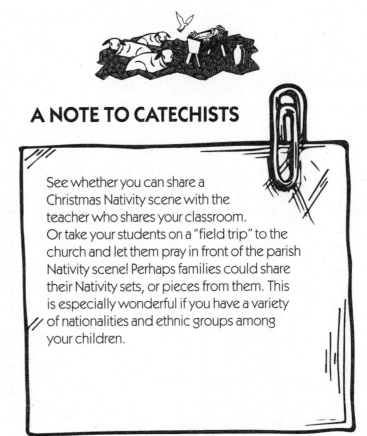

A NOTE TO CATECHISTS

See whether you can share a Christmas Nativity scene with the teacher who shares your classroom. Or take your students on a "field trip" to the church and let them pray in front of the parish Nativity scene! Perhaps families could share their Nativity sets, or pieces from them. This is especially wonderful if you have a variety of nationalities and ethnic groups among your children.

GRACE BEFORE MEALS

CHRISTMAS TIME

LEADER:

"For a child has been born for us,"

ALL: "a son given to us."

✚ All make the Sign of the Cross.

In the name of the Father, and of the Son, and of the Holy Spirit. Amen.

LEADER:

Heavenly Father,
may the food we are about to share
help to nourish our bodies and minds,
just as you nurture us always
with the gift of your Son
and your everlasting Spirit.
May we be a living sign of the
presence of Jesus,
who is hope for the world.
We ask this through Christ our Lord.

ALL: Amen.

✚ All make the Sign of the Cross.

In the name of the Father, and of the Son, and of the Holy Spirit. Amen.

PRAYER AT DAY'S END

CHRISTMAS TIME

LEADER:
Sing to the Lord a new song,

ALL: for he has done wondrous deeds!

✛ All make the Sign of the Cross.

In the name of the Father, and of the Son, and of the Holy Spirit. Amen.

LEADER:
Heavenly Father,
the gift of your Son
gives us so much joy!
We thank you for this day,
filled with wonder and small adventures.
May we always remember that you
are the source of all goodness
as we praise the miracle of Jesus,
whom you sent to us
to lead the way back to you.
We ask this through Christ our Lord
and Savior.

ALL: Amen.

✛ All make the Sign of the Cross.

In the name of the Father, and of the Son, and of the Holy Spirit. Amen.

PRAYER SERVICE
EPIPHANY

Prepare six leaders and a song leader for this service. The second and fourth leaders will need Bibles to read the Scripture passages and may need help finding and practicing them. Before you begin, remove the figures of shepherds and the three kings from your Nativity scene. Put the shepherds away until next year. Place the kings a short distance from the Nativity scene. Then gather the class near it. This service calls for two songs. Help the song leader prepare to lead the singing.

SONG LEADER:

Please stand and join in singing our opening song, "We Three Kings."

FIRST LEADER:

✚ All make the Sign of the Cross.

May the light of our Creator guide us in this prayer of praise.

ALL: Amen.

Let us pray:
Almighty God,
You are the light of the world!
Guide us with your radiance
as we reflect your goodness in our lives.
We ask this through Christ our Lord.

ALL: Amen.

◆ Gesture for all to sit.

SECOND LEADER: Isaiah 9:2–7

A reading from the Book of the Prophet Isaiah.

◆ Read the Scripture passage from the Bible.

The Word of the Lord.

◆ All observe silence.

THIRD LEADER: Psalm 148:1–2, 3–4, 9–10, 11–12, 13

Our refrain is: Praise the LORD!

ALL: Praise the LORD!

Praise the LORD from the heavens;
   praise him in the heights!
Praise him, all his angels;
   praise him, all his host!

ALL: Praise the LORD!

Praise him, sun and moon;
   praise him, all you shining stars!
Praise him, you highest heavens,
   and you waters above the heavens!

ALL: Praise the LORD!

Mountains and all hills,
   fruit trees and all cedars!
Wild animals and all cattle,
   creeping things and flying birds!

ALL: Praise the LORD!

Kings of the earth and all peoples,
   princes and all rulers of the earth!
Young men and women alike,
   old and young together!

ALL: Praise the LORD!

   ◆ All stand and sing **Alleluia.**

FOURTH LEADER: Matthew 2:9b–12

A reading from the holy Gospel according
to Matthew.

   ◆ Read the Scripture passage from a Bible.

The Gospel of the Lord.

   ◆ All sit and observe silence.

   ◆ In silence, an adult slowly moves the three figures
    of the Wise Men, one at a time, into the stable.

SONG LEADER:
Let us stand and sing, "Joy to the World."

FIFTH LEADER:
Heavenly Father,
you created the sun, planets,
moon, and stars,
and everything that breathes
to give you glory.
You are almighty and powerful,
yet you are as close to us as our breath,
and you live within our hearts.
Inspire us more with your
gentle Spirit and direction
just as you did the wise men
who traveled far to
see your glory in the Christ child.
We ask this through your Son Jesus.

Amen.

Let us pray: **Our Father . . . Amen.**

SIXTH LEADER:
May God's love, found in the Trinity of
Father, Son, and Spirit,
always surround us on our journey.

ALL: Amen.

   ✛ All make the Sign of the Cross.

PRAYER FOR
THURSDAY, JANUARY 2, 2020

PENING

The celebration of Christmas continues. We need time to let the joy of Jesus' Incarnation sink into our hearts. Isaiah prophesized a child would grow up and be light for the world. He would act with righteousness; that is, with concern for the good of all people. Today is the Memorial of Sts. Basil the Great and Gregory Nazianzen, bishops who wrote much about the Holy Spirit and the Trinity.

✚ All make the Sign of the Cross.

In the name of the Father, and of the Son, and of the Holy Spirit. Amen.

PSALM

(For a longer psalm, see page xiii.)
Psalm 96:1–2a, 2b–3, 5b–6, 11a

Let the heavens be glad and the earth rejoice!

Let the heavens be glad and the earth rejoice!

O sing to the LORD a new song;
    sing to the LORD, all the earth.
Sing to the LORD; bless his name.

Let the heavens be glad and the earth rejoice!

READING

Isaiah 9:1a, 2–3ac, 6–7ab

A reading from the Book of the prophet Isaiah.

But there will be no gloom for those who were in anguish. The people who walked in darkness have seen a great light; those who lived in a land of deep darkness—on them light has shined. You have multiplied the nation, you have increased its joy; they rejoice before you as with joy at the harvest. For a child has been born for us, a son given to us; authority rests upon his shoulders; and he is named Wonderful Counselor, Mighty God, Everlasting Father, Prince of Peace. His authority shall grow continually, and there shall be endless peace for the throne of David and his kingdom. He will establish and uphold it with justice and with righteousness from this time onward and forevermore.

The Word of the Lord.

◆ All observe silence.

FOR SILENT REFLECTION

Think about this silently in your heart. The child is named Wonderful Counselor, Mighty God, Everlasting Father, Prince of Peace. How great this child Jesus must be!

CLOSING PRAYER

Let us pray to God for our needs and the needs of others: our family, neighborhood, and the world. For each need we say, "Lord, hear our prayer."

◆ All may add their own prayers here.

Let us pray: **Our Father . . . Amen.**

Glory to you, O God;
you have given us the best gift!
Help us see Jesus in one another
as clearly as the shepherds and the Magi
saw him in the manger.
We ask this in Christ's name.

Amen.

✚ All make the Sign of the Cross.

OPENING

Today we celebrate the Most Holy Name of Jesus, which is not only his identity but also his mission. We will again hear the story of the announcement of Jesus' birth to the shepherds. The image of a shepherd is important in the Bible. We know that the child who was born in Bethlehem will become the Good Shepherd who cares for each sheep of his flock.

✦ All make the Sign of the Cross.

In the name of the Father, and of the Son, and of the Holy Spirit. Amen.

PSALM

(For a longer psalm, see page xiii.)
Psalm 96:1–2a, 2b–3, 5b–6, 11a

Let the heavens be glad and the earth rejoice!

Let the heavens be glad and the earth rejoice!

O sing to the LORD a new song;
    sing to the LORD, all the earth.
Sing to the LORD; bless his name.

Let the heavens be glad and the earth rejoice!

◆ All stand and sing **Alleluia.**

GOSPEL

Luke 2:8–14

A reading from the holy Gospel according to Luke.

In that region there were shepherds living in the fields, keeping watch over their flock by night. Then an angel of the Lord stood before them, and the glory of the Lord shone around them, and they were terrified. But the angel said to them, "Do not be afraid; for see—I am bringing you good news of great joy for all the people: to you is born this day in the city of David a Savior, who is the Messiah, the Lord. This will be a sign for you: you will find a child wrapped in bands of cloth and lying in a manger." And suddenly there was with the angel a multitude of the heavenly host, praising God and saying, "Glory to God in the highest heaven, and on earth peace among those whom he favors!"

The Gospel of the Lord.

◆ All sit and observe silence.

FOR SILENT REFLECTION

Think about this silently in your heart. Why did the angels announce the birth of the Messiah, the Savior, to the shepherds first?

CLOSING PRAYER

Let us pray to God for our needs and the needs of others: our family, neighborhood, and the world. For each need we say, "Lord, hear our prayer."

◆ All may add their own prayers here.

Let us pray: **Our Father . . . Amen.**

With the shepherds of long ago, we rejoice
at your coming, O Lord.
With the angels who announced your birth,
we say: Glory to God in the highest,
and peace to all people on earth!
We give you thanks and praise
in Christ Jesus' name.

Amen.

✦ All make the Sign of the Cross.

PRAYER FOR THE WEEK

WITH A READING FROM THE GOSPEL FOR **SUNDAY, JANUARY 5, 2020**

OPENING

Today we celebrate the Solemnity of the Epiphany [ih-PIF-uh-nee]. Epiphany means "to show forth." The star showed the Wise Men the way to Jesus. They recognized Jesus as King and worshiped him.

✚ All make the Sign of the Cross.

In the name of the Father, and of the Son, and of the Holy Spirit. Amen.

PSALM

(For a longer psalm, see page xiii.)
Psalm 96:1–2a, 2b–3, 5b–6, 11a

Let the heavens be glad and the earth rejoice!

Let the heavens be glad and the earth rejoice!

O sing to the Lord a new song;
    sing to the Lord, all the earth.
Sing to the Lord; bless his name.

Let the heavens be glad and the earth rejoice!

◆ All stand and sing **Alleluia.**

GOSPEL

Matthew 2:1–2, 8ab, 9–11

A reading from the holy Gospel according to Matthew.

In the time of King Herod, after Jesus was born in Bethlehem of Judea, wise men from the East came to Jerusalem, asking, "Where is the child who has been born king of the Jews? For we observed his star at its rising, and have come to pay him homage." Then King Herod sent them to Bethlehem, saying, "Go and search diligently for the child." When they had heard the king, they set out; and there, ahead of them, went the star that they had seen at its rising, until it stopped over the place where the child was. When they saw that the star had stopped, they were overwhelmed with joy. On entering the house, they saw the child with Mary his mother; and they knelt down and paid him homage. Then, opening their treasure chests, they offered him gifts of gold, frankincense, and myrrh.

The Gospel of the Lord.

◆ All sit and observe silence.

FOR SILENT REFLECTION

Think about this silently in your heart. What gift can you give to Jesus?

CLOSING PRAYER

Let us pray to God for our needs and the needs of others: our family, neighborhood, and the world. For each need we say, "Lord, hear our prayer."

◆ All may add their own prayers here.

Let us pray: **Our Father . . . Amen.**

Kings and shepherds looked for you, O Lord.
As the Wise Men brought gifts of gold, frankincense, and myrrh,
may we offer you our gifts of praise and thanksgiving.
You live and reign with God the Father
in the unity of the Holy Spirit,
one God, for ever and ever.

Amen.

✚ All make the Sign of the Cross.

OPENING

The Wise Men, or Magi, are also witnesses to Jesus' birth. Instead of hearing angels sing, they were led by a star. Yesterday we celebrated the Solemnity of the Epiphany. Today we again hear how the Wise Men sought the infant Jesus, and tomorrow we will hear more of what happened.

✣ All make the Sign of the Cross.

In the name of the Father, and of the Son, and of the Holy Spirit. Amen.

PSALM
(For a longer psalm, see page xiii.)
Psalm 96:1–2a, 2b–3, 5b–6, 11a

Let the heavens be glad and the earth rejoice!

Let the heavens be glad and the earth rejoice!

O sing to the Lord a new song;
  sing to the Lord, all the earth.
Sing to the Lord; bless his name.

Let the heavens be glad and the earth rejoice!

◆ All stand and sing **Alleluia.**

GOSPEL
Matthew 2:1–2, 8ab, 9–11

A reading from the holy Gospel according to Matthew.

In the time of King Herod, after Jesus was born in Bethlehem of Judea, wise men from the East came to Jerusalem, asking, "Where is the child who has been born king of the Jews? For we observed his star at its rising, and have come to pay him homage." Then King Herod sent them to Bethlehem, saying, "Go and search diligently for the child." When they had heard the king, they set out; and there, ahead of them, went the star that they had seen at its rising, until it stopped over the place where the child was. When they saw that the star had stopped, they were overwhelmed with joy. On entering the house, they saw the child with Mary his mother; and they knelt down and paid him homage. Then, opening their treasure chests, they offered him gifts of gold, frankincense, and myrrh.

The Gospel of the Lord.

◆ All sit and observe silence.

FOR SILENT REFLECTION

Think about this silently in your heart. How do you actively seek Jesus in your life?

CLOSING PRAYER

Let us pray to God for our needs and the needs of others: our family, neighborhood, and the world. For each need we say, "Lord, hear our prayer."

◆ All may add their own prayers here.

Let us pray: **Our Father . . . Amen.**

Glory to you, O God;
you have given us the best gift!
Help us see Jesus in one another
as clearly as the shepherds and the Magi
saw him in the manger.
We ask this in Christ's name.

Amen.

✣ All make the Sign of the Cross.

PRAYER FOR
TUESDAY, JANUARY 7, 2020

OPENING

We know that not everyone rejoiced at Jesus' birth. The powerful king Herod was threatened by the idea that a new king of the Jews had been born and sought to kill him. An angel appeared to Joseph and warned him to flee with Mary and the child to Egypt, where they would be safe. We remember St. Raymond of Penyafort, the patron saint of canon lawyers, today.

✝ All make the Sign of the Cross.

In the name of the Father, and of the Son, and of the Holy Spirit. Amen.

PSALM

(For a longer psalm, see page xiii.)
Psalm 96:1–2a, 2b–3, 5b–6, 11a

Let the heavens be glad and the earth rejoice!

Let the heavens be glad and the earth rejoice!

O sing to the LORD a new song;
   sing to the LORD, all the earth.
Sing to the LORD; bless his name.

Let the heavens be glad and the earth rejoice!

◆ All stand and sing **Alleluia.**

GOSPEL

Matthew 2:13–15a, 19–20, 23

A reading from the holy Gospel according to Matthew.

Now after the wise men had left, an angel of the Lord appeared to Joseph in a dream and said, "Get up, take the child and his mother, and flee to Egypt, and remain there until I tell you; for Herod is about to search for the child, to destroy him." Then Joseph got up, took the child and his mother by night, and went to Egypt, and remained there until the death of Herod. When Herod died, an angel of the Lord suddenly appeared in a dream to Joseph in Egypt and said, "Get up, take the child and his mother, and go to the land of Israel, for those who were seeking the child's life are dead." There he made his home in a town called Nazareth, so that what had been spoken through the prophets might be fulfilled, "He will be called a Nazorean."

The Gospel of the Lord.

◆ All sit and observe silence.

FOR SILENT REFLECTION

Think about this silently in your heart. Pray today for refugees who have to leave their countries to save their lives.

CLOSING PRAYER

Let us pray to God for our needs and the needs of others: our family, neighborhood, and the world. For each need we say, "Lord, hear our prayer."

◆ All may add their own prayers here.

Let us pray: **Our Father . . . Amen.**

We pray, O God, for all those who have had to flee their homes and their countries. We ask you to guide them to safety and peace, as your Holy Spirit guided Joseph, Mary, and Jesus.
We ask this in Christ's name.

Amen.

✝ All make the Sign of the Cross.

OPENING

Eight days after Jesus' birth, according to the Law of Moses, Mary and Joseph brought Jesus to the Temple in Jerusalem to present him to the Lord. At the Temple were the holy man Simeon and a widow Anna. Both Simeon and Anna had been praying for the coming of the Messiah for many years. Today we hear about when Anna sees the child Jesus.

✚ All make the Sign of the Cross.

In the name of the Father, and of the Son, and of the Holy Spirit. Amen.

PSALM

(For a longer psalm, see page xiii.)
Psalm 96:1–2a, 2b–3, 5b–6, 11a

Let the heavens be glad and the earth rejoice!

Let the heavens be glad and the earth rejoice!

O sing to the LORD a new song;
  sing to the LORD, all the earth.
Sing to the LORD; bless his name.

Let the heavens be glad and the earth rejoice!

◆ All stand and sing **Alleluia.**

GOSPEL

Luke 2:36–38

A reading from the holy Gospel according to Luke.

In the temple, there was also a prophet, Anna the daughter of Phanuel, of the tribe of Asher. She was of a great age, having lived with her husband seven years after her marriage, then as a widow to the age of eighty-four. She never left the temple but worshiped there with fasting and prayer night and day. At that moment she came, and began to praise God and to speak about the child to all who were looking for the redemption of Jerusalem.

The Gospel of the Lord.

◆ All sit and observe silence.

FOR SILENT REFLECTION

Think about this silently in your heart. How do you think that Anna was able to recognize Jesus as the Messiah?

CLOSING PRAYER

Let us pray to God for our needs and the needs of others: our family, neighborhood, and the world. For each need we say, "Lord, hear our prayer."

◆ All may add their own prayers here.

Let us pray: **Our Father . . . Amen.**

Holy and gracious God,
you heard the prayers of your servant Anna.
We ask that you hear our prayers.
Help us to welcome Jesus into our hearts
as Anna welcomed him in the Temple.
This we ask in Christ's name.

Amen.

✚ All make the Sign of the Cross.

THURSDAY, JANUARY 9, 2020

OPENING

Today's Gospel reading is one of the few stories in the Bible about Jesus when he was a boy. Jesus had a clear sense of his calling. Even at the age of twelve he started to reveal who he was to the elders in the Temple. Passover was the major religious feast at the beginning of the Jewish year.

✚ All make the Sign of the Cross.

In the name of the Father, and of the Son, and of the Holy Spirit. Amen.

PSALM

(For a longer psalm, see page xiii.)
Psalm 96:1–2a, 2b–3, 5b–6, 11a

Let the heavens be glad and the earth rejoice!

Let the heavens be glad and the earth rejoice!

O sing to the LORD a new song;
  sing to the LORD, all the earth.
Sing to the LORD; bless his name.

Let the heavens be glad and the earth rejoice!

◆ All stand and sing **Alleluia.**

GOSPEL

Luke 2:41–47

A reading from the holy Gospel according to Luke.

Now every year Jesus' parents went to Jerusalem for the festival of Passover. And when Jesus was twelve years old, they went up as usual for the festival. When the festival ended and they started to return, the boy Jesus stayed behind in Jerusalem, but his parents did not know it. Assuming that he was in the group of travelers, they went a day's journey. Then they started to look for him among their rela-tives and friends. When they did not find him, they returned to Jerusalem to search for him. After three days they found Jesus in the temple, sitting among the teachers, listening to them and asking them questions. And all who heard him were amazed at this understanding and his answers.

The Gospel of the Lord.

◆ All sit and observe silence.

FOR SILENT REFLECTION

Think about this silently in your heart. How do you think Jesus' parents, Joseph and Mary, felt as they listened to Jesus talk with the religious teachers?

CLOSING PRAYER

Let us pray to God for our needs and the needs of others: our family, neighborhood, and the world. For each need we say, "Lord, hear our prayer."

◆ All may add their own prayers here.

Let us pray: **Our Father . . . Amen.**

Walk with us, O God, and guide us.
Help us to love your teachings
and seek to understand your will.
We ask this in the name of Christ our Lord.

Amen.

✚ All make the Sign of the Cross.

OPENING

Today we hear how Jesus' cousin, John the Baptist, taught the people about Jesus. John recognizes that Jesus was sent by God to redeem the world.

✠ All make the Sign of the Cross.

In the name of the Father, and of the Son, and of the Holy Spirit. Amen.

PSALM

(For a longer psalm, see page xiii.)
Psalm 96:1–2a, 2b–3, 5b–6, 11a

Let the heavens be glad and the earth rejoice!

Let the heavens be glad and the earth rejoice!

O sing to the LORD a new song;
  sing to the LORD, all the earth.
Sing to the LORD; bless his name.

Let the heavens be glad and the earth rejoice!

◆ All stand and sing **Alleluia.**

GOSPEL

John 1:29–34

A reading from the holy Gospel according to John.

The next day John saw Jesus coming toward him and declared, "Here is the Lamb of God who takes away the sin of the world! This is he of whom I said, 'After me comes a man who ranks ahead of me because he was before me.' I myself did not know him; but I came baptizing with water for this reason, that he might be revealed to Israel. And John testified, "I saw the Spirit descending from heaven like a dove, and it remained on him. I myself did not know him, but the one who sent me to baptize with water said to me, 'He on whom you see the Spirit descend and remain is the one who baptizes with the Holy Spirit.' And I myself have seen and have testified that this is the Son of God."

The Gospel of the Lord.

◆ All sit and observe silence.

FOR SILENT REFLECTION

Think about this silently in your heart. When do you hear the words that John said about Jesus, ". . . the Lamb of God who takes away the sin of the world"?

CLOSING PRAYER

Let us pray to God for our needs and the needs of others: our family, neighborhood, and the world. For each need we say, "Lord, hear our prayer."

◆ All may add their own prayers here.

Let us pray: **Our Father . . . Amen.**

We thank and praise you, O God,
for sending Jesus to the world.
May we learn to follow his example
and help to build your Kingdom
of peace and justice on earth.
We pray this in Christ's name.

Amen.

✠ All make the Sign of the Cross.

PRAYER FOR THE WEEK
WITH A READING FROM THE GOSPEL FOR **SUNDAY, JANUARY 12, 2020**

OPENING

Today we celebrate the Solemnity of the Baptism of the Lord, and our Gospel is the story of Jesus' baptism by his cousin John the Baptist. When Jesus came out of the water, the Spirit of God appeared to him in the form of a dove. We are also baptized with water. The white garment and the baptismal candle symbolize the spirit of God that comes to us in the Sacrament of Baptism. The words that God said to Jesus are true about us as well: we are God's beloved daughters and sons.

◆ All make the Sign of the Cross.

In the name of the Father, and of the Son, and of the Holy Spirit. Amen.

PSALM

(For a longer psalm, see page xiii.)
Psalm 96:1–2a, 2b–3, 5b–6, 11a

Let the heavens be glad and the earth rejoice!

Let the heavens be glad and the earth rejoice!

O sing to the LORD a new song;
   sing to the LORD, all the earth.
Sing to the LORD; bless his name.

Let the heavens be glad and the earth rejoice!

◆ All stand and sing **Alleluia.**

GOSPEL

Matthew 3:13–17

A reading of the holy Gospel according to Matthew.

Then Jesus came from Galilee to John at the Jordan, to be baptized by him. John would have prevented him, saying, "I need to be baptized by you, and do you come to me?" But Jesus answered him, "Let it be so now; for it is proper for us in this way to fulfill all righteousness." Then John consented. And when Jesus had been baptized, just as he came up from the water, suddenly the heavens were opened to him and he saw the Spirit of God descending like a dove and alighting on him. And a voice from heaven said, "This is my Son, the Beloved, with whom I am well pleased."

The Gospel of the Lord.

◆ All sit and observe silence.

FOR SILENT REFLECTION

Think about this silently in your heart. You are God's beloved daughter or son in whom God is well pleased. How does that make you feel?

CLOSING PRAYER

Let us pray to God for our needs and the needs of others: our family, neighborhood, and the world. For each need we say, "Lord, hear our prayer."

◆ All may add their own prayers here.

Let us pray: **Our Father . . . Amen.**

O God, our loving Father,
we thank you for caring for us as your sons and daughters.
We give you honor and praise
in the name of Jesus Christ, our Lord.

Amen.

◆ All make the Sign of the Cross.

ORDINARY TIME WINTER

MONDAY, JANUARY 13 — TUESDAY, FEBRUARY 25

WINTER **ORDINARY TIME**

THE MEANING OF ORDINARY TIME

We've just celebrated the two great seasons of Advent and Christmas and now move back into Ordinary Time. Our seasons celebrate certain aspects of what we call Christ's "Paschal Mystery." For example, during the four weeks of Advent we focused on preparing to celebrate Christ's first coming in the Incarnation and preparing for Christ's Second Coming at the Parousia [par-oo-SEE-u]. The several weeks of Christmas focus on the wonder and joy of that first reality of God-with-us in Jesus. Now we move into the beginning of this year's ordered— that is, counted—Sundays of Ordinary Time. Each celebrates the Paschal Mystery in its entirety: Christ has died and is risen and will come again. Winter Ordinary Time is usually quite short, lasting only a few weeks.

The Prayers for the Week will reflect the Sunday Gospels, but during the week we will again "walk through the Bible." In week one we'll hear about Jesus' early years with the great stories of the Presentation in the Temple (an epiphany for Simeon and Anna), the finding in the Temple, and Jesus' baptism. We end the week with Jesus' instruction to the Apostles and to us to go out and proclaim the Gospel, the "good news." Week two examines the theme of abundance, from the concrete need for water to God's ineffable Word. Week three looks at the Transfiguration of Jesus by introducing Elijah and Moses in the Old Testament, relating St. Luke's story of the Transfiguration and its implications for Jesus. Week four is about "light" and we look at its biblical varieties in the books of Proverbs and Baruch, the Gospel of Luke, and letters to the Romans and Ephesians.

PREPARING TO CELEBRATE ORDINARY TIME IN THE CLASSROOM

You will need to replace your white cloth with a green one, now that it is Ordinary Time again. Plan another procession with your students if they respond well to them. Otherwise, you might ask them if they have any ideas about how to change the cloths with care and dignity. You might be surprised at the depth of their suggestions.

SACRED SPACE

Place a clear bowl with water in the prayer space for the first week to honor the baptism of Jesus and our own.

A plain vase with a bunch of bare branches would be appropriate, or a potted plant. A spider plant or an ivy will withstand long weekends without too much attention. Give its care and watering to your students. Make a job chart and allow them to take turns watering the plant. Watching the plant grow will provide a concrete sign of the growth that can take place in our hearts during this liturgical season.

In February consider placing two candles tied with a red ribbon for St. Blaise (February 3) in the space.

MOVEMENT AND GESTURE

Integrate the bowl of water into the daily prayer by bringing the bowl to the children or having them go to the bowl to make the Sign of the Cross. You might get holy water from the parish church but using tap water is also fine. Water is intrinsically holy. If the water becomes dirty it should be used to water plants or poured into the earth because it is holy by God's creation and by our use. See the suggestions for February 2, the Presentation of the Lord, below.

FESTIVITY IN SCHOOL AND HOME

From January 18 through 25, the Church joins with our Protestant brothers and sisters in the Week of Prayer for Christian Unity. A special prayer service, which may be used anytime during the week, is provided on page 167.

On February 2 we celebrate the feast of the Presentation of the Lord, also known as Candlemas. This is a beautiful feast to celebrate with children. If your school does not attend Mass that day, you might use the Scriptures from Monday and Tuesday of the first week of Ordinary Time. Before you begin prayer that day, dim the classroom lights and light a candle. Help the student proclaiming the Scripture to practice so that it can be done well, and allow time for the class to ponder the story together. If the children are old enough they might light and hold congregational candles (tapers) during the Gospel. (See more, under Prayers for Ordinary Time and A Note to Catechists.)

SACRED MUSIC

This would be the perfect time to learn how to sing one of the psalms. Psalm 27 ("The Lord Is My Light and My Salvation") and Psalm 23 ("The Lord Is My Shepherd") are two beautiful psalms that have many different musical settings. Children might also enjoy "This Little Light of Mine" and "I Want to Walk as a Child of the Light." Invite children to share favorite spiritual songs from their ethnic backgrounds and try singing songs from other countries ("We are Marching in the Light," "Pan de Vida," the round "Shalom Chevarim"). Also, don't forget to sing Alleluia often during these days. When Lent arrives, we will have to wait a long time before Easter when we can sing it again. The best Alleluia to sing is the one your parish uses before the Sunday Gospel.

PRAYERS FOR ORDINARY TIME

A tradition from the Liturgy of the Hours is to pray the *Canticle of Simeon* before going to bed. This is the prayer of the elderly man Simeon, who met the Holy Family in the Temple of Jerusalem when Mary and Joseph brought Jesus there as a baby. God had promised Simeon he would not die before he saw the Messiah. Simeon took the child Jesus in his arms and said this prayer:

"Master, now you are dismissing your servant
     in peace,
    according to your word;
for my eyes have seen your salvation,
    which you have prepared in the presence
      of all peoples,
    a light for revelation to the Gentiles
      and for glory to your people Israel."
        (Luke 2:29–32)

Introduce this prayer on February 2, the feast of the Presentation of the Lord. You may want to ask the children about certain key words in the prayer. Possible "wondering" questions could include: Why does Simeon call himself God's "servant"? Does the word "servant" recall anything that Mary once said? How did Simeon know that Jesus was a special baby? How is this small baby a "light" and a "glory"?

A NOTE TO CATECHISTS

Sometimes building codes will not allow school teachers or catechists to burn matches or light candles in the classroom. If possible, for February 2, plan a visit to a room where fire is permitted so that your celebration of the feast of the Presentation of the Lord will be set apart from the days surrounding it.

GRACE BEFORE MEALS

ORDINARY TIME • WINTER

LEADER:

Who is this King of glory?

ALL: The Lord, strong and mighty.

✚ All make the Sign of the Cross.

In the name of the Father, and of the Son, and of the Holy Spirit. Amen.

LEADER:

Heavenly Father,
we thank you for
the food we are about to share.
The abundance of this meal
reflects your goodness,
and how you provide for us
every day, in so many ways.
We ask this through Christ our Lord.

All: Amen.

✚ All make the Sign of the Cross.

In the name of the Father, and of the Son, and of the Holy Spirit. Amen.

PRAYER AT DAY'S END

ORDINARY TIME • WINTER

LEADER:
Your word is a light to my feet,

ALL: and a light to my path.

✚ All make the Sign of the Cross.

In the name of the Father, and of the Son, and of the Holy Spirit. Amen.

LEADER:
Heavenly Father,
thank you for this day of learning.
As we make our way home or
to other activities,
help us turn to you
for guidance in everything we do.
Keep us safe as we respond
to your Word in our hearts
as we meet with family and friends.
We ask this through Christ our Lord.

All: Amen.

✚ All make the Sign of the Cross.

In the name of the Father, and of the Son, and of the Holy Spirit. Amen.

OPENING

The Gospel today is the story of Jesus' baptism by John the Baptist. When Jesus came out of the water, the Spirit of God appeared to him in the form of a dove. We are baptized with water too. The white garment and the baptismal candle symbolize the spirit of God that comes to each of us in the Sacrament of Baptism. The words that God said to Jesus are true about us. We are also God's beloved daughters and sons.

✚ All make the Sign of the Cross.

In the name of the Father, and of the Son, and of the Holy Spirit. Amen.

PSALM
(For a longer psalm, see page xiii.)
Psalm 23:1–3a, 3b–4, 5, 6

I shall dwell in the house of the LORD my
   whole life long.

I shall dwell in the house of the LORD my whole life long.

The LORD is my shepherd, I shall not want.
   He makes me lie down in green pastures;
he leads me beside still waters;
   he restores my soul.

I shall dwell in the house of the LORD my whole life long.

◆ All stand and sing **Alleluia.**

GOSPEL
Matthew 3:13–17

A reading from the holy Gospel according to Matthew.

Then Jesus came from Galilee to John at the Jordan, to be baptized by him. John would have prevented him, saying, "I need to be bap-tized by you, and do you come to me?" But Jesus answered him, "Let it be so now; for it is proper for us in this way to fulfill all righteous-ness." Then he consented. And when Jesus had been baptized, just as he came up from the water, suddenly the heavens were opened to him and he saw the Spirit of God descending like a dove and alighting on him. And a voice from heaven said, "This is my Son, the Beloved, with whom I am well pleased."

The Gospel of the Lord.

◆ All sit and observe silence.

FOR SILENT REFLECTION

Think about this silently in your heart. You are God's beloved son or daughter in whom God is well pleased. How does that make you feel?

CLOSING PRAYER

Let us pray to God for our needs and the needs of others: our family, neighborhood, and the world. For each need we say, "Lord, hear our prayer."

◆ All may add their own prayers here.

Let us pray: **Our Father . . . Amen.**

How blessed we are, O God,
to be your children, your daughters and sons.
May we be pleasing to you in our words
and our actions as Jesus was.
We ask this through Christ our Lord.

Amen.

✚ All make the Sign of the Cross.

OPENING

On the eighth day after Jesus' birth, according to the Law of Moses, Mary and Joseph brought Jesus to the Temple in Jerusalem to present him to the Lord. It had been revealed to the holy man Simeon that he would see the Messiah before he died. When Simeon took Jesus in his arms, he praised God, saying, "Master, my eyes have seen your salvation, a light for revelation to the Gentiles and for glory to your people Israel." Today we hear about Anna, who was with Simeon in the Temple.

✦ All make the Sign of the Cross.

In the name of the Father, and of the Son, and of the Holy Spirit. Amen.

PSALM

(For a longer psalm, see page xiii.)
Psalm 23:1–3a, 3b–4, 5, 6

I shall dwell in the house of the LORD my
 whole life long.

I shall dwell in the house of the LORD my whole life long.

The LORD is my shepherd, I shall not want.
 He makes me lie down in green pastures;
he leads me beside still waters;
 he restores my soul.

I shall dwell in the house of the LORD my whole life long.

✦ All stand and sing Alleluia.

GOSPEL

Luke 2:36–38

A reading from the holy Gospel according to Luke.

In the temple, there was also a prophet, Anna the daughter of Phanuel, of the tribe of Asher.

She was of a great age, having lived with her husband seven years after her marriage, then as a widow to the age of eighty-four. She never left the temple but worshiped there with fasting and prayer night and day. At that moment she came, and began to praise God and to speak about the child to all who were looking for the redemption of Jerusalem.

The Gospel of the Lord.

◆ All sit and observe silence.

FOR SILENT REFLECTION

Think about this silently in your heart. Simeon and Anna both recognized Jesus as a light for the world. Why is Jesus a light for all?

CLOSING PRAYER

Let us pray to God for our needs and the needs of others: our family, neighborhood, and the world. For each need we say, "Lord, hear our prayer."

◆ All may add their own prayers here.

Let us pray: **Our Father . . . Amen.**

Holy and loving God,
you sent your son Jesus to be a light
for the world.
Help us to follow his example
and to let his light shine in each of us.
We ask this in his name.

Amen.

✦ All make the Sign of the Cross.

OPENING

Today's Gospel reading is one of the few stories in the Bible about Jesus when he was a young boy. Jesus had a clear sense of his calling. Even at the age of twelve he started revealing who he was to the elders in the Temple. Passover was the major religious feast at the beginning of the Jewish year.

✝ All make the Sign of the Cross.

In the name of the Father, and of the Son, and of the Holy Spirit. Amen.

PSALM

(For a longer psalm, see page xiii.)
Psalm 23:1–3a, 3b–4, 5, 6

I shall dwell in the house of the LORD my
whole life long.

**I shall dwell in the house of the LORD my
whole life long.**

The LORD is my shepherd, I shall not want.
He makes me lie down in green pastures;
he leads me beside still waters;
he restores my soul.

**I shall dwell in the house of the LORD my
whole life long.**

◆ All stand and sing **Alleluia.**

GOSPEL

Luke 2:41–47

A reading from the holy Gospel according to Luke.

Now every year Jesus' parents went to Jerusalem for the festival of the Passover. And when Jesus was twelve years old, they went up as usual for the festival. When the festival was ended and they started to return, the boy Jesus stayed behind in Jerusalem, but his parents did not know it. Assuming that he was in the group of travelers, they went a day's journey. Then they started to look for him among their relatives and friends. When they did not find him, they returned to Jerusalem to search for him. After three days they found Jesus in the temple, sitting among the teachers, listening to them and asking them questions. And all who heard him were amazed at his understanding and his answers.

The Gospel of the Lord.

◆ All sit and observe silence.

FOR SILENT REFLECTION

Think about this silently in your heart. How do you think Jesus' parents felt listening to him talk with the religious leaders?

CLOSING PRAYER

Let us pray to God for our needs and the needs of others: our family, neighborhood, and the world. For each need we say, "Lord, hear our prayer."

◆ All may add their own prayers here.

Let us pray: **Our Father . . . Amen.**

Heavenly Father,
from a young age, Jesus listened and learned from his teachers.
May we open our hearts and minds to those who help us to understand your word.
We ask this in Christ's name.

Amen.

✝ All make the Sign of the Cross.

OPENING

In today's Gospel, we hear how John the Baptist recognizes Jesus as sent by God. John calls him the "Lamb of God." In the Mass, we call on Jesus, the Lamb of God, to take away our sins and to give us peace.

✚ All make the Sign of the Cross.

In the name of the Father, and of the Son, and of the Holy Spirit. Amen.

PSALM

(For a longer psalm, see page xiii.)
Psalm 23:1–3a, 3b–4, 5, 6

I shall dwell in the house of the LORD my
　　whole life long.

I shall dwell in the house of the LORD my whole life long.

The LORD is my shepherd, I shall not want.
　He makes me lie down in green pastures;
he leads me beside still waters;
　he restores my soul.

I shall dwell in the house of the LORD my whole life long.

◆ All stand and sing **Alleluia.**

GOSPEL

John 1:29–34

A reading from the holy Gospel according to John.

The next day John the Baptist saw Jesus coming toward him and declared, "Here is the Lamb of God who takes away the sin of the world! This is he of whom I said, 'After me comes a man who ranks ahead of me because he was before me.' I myself did not know him; but I came baptizing with water for this reason, that he might be revealed to Israel." And John testified, "I saw the Spirit descending from heaven like a dove, and it remained on him. I myself did not know him, but the one who sent me to baptize with water said to me, 'He on whom you see the Spirit descend and remain is the one who baptizes with the Holy Spirit.' And I myself have seen and have testified that this is the Son of God."

The Gospel of the Lord.

◆ All sit and observe silence.

FOR SILENT REFLECTION

Think about this silently in your heart. Remember that when you were baptized you also became a child of God.

CLOSING PRAYER

Let us pray to God for our needs and the needs of others: our family, neighborhood, and the world. For each need we say, "Lord, hear our prayer."

◆ All may add their own prayers here.

Let us pray: **Our Father . . . Amen.**

We give you thanks, O God,
for the gift of Baptism.
We thank you for calling us to be your children, and for sending the Holy Spirit to guide us.
We pray in the name of your Son,
Jesus Christ, our Lord.

Amen.

✚ All make the Sign of the Cross.

OPENING

Today is the feast of St. Anthony of Egypt (251–356). St. Anthony lived a life of prayer alone in the desert for many years. But he realized that he needed to live in community, so he founded the first group of monks who lived together and dedicated themselves to prayer. In today's reading, the Apostle Peter announces that Jesus' teachings are for all people in every nation.

✚ All make the Sign of the Cross.

In the name of the Father, and of the Son, and of the Holy Spirit. Amen.

PSALM

(For a longer psalm, see page xiii.)
Psalm 23:1–3a, 3b–4, 5, 6

I shall dwell in the house of the LORD my
    whole life long.

I shall dwell in the house of the LORD my whole life long.

The LORD is my shepherd, I shall not want.
   He makes me lie down in green pastures;
he leads me beside still waters;
   he restores my soul.

I shall dwell in the house of the LORD my whole life long.

READING

Acts 10:34–38

A reading from the Acts of the Apostles.

Then Peter began to speak to them: "I truly understand that God shows no partiality, but in every nation anyone who fears him and does what is right is acceptable to him. You know the message he sent to the people of Israel, preaching peace by Jesus Christ—he is Lord of all. That message spread throughout Judea, beginning in Galilee after the baptism that John announced: how God anointed Jesus of Nazareth with the Holy Spirit and with power; how he went about doing good and healing all who were oppressed by the devil, for God was with him."

The Word of the Lord.

◆ All observe silence.

FOR SILENT REFLECTION

Think about this silently in your heart. Jesus went about doing good because God was with him. What acts of goodness can you do for someone today?

CLOSING PRAYER

Let us pray to God for our needs and the needs of others: our family, neighborhood, and the world. For each need we say, "Lord, hear our prayer."

◆ All may add their own prayers here.

Let us pray: **Our Father . . . Amen.**

Holy and almighty God,
in Jesus we see your will for all people.
He taught peace,
he healed those who were suffering, and
he offered hope and freedom
to the oppressed.
We give you thanks for sending Jesus to us.
We pray in his name.

Amen.

✚ All make the Sign of the Cross.

WEEK OF PRAYER FOR CHRISTIAN UNITY

Prepare four leaders and a song leader for this service. The second leader will need a Bible to read the Scripture passage and may need help finding and practicing it.

FIRST LEADER:
May the peace of Christ, who unites brothers and sisters around the world in his name, be with us, now and for ever.

ALL: Amen.

✚ All make the Sign of the Cross.

Let us pray:
Almighty God,
Creator of all wisdom,
you have made each of us
in your image
to reflect your many gifts.
We have been blessed through the
waters of Baptism,
to join with all Christians in the
loving power of
Father, Son, and Spirit.
Send your Spirit to guide us
as we seek your truth
and become united with Jesus
as our leader in faith.
We ask this through Christ our Lord.

ALL: Amen.

◆ All stand and sing **Alleluia.**

SECOND LEADER: John 15:12–17
A reading from the holy Gospel according to John.

◆ Read the Gospel passage from the Bible.

The Gospel of the Lord.

Let us pause and pray in silence for peace and unity among all Christians.

◆ Observe a time of silence.

THIRD LEADER:
Lord God,
you have made yourself known
to all the nations.
We declare your handiwork through
acts of peace and social justice
that assist all in need.
Guide us with your ways of peace.
Give us the courage to seek solutions
that benefit all
and that serve people
to build dignity and respect
for one another.
We ask this through Christ our Lord.

ALL: Amen.

FOURTH LEADER:
Now let us offer to one another a sign of Christ's peace.

◆ All offer one another a sign of peace.

And may the Lord bless us,

✚ All make the Sign of the Cross.

protect us from all evil,
and bring us to everlasting life.

ALL: Amen.

PRAYER FOR THE WEEK

WITH A READING FROM THE GOSPEL FOR **SUNDAY, JANUARY 19, 2020**

OPENING

In today's Gospel, John the Baptist declares that Jesus, the Lamb of God, takes away the sin of the world. We say this prayer every time we go to Mass.

✚ All make the Sign of the Cross.

In the name of the Father, and of the Son, and of the Holy Spirit. Amen.

PSALM

(For a longer psalm, see page xiii.)
Psalm 23:1–3a, 3b–4, 5, 6

I shall dwell in the house of the LORD my
　　whole life long.

**I shall dwell in the house of the LORD my
whole life long.**

The LORD is my shepherd, I shall not want.
　He makes me lie down in green pastures;
he leads me beside still waters;
　he restores my soul.

**I shall dwell in the house of the LORD my
whole life long.**

◆ All stand and sing **Alleluia.**

GOSPEL

John 1:29–34

A reading from the holy Gospel according to John.

The next day John the Baptist saw Jesus coming toward him and declared, "Here is the Lamb of God who takes away the sin of the world! This is he of whom I said, 'After me comes a man who ranks ahead of me because he was before me.' I myself did not know him; but I came baptizing with water for this reason, that he might be revealed to Israel." And John testified, "I saw the Spirit descending from heaven like a dove, and it remained on him. I myself did not know him, but the one who sent me to baptize with water said to me, 'He on whom you see the Spirit descend and remain is the one who baptizes with the Holy Spirit.' And I myself have seen and have testified that this is the Son of God."

The Gospel of the Lord.

◆ All sit and observe silence.

FOR SILENT REFLECTION

Think about this silently in your heart. John describes the Holy Spirit as a dove that descended on Jesus. How do you imagine the Holy Spirit?

CLOSING PRAYER

Let us pray to God for our needs and the needs of others: our family, neighborhood, and the world. For each need we say, "Lord, hear our prayer."

◆ All may add their own prayers here.

Let us pray: **Our Father . . . Amen.**

We thank you, O God,
for the gift of the Holy Spirit.
The Holy Spirit guides us and strengthens us.
Help us to listen to the Spirit's voice,
as John the Baptist did.
We ask this in Christ's name.

Amen.

✚ All make the Sign of the Cross.

OPENING

Today is the feast of St. Fabian who was pope from 236 to 250. He is famous for the miraculous nature of his election, in which a dove is said to have descended on his head, marking him as the Holy Spirit's choice for pope. In today's reading, Jesus gives us good advice on how to live.

✚ All make the Sign of the Cross.

In the name of the Father, and of the Son, and of the Holy Spirit. Amen.

PSALM

(For a longer psalm, see page xiii.)
Psalm 23:1–3a, 3b–4, 5, 6

I shall dwell in the house of the LORD my
    whole life long.

I shall dwell in the house of the LORD my whole life long.

The LORD is my shepherd, I shall not want.
   He makes me lie down in green pastures;
he leads me beside still waters;
   he restores my soul.

I shall dwell in the house of the LORD my whole life long.

◆ All stand and sing **Alleluia.**

GOSPEL

Matthew 7:15–20

A reading from the holy Gospel according to Matthew.

"Beware of false prophets, who come to you in sheep's clothing but inwardly are ravenous wolves. You will know them by their fruits. Are grapes gathered from thorns, or figs from thistles? In the same way, every good tree bears good fruit, but the bad tree bears bad fruit. A good tree cannot bear bad fruit, nor can a bad tree bear good fruit. Every tree that does not bear good fruit is cut down and thrown into the fire. Thus you will know them by their fruits."

The Gospel of the Lord.

◆ All sit and observe silence.

FOR SILENT REFLECTION

Think about this silently in your heart. Think of someone you know who bears good fruit; that is, does good actions in their life.

CLOSING PRAYER

Let us pray to God for our needs and the needs of others: our family, neighborhood, and the world. For each need we say, "Lord, hear our prayer."

◆ All may add their own prayers here.

Let us pray: **Our Father . . . Amen.**

We pray, O Lord, that through our words and our actions we may bear good fruit in our world.
We ask this in Christ Jesus' name.

Amen.

✚ All make the Sign of the Cross.

PRAYER FOR
TUESDAY, JANUARY 21, 2020

OPENING

In today's reading, Jesus helps us recognize what our real treasure is. The reading mentions that moths and rust ruin earthly treasure. In Jesus' time, wealthy people had fine clothes made of silk, which the moth could destroy. Precious metals such as copper and bronze, can be eaten away by rust. No matter how valuable, these earthly things will not last. Today we celebrate St. Agnes, an early Christian martyr. She is the patron saint of virtue.

✚ All make the Sign of the Cross.

In the name of the Father, and of the Son, and of the Holy Spirit. Amen.

PSALM

(For a longer psalm, see page xiii.)
Psalm 23:1–3a, 3b–4, 5, 6

I shall dwell in the house of the Lord my
    whole life long.

I shall dwell in the house of the Lord my whole life long.

The Lord is my shepherd, I shall not want.
    He makes me lie down in green pastures;
he leads me beside still waters;
    he restores my soul.

I shall dwell in the house of the Lord my whole life long.

◆ All stand and sing **Alleluia.**

GOSPEL

Matthew 6:19–21, 24ad

A reading from the holy Gospel according to Matthew.

"Do not store up for yourselves treasures on earth, where moth and rust consume and where thieves break in and steal; but store up for yourselves treasures in heaven, where neither moth nor rust consumes and where thieves do not break in and steal. For where your treasure is, there your heart will be also. No one can serve two masters; you cannot serve God and wealth."

The Gospel of the Lord.

◆ All sit and observe silence.

FOR SILENT REFLECTION

Think about this silently in your heart. What kind of treasure does Jesus say is really important? What is heavenly treasure?

CLOSING PRAYER

Let us pray to God for our needs and the needs of others: our family, neighborhood, and the world. For each need we say, "Lord, hear our prayer."

◆ All may add their own prayers here.

Let us pray: **Our Father . . . Amen.**

Loving and faithful God,
you have blessed us
with the gift of faith in you.
May we always treasure this great gift.
May our lives show that we are storing
our treasure in heaven.
We ask this in Christ's name.

Amen.

✚ All make the Sign of the Cross.

OPENING

This week we are hearing several of Jesus' maxims. A maxim is a short, basic truth about life. Maxims are words of wisdom that help people understand how to live better. Today's maxim is simple. Jesus says God loves us and wants to help us. We should ask for what we need. Today we also pray for the legal protection of unborn children.

✜ All make the Sign of the Cross.

In the name of the Father, and of the Son, and of the Holy Spirit. Amen.

PSALM

(For a longer psalm, see page xiii.)
Psalm 23:1–3a, 3b–4, 5, 6

I shall dwell in the house of the LORD my
whole life long.

I shall dwell in the house of the LORD my whole life long.

The LORD is my shepherd, I shall not want.
He makes me lie down in green pastures;
he leads me beside still waters;
he restores my soul.

I shall dwell in the house of the LORD my whole life long.

◆ All stand and sing **Alleluia.**

GOSPEL

Matthew 7:7–11

A reading from the holy Gospel according to Matthew.

"Ask, and it will be given you; search, and you will find; knock, and the door will be opened for you. For everyone who asks receives, and everyone who searches finds, and for everyone who knocks, the door will be opened. Is there anyone among you who, if your child asks for bread, will give a stone? Or if the child asks for a fish, will give a snake? If you then, who are evil, know how to give good gifts to your children, how much more will your Father in heaven give good things to those who ask him!"

The Gospel of the Lord.

◆ All sit and observe silence.

FOR SILENT REFLECTION

Think about this silently in your heart. What would you like to say to God now?

CLOSING PRAYER

Let us pray to God for our needs and the needs of others: our family, neighborhood, and the world. For each need we say, "Lord, hear our prayer."

◆ All may add their own prayers here.

Let us pray: **Our Father . . . Amen.**

We give you thanks, O God,
for the gift of life.
We pray for mothers, fathers, and all children, those yet unborn and all who need your special protection.
We ask this in Christ's name.

Amen.

✜ All make the Sign of the Cross.

OPENING

Today we remember St. Marianne Cope. After ministering to the sick in New York, she joined a mission to Hawaii. Working with St. Damien of Moloka'i, she cared for people with Hansen's disease, also known as leprosy. In today's reading, Jesus reminds us that sometimes we are critical of other people and don't see our own mistakes or weaknesses. A hypocrite engages in the same behaviors for which he or she criticizes others.

✚ All make the Sign of the Cross.

In the name of the Father, and of the Son, and of the Holy Spirit. Amen.

PSALM

(For a longer psalm, see page xiii.)
Psalm 23:1–3a, 3b–4, 5, 6

I shall dwell in the house of the LORD my
    whole life long.

I shall dwell in the house of the LORD my whole life long.

The LORD is my shepherd, I shall not want.
    He makes me lie down in green pastures;
he leads me beside still waters;
    he restores my soul.

I shall dwell in the house of the LORD my whole life long.

◆ All stand and sing **Alleluia.**

GOSPEL

Matthew 7:1–5

A reading from the holy Gospel according to Matthew.

"Do not judge, so that you may not be judged. For with the judgment you make you will be judged, and the measure you give will be the measure you get. Why do you see the speck in your neighbor's eye, but do not notice the log in your own eye? Or how can you say to your neighbor, 'Let me take the speck out of your eye,' while the log is in your own eye? You hypocrite, first take the log out of your own eye, and then you will see clearly to take the speck out of your neighbor's eye."

The Gospel of the Lord.

◆ All sit and observe silence.

FOR SILENT REFLECTION

Think about this silently in your heart. Do you criticize people for making fun of others or for bullying but do the same things yourself?

CLOSING PRAYER

Let us pray to God for our needs and the needs of others: our family, neighborhood, and the world. For each need we say, "Lord, hear our prayer."

◆ All may add their own prayers here.

Let us pray: **Our Father . . . Amen.**

Help us to have the courage
to do what is right, O God.
Help us to be kind
and caring of others.
We ask this in Christ's name.

Amen.

✚ All make the Sign of the Cross.

OPENING

In today's reading, Jesus uses the image of the vine to help us understand how close he is to us and we are to him. He says that he is the vine and we are its branches. Jesus uses the word *abide*, which means both "to stay with" and "to follow." Today we celebrate the Memorial of St. Francis de Sales. His book *An Introduction to the Devout Life* was a primer for all people to live holy lives.

✚ All make the Sign of the Cross.

In the name of the Father, and of the Son, and of the Holy Spirit. Amen.

PSALM (For a longer psalm, see page xiii.) Psalm 23:1–3a, 3b–4, 5, 6

I shall dwell in the house of the LORD my
    whole life long.

I shall dwell in the house of the LORD my whole life long.

The LORD is my shepherd, I shall not want.
   He makes me lie down in green pastures;
he leads me beside still waters;
   he restores my soul.

I shall dwell in the house of the LORD my whole life long..

◆ All stand and sing **Alleluia**.

GOSPEL
John 15:1–7

A reading of the holy Gospel according to John.

"I am the true vine, and my Father is the vine-grower. He removes every branch in me that bears no fruit. Every branch that bears fruit he prunes to make it bear more fruit. You have already been cleansed by the word that I have spoken to you. Abide in me as I abide in you. Just as the branch cannot bear fruit by itself unless it abides in the vine, neither can you unless you abide in me. I am the vine, you are the branches. Those who abide in me and I in them bear much fruit, because apart from me you can do nothing. Whoever does not abide in me is thrown away like a branch and withers; such branches are gathered, thrown into the fire and burned. If you abide in me, and my words abide in you, ask for whatever you wish, and it will be done for you."

The Gospel of the Lord.

◆ All sit and observe silence.

FOR SILENT REFLECTION

Think about this silently in your heart. How do you stay connected to Jesus?

CLOSING PRAYER

Let us pray to God for our needs and the needs of others: our family, neighborhood, and the world. For each need we say, "Lord, hear our prayer."

◆ All may add their own prayers here.

Let us pray: **Our Father . . . Amen.**

Your love for us is so great, O God!
We are joined to you through Jesus.
Help us to stay on the vine, and
to always be close to you.
We ask this in the name of your Son
Jesus Christ our Lord.

Amen.

✚ All make the Sign of the Cross.

OPENING

Today we hear Jesus call his first disciples, ordinary men who recognized that Jesus was calling them to a new life.

✚ All make the Sign of the Cross.

In the name of the Father, and of the Son, and of the Holy Spirit. Amen.

PSALM

(For a longer psalm, see page xiii.)
Psalm 23:1–3a, 3b–4, 5, 6

I shall dwell in the house of the LORD my
whole life long.

I shall dwell in the house of the LORD my whole life long.

The LORD is my shepherd, I shall not want.
He makes me lie down in green pastures;
he leads me beside still waters;
he restores my soul.

I shall dwell in the house of the LORD my whole life long.

◆ All stand and sing **Alleluia.**

GOSPEL

Matthew 4:12, 17–21abd, 22–23

A reading from the holy Gospel according to Matthew.

Now when Jesus heard that John had been arrested, he withdrew to Galilee. From that time Jesus began to proclaim, "Repent, for the kingdom of heaven has come near." As he walked by the Sea of Galilee, he saw two brothers, Simon, who is called Peter, and Andrew his brother, casting a net into the sea—for they were fishermen. And he said to them, "Follow me, and I will make you fish for people."

Immediately they left their nets and followed him. As he went from there, he saw two other brothers, James son of Zebedee and his brother John, mending their nets, and he called them. Immediately they left the boat and their father, and followed him. Jesus went throughout Galilee, teaching in their synagogues and proclaiming the good news of the kingdom and curing every disease and every sickness among the people.

The Gospel of the Lord.

◆ All sit and observe silence.

FOR SILENT REFLECTION

Think about this silently in your heart. How can you follow Jesus?

CLOSING PRAYER

Let us pray to God for our needs and the needs of others: our family, neighborhood, and the world. For each need we say, "Lord, hear our prayer."

◆ All may add their own prayers here.

Let us pray: **Our Father . . . Amen.**

Walk with us, Loving God, and guide us.
Show us your path of goodness
so our words and actions may help build
your Kingdom of peace and justice.
We ask this in Christ's name.

Amen.

✚ All make the Sign of the Cross.

OPENING

Mountains have been viewed as a place to be close to God or to have a spiritual experience. This was certainly true for the prophet Elijah, who was told to go to the mountain to see the Lord. Today we remember St. Angela Merici. She dedicated her life to helping young girls have a Christian education.

✝ All make the Sign of the Cross.

In the name of the Father, and of the Son, and of the Holy Spirit. Amen.

PSALM

(For a longer psalm, see page xiii.)
Psalm 23:1–3a, 3b–4, 5, 6

I shall dwell in the house of the LORD my
  whole life long.

I shall dwell in the house of the LORD my whole life long.

The LORD is my shepherd, I shall not want.
  He makes me lie down in green pastures;
he leads me beside still waters;
  he restores my soul.

I shall dwell in the house of the LORD my whole life long.

READING

1 Kings 19:11–14

A reading from the First Book of Kings.

The angel of the LORD said to Elijah, "Go out and stand on the mountain before the LORD, for the LORD is about to pass by." Now there was a great wind, so strong that it was splitting mountains and breaking rocks in pieces before the LORD, but the LORD was not in the wind; and after the wind an earthquake, but the LORD was not in the earthquake; and after the earthquake a fire, but the LORD was not in the fire; and after the fire a sound of sheer silence. When Elijah heard it, he wrapped his face in his mantle and went out and stood at the entrance of the cave. Then there came a voice to him that said, "What are you doing here, Elijah?" He answered, "I have been very zealous for the LORD, the God of hosts; for the Israelites have forsaken your covenant, thrown down your altars, and killed your prophets with the sword. I alone am left, and they are seeking my life, to take it away."

The Word of the Lord.

◆ All observe silence.

FOR SILENT REFLECTION

Think about this silently in your heart. When does God speak to you? Do you have to be very still to hear God's voice?

CLOSING PRAYER

Let us pray to God for our needs and the needs of others: our family, neighborhood, and the world. For each need we say, "Lord, hear our prayer."

◆ All may add their own prayers here.

Let us pray: **Our Father . . . Amen.**

May we listen for your voice,
O Lord, in our everyday moments.
May we trust that you will always guide us.
We ask this in Christ's name.

Amen.

✝ All make the Sign of the Cross.

PRAYER FOR
TUESDAY, JANUARY 28, 2020

OPENING

God gave the commandments to Moses on Mount Horeb. Moses reminds the people that they have a covenant, an agreement of love, with God. We also have a covenant with God through Jesus. Today we celebrate the feast of St. Thomas Aquinas. He was a learned scholar of philosophy and theology, and his works are still studied today.

✦ All make the Sign of the Cross.

In the name of the Father, and of the Son, and of the Holy Spirit. Amen.

PSALM

(For a longer psalm, see page xiii.)
Psalm 23:1–3a, 3b–4, 5, 6

I shall dwell in the house of the LORD my whole life long.

I shall dwell in the house of the LORD my whole life long.

The LORD is my shepherd, I shall not want.
  He makes me lie down in green pastures;
he leads me beside still waters;
  he restores my soul.

I shall dwell in the house of the LORD my whole life long.

READING

Deuteronomy 5:1–5

A reading from the Book of Deuteronomy.

Moses convened all Israel, and said to them: Hear, O Israel, the statutes and ordinances that I am addressing to you today; you shall learn them and observe them diligently. The LORD our God made a covenant with us at Horeb. Not with our ancestors did the LORD make this covenant, but with us, who are all of us here alive today. The LORD spoke with you face to face at the mountain, out of the fire. (At that time I was standing between the LORD and you to declare to you the words of the LORD; for you were afraid because of the fire and did not go up the mountain.)

The Word of the Lord.

◆ All observe silence.

FOR SILENT REFLECTION

Think about this silently in your heart. How do the Ten Commandments help us keep our covenant, our loving agreement, with God?

CLOSING PRAYER

Let us pray to God for our needs and the needs of others: our family, neighborhood, and the world. For each need we say, "Lord, hear our prayer."

◆ All may add their own prayers here.

Let us pray: **Our Father . . . Amen.**

Holy God, in making a covenant with
Israel you revealed your desire
to be in close relationship to us.
Help us to follow your will.
We ask this through Christ our Lord.

Amen.

✦ All make the Sign of the Cross.

OPENING

Jesus and his disciples had a significant mountaintop experience when Jesus revealed his true nature to Peter, James, and John because Jesus' divine form was revealed to his companions, who had only seen his human form.

✛ All make the Sign of the Cross.

In the name of the Father, and of the Son, and of the Holy Spirit. Amen.

PSALM

(For a longer psalm, see page xiii.)
Psalm 23:1–3a, 3b–4, 5, 6

I shall dwell in the house of the LORD my
    whole life long.

I shall dwell in the house of the LORD my whole life long.

The LORD is my shepherd, I shall not want.
    He makes me lie down in green pastures;
he leads me beside still waters;
    he restores my soul.

I shall dwell in the house of the LORD my whole life long.

◆ All stand and sing **Alleluia.**

GOSPEL

Mark 9:2–8

A reading from the holy Gospel according to Mark.

Six days later, Jesus took with him Peter and James and John, and led them up a high mountain apart, by themselves. And he was transfigured before them, and his clothes became dazzling white, such as no one on earth could bleach them. And there appeared to them Elijah with Moses, who were talking with Jesus. Then Peter said to Jesus, "Rabbi, it is good for us to be here; let us make three dwellings, one for you, one for Moses, and one for Elijah." He did not know what to say, for they were terrified. Then a cloud overshadowed them, and from the cloud there came a voice, "This is my Son, the Beloved; listen to him!" Suddenly when they looked around, they saw no one with them anymore, but only Jesus.

The Gospel of the Lord.

◆ All sit and observe silence.

FOR SILENT REFLECTION

Think about this silently in your heart. How would you have felt if you had seen Jesus' Transfiguration?

CLOSING PRAYER

Let us pray to God for our needs and the needs of others: our family, neighborhood, and the world. For each need we say, "Lord, hear our prayer."

◆ All may add their own prayers here.

Let us pray: **Our Father . . . Amen.**

Holy God,
Jesus showed his disciples
that he was the Son of God.
Help us to open our eyes so that we may grow in your image.
We ask this through Christ our Lord.

Amen.

✛ All make the Sign of the Cross.

PRAYER FOR
THURSDAY, JANUARY 30, 2020

OPENING

Mountaintop experiences are wonderful, but we cannot live there. We have to come back down to our daily life. Jesus prepares his disciples for his death and for them to take up his ministry of proclaiming God's love.

✝ All make the Sign of the Cross.

In the name of the Father, and of the Son, and of the Holy Spirit. Amen.

PSALM

(For a longer psalm, see page xiii.)
Psalm 23:1–3a, 3b–4, 5, 6

I shall dwell in the house of the LORD my
    whole life long.

I shall dwell in the house of the LORD my whole life long.

The LORD is my shepherd, I shall not want.
    He makes me lie down in green pastures;
he leads me beside still waters;
    he restores my soul.

I shall dwell in the house of the LORD my whole life long.

◆ All stand and sing **Alleluia.**

GOSPEL

Mark 9:9–10, 30–32

A reading from the holy Gospel according to Mark.

As they were coming down the mountain, Jesus ordered them to tell no one about what they had seen, until after the Son of Man had risen from the dead. So they kept the matter to themselves, questioning what this rising from the dead could mean. Jesus and his disciples went on from there and passed through Galilee.

He did not want anyone to know it; for he was teaching his disciples, saying to them, "The Son of Man is to be betrayed into human hands, and they will kill him, and three days after being killed, he will rise again." But they did not understand what he was saying and were afraid to ask him.

The Gospel of the Lord.

◆ All sit and observe silence.

FOR SILENT REFLECTION

Think about this silently in your heart. What hard things do you have to face? Ask Jesus to help you.

CLOSING PRAYER

Let us pray to God for our needs and the needs of others: our family, neighborhood, and the world. For each need we say, "Lord, hear our prayer."

◆ All may add their own prayers here.

Let us pray: **Our Father . . . Amen.**

Be with us, O Lord, when we face challenges and difficult times.
When we struggle, help us to believe in you and your love.
We ask this in Christ's name.

Amen.

✝ All make the Sign of the Cross.

OPENING

After coming down from the mountain, the disciples began to argue. Jesus responds to them by placing a small child on his lap. Today we remember St. John Bosco, who devoted his life to caring for the emotional and spiritual needs of young people.

✝ All make the Sign of the Cross.

In the name of the Father, and of the Son, and of the Holy Spirit. Amen.

PSALM

(For a longer psalm, see page xiii.)
Psalm 23:1–3a, 3b–4, 5, 6

I shall dwell in the house of the LORD my
　　whole life long.

I shall dwell in the house of the LORD my whole life long.

The LORD is my shepherd, I shall not want.
　　He makes me lie down in green pastures;
he leads me beside still waters;
　　he restores my soul.

I shall dwell in the house of the LORD my whole life long.

◆ All stand and sing **Alleluia.**

GOSPEL

Mark 9:33–37

A reading from the holy Gospel according to Mark.

Then they came to Capernaum; and when he was in the house he asked them, "What were you arguing about on the way?" But they were silent, for on the way they had argued with one another about who was the greatest. He sat down, called the twelve, and said to them, "Whoever wants to be first must be last of all and servant of all." Then he took a little child and put it among them; and taking it in his arms, he said to them, "Whoever welcomes one such child in my name welcomes me, and whoever welcomes me welcomes not me but the one who sent me."

The Gospel of the Lord.

◆ All sit and observe silence.

FOR SILENT REFLECTION

Think about this silently in your heart. What do you think Jesus is trying to teach the disciples and us?

CLOSING PRAYER

Let us pray to God for our needs and the needs of others: our family, neighborhood, and the world. For each need we say, "Lord, hear our prayer."

◆ All may add their own prayers here.

Let us pray: **Our Father . . . Amen.**

God, our Father,
you welcome and love all your children.
By the example of St. John Bosco,
help us to remember
that all of your children are important.
We ask this in Christ's name.

Amen.

✝ All make the Sign of the Cross.

PRAYER FOR THE WEEK
WITH A READING FROM THE GOSPEL FOR **SUNDAY, FEBRUARY 2, 2020**

OPENING

This Sunday we celebrate the Presentation of the Lord in the Temple. Our Gospel reading is taken from St. Luke's account of when Joseph and Mary took their son Jesus to present him to God. This was a Jewish custom, and Mary and Joseph observed the law. Listen to what Simeon says when he sees Jesus.

✚ All make the Sign of the Cross.

In the name of the Father, and of the Son, and of the Holy Spirit. Amen.

PSALM

(For a longer psalm, see page xiii.)
Psalm 23:1–3a, 3b–4, 5, 6

I shall dwell in the house of the LORD my
    whole life long.

**I shall dwell in the house of the LORD my
    whole life long.**

The LORD is my shepherd, I shall not want.
    He makes me lie down in green pastures;
he leads me beside still waters;
    he restores my soul.

**I shall dwell in the house of the LORD my
    whole life long..**

◆ All stand and sing **Alleluia.**

GOSPEL

Luke 2:27–32

A reading from the holy Gospel according to Luke.

Guided by the Spirit, Simeon came into the temple; and when the parents brought in the child Jesus, to do for him what was customary under the law, Simeon took him in his arms and praised God, saying, "Master, now you are dismissing your servant in peace, according to your word; for my eyes have seen your salvation, which you have prepared in the presence of all peoples, a light for revelation to the Gentiles and glory to your people Israel."

The Gospel of the Lord.

◆ All sit and observe silence.

FOR SILENT REFLECTION

Think about this silently in your heart. Simeon had prayed for many years to see the Messiah, the savior. How do you think he was feeling when he finally saw the child Jesus?

CLOSING PRAYER

Let us pray to God for our needs and the needs of others: our family, neighborhood, and the world. For each need we say, "Lord, hear our prayer."

◆ All may add their own prayers here.

Let us pray: **Our Father . . . Amen.**

May we be faithful in our prayer, O God,
so that we might recognize you in our midst.
May we trust in your saving power.
This we ask this in Christ Jesus' name.

Amen.

✚ All make the Sign of the Cross.

OPENING

This week we will look at the role of ministers in the early Church. In today's reading from the Acts of the Apostles, we hear how the Apostles chose people to help them. Today we celebrate the feast of St. Blaise. On this day, it is traditional to have our throats blessed and to pray for good health.

✝ All make the Sign of the Cross.

In the name of the Father, and of the Son, and of the Holy Spirit. Amen.

PSALM

(For a longer psalm, see page xiii.)
Psalm 23:1–3a, 3b–4, 5, 6

I shall dwell in the house of the LORD my
    whole life long.

I shall dwell in the house of the LORD my whole life long.

The LORD is my shepherd, I shall not want.
    He makes me lie down in green pastures;
he leads me beside still waters;
    he restores my soul.

I shall dwell in the house of the LORD my whole life long.

READING

Acts 6:1–2a, 3–5ab, 6

A reading from the Acts of the Apostles.

Now during those days, when the disciples were increasing in number, the Hellenists complained against the Hebrews because their widows were being neglected in the daily distribution of food. And the twelve called together the whole community of the disciples and said, "Friends, select from among yourselves seven men of good standing, full of the Spirit and of wisdom, whom we may appoint to this task, while we, for our part, will devote ourselves to prayer and to serving the word." What they said pleased the whole community, and they chose Stephen, a man full of faith and the Holy Spirit, together with Philip, Prochorus [PRAH-kuh-ruhs], Nicanor [NICK-ah-nor], Timon [TĪ-muhn], Parmenas [PAHR-muh-nuhs], and Nicolaus. They had these men stand before the apostles, who prayed and laid their hands on them.

The Word of the Lord.

◆ All observe silence.

FOR SILENT REFLECTION

Think about this silently in your heart. All Christians are called to serve others. How can you serve others today?

CLOSING PRAYER

Let us pray to God for our needs and the needs of others: our family, neighborhood, and the world. For each need we say, "Lord, hear our prayer."

◆ All may add their own prayers here.

Let us pray: **Our Father . . . Amen.**

Today we pray for priests, deacons, sisters, and all ministers who serve God
by serving his people.
May they be blessed.
We ask this in Christ Jesus' name.

Amen.

✝ All make the Sign of the Cross.

PRAYER FOR
TUESDAY, FEBRUARY 4, 2020

OPENING

Today we hear of Phoebe [FEE-be], and other men and women who ministered as missionaries, preachers of the Gospel, and leaders of their churches.

✚ All make the Sign of the Cross.

In the name of the Father, and of the Son, and of the Holy Spirit. Amen.

PSALM

(For a longer psalm, see page xiii.)
Psalm 23:1–3a, 3b–4, 5, 6

I shall dwell in the house of the LORD my
    whole life long.

I shall dwell in the house of the LORD my whole life long.

The LORD is my shepherd, I shall not want.
    He makes me lie down in green pastures;
he leads me beside still waters;
    he restores my soul.

I shall dwell in the house of the LORD my whole life long.

READING

Romans 16:1–2ac, 3–4a, 5a, 6–7, 12, 16b

A reading from the Letter of Paul to the Romans.

I commend to you our sister Phoebe, a deacon of the church at Cenchreae [SEN-kruh-ee], so that you may welcome her in the Lord as is fitting for the saints, for she has been a benefactor of many and of myself as well. Greet Prisca and Aquila [AK-wih-luh], who work with me in Christ Jesus, and who risked their necks for my life. Greet also the church in their house. Greet Mary, who has worked very hard among you. Greet Andronicus [an-DRAHN-uh-kuhs] and Junia, my relatives who were in prison with me; they are prominent among the apostles, and they were in Christ before I was. Greet those workers in the Lord, Tryphaena [tray-FI-nuh] and Tryphosa [tri-FO-suh]. Greet the beloved Persis, who has worked hard in the Lord. All the churches of Christ greet you.

The Word of the Lord.

◆ All observe silence.

FOR SILENT REFLECTION

Think about this silently in your heart. In what small ways are you called to minister; that is, to care for others?

CLOSING PRAYER

Let us pray to God for our needs and the needs of others: our family, neighborhood, and the world. For each need we say, "Lord, hear our prayer."

◆ All may add their own prayers here.

Let us pray: **Our Father . . . Amen.**

Loving God,
We pray that each of us will know
that we are called to minister to others.
We ask this in the name of Christ our Lord.

Amen.

✚ All make the Sign of the Cross.

OPENING

Today we hear about the qualities needed to be a good deacon or minister. To be a good minister to others requires learning to live a virtuous and holy life. St. Agatha, whose memorial we celebrate today, was tortured for choosing to live a virtuous life. She was martyred in 253.

✝ All make the Sign of the Cross.

In the name of the Father, and of the Son, and of the Holy Spirit. Amen.

PSALM

(For a longer psalm, see page xiii.)
Psalm 23:1–3a, 3b–4, 5, 6

I shall dwell in the house of the LORD my
  whole life long.

**I shall dwell in the house of the LORD my
whole life long.**

The LORD is my shepherd, I shall not want.
  He makes me lie down in green pastures;
he leads me beside still waters;
  he restores my soul.

**I shall dwell in the house of the LORD my
whole life long.**

READING

1 Timothy 3:8–13

A reading from the First Letter of Paul to Timothy.

Deacons likewise must be serious, not double-tongued, not indulging in much wine, not greedy for money; they must hold fast to the mystery of the faith with a clear conscience. And let them first be tested; then, if they prove themselves blameless, let them serve as deacons. Women likewise must be serious, not slanderers, but temperate, faithful in all things. Let deacons be married only once, and let them manage their children and their households well; for those who serve well as deacons gain a good standing for themselves and great boldness in the faith that is in Christ Jesus.

The Word of the Lord.

◆ All observe silence.

FOR SILENT REFLECTION

Think about this silently in your heart. What virtue or quality do you need to develop to live your Christian life more fully?

CLOSING PRAYER

Let us pray to God for our needs and the needs of others: our family, neighborhood, and the world. For each need we say, "Lord, hear our prayer."

◆ All may add their own prayers here.

Let us pray: **Our Father . . . Amen.**

Walk with us, Loving God, and guide us.
Show us your path of goodness
so our words and actions may help build
your Kingdom of peace and justice.
We ask this in Christ's name.

Amen.

✝ All make the Sign of the Cross.

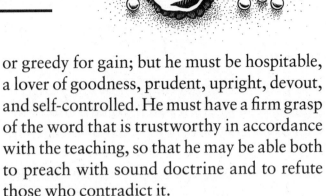

OPENING

In today's reading we hear about the ministry of the bishop. St. Paul describes the characteristics for a bishop. The word *bishop* means "overseer." Today we remember St. Paul Miki and Companions, who were Christians martyred in Japan.

✝ All make the Sign of the Cross.

In the name of the Father, and of the Son, and of the Holy Spirit. Amen.

PSALM

(For a longer psalm, see page xiii.)
Psalm 23:1–3a, 3b–4, 5, 6

I shall dwell in the house of the LORD my
    whole life long.

**I shall dwell in the house of the LORD my
whole life long.**

The LORD is my shepherd, I shall not want.
   He makes me lie down in green pastures;
he leads me beside still waters;
   he restores my soul.

**I shall dwell in the house of the LORD my
whole life long.**

READING

Titus 1:5–9

A reading from the Letter of Paul to Titus.

I left you behind in Crete for this reason, so that you should put in order what remained to be done, and should appoint elders in every town, as I directed you: someone who is blameless, married only once, whose children are believers, not accused of debauchery and not rebellious. For a bishop, as God's steward, must be blameless; he must not be arrogant or quick-tempered or addicted to wine or violent or greedy for gain; but he must be hospitable, a lover of goodness, prudent, upright, devout, and self-controlled. He must have a firm grasp of the word that is trustworthy in accordance with the teaching, so that he may be able both to preach with sound doctrine and to refute those who contradict it.

The Word of the Lord.

◆ All observe silence.

FOR SILENT REFLECTION

Think about this silently in your heart. Pray for the bishop of your diocese, that he may be a good and faithful leader.

CLOSING PRAYER

Let us pray to God for our needs and the needs of others: our family, neighborhood, and the world. For each need we say, "Lord, hear our prayer."

◆ All may add their own prayers here.

Let us pray: **Our Father . . . Amen.**

Holy God,
you entrust the bishops
with the care of the people.
Help them to be good shepherds of their
flocks and to lead them to you.
We ask this in Christ's name.

Amen.

✝ All make the Sign of the Cross.

OPENING

St. Paul is put in prison for his preaching about Jesus. Other faithful people continue his ministry, and Paul writes letters as a way to continue his work.

✠ All make the Sign of the Cross.

In the name of the Father, and of the Son, and of the Holy Spirit. Amen.

PSALM

(For a longer psalm, see page xiii.)
Psalm 23:1–3a, 3b–4, 5, 6

I shall dwell in the house of the LORD my
    whole life long.

**I shall dwell in the house of the LORD my
whole life long.**

The LORD is my shepherd, I shall not want.
   He makes me lie down in green pastures;
he leads me beside still waters;
   he restores my soul.

**I shall dwell in the house of the LORD my
whole life long.**

READING

Colossians 4:2–3, 7–9, 15

A reading from the Letter of Paul to
the Colossians.

Devote yourselves to prayer, keeping alert in it with thanksgiving. At the same time pray for us as well that God will open to us a door for the word, that we may declare the mystery of Christ, for which I am in prison. Tychicus [TIK-uh-kuhs] will tell you all the news about me; he is a beloved brother, a faithful minister, and a fellow servant in the Lord. I have sent him to you for this very purpose, so that you may know how we are and that he may encour-age your hearts; he is coming with Onesimus [oh-NES-uh-muhs], the faithful and beloved brother, who is one of you. They will tell you about everything here. Give my greetings to the brothers and sisters in Laodicea [lay-ahd-ih-SEE-uh], and to Nympha [NIM-fah] and the church in her house.

The Word of the Lord.

◆ All observe silence.

FOR SILENT REFLECTION

Think about this silently in your heart. What does it mean to be a "sister" or "brother" in Jesus, even with people we don't know?

CLOSING PRAYER

Let us pray to God for our needs and the needs of others: our family, neighborhood, and the world. For each need we say, "Lord, hear our prayer."

◆ All may add their own prayers here.

Let us pray: **Our Father . . . Amen.**

Because you are our father, O God,
we are all your children.
May we learn to love one another as our
brothers and sisters in faith.
We ask this in the name of our brother,
Jesus Christ.

Amen.

✠ All make the Sign of the Cross.

PRAYER FOR THE WEEK

OPENING

At our Baptism, we are given a small candle lit from the Paschal candle. It is reminder that as Christians we are called to be a light for the world. We hear more about this image of light, and of the image of salt, in the Gospel reading today.

✛ All make the Sign of the Cross.

> **In the name of the Father, and of the Son, and of the Holy Spirit. Amen.**

PSALM

(For a longer psalm, see page xiii.)
Psalm 23:1–3a, 3b–4, 5, 6

I shall dwell in the house of the LORD my
    whole life long.

**I shall dwell in the house of the LORD my
whole life long.**

The LORD is my shepherd, I shall not want.
    He makes me lie down in green pastures;
he leads me beside still waters;
    he restores my soul.

**I shall dwell in the house of the LORD my
whole life long.**

◆ All stand and sing **Alleluia.**

GOSPEL

Matthew 5:13–16

A reading from the holy Gospel according to Matthew.

Jesus said to the disciples, "You are the salt of the earth; but if salt has lost its taste, how can its saltiness be restored? It is no longer good for anything, but is thrown out and trampled underfoot. You are the light of the world. A city built on a hill cannot be hid. No one after lighting a lamp puts it under the bushel basket, but on the lampstand, and it gives light to all in the house. In the same way, let your light shine before others, so that they may see your good works and give glory to your Father in heaven."

The Gospel of the Lord.

◆ All sit and observe silence.

FOR SILENT REFLECTION

Think about this silently in your heart. How can you let your light shine at school and at home this week?

CLOSING PRAYER

Let us pray to God for our needs and the needs of others: our family, neighborhood, and the world. For each need we say, "Lord, hear our prayer."

◆ All may add their own prayers here.

Let us pray: **Our Father . . . Amen.**

O God,
thank you for the different gifts
you have given to each of us.
May we use them to give you glory.
Let us be a light for the world.
We ask this in Christ Jesus' name.

Amen.

✛ All make the Sign of the Cross.

OPENING

The Church is called "the Body of Christ" because we are Jesus' hands, feet, and face in the world. A body is best when all the parts are working. Christ's Body is best when each of us does our part and uses our gifts in service of others.

✝ All make the Sign of the Cross.

In the name of the Father, and of the Son, and of the Holy Spirit. Amen.

PSALM

(For a longer psalm, see page xiii.)
Psalm 23:1–3a, 3b–4, 5, 6

I shall dwell in the house of the Lord my
   whole life long.

I shall dwell in the house of the Lord my whole life long.

The Lord is my shepherd, I shall not want.
   He makes me lie down in green pastures;
he leads me beside still waters;
   he restores my soul.

I shall dwell in the house of the Lord my whole life long.

READING

1 Corinthians 12:4–11

A reading from the First Letter of Paul to the Corinthians [kohr-IN-thee-uhnz].

Now there are varieties of gifts, but the same Spirit; and there are varieties of services, but the same Lord; and there are varieties of activities, but it is the same God who activates all of them in everyone. To each is given the manifestation of the Spirit for the common good. To one is given through the Spirit the utterance of wisdom, and to another the utterance of knowledge according to the same Spirit, to another faith by the same Spirit, to another gifts of healing by the one Spirit, to another the working of miracles, to another prophecy, to another the discernment of spirits, to another various kinds of tongues, to another the interpretation of tongues. All these are activated by one and the same Spirit, who allots to each one individually just as the Spirit chooses.

The Word of the Lord.

◆ All observe silence.

FOR SILENT REFLECTION

Think about this silently in your heart. St. Paul says we all have gifts to share. What do you think is your gift to share?

CLOSING PRAYER

Let us pray to God for our needs and the needs of others: our family, neighborhood, and the world. For each need we say, "Lord, hear our prayer."

◆ All may add their own prayers here.

Let us pray: **Our Father . . . Amen.**

In your wisdom, O God,
you have given us a variety of gifts.
Help us to honor you by using our talents
and strengths to help one another.
We ask this through Christ our Lord.

Amen.

✝ All make the Sign of the Cross.

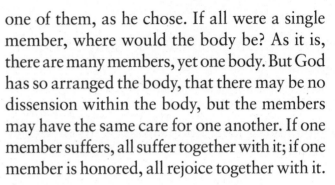

OPENING

In the human body if an arm is broken or a stomach is sick the whole person suffers. This is the same with the Body of Christ. Just as we do the work of Jesus together, so we suffer with others who are in pain and we rejoice with others who are happy. Today we honor Mary, Our Lady of Lourdes, to whom we pray for healing from illness of all kinds.

✦ All make the Sign of the Cross.

In the name of the Father, and of the Son, and of the Holy Spirit. Amen.

PSALM
(For a longer psalm, see page xiii.)
Psalm 23:1–3a, 3b–4, 5, 6

I shall dwell in the house of the LORD my
    whole life long.

I shall dwell in the house of the LORD my whole life long.

The LORD is my shepherd, I shall not want.
    He makes me lie down in green pastures;
he leads me beside still waters;
    he restores my soul.

I shall dwell in the house of the LORD my whole life long.

READING
1 Corinthians 12:12–13ab, 18–20, 24b, 25–26

A reading from the First Letter of Paul to the Corinthians [kohr-IN-thee-uhnz].

For just as the body is one and has many members, and all the members of the body, though many, are one body, so it is with Christ. For in the one Spirit we were all baptized into one body—Jews or Greeks, slaves or free. But as it is, God arranged the members in the body, each one of them, as he chose. If all were a single member, where would the body be? As it is, there are many members, yet one body. But God has so arranged the body, that there may be no dissension within the body, but the members may have the same care for one another. If one member suffers, all suffer together with it; if one member is honored, all rejoice together with it.

The Word of the Lord.

◆ All observe silence.

FOR SILENT REFLECTION

Think about this silently in your heart. How can you let someone who is suffering know that you care about him or her?

CLOSING PRAYER

Let us pray to God for our needs and the needs of others: our family, neighborhood, and the world. For each need we say, "Lord, hear our prayer."

◆ All may add their own prayers here.

Let us pray: **Our Father . . . Amen.**

God of hope and healing,
we pray for all who are ill and suffering
from physical, mental, or spiritual disease.
Please strengthen them and give them courage.
We ask this in Christ's name.

Amen.

✦ All make the Sign of the Cross.

OPENING

St. Paul firmly states that we are all part of Christ's Body, and each of us is necessary and important. Sometimes we believe we're not important, especially if we compare ourselves to others. St. Paul says we don't have to be like anyone else. We just have to try to be our best selves.

✦ All make the Sign of the Cross.

In the name of the Father, and of the Son, and of the Holy Spirit. Amen.

PSALM

(For a longer psalm, see page xiii.)
Psalm 23:1–3a, 3b–4, 5, 6

I shall dwell in the house of the LORD my
    whole life long.

I shall dwell in the house of the LORD my whole life long.

The LORD is my shepherd, I shall not want.
    He makes me lie down in green pastures;
he leads me beside still waters;
    he restores my soul.

I shall dwell in the house of the LORD my whole life long.

READING

1 Corinthians 12:14–17, 21, 27

A reading from the First Letter of Paul to the Corinthians [kohr-IN-thee-uhnz].

Indeed, the body does not consist of one member but of many. If the foot would say, "Because I am not a hand, I do not belong to the body," that would not make it any less a part of the body. And if the ear would say, "Because I am not an eye, I do not belong to the body," that would not make it any less a part of the body.

If the whole body were an eye, where would the hearing be? If the whole body were hearing, where would the sense of smell be? The eye cannot say to the hand, "I have no need of you," nor again the head to the feet, "I have no need of you." Now you are the body of Christ and individually members of it.

The Word of the Lord.

◆ All observe silence.

FOR SILENT REFLECTION

Think about this silently in your heart. Where am I needed this week and who needs me?

CLOSING PRAYER

Let us pray to God for our needs and the needs of others: our family, neighborhood, and the world. For each need we say, "Lord, hear our prayer."

◆ All may add their own prayers here.

Let us pray: **Our Father . . . Amen.**

Creator God,
in your wisdom and goodness
you made us
and blessed us with different gifts.
May we share our gifts with one another and build up the Body of Christ,
in whose name we pray.

Amen.

✦ All make the Sign of the Cross.

THURSDAY, FEBRUARY 13, 2020

OPENING

The most important gift we can bring to the Body of Christ is our love! All other gifts are good and necessary, but the first gift is love.

✦ All make the Sign of the Cross.

In the name of the Father, and of the Son, and of the Holy Spirit. Amen.

PSALM

(For a longer psalm, see page xiii.)
Psalm 23:1–3a, 3b–4, 5, 6

I shall dwell in the house of the LORD my
    whole life long.

I shall dwell in the house of the LORD my whole life long.

The LORD is my shepherd, I shall not want.
    He makes me lie down in green pastures;
he leads me beside still waters;
    he restores my soul.

I shall dwell in the house of the LORD my whole life long.

READING

1 Corinthians 12:27–31; 13:8

A reading from the First Letter of Paul to the Corinthians [kohr-IN-thee-uhnz].

Now you are the body of Christ and individually members of it. And God has appointed in the church first apostles, second prophets, third teachers; then deeds of power, then gifts of healing, forms of assistance, forms of leadership, various kinds of tongues. Are all apostles? Are all prophets? Are all teachers? Do all work miracles? Do all possess gifts of healing? Do all speak in tongues? Do all interpret? But strive for the greater gifts. And I will show you a still more excellent way. Love never ends. But

as for prophecies, they will come to an end; as for tongues, they will cease; as for knowledge, it will come to an end.

The Word of the Lord.

◆ All observe silence.

FOR SILENT REFLECTION

Think about this silently in your heart. How can we show our family and friends that we love them?

CLOSING PRAYER

Let us pray to God for our needs and the needs of others: our family, neighborhood, and the world. For each need we say, "Lord, hear our prayer."

◆ All may add their own prayers here.

Let us pray: **Our Father . . . Amen.**

Holy and loving God,
because you love us,
we love you and all you have created.
Help us always to remember that the first and most important gift is love.
We ask this in the name of Christ our Lord.

Amen.

✦ All make the Sign of the Cross.

OPENING

St. Paul preaches that the gift of love is more important than any other talent or gift. Without love, our actions will not bear good fruit. If we love, we will act rightly. Today is Valentine's Day, when we celebrate Christian values of thoughtfulness and tender care.

✦ All make the Sign of the Cross.

In the name of the Father, and of the Son, and of the Holy Spirit. Amen.

PSALM

(For a longer psalm, see page xiii.)
Psalm 23:1–3a, 3b–4, 5, 6

I shall dwell in the house of the LORD my
    whole life long.

I shall dwell in the house of the LORD my whole life long.

The LORD is my shepherd, I shall not want.
    He makes me lie down in green pastures;
he leads me beside still waters;
    he restores my soul.

I shall dwell in the house of the LORD my whole life long.

READING

1 Corinthians 13:1–7

A reading from the First Letter of Paul to the Corinthians [kohr-IN-thee-uhnz].

If I speak in the tongues of mortals and of angels, but do not have love, I am a noisy gong or a clanging cymbal. And if I have prophetic powers, and understand all mysteries and all knowledge, and if I have all faith, so as to remove mountains, but do not have love, I am nothing. If I give away all my possessions, and if I hand over my body so that I may boast, but

do not have love, I gain nothing. Love is patient; love is kind; love is not envious or boastful or arrogant or rude. It does not insist on its own way; it is not irritable or resentful; it does not rejoice in wrongdoing, but rejoices in the truth. It bears all things, believes all things, hopes all things, endures all things.

The Word of the Lord.

◆ All observe silence.

FOR SILENT REFLECTION

Think about this silently in your heart. When you love someone or something, how do you act toward them?

CLOSING PRAYER

Let us pray to God for our needs and the needs of others: our family, neighborhood, and the world. For each need we say, "Lord, hear our prayer."

◆ All may add their own prayers here.

Let us pray: **Our Father . . . Amen.**

We give you thanks,
gracious and loving God,
for all who love us and whom we love.
Help us to be kind, generous,
and loving to all.
We ask this in Christ's name.

Amen.

✦ All make the Sign of the Cross.

PRAYER FOR THE WEEK

WITH A READING FROM THE GOSPEL FOR **SUNDAY, FEBRUARY 16, 2020**

OPENING

In the Gospel Jesus says that he is the fulfillment of the law. He is talking about the covenant God made with Moses and the Israelites. Jesus, a good Jewish man who is faithful to the law, wants people to understand that keeping the covenant will bring about the Kingdom of God.

✝ All make the Sign of the Cross.

In the name of the Father, and of the Son, and of the Holy Spirit. Amen.

PSALM

(For a longer psalm, see page xiii.)
Psalm 23:1–3a, 3b–4, 5, 6

I shall dwell in the house of the LORD my whole life long.

I shall dwell in the house of the LORD my whole life long.

The LORD is my shepherd, I shall not want.
  He makes me lie down in green pastures;
he leads me beside still waters;
  he restores my soul.

I shall dwell in the house of the LORD my whole life long.

◆ All stand and sing **Alleluia.**

GOSPEL

Matthew 5:17–20

A reading from the holy Gospel according to Matthew.

Jesus said to the disciples, "Do not think that I have come to abolish the law or the prophets; I have come not to abolish but to fulfill. For truly I tell you, until heaven and earth pass away, not one letter, not one stroke of a letter, will pass from the law until all is accomplished. Therefore, whoever breaks one of the least of these commandments, and teaches others to do the same, will be called least in the kingdom of heaven; but whoever does them and teaches them will be called great in the kingdom of heaven. For I tell you, unless your righteousness exceeds that of the scribes and Pharisees, you will never enter the kingdom of heaven.

The Gospel of the Lord.

◆ All sit and observe silence.

FOR SILENT REFLECTION

Think about this silently in your heart. How do the Ten Commandments help us to love God and others better?

CLOSING PRAYER

Let us pray to God for our needs and the needs of others: our family, neighborhood, and the world. For each need we say, "Lord, hear our prayer."

◆ All may add their own prayers here.

Let us pray: **Our Father . . . Amen.**

Loving and faithful God,
you sent Jesus to teach us
about your Kingdom.
May we do your will here on earth
as it is done in heaven.
We ask this in Christ's name.

Amen.

✝ All make the Sign of the Cross.

OPENING

This week we'll focus on Jesus' miracles of healing. Jesus showed compassion and concern for those who suffered. Many people sought him out and had faith that he could heal them.

✚ All make the Sign of the Cross.

In the name of the Father, and of the Son, and of the Holy Spirit. Amen.

PSALM

(For a longer psalm, see page xiii.)
Psalm 23:1–3a, 3b–4, 5, 6

I shall dwell in the house of the LORD my
    whole life long.

I shall dwell in the house of the LORD my whole life long.

The LORD is my shepherd, I shall not want.
    He makes me lie down in green pastures;
he leads me beside still waters;
    he restores my soul.

I shall dwell in the house of the LORD my whole life long.

◆ All stand and sing **Alleluia.**

GOSPEL

Matthew 8:1–3, 14–17

A reading from the holy Gospel according to Matthew.

When Jesus had come down from the mountain, great crowds followed him; and there was a leper who came to him and knelt before him, saying, "Lord, if you choose, you can make me clean." He stretched out his hand and touched him, saying, "I do choose. Be made clean!" Immediately his leprosy was cleansed. When Jesus entered Peter's house, he saw his mother-in-law lying in bed with a fever; he touched her hand, and the fever left her, and she got up and began to serve him. That evening they brought to him many who were possessed with demons; and he cast out the spirits with a word, and cured all who were sick. This was to fulfill what had been spoken through the prophet Isaiah, "He took our infirmities and bore our diseases."

The Gospel of the Lord.

◆ All sit and observe silence.

FOR SILENT REFLECTION

Think about this silently in your heart. What in your life needs healing?

CLOSING PRAYER

Let us pray to God for our needs and the needs of others: our family, neighborhood, and the world. For each need we say, "Lord, hear our prayer."

◆ All may add their own prayers here.

Let us pray: **Our Father . . . Amen.**

God of hope and healing,
we pray for the faith of the leper,
who reached out and asked for help.
May we trust in your healing power to save.
We ask this in the name of your Son,
Jesus Christ our Lord.

Amen.

✚ All make the Sign of the Cross.

OPENING

In Jesus' time people thought mental illness was caused by a demon. Sometimes we talk about our demons; that is, the things that keep us from being our best selves. Jesus' compassion allowed him to cast out demons.

✦ All make the Sign of the Cross.

In the name of the Father, and of the Son, and of the Holy Spirit. Amen.

PSALM

(For a longer psalm, see page xiii.)
Psalm 23:1–3a, 3b–4, 5, 6

I shall dwell in the house of the LORD my whole life long.

I shall dwell in the house of the LORD my whole life long.

The LORD is my shepherd, I shall not want.
   He makes me lie down in green pastures;
he leads me beside still waters;
   he restores my soul.

I shall dwell in the house of the LORD my whole life long.

◆ All stand and sing **Alleluia.**

GOSPEL

Matthew 9:32–38

A reading from the holy Gospel according to Matthew.

After they had gone away, a demoniac who was mute was brought to him. And when the demon had been cast out, the one who had been mute spoke; and the crowds were amazed and said, "Never has anything like this been seen in Israel." But the Pharisees said, "By the ruler of the demons he casts out the demons."

Then Jesus went about all the cities and villages, teaching in their synagogues, and proclaiming the good news of the kingdom, and curing every disease and every sickness. When he saw the crowds, he had compassion for them, because they were harassed and helpless, like sheep without a shepherd. Then he said to his disciples, "The harvest is plentiful, but the laborers are few; therefore ask the Lord of the harvest to send out laborers into his harvest."

The Gospel of the Lord.

◆ All sit and observe silence.

FOR SILENT REFLECTION

Think about this silently in your heart. What bad habit or attitude hurts you or others? How can you refrain from them?

CLOSING PRAYER

Let us pray to God for our needs and the needs of others: our family, neighborhood, and the world. For each need we say, "Lord, hear our prayer."

◆ All may add their own prayers here.

Let us pray: **Our Father . . . Amen.**

Good and gracious God,
you care for us as a shepherd
cares for the sheep.
You have compassion for those in need.
May we follow your example.
We ask this in Christ's name.

Amen.

✦ All make the Sign of the Cross.

OPENING

Jewish law did not allow work on the Sabbath. When Jesus heals on the Sabbath, he is challenged by the Pharisee. Jesus responds that taking care of people is the more important law. God wants us to be merciful all the time.

✚ All make the Sign of the Cross.

In the name of the Father, and of the Son, and of the Holy Spirit. Amen.

PSALM

(For a longer psalm, see page xiii.)
Psalm 23:1–3a, 3b–4, 5, 6

I shall dwell in the house of the LORD my whole life long.

I shall dwell in the house of the LORD my whole life long.

The LORD is my shepherd, I shall not want.
  He makes me lie down in green pastures;
he leads me beside still waters;
  he restores my soul.

I shall dwell in the house of the LORD my whole life long.

◆ All stand and sing **Alleluia.**

GOSPEL

Matthew 12:3a, 6–7, 9–13

A reading from the holy Gospel according to Matthew.

Jesus said to the Pharisees, "I tell you, something greater than the temple is here. But if you had known what this means, 'I desire mercy and not sacrifice,' you would not have condemned the guiltless." He left that place and entered their synagogue; a man was there with a withered hand, and the Pharisees asked him, "Is it lawful to cure on the sabbath?" so that they might accuse Jesus. He said to them, "Suppose one of you has only one sheep and it falls into a pit on the sabbath; will you not lay hold of it and lift it out? How much more valuable is a human being than a sheep! So it is lawful to do good on the sabbath." Then he said to the man, "Stretch out your hand." He stretched it out, and it was restored, as sound as the other.

The Gospel of the Lord.

◆ All sit and observe silence.

FOR SILENT REFLECTION

Think about this silently in your heart. Why do you think Jesus uses the example of the sheep that has fallen into a pit?

CLOSING PRAYER

Let us pray to God for our needs and the needs of others: our family, neighborhood, and the world. For each need we say, "Lord, hear our prayer."

◆ All may add their own prayers here.

Let us pray: **Our Father . . . Amen.**

In your great mercy, O Lord,
you sent Jesus to teach us
about your Kingdom.
Help us to value and care for human life and
for all that you created.
We ask this in Christ's name.

Amen.

✚ All make the Sign of the Cross.

THURSDAY, FEBRUARY 20, 2020

OPENING

Compassion means to feel the suffering of another person. When Jesus seeks some time alone after John the Baptist's death, he is followed by the crowd. Jesus feels their suffering, and in his compassion he responds to their needs.

✣ All make the Sign of the Cross.

In the name of the Father, and of the Son, and of the Holy Spirit. Amen.

PSALM

(For a longer psalm, see page xiii.)
Psalm 23:1–3a, 3b–4, 5, 6

I shall dwell in the house of the Lord my
    whole life long.

I shall dwell in the house of the Lord my whole life long.

The Lord is my shepherd, I shall not want.
   He makes me lie down in green pastures;
he leads me beside still waters;
   he restores my soul.

I shall dwell in the house of the Lord my whole life long.

◆ All stand and sing **Alleluia.**

GOSPEL

Matthew 14:10, 12–14, 34–36

A reading from the holy Gospel according to Matthew.

King Herod sent and had John the Baptist beheaded in the prison. His disciples came and took the body and buried it; then they went and told Jesus. Now when Jesus heard this he withdrew from there in a boat to a deserted place by himself. But when the crowds heard it, they followed him on foot from the towns.

When he went ashore, he saw a great crowd; and he had compassion for them and cured their sick. When they had crossed over, they came to land at Gennesaret. After the people of that place recognized him, they sent word throughout the region and brought all who were sick to him, and begged him that they might touch even the fringe of his cloak; and all who touched it were healed.

The Gospel of the Lord.

◆ All sit and observe silence.

FOR SILENT REFLECTION

Think about this silently in your heart. Do you know someone who is suffering? How can you show compassion for that person?

CLOSING PRAYER

Let us pray to God for our needs and the needs of others: our family, neighborhood, and the world. For each need we say, "Lord, hear our prayer."

◆ All may add their own prayers here.

Let us pray: **Our Father . . . Amen.**

Make us as compassionate as you are,
O God.
Help us to know when to put the needs
of others before our own.
Jesus is our model, and
we pray in his name.

Amen.

✣ All make the Sign of the Cross.

OPENING

Today we remember St. Peter Damian, a bishop and Doctor of the Church who dedicated his life to penance and study of Scripture. Our Church has great compassion for those who are ill. We pray for the sick every Sunday in our intercessions. We celebrate the Sacrament of Anointing that has many prayers for healing both body and spirit. We visit and send cards to the sick. This is continuing Jesus' work.

✚ All make the Sign of the Cross.

In the name of the Father, and of the Son, and of the Holy Spirit. Amen.

PSALM

(For a longer psalm, see page xiii.)
Psalm 23:1–3a, 3b–4, 5, 6

I shall dwell in the house of the LORD my
    whole life long.

I shall dwell in the house of the LORD my whole life long.

The LORD is my shepherd, I shall not want.
  He makes me lie down in green pastures;
he leads me beside still waters;
  he restores my soul.

I shall dwell in the house of the LORD my whole life long.

◆ All stand and sing **Alleluia.**

GOSPEL

Matthew 20:29–34

A reading from the holy Gospel according to Matthew.

As they were leaving Jericho, a large crowd followed him. There were two blind men sitting by the roadside. When they heard that Jesus was passing by, they shouted, "Lord, have mercy on us, Son of David!" The crowd sternly ordered them to be quiet; but they shouted even more loudly, "Have mercy on us, Lord, Son of David!" Jesus stood still and called them, saying, "What do you want me to do for you?" They said to him, "Lord, let our eyes be opened." Moved with compassion, Jesus touched their eyes. Immediately they regained their sight and followed him.

The Gospel of the Lord.

◆ All sit and observe silence.

FOR SILENT REFLECTION

Think about this silently in your heart. Do you know someone who's sick? Say a prayer for that person.

CLOSING PRAYER

Let us pray to God for our needs and the needs of others: our family, neighborhood, and the world. For each need we say, "Lord, hear our prayer."

◆ All may add their own prayers here.

Let us pray: **Our Father . . . Amen.**

O God,
may our eyes be open
to see your good works.
Have mercy on us and grant us your grace.
We ask this in Christ's name.

Amen.

✚ All make the Sign of the Cross.

PRAYER FOR THE WEEK

WITH A READING FROM THE GOSPEL FOR **SUNDAY, FEBRUARY 23, 2020**

OPENING

We do not earn God's love. God loves us just as we are. Jesus asks us to be like God and to love everyone, even our enemies. Imagine a world where people did not dislike, hurt, or hate each other.

✛ All make the Sign of the Cross.

In the name of the Father, and of the Son, and of the Holy Spirit. Amen.

PSALM
(For a longer psalm, see page xiii.)
Psalm 23:1–3a, 3b–4, 5, 6

I shall dwell in the house of the LORD my
    whole life long.

I shall dwell in the house of the LORD my whole life long.

The LORD is my shepherd, I shall not want.
  He makes me lie down in green pastures;
he leads me beside still waters;
  he restores my soul.

I shall dwell in the house of the LORD my whole life long.

◆ All stand and sing **Alleluia.**

GOSPEL
Matthew 5:43–48

A reading from the holy Gospel according to Matthew.

"You have heard that it was said, 'You shall love your neighbor and hate your enemy.' But I say to you, Love your enemies and pray for those who persecute you, so that you may be children of your Father in heaven; for he makes his sun rise on the evil and on the good, and sends rain on the righteous and on the unrigh-teous. For if you love those who love you, what reward do you have? Do not even the tax collectors do the same? And if you greet only your brothers and sisters, what more are you doing than others? Do not even the Gentiles do the same? Be perfect, therefore, as your heavenly Father is perfect."

The Gospel of the Lord.

◆ All sit and observe silence.

FOR SILENT REFLECTION

Think about this silently in your heart. Is there someone you call an "enemy"? Pray that you learn to love that person.

CLOSING PRAYER

Let us pray to God for our needs and the needs of others: our family, neighborhood, and the world. For each need we say, "Lord, hear our prayer."

◆ All may add their own prayers here.

Let us pray: **Our Father . . . Amen.**

All good and loving God,
it is not easy to love our enemies.
Help us to have the courage to pray for those we do not like or who do not like us.
We ask this is Christ's name.

Amen.

✛ All make the Sign of the Cross.

OPENING

The Church uses symbols in the sacraments to express their deeper meaning, such as water in Baptism. This week we'll see that Jesus is the first symbol for all sacraments. In today's reading Jesus calls himself "living water" that quenches people's thirst for God.

✦ All make the Sign of the Cross.

In the name of the Father, and of the Son, and of the Holy Spirit. Amen.

PSALM

(For a longer psalm, see page xiii.)
Psalm 23:1–3a, 3b–4, 5, 6

I shall dwell in the house of the LORD my
    whole life long.

**I shall dwell in the house of the LORD my
whole life long.**

The LORD is my shepherd, I shall not want.
   He makes me lie down in green pastures;
he leads me beside still waters;
   he restores my soul.

**I shall dwell in the house of the LORD my
whole life long.**

◆ All stand and sing **Alleluia.**

GOSPEL

John 7:37acd, 38–41

A reading from the holy Gospel according to John.

On the last day of the festival, while Jesus was standing there, he cried out, "Let anyone who is thirsty come to me, and let the one who believes in me drink. As the scripture has said, 'Out of the believer's heart shall flow rivers of living water.'" Now he said this about the Spirit, which believers in him were to receive; for as yet there was no Spirit, because Jesus was not yet glorified. When they heard these words, some in the crowd said, "This is really the prophet." Others said, "This is the Messiah."

The Gospel of the Lord.

◆ All sit and observe silence.

FOR SILENT REFLECTION

Think about this silently in your heart. For what do you thirst; that is, what do you desire? Bring that to God in prayer.

CLOSING PRAYER

Let us pray to God for our needs and the needs of others: our family, neighborhood, and the world. For each need we say, "Lord, hear our prayer."

◆ All may add their own prayers here.

Let us pray: **Our Father . . . Amen.**

We thirst, O God, for you.
You know our needs even better than we do.
Help us to trust in you.
We ask this through Jesus Christ,
the Living Water.

Amen.

✦ All make the Sign of the Cross.

OPENING

Mary anoints Jesus' feet with nard, a sweet-smelling oil. Anointing is an ancient way of indicating that a person is chosen for a special work. In Baptism we are anointed with a fragrant, sacred oil called chrism. As Christians, we have important work to do.

✝ All make the Sign of the Cross.

In the name of the Father, and of the Son, and of the Holy Spirit. Amen.

PSALM

(For a longer psalm, see page xiii.)
Psalm 23:1–3a, 3b–4, 5, 6

I shall dwell in the house of the LORD my
    whole life long.

I shall dwell in the house of the LORD my whole life long.

The LORD is my shepherd, I shall not want.
    He makes me lie down in green pastures;
he leads me beside still waters;
    he restores my soul.

I shall dwell in the house of the LORD my whole life long.

◆ All stand and sing **Alleluia.**

GOSPEL

John 12:1–4abd, 5, 7–8

A reading from the holy Gospel according to John.

Six days before the Passover Jesus came to Bethany, the home of Lazarus, whom he had raised from the dead. There they gave a dinner for him. Martha served, and Lazarus was one of those at the table with him. Mary took a pound of costly perfume made of pure nard, anointed Jesus' feet, and wiped them with her hair. The house was filled with the fragrance of the perfume. But Judas Iscariot [ih-SKAYR-ee-uht], one of his disciples, said, "Why was this perfume not sold for three hundred denarii and the money given to the poor?" Jesus said, "Leave her alone. She bought it so that she might keep it for the day of my burial. You always have the poor with you, but you do not always have me."

The Gospel of the Lord.

◆ All sit and observe silence.

FOR SILENT REFLECTION

Think about this silently in your heart. At Baptism you were anointed with chrism. What have we been anointed to do?

CLOSING PRAYER

Let us pray to God for our needs and the needs of others: our family, neighborhood, and the world. For each need we say, "Lord, hear our prayer."

◆ All may add their own prayers here.

Let us pray: **Our Father . . . Amen.**

In anointing Jesus with oil,
Mary showed her love for him.
In caring for others and doing your will,
we show our love for you, O God.
Help us to be generous in our love.
We ask this in Christ's name.

Amen.

✝ All make the Sign of the Cross.

LENT

WEDNESDAY, FEBRUARY 26 — WEDNESDAY, APRIL 8

LENT

THE MEANING OF LENT

On Ash Wednesday the Church enters into her great retreat time called Lent. It is a time to reflect on how we are with God, with our neighbor, and with ourselves and to make some changes in our attitudes or speech or actions if we need to. We should do this often throughout the year, but we do it more consciously in Lent to prepare for the celebration of Easter when some people will be baptized and the rest of us will renew our Baptismal promises.

We have six weeks to concentrate on this conversion of heart, this turning back to or moving closer to God. During this time we might ask ourselves a simple question: "What do I need to stop doing or start doing to be the very good person God made me?" If we find we have some bad habits or have hurt someone (even ourselves) or have neglected to do something we should, we can express our sincere regret and willingness to change in the Sacrament of Reconciliation.

The three Lenten disciplines can help us to train our hearts in love. We are called to pray, fast, and give alms. We pray more regularly and perhaps for longer periods of time. Praying is a conversation with God and a way to be closer to God.

We fast to remind ourselves that there is nothing more important than God and the needs of God's people. Perhaps we give up a certain food and give the money we save to the poor. We might give up playing video games and use the time to help around the house. Part of fasting is abstaining from meat on Fridays of Lent so we eat simply and sparingly as poor people must.

The third discipline is almsgiving. The word comes from the Greek meaning "compassion" and is associated with giving food, money, or clothing to the poor. The money we save by giving up a favorite food or activity might be used this way. We may have a toy, games, or clothes we no longer use very often that we could give to someone else.

Lent's purpose of preparing us to celebrate Easter becomes more focused as we enter into Holy Week. Lent ends with the Mass of the Lord's Supper on Holy Thursday evening. At that moment we enter the Triduum, the three holiest days of the Church year.

PREPARING TO CELEBRATE LENT IN THE CLASSROOM

SACRED SPACE

Remember that on Ash Wednesday, you will need to change your prayer tablecloth from green to purple. If you have a growing plant in the prayer space, remove it. Ask the children to bring in their family's dried palms from last year and put them in a simple vase. A clear bowl full of ashes would be appropriate. They are available through local religious goods stores. (Use the same bowl to hold water in Easter.)

MOVEMENT AND GESTURE

You may want to use some incense during some of the prayers. Ask the parish priest or deacon for some charcoal and incense. You'll also need a pot full of sand to place the charcoal in. An altar server can help you light the charcoal about ten minutes before the prayer. Then the leader can place just enough incense on the charcoal before the Scripture is proclaimed. Be sure to have open windows and let people know you are using the incense. Ask the children with allergies and asthma to stand in the back of the space in case the smoke bothers them. At the end of the prayer cover the charcoal with sand to stop it from smoking.

FESTIVITY IN SCHOOL AND HOME

Lent is a more solemn time. Festivity is kept to a minimum, although there may be special feasts such as St. Joseph's Day or St. Patrick's Day, where it is the custom to celebrate and honor these saints. Because we are not in school during the three sacred days leading up to Easter, we have provided prayers the children can bring home. You will find Home Prayer pages to copy and send home so that families can keep Holy Thursday and Good Friday (pages 249–250). The Prayer Service for Ash Wednesday (pages 206–207) can be used for the classroom or for a larger group.

SACRED MUSIC

Lent is a more solemn time and our music reflects this. Our songs are more plaintive and contemplative. Children love to sing "Jesus, Remember Me," and "What Wondrous Love Is This?" Other songs for Lent are "Amazing Grace," the African American spiritual "Somebody's Knockin' at Your Door," and the Latin hymn "Ubi Caritas." We don't sing "Alleluia" during Lent. Tell the children we are saving all our Alleluia joy for Easter. For the Prayer for the Week, and during the week where there is a Gospel, we sing an acclamation, such as "Praise to you, Lord Jesus Christ" to whatever tune the parish is using.

PRAYERS FOR LENT

Lent is the perfect time to learn or to review an Act of Contrition. Psalm 51 is also a beautiful prayer for this season of penance and conversion.

A NOTE TO CATECHISTS

If any children in your group are preparing to celebrate the sacraments of initiation at the Easter Vigil, gather them to read the following three great accounts from the Gospel of John: (1) Jesus teaches the Woman at the Well who finally understands Jesus is the Messiah (John 4:5–15, 19b–26, 39a, 40–42); (2) Jesus cures the Man Born Blind of physical blindness and the man "sees" and follow him (John 9:1, 6–9, 13–17, 34–38); and (3) Jesus raises Lazarus from the dead (John 11:3–7, 17, 20–27, 33b–45). These are long passages and may require some time to read and discuss with your students, but fight the temptation to rush through them!

GRACE BEFORE MEALS

LENT

LEADER:

We adore you, O Christ, and we praise you

ALL: because by your holy Cross you have redeemed the world.

✚ All make the Sign of the Cross.

In the name of the Father, and of the Son, and of the Holy Spirit. Amen.

LEADER:

God of compassion,
we thank you for this meal
and for those who prepared it.
May we be nourished by this food
and by the love and friendship we share.
Help us to be mindful of people
in our community and other regions
who will remain hungry today.
May we become your true food for others
through gifts of your Spirit and our works
    of charity.
We ask this through Christ our Lord.

All: Amen.

✚ All make the Sign of the Cross.

In the name of the Father, and of the Son, and of the Holy Spirit. Amen.

PRAYER AT DAY'S END

LENT

LEADER:
Blessed be the Lord,

ALL: for he has heard the sound of my pleadings.

✠ All make the Sign of the Cross.

In the name of the Father, and of the Son, and of the Holy Spirit. Amen.

LEADER:
Merciful Lord,
sometimes we fail in what
we say or do.
As our school day ends,
help us to remember that
your mercy and love
are never-ending.
Guide us as we renew our
commitment
to deepen our relationship with you
throughout this season of Lent.
We ask this in your name.

All: Amen.

✠ All make the Sign of the Cross.

In the name of the Father, and of the Son, and of the Holy Spirit. Amen.

PRAYER SERVICE
ASH WEDNESDAY

Prepare eight leaders for this service. Before you begin, prepare a long piece of butcher-block paper or cloth banner with the word "Alleluia" written on it. The inside of the first three letters, "A-l-l" should be colored in, but you should only be able to see an outline of the rest of the word's letters, "e-l-u-i-a." Hang this banner for all to see, but make it accessible so that an additional letter can be colored each week of Lent. On Fridays during Lent, you may want to incorporate coloring the additional letters when you do Prayer at Day's End for Lent, found on page 205.

The fifth and sixth leaders of this Prayer Service will need Bibles for the Scripture passages and may need help practicing them. You may wish to begin by singing "From Ashes to the Living Font" and end with "Soon and Very Soon." If the group will sing, prepare a song leader.

FIRST LEADER:

✚ All make the sign of the Cross.

In the name of the Father, and of the Son, and of the Holy Spirit. Amen.

Today we embark together on a journey through Lent. It is a time for self-discovery as we remember how Jesus went into the desert for forty days and was tempted by the devil. During our Lenten experience, we pray more, eat less, and give to the poor to prepare ourselves for what is at the heart of our Christian faith—Christ's Resurrection at Easter! But we must make ready our hearts and minds, like an athlete trains for a key game or race. We need to strengthen our good habits as we remain God's sons and daughters through the waters of Baptism.

SECOND LEADER:

Each year, on Ash Wednesday, Catholics are marked with ashes in the Sign of the Cross as a reminder that we are entering into Lent. This ashen sign reminds us of our humanness, and that sometimes we fail. We need God's help to succeed. That's why prayer is so vital in our lives.

THIRD LEADER:

During Lent, we also fast from the word "Alleluia," which means "Praise the Lord" in Hebrew. We've prepared this banner with only three of the letters colored in. But you'll see that on this special day, we are *all* in this together! Lent can be a time for us *all* to get closer to Christ. Just like a team trains for a big game, we *all* can do this through prayer and sacrifice. So at the end of each week in Lent, we will color in one more letter to mark another week closer to our declaring this joyous word!

FOURTH LEADER:

Let us pray:
Almighty Father,
through the waters of Baptism,
you claimed us as
your sons and daughters.

You love us without condition.
May our prayers, fasting, and
works of charity deepen
our connection with you
as we better understand the suffering of
our brothers and sisters around the world.
May we remember how
Jesus was tempted in the desert
and that *all* of us need to make
you our priority
in word and deed.
We ask this through Christ our Lord.

ALL: Amen.

◆ All stand and sing **Praise to you, Lord Jesus Christ** . . .

FIFTH LEADER: Matthew 4:1–11
A reading from the holy Gospel according
to Matthew.

◆ Read the Scripture passage from a Bible.

The Gospel of the Lord.

◆ All remain standing and observe silence.

SIXTH LEADER: Matthew 6:1–2
A reading from the holy Gospel according
to Matthew.

◆ Read the Scripture passage from a Bible.

The Gospel of the Lord.

◆ All sit and observe silence.

*POF *
SEVENTH LEADER:
Let us pray as Jesus taught us:

ALL: Our Father . . . Amen.

Fr. H
Lord God,
help us to be one with you
during this season of Lent.
Guide us as you led
Jesus through the
trying times in his life.
May we let go of
our negative habits and thoughts
that make us feel distant
from your loving presence.
We look forward to
the joy of Easter,
for our hope is Jesus
in this time of preparation.
We ask this through Christ our Lord.

ALL: Amen.

EIGHTH LEADER:
Let us offer to one another a sign of
Christ's peace:

◆ All offer one another a sign of peace.

And may the Lord bless us,

✝ All make the Sign of the Cross.

protect us from all evil,
and bring us to everlasting life.

ALL: Amen.

PRAYER FOR
WEDNESDAY, FEBRUARY 26, 2020

OPENING

We begin Lent with a cross of ashes placed on our foreheads. Prayer and almsgiving are two of our "disciplines"; that is, our Christian training activities that will help us to follow Jesus more closely. *Alms* is a special word for money given to the poor.

✚ All make the Sign of the Cross.

In the name of the Father, and of the Son, and of the Holy Spirit. Amen.

PSALM

(For a longer psalm, see page xiv.)
Psalm 34:4–5, 6–7, 16–17, 18–19

The LORD saves the crushed in spirit.

The LORD saves the crushed in spirit.

I sought the LORD, and he answered me,
 and delivered me from all my fears.
Look to him, and be radiant;
 so your faces shall never be ashamed.

The LORD saves the crushed in spirit.

◆ All stand and sing **Praise to you, Lord Jesus Christ . . .**

GOSPEL

Matthew 6:2ac, 3–5ab, 6

A reading from the holy Gospel according to Matthew.

Jesus said, "So whenever you give alms, do not sound a trumpet before you, as the hypocrites do in the synagogues and in the streets. Truly I tell you, they have received their reward. But when you give alms, do not let your left hand know what your right hand is doing, so that your alms may be done in secret; and your Father who sees in secret will reward you. And whenever you pray, do not be like the hypocrites; for they love to stand and pray in the synagogues and at the street corners, so that they may be seen by others. But whenever you pray, go into your room and shut the door and pray to your Father who is in secret; and your Father who sees in secret will reward you."

The Gospel of the Lord.

◆ All sit and observe silence.

FOR SILENT REFLECTION

Think about this silently in your heart. For whom or for what will you pray this week?

CLOSING PRAYER

Let us pray to God for our needs and the needs of others: our family, neighborhood, and the world. For each need we say, "Lord, hear our prayer."

◆ All may add their own prayers here.

Let us pray: **Our Father . . . Amen.**

O God, during this holy season
help us to come closer to you.
Help us to fast from those things
that separate us from your love,
to give generously to others,
and to pray always.
We ask this in Christ's name.

Amen.

✚ All make the Sign of the Cross.

OPENING

Jesus instructs us about "piety" or the way we show our religiousness or reverence. We're not supposed to be showy about it. Jesus also assumes we are fasting. Fasting is how we train ourselves to put God and people before things.

✠ All make the Sign of the Cross.

In the name of the Father, and of the Son, and of the Holy Spirit. Amen.

PSALM

(For a longer psalm, see page xiv.)
Psalm 34:4–5, 6–7, 16–17, 18–19

The LORD saves the crushed in spirit.

The LORD saves the crushed in spirit.

I sought the LORD, and he answered me,
 and delivered me from all my fears.
Look to him, and be radiant;
 so your faces shall never be ashamed.

The LORD saves the crushed in spirit.

◆ All stand and sing **Praise to you, Lord Jesus Christ . . .**

GOSPEL

Matthew 6:1, 7–8, 16–18

A reading from the holy Gospel according to Matthew.

Jesus also said, "Beware of practicing your piety before others in order to be seen by them; for then you have no reward from your Father in heaven. When you are praying, do not heap up empty phrases as the Gentiles do; for they think that they will be heard because of their many words. Do not be like them, for your Father knows what you need before you ask him. And whenever you fast, do not look dismal, like the hypocrites, for they disfigure their faces so as to show others that they are fasting. Truly I tell you, they have received their reward. But when you fast, put oil on your head and wash your face, so that your fasting may be seen not by others but by your Father who is in secret; and your Father who sees in secret will reward you."

The Gospel of the Lord.

◆ All sit and observe silence.

FOR SILENT REFLECTION

Think about this silently in your heart. Why would Jesus tell us to keep our fasting and praying private or a secret?

CLOSING PRAYER

Let us pray to God for our needs and the needs of others: our family, neighborhood, and the world. For each need we say, "Lord, hear our prayer."

◆ All may add their own prayers here.

Let us pray: **Our Father . . . Amen.**

As we begin this season of Lent,
we pray that we may come closer to you,
O God.
May we be strong and steadfast during these forty days.
We ask this in Christ's name.

Amen.

✠ All make the Sign of the Cross.

PRAYER FOR
FRIDAY, FEBRUARY 28, 2020

OPENING

Isaiah speaks about what type of fast God really wants. He wants us to fast or refrain from sin and what is evil. God wants us to care for others, especially those who are poor, homeless, or hungry.

✚ All make the Sign of the Cross.

In the name of the Father, and of the Son, and of the Holy Spirit. Amen.

PSALM

(For a longer psalm, see page xiv.)
Psalm 34:4–5, 6–7, 16–17, 18–19

The Lord saves the crushed in spirit.

The Lord saves the crushed in spirit.

I sought the Lord, and he answered me,
    and delivered me from all my fears.
Look to him, and be radiant;
    so your faces shall never be ashamed.

The Lord saves the crushed in spirit.

READING

Isaiah 58:6ac, 7ab, 8a, 9–10

A reading from the Book of the prophet Isaiah.

Is not this the fast that I choose: to loose the bonds of injustice, to let the oppressed go free? Is it not to share your bread with the hungry, and bring the homeless poor into your house; when you see the naked, to cover them? Then your light shall break forth like the dawn. Then you shall call, and the Lord will answer; you shall cry for help, and he will say, Here I am. If you remove the yoke from among you, the pointing of the finger, the speaking of evil, if you offer your food to the hungry and satisfy the needs of the afflicted, then your light shall rise in the darkness and your gloom be like the noonday.

The Word of the Lord.

◆ All observe silence.

FOR SILENT REFLECTION

Think about this silently in your heart. Who is hungry for something they need, or who is hurting? How can you be a light for them?

CLOSING PRAYER

Let us pray to God for our needs and the needs of others: our family, neighborhood, and the world. For each need we say, "Lord, hear our prayer."

◆ All may add their own prayers here.

Let us pray: **Our Father . . . Amen.**

From ancient times until now, O God,
your message is clear.
We serve you by caring for those in need.
Help us to find even small ways to be just
and charitable.
We pray in the name
of Jesus Christ, our Lord.

Amen.

✚ All make the Sign of the Cross.

PRAYER FOR THE WEEK
WITH A READING FROM THE GOSPEL FOR **SUNDAY, MARCH 1, 2020**

OPENING

We have begun our the first week of Lent, our time of penance and prayer. Like Jesus we fast and we pray. These remind us that God is first in our lives. Even Jesus was tempted and had to resist temptation.

✝ All make the Sign of the Cross.

In the name of the Father, and of the Son, and of the Holy Spirit. Amen.

PSALM

(For a longer psalm, see page xiv.)
Psalm 34:4–5, 6–7, 16–17, 18–19

The Lord saves the crushed in spirit.

The Lord saves the crushed in spirit.

I sought the Lord, and he answered me,
  and delivered me from all my fears.
Look to him, and be radiant;
  so your faces shall never be ashamed.

The Lord saves the crushed in spirit.

◆ All stand and sing **Praise to you, Lord Jesus Christ . . .**

GOSPEL

Matthew 4:1–4, 8–11

A reading from the holy Gospel according to Matthew.

Jesus was led up by the Spirit into the wilderness to be tempted by the devil. He fasted forty days and forty nights, and afterwards he was famished. The tempter came and said to him, "If you are the Son of God, command these stones to become loaves of bread." But he answered, "It is written, 'One does not live by bread alone, but by every word that comes from the mouth of God.'" Again, the devil took him to a very high mountain and showed him all the kingdoms of the world and their splendor; and he said to him, "All these I will give you, if you will fall down and worship me." Jesus said to him, "Away with you, Satan! for it is written, 'Worship the Lord your God, and serve only him.'" Then the devil left him, and suddenly angels came and waited on him.

The Gospel of the Lord.

◆ All sit and observe silence.

FOR SILENT REFLECTION

Think about this silently in your heart. What can you give up this week that will make you stronger? Can you find more time to pray?

CLOSING PRAYER

Let us pray to God for our needs and the needs of others: our family, neighborhood, and the world. For each need we say, "Lord, hear our prayer."

◆ All may add their own prayers here.

Let us pray: **Our Father . . . Amen.**

Heavenly Father,
even Jesus knew temptation,
and when he overcame it,
angels came to help him.
We pray that we may overcome temptation
to do wrong
and that we might be strengthened as he was.
Through Christ our Lord.

Amen.

✝ All make the Sign of the Cross.

OPENING

This week we'll see what the Scriptures teach us about forgiveness. The Jewish prophet Nehemiah called the people to a fast to show they were sorry for their sins.

✚ All make the Sign of the Cross.

In the name of the Father, and of the Son, and of the Holy Spirit. Amen.

PSALM

(For a longer psalm, see page xiv.)
Psalm 34:4–5, 6–7, 16–17, 18–19

The LORD saves the crushed in spirit.

The LORD saves the crushed in spirit.

I sought the LORD, and he answered me,
    and delivered me from all my fears.
Look to him, and be radiant;
    so your faces shall never be ashamed.

The LORD saves the crushed in spirit.

READING

Nehemiah 9:1a, 2–3, 6ab, 9, 17c

A reading from the Book of the prophet Nehemiah.

Now on the twenty-fourth day of this month the people of Israel were assembled with fasting and in sackcloth. Then those of Israelite descent separated themselves from all foreigners, and stood and confessed their sins and the iniquities of their ancestors. They stood up in their place and read from the book of the law of the LORD their God for a fourth part of the day, and for another fourth they made confession and worshiped the LORD their God. And Ezra said: "You are the LORD, you alone. And you saw the distress of our ancestors in Egypt and heard their cry at the Red Sea. But you are a God ready to forgive, gracious and merciful, slow to anger and abounding in steadfast love, and you did not forsake them."

The Word of the Lord.

◆ All observe silence.

FOR SILENT REFLECTION

Think about this silently in your heart. For what do you need forgiveness?

CLOSING PRAYER

Let us pray to God for our needs and the needs of others: our family, neighborhood, and the world. For each need we say, "Lord, hear our prayer."

◆ All may add their own prayers here.

Let us pray: **Our Father . . . Amen.**

Forgiving Father,
we ask you to forgive us our sins,
in thought, or words, or actions.
We thank you for your mercy and goodness.
We pray in the name of Christ our Lord.

Amen.

✚ All make the Sign of the Cross.

OPENING

The Old Testament prophet Ezekiel lists all the things a righteous, or good, person does out of love for God. He says it is never too late to change from our selfish ways. God is always forgiving. St. Katharine Drexel, whose feast we celebrate today, is an American saint who founded Xavier University in New Orleans, a college to train teachers and the first Catholic American university for African Americans. Mother Drexel also founded fifty missions for Indians in the United States.

✚ All make the Sign of the Cross.

In the name of the Father, and of the Son, and of the Holy Spirit. Amen.

PSALM

(For a longer psalm, see page xiv.)
Psalm 34:4–5, 6–7, 16–17, 18–19

The LORD saves the crushed in spirit.

The LORD saves the crushed in spirit.

I sought the LORD, and he answered me,
   and delivered me from all my fears.
Look to him, and be radiant;
   so your faces shall never be ashamed.

The LORD saves the crushed in spirit.

READING

Ezekiel 18:5–6a, 7acd, 8–9, 21

A reading from the Book of the prophet Ezekiel.

If a man is righteous and does what is lawful and right—if he does not eat upon the mountains or lift up his eyes to the idols of the house of Israel, does not oppress anyone, commits no robbery, gives his bread to the hungry and covers the naked with a garment, does not take advance or accrued interest, withholds his hand from iniquity, executes true justice between contending parties, follows my statutes, and is careful to observe my ordinances, acting faithfully—such a one is righteous; he shall surely live, says the Lord GOD. But if the wicked turn away from all their sins that they have committed and keep all my statutes and do what is lawful and right, they shall surely live; they shall not die.

The Word of the Lord.

◆ All observe silence.

FOR SILENT REFLECTION

Think about this silently in your heart. Do you know someone who is a righteous person? What can you learn from her or him?

CLOSING PRAYER

Let us pray to God for our needs and the needs of others: our family, neighborhood, and the world. For each need we say, "Lord, hear our prayer."

◆ All may add their own prayers here.

Let us pray: **Our Father . . . Amen.**

During this Lenten season, O Lord,
we pray that we will do what is right.
Help us to be obedient to our parents,
kind to our classmates,
and respectful of all.
We ask this in Christ's name.

Amen.

✚ All make the Sign of the Cross.

PRAYER FOR
WEDNESDAY, MARCH 4, 2020

OPENING

Jesus teaches that we need to ask for forgiveness when we've hurt someone. When he says "brother" and "sister," Jesus is referring to everyone, not only our family members. In Christ we are all brothers and sisters. Today we remember St. Casimir. He ruled Poland and Lithuania. He understood that we are all family in Christ by caring for his people.

✚ All make the Sign of the Cross.

In the name of the Father, and of the Son, and of the Holy Spirit. Amen.

PSALM

(For a longer psalm, see page xiv.)
Psalm 34:4–5, 6–7, 16–17, 18–19

The Lord saves the crushed in spirit.

The Lord saves the crushed in spirit.

I sought the Lord, and he answered me,
    and delivered me from all my fears.
Look to him, and be radiant;
    so your faces shall never be ashamed.

The Lord saves the crushed in spirit.

◆ All stand and sing **Praise to you, Lord Jesus Christ . . .**

GOSPEL

Matthew 5:21–24

A reading from the holy Gospel according to Matthew.

Jesus said, "You have heard that it was said to those of ancient times, 'You shall not murder'; and 'whoever murders shall be liable to judgment.' But I say to you that if you are angry with a brother or sister, you will be liable to judgment; and if you insult a brother or sister,

you will be liable to the council; and if you say, 'You fool,' you will be liable to the hell of fire. So when you are offering your gift at the altar, if you remember that your brother or sister has something against you, leave your gift there before the altar and go; first be reconciled to your brother or sister, and then come and offer your gift."

The Gospel of the Lord.

◆ All sit and observe silence.

FOR SILENT REFLECTION

Think about this silently in your heart. Is there someone you need to ask to forgive you? Or is there someone you need to forgive?

CLOSING PRAYER

Let us pray to God for our needs and the needs of others: our family, neighborhood, and the world. For each need we say, "Lord, hear our prayer."

◆ All may add their own prayers here.

Let us pray: **Our Father . . . Amen.**

Loving God,
often it is hard to ask for forgiveness
and to forgive others.
Grant us the humility to ask for forgiveness
when we have sinned
and a generous heart to forgive.
Through Christ our Lord.

Amen.

✚ All make the Sign of the Cross.

OPENING

Today Jesus insists we must forgive people who have hurt us. We have to try to let go of anger, bitterness, or revenge. Jesus says to forgive seventy-seven times. The number seven stands for something perfect or complete, so seventy-seven times is a lot of forgiving!

✝ All make the Sign of the Cross.

In the name of the Father, and of the Son, and of the Holy Spirit. Amen.

PSALM

(For a longer psalm, see page xiv.)
Psalm 34:4–5, 6–7, 16–17, 18–19

The LORD saves the crushed in spirit.

The LORD saves the crushed in spirit.

I sought the LORD, and he answered me,
and delivered me from all my fears.
Look to him, and be radiant;
so your faces shall never be ashamed.

The LORD saves the crushed in spirit.

◆ All stand and sing **Praise to you, Lord Jesus Christ . . .**

GOSPEL

Matthew 18:21–27

A reading from the holy Gospel according to Matthew.

Then Peter came and said to Jesus, "Lord, if another member of the church sins against me, how often should I forgive? As many as seven times?" Jesus said to him, "Not seven times, but, I tell you, seventy-seven times. For this reason the kingdom of heaven may be compared to a king who wished to settle accounts with his slaves. When he began the reckoning, one who owed him ten thousand talents was brought to him; and, as he could not pay, his lord ordered him to be sold, together with his wife and children and all his possessions, and payment to be made. So the slave fell on his knees before him, saying, 'Have patience with me, and I will pay you everything.' And out of pity for him, the lord of that slave released him and forgave him the debt."

The Gospel of the Lord.

◆ All sit and observe silence.

FOR SILENT REFLECTION

Think about this silently in your heart. Is it easy to keep forgiving someone? Pray for the strength and courage to forgive.

CLOSING PRAYER

Let us pray to God for our needs and the needs of others: our family, neighborhood, and the world. For each need we say, "Lord, hear our prayer."

◆ All may add their own prayers here.

Let us pray: **Our Father . . . Amen.**

Gracious and forgiving Father,
it is not always easy for us to forgive
those who have hurt us.
We ask you to grant us the courage to be
generous in forgiving others.
We ask this in Christ's name.

Amen.

✝ All make the Sign of the Cross.

OPENING

Today's reading continues the story we heard yesterday. Jesus' parable teaches that because God forgives us we must do the same for others. The slave didn't do this. Thankfully, God's love for us is great and God is merciful even when we aren't.

✚ All make the Sign of the Cross.

In the name of the Father, and of the Son, and of the Holy Spirit. Amen.

PSALM

(For a longer psalm, see page xiv.)
Psalm 34:4–5, 6–7, 16–17, 18–19

The LORD saves the crushed in spirit.

The LORD saves the crushed in spirit.

I sought the LORD, and he answered me,
    and delivered me from all my fears.
Look to him, and be radiant;
    so your faces shall never be ashamed.

The LORD saves the crushed in spirit.

◆ All stand and sing **Praise to you, Lord Jesus Christ** . . .

GOSPEL

Matthew 18:28–29ab, 30–31ac, 32–34

A reading from the holy Gospel according to Matthew.

"But that same slave as he went out, came upon one of his fellow slaves who owed him a hundred denarii; and seizing him by the throat, he said, 'Pay what you owe.' Then his fellow slave fell down and pleaded with him, 'Have patience with me.' But he refused; then he went and threw him into prison until he would pay the debt. When his fellow slaves saw what had happened, they went and reported to their lord all that had taken place. Then his lord summoned him and said to him, 'You wicked slave! I forgave you all that debt because you pleaded with me. Should you not have had mercy on your fellow slave, as I had mercy on you?' And in anger his lord handed him over to be tortured until he would pay his entire debt."

The Gospel of the Lord.

◆ All sit and observe silence.

FOR SILENT REFLECTION

Think about this silently in your heart. What prevents us from forgiving someone who has hurt us?

CLOSING PRAYER

Let us pray to God for our needs and the needs of others: our family, neighborhood, and the world. For each need we say, "Lord, hear our prayer."

◆ All may add their own prayers here.

Let us pray: **Our Father . . . Amen.**

Holy God,
during this season of Lent,
help us to believe in the power of forgiveness.
May we forgive those who have offended us,
and may we ask forgiveness
when we have been the offender.
We ask this in Christ's name.

Amen.

✚ All make the Sign of the Cross.

PRAYER FOR THE WEEK

WITH A READING FROM THE GOSPEL FOR **SUNDAY, MARCH 8, 2020**

OPENING

Sometimes we have experiences when we clearly know God is present in our lives. It could be when we are praying or at Mass, in nature, or being hugged by someone we love. We call those "mountaintop experiences." Today's Gospel is about a mountaintop experiences that the disciples had.

✚ All make the Sign of the Cross.

In the name of the Father, and of the Son, and of the Holy Spirit. Amen.

PSALM

(For a longer psalm, see page xiv.)
Psalm 34:4–5, 6–7, 16–17, 18–19

The LORD saves the crushed in spirit.

The LORD saves the crushed in spirit.

I sought the LORD, and he answered me,
  and delivered me from all my fears.
Look to him, and be radiant;
  so your faces shall never be ashamed.

The LORD saves the crushed in spirit.

◆ All stand and sing **Praise to you, Lord Jesus Christ . . .**

GOSPEL

Matthew 17:1–5

A reading from the holy Gospel according to Matthew.

Jesus took with him Peter and James and his brother John and led them up a high mountain, by themselves. And he was transfigured before them, and his face shone like the sun, and his clothes became dazzling white. Suddenly there appeared to them Moses and Elijah, talking with him. Then Peter said to Jesus, "Lord, it is good for us to be here; if you wish, I will make three dwellings here, one for you, one for Moses, and one for Elijah." While he was still speaking, suddenly a bright cloud overshadowed them, and from the cloud a voice said, "This is my Son, the Beloved; with him I am well pleased; listen to him!"

The Gospel of the Lord.

◆ All sit and observe silence.

FOR SILENT REFLECTION

Think about this silently in your heart. When did you feel God particularly present in your life?

CLOSING PRAYER

Let us pray to God for our needs and the needs of others: our family, neighborhood, and the world. For each need we say, "Lord, hear our prayer."

◆ All may add their own prayers here.

Let us pray: **Our Father . . . Amen.**

Almighty God,
help us to trust that you are present
and with us always.
We ask this in the name of your Son,
Jesus Christ our Lord.

Amen.

✚ All make the Sign of the Cross.

OPENING

Lent gives us time to think about how we can live our lives more fully in the way that Jesus taught us to live. No matter what we have done, Jesus always forgives us if we say we are sorry. Today's reading is a parable that Jesus told to explain that God's love and forgiveness are given to everyone. Today we remember St. Frances of Rome, a woman of wealth who lived a life faithful to God and in service to others. She cared for the poor and ill in Rome.

✝ All make the Sign of the Cross.

In the name of the Father, and of the Son, and of the Holy Spirit. Amen.

PSALM

(For a longer psalm, see page xiv.)
Psalm 34:4–5, 6–7, 16–17, 18–19

The LORD saves the crushed in spirit.

The LORD saves the crushed in spirit.

I sought the LORD, and he answered me,
 and delivered me from all my fears.
Look to him, and be radiant;
 so your faces shall never be ashamed.

The LORD saves the crushed in spirit.

◆ All stand and sing **Praise to you, Lord Jesus Christ . . .**

GOSPEL

Luke 15:1–7

A reading from the holy Gospel according to Luke.

Now all the tax collectors and sinners were coming near to listen to Jesus. And the Pharisees and the scribes were grumbling and saying, "This fellow welcomes sinners and eats with them." So Jesus told them this parable: "Which one of you, having a hundred sheep and losing one of them, does not leave the ninety-nine in the wilderness and go after the one that is lost until he finds it? When he has found it, he lays it on his shoulders and rejoices. And when he comes home, he calls together his friends and neighbors, saying to them, 'Rejoice with me, for I have found my sheep that was lost.' Just so, I tell you, there will be more joy in heaven over one sinner who repents than over ninety-nine righteous persons who need no repentance."

The Gospel of the Lord.

◆ All sit and observe silence.

FOR SILENT REFLECTION

Think about this silently in your heart. Why do you think there is such great joy when the lost sheep is found?

CLOSING PRAYER

Let us pray to God for our needs and the needs of others: our family, neighborhood, and the world. For each need we say, "Lord, hear our prayer."

◆ All may add their own prayers here.

Let us pray: **Our Father . . . Amen.**

How great is your care for each of us, O God.
You call us by name
and search for us.
Help us to know the sound of your voice
and to respond when you call.
We ask this in the name of our Good
Shepherd, Jesus Christ our Lord.

Amen.

✝ All make the Sign of the Cross.

OPENING

In Jesus' time, tax collectors were considered sinners because the monies they collected went to the occupying Romans. But Jesus befriended them. Today's reading is another parable that Jesus told to explain how precious all God's people are and how happy God is when anyone changes their life to do better.

✚ All make the Sign of the Cross.

In the name of the Father, and of the Son, and of the Holy Spirit. Amen.

PSALM

(For a longer psalm, see page xiv.)
Psalm 34:4–5, 6–7, 16–17, 18–19

The LORD saves the crushed in spirit.

The LORD saves the crushed in spirit.

I sought the LORD, and he answered me,
 and delivered me from all my fears.
Look to him, and be radiant;
 so your faces shall never be ashamed.

The LORD saves the crushed in spirit.

◆ All stand and sing **Praise to you, Lord Jesus Christ . . .**

GOSPEL

Luke 15:1–3, 8–10

A reading from the holy Gospel according to Luke.

Now all the tax collectors and sinners were coming near to listen to him. And the Pharisees and the scribes were grumbling and saying, "This fellow welcomes sinners and eats with them." So he told them this parable: "What woman having ten silver coins, if she loses one of them, does not light a lamp, sweep the house, and search carefully until she finds it? When she has found it, she calls together her friends and neighbors, saying, 'Rejoice with me, for I have found the coin that I had lost.' Just so, I tell you, there is joy in the presence of the angels of God over one sinner who repents."

The Gospel of the Lord.

◆ All sit and observe silence.

FOR SILENT REFLECTION

Think about this silently in your heart. Can you say a prayer of thanksgiving for God's love and forgiveness?

CLOSING PRAYER

Let us pray to God for our needs and the needs of others: our family, neighborhood, and the world. For each need we say, "Lord, hear our prayer."

◆ All may add their own prayers here.

Let us pray: **Our Father . . . Amen.**

Loving God,
you care for each of us.
When we are lost, you search for us.
When we come back to you, you rejoice.
May we always stay close to you.
We ask this in Christ's name.

Amen.

✚ All make the Sign of the Cross.

OPENING

Over the next three days we will hear the parable of the forgiving father, sometimes called the prodigal son. The word *prodigal* means "wasteful or reckless with money."

✦ All make the Sign of the Cross.

In the name of the Father, and of the Son, and of the Holy Spirit. Amen.

PSALM

(For a longer psalm, see page xiv.)
Psalm 34:4–5, 6–7, 16–17, 18–19

The LORD saves the crushed in spirit.

The LORD saves the crushed in spirit.

I sought the LORD, and he answered me,
and delivered me from all my fears.
Look to him, and be radiant;
so your faces shall never be ashamed.

The LORD saves the crushed in spirit.

◆ All stand and sing **Praise to you, Lord Jesus Christ . . .**

GOSPEL

Luke 15:11–13a, 14ac, 15–17a, 18–19

A reading from the holy Gospel according to Luke.

Jesus said, "There was a man who had two sons. The younger of them said to his father, 'Father, give me the share of the property that will belong to me.' So the father divided his property between them. A few days later the younger son gathered all he had and traveled to a distant country. When he had spent everything, he began to be in need. So he went and hired himself out to one of the citizens of that country, who sent him to his fields to feed the pigs. He would gladly have filled himself with the pods that the pigs were eating; and no one gave him anything. But when he came to himself he said, 'I will get up and go to my father, and I will say to him, "Father, I have sinned against heaven and before you; I am no longer worthy to be called your son; treat me like one of your hired hands."'"

The Gospel of the Lord.

◆ All sit and observe silence.

FOR SILENT REFLECTION

Think about this silently in your heart. What do you think of the son in the part of the story we heard today?

CLOSING PRAYER

Let us pray to God for our needs and the needs of others: our family, neighborhood, and the world. For each need we say, "Lord, hear our prayer."

◆ All may add their own prayers here.

Let us pray: **Our Father . . . Amen.**

God, our Father,
sometimes we are like the son
in today's Gospel.
When we wander away from you,
help us to return.
We trust you will welcome us back always.
We pray through Christ our Lord.

Amen.

✦ All make the Sign of the Cross.

OPENING

Today we continue the story of the forgiving father, or the prodigal son. Remember, the younger son took his inheritance from his father and wasted it. Then he had to take care of pigs, which was considered one of the worst jobs. He was so unhappy that he decided to go back home to his father and apologize.

✚ All make the Sign of the Cross.

In the name of the Father, and of the Son, and of the Holy Spirit. Amen.

PSALM

(For a longer psalm, see page xiv.)
Psalm 34:4–5, 6–7, 16–17, 18–19

The LORD saves the crushed in spirit.

The LORD saves the crushed in spirit.

I sought the LORD, and he answered me,
  and delivered me from all my fears.
Look to him, and be radiant;
  so your faces shall never be ashamed.

The LORD saves the crushed in spirit.

◆ All stand and sing **Praise to you, Lord Jesus Christ . . .**

GOSPEL

Luke 15:20–24

A reading from the holy Gospel according to Luke.

Jesus said, "So the son set off and went to his father. But while he was still far off, his father saw him and was filled with compassion; he ran and put his arms around his son and kissed him. Then the son said to him, 'Father, I have sinned against heaven and before you; I am no longer worthy to be called your son.' But the father said to his slaves, 'Quickly, bring out a robe—the best one—and put it on him; put a ring on his finger and sandals on his feet. And get the fatted calf and kill it, and let us eat and celebrate; for this son of mine was dead and is alive again; he was lost and is found!' And they began to celebrate."

The Gospel of the Lord.

◆ All sit and observe silence.

FOR SILENT REFLECTION

Think about this silently in your heart. What do you think of the father's response to the son when he returned?

CLOSING PRAYER

Let us pray to God for our needs and the needs of others: our family, neighborhood, and the world. For each need we say, "Lord, hear our prayer."

◆ All may add their own prayers here.

Let us pray: **Our Father . . . Amen.**

O compassionate God,
we pray that we will grow closer to you this Lent.
Help us to fast from all that separates us from you.
We ask this in Christ's name.

Amen.

✚ All make the Sign of the Cross.

PRAYER FOR
FRIDAY, MARCH 13, 2020

OPENING

Jesus told parables to teach us about the nature of God. Jesus' parable about the father and his sons reveals something about God. There is another part of the parable that we will hear today. It is about the older son who stayed home with his father.

✚ All make the Sign of the Cross.

In the name of the Father, and of the Son, and of the Holy Spirit. Amen.

PSALM

(For a longer psalm, see page xiv.)
Psalm 34:4–5, 6–7, 16–17, 18–19

The LORD saves the crushed in spirit.

The LORD saves the crushed in spirit.

I sought the LORD, and he answered me,
  and delivered me from all my fears.
Look to him, and be radiant;
  so your faces shall never be ashamed.

The LORD saves the crushed in spirit.

◆ All stand and sing **Praise to you, Lord Jesus Christ** . . .

GOSPEL

Luke 15:25–29, 31–32

A reading from the holy Gospel according to Luke.

"Now the elder son was in the field; and when he came and approached the house, he heard music and dancing. He called one of the slaves and asked what was going on. The slave replied, 'Your brother has come, and your father has killed the fatted calf, because he has got him back safe and sound.' Then the older brother became angry and refused to go in. His father came out and began to plead with him. The father said to him, 'Son, you are always with me, and all that is mine is yours. But we had to celebrate and rejoice, because this brother of yours was dead and has come to life; he was lost and has been found.'"

The Gospel of the Lord.

◆ All sit and observe silence.

FOR SILENT REFLECTION

Think about this silently in your heart. What do you think about how the older son felt and about what the father said to him?

CLOSING PRAYER

Let us pray to God for our needs and the needs of others: our family, neighborhood, and the world. For each need we say, "Lord, hear our prayer."

◆ All may add their own prayers here.

Let us pray: **Our Father . . . Amen.**

Loving God,
like the older brother we sometimes feel angry or envious of others.
Help us to know that you love each of us and that we are all your children.
We pray through Christ our Lord.

Amen.

✚ All make the Sign of the Cross.

OPENING

In Jesus' time, Jews hated people from Samaria and had nothing to do with them. In today's Gospel, Jesus teaches that God's love and forgiveness are for everyone.

✚ All make the Sign of the Cross.

In the name of the Father, and of the Son, and of the Holy Spirit. Amen.

PSALM

(For a longer psalm, see page xiv.)
Psalm 34:4–5, 6–7, 16–17, 18–19

The LORD saves the crushed in spirit.

The LORD saves the crushed in spirit.

I sought the LORD, and he answered me,
 and delivered me from all my fears.
Look to him, and be radiant;
 so your faces shall never be ashamed.

The LORD saves the crushed in spirit.

◆ All stand and sing **Praise to you, Lord Jesus Christ . . .**

GOSPEL

John 4:7, 9ab, 10–14a

A reading from the holy Gospel according to John.

A Samaritan woman came to draw water, and Jesus said to her, "Give me a drink." The Samaritan woman said to him, "How is it that you, a Jew, ask a drink of me, a woman of Samaria?" Jesus answered her, "If you knew the gift of God, and who it is that is saying to you, 'Give me a drink,' you would have asked him, and he would have given you living water." The woman said to him, "Sir, you have no bucket, and the well is deep. Where do you get that living water? Are you greater than our ancestor Jacob, who gave us the well, and with his sons and his flocks drank from it?" Jesus said to her, "Everyone who drinks of this water will be thirsty again, but those who drink of the water that I will give them will never be thirsty."

The Gospel of the Lord.

◆ All sit and observe silence.

FOR SILENT REFLECTION

Think about this silently in your heart. Jesus is like life-giving water. Receiving the Body of Christ in Holy Communion keeps us spiritually alive.

CLOSING PRAYER

Let us pray to God for our needs and the needs of others: our family, neighborhood, and the world. For each need we say, "Lord, hear our prayer."

◆ All may add their own prayers here.

Let us pray: **Our Father . . . Amen.**

God our Creator,
you sent your Son Jesus
to show us the way to you.
May our thirst for you be quenched
by the Living Water that is Christ Jesus,
in whose name we pray.

Amen.

✚ All make the Sign of the Cross.

PRAYER FOR
MONDAY, MARCH 16, 2020

OPENING

The Sadducees and the Pharisees were the ruling class and religious leaders of Israel. They taught the importance of religious law. In today's reading, the lawyer who questioned Jesus was really trying to trip him up because to choose one law as the greatest would be a challenge to those who chose another law as greatest. Jesus did not choose any law that was written at the time. He said the greatest rule is the love of God and love of neighbor on which all religious law is built.

✛ All make the Sign of the Cross.

In the name of the Father, and of the Son, and of the Holy Spirit. Amen.

PSALM

(For a longer psalm, see page xiv.)
Psalm 34:4–5, 6–7, 16–17, 18–19

The Lord saves the crushed in spirit.

The Lord saves the crushed in spirit.

I sought the Lord, and he answered me,
  and delivered me from all my fears.
Look to him, and be radiant;
  so your faces shall never be ashamed.

The Lord saves the crushed in spirit.

◆ All stand and sing **Praise to you, Lord Jesus Christ . . .**

GOSPEL

Matthew 22:34–40

A reading from the holy Gospel according to Matthew.

When the Pharisees heard that Jesus had silenced the Sadducees, they gathered together, and one of them, a lawyer, asked him a question to test him. "Teacher, which commandment in the law is the greatest?" He said to him, "'You shall love the Lord your God with all your heart, and with all your soul, and with all your mind.' This is the greatest and first commandment. And a second is like it: 'You shall love your neighbour as yourself.' On these two commandments hang all the law and the prophets."

The Gospel of the Lord.

◆ All sit and observe silence.

FOR SILENT REFLECTION

Think about this silently in your heart. How do you follow the two greatest commandments?

CLOSING PRAYER

Let us pray to God for our needs and the needs of others: our family, neighborhood, and the world. For each need we say, "Lord, hear our prayer."

◆ All may add their own prayers here.

Let us pray: **Our Father . . . Amen.**

Once again, O God,
you call us to love.
During this Lenten season,
help us to grow in love for you,
and to treat our neighbors
as we wish to be treated.
We pray in the name of Jesus Christ, our Lord.

Amen.

✛ All make the Sign of the Cross.

OPENING

The traditional religious laws of Jesus' time focused on rules about what you ate, or how you dressed, or when you prayed. Jesus had a different focus, as we will hear today. Today we celebrate the Irish saint, Patrick. He is revered in Ireland because he converted the people there to Christianity.

✝ All make the Sign of the Cross.

In the name of the Father, and of the Son, and of the Holy Spirit. Amen.

PSALM
(For a longer psalm, see page xiv.)
Psalm 34:4–5, 6–7, 16–17, 18–19

The LORD saves the crushed in spirit.

The LORD saves the crushed in spirit.

I sought the LORD, and he answered me,
    and delivered me from all my fears.
Look to him, and be radiant;
    so your faces shall never be ashamed.

The LORD saves the crushed in spirit.

◆ All stand and sing **Praise to you, Lord Jesus Christ . . .**

GOSPEL
Matthew 25:34–37, 40

A reading from the holy Gospel according to Matthew.

The king will say to those at his right hand, "Come, you that are blessed by my Father, inherit the kingdom prepared for you from the foundation of the world; for I was hungry and you gave me food, I was thirsty and you gave me something to drink, I was a stranger and you welcomed me, I was naked and you gave me clothing, I was sick and you took care of me, I was in prison and you visited me." Then the righteous will answer him, "Lord, when was it that we saw you hungry and gave you food, or thirsty and gave you something to drink?" And the king will answer them, "Truly I tell you, just as you did it to one of the least of these who are members of my family, you did it to me."

The Gospel of the Lord.

◆ All sit and observe silence.

FOR SILENT REFLECTION

Think about this silently in your heart. How does God want us to treat those who have less than we do?

CLOSING PRAYER

Let us pray to God for our needs and the needs of others: our family, neighborhood, and the world. For each need we say, "Lord, hear our prayer."

◆ All may add their own prayers here.

Let us pray: **Our Father . . . Amen.**

God of love and compassion,
in caring for others we honor you.
May we each know how to respond
to the needs of those who are suffering.
We ask this in Christ's name.

Amen.

✝ All make the Sign of the Cross.

PRAYER SERVICE
MEMORIAL OF ST. PATRICK

Prepare six leaders for this service. The third reader will need a Bible for the Gospel passage and may need help finding it and practicing. After the story of St. Patrick, you may wish to begin by singing "Lord of All Hopefulness," and end with "Christ Be Beside Me" (to the tune of "Morning Has Broken") or "The Summons." If there will be singing, prepare a song leader.

◆ All make the Sign of the Cross.

In the name of the Father, and of the Son, and of the Holy Spirit. Amen.

FIRST LEADER:

Praise be to God,
who in every age sends great missionaries
    like St. Patrick
to preach the Good News of Jesus Christ!

ALL: Amen.

Listen now to the story of St. Patrick, who lived in the fifth century: As a teen, St. Patrick was kidnapped from Scotland and sold as a slave in Ireland. Several years later, with God's help, he escaped to Britain, where he studied to become a priest and later was ordained a bishop. Then he went back to Ireland and brought the faith of Jesus to all the Irish people. He helped them believe that God didn't live in the trees of the forest, but in the hearts of all people.

SONG LEADER:

Please join in singing our opening song.

SECOND LEADER:
Let us pray:
Holy Trinity, one God in three persons,
we thank you for sending us holy men
     and women
who help people to know you.
May we always look for guides who will
     give us a deeper knowledge of
     your mysteries.
We ask this through Christ our Lord.

ALL: Amen.

◆ All stand and sing **Praise to you,
Lord Jesus Christ** . . .

THIRD LEADER: Matthew 28:18–20
A reading from the holy Gospel according
to Matthew.

◆ Read the Gospel passage from the Bible.

The Gospel of the Lord.

◆ All observe silence.

FOURTH LEADER:
Let us bring our hopes and needs to God as
we pray, "Lord, hear our prayer."

For all the children of the world, may we
find good guides and models of faith. May
we develop our talents and use them wisely,
we pray to the Lord.

For our Irish ancestors and all those who
came before us. May we live the faith they
passed on to us and treasure the heritage they
have given us, we pray to the Lord.

For the homeless and the hungry, for those
who are sick or suffering in any way, and for
those who have died, we pray to the Lord.

FIFTH LEADER:
Let us pray as Jesus taught us:
Our Father . . . Amen.

◆ Pause, and then say:

Let us offer one another a sign of
Christ's peace.

◆ All offer one another a sign of peace.

SIXTH LEADER:
Let us pray:
God of our ancestors,
give us the strength and courage
     of St. Patrick
so that we may bring the love and joy
     of your Kingdom
to all the world.
We ask this through Christ our Lord.

ALL: Amen.

✝ All make the Sign of the Cross.

**In the name of the Father, and of the
Son, and of the Holy Spirit. Amen.**

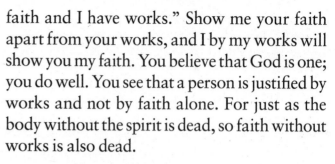

OPENING

Jesus said the greatest commandment is to love God and love your neighbor as yourself. In today's reading, St. Paul says that it is not enough to just have faith—to believe in the teachings of Jesus. We must prove that we believe by our actions. The word *works* means "actions." St. Cyril of Jerusalem, whose memorial we celebrate today, sold gifts from the emperor to raise money for the poor. He was well loved for his charity and generosity.

✛ All make the Sign of the Cross.

In the name of the Father, and of the Son, and of the Holy Spirit. Amen.

PSALM

(For a longer psalm, see page xiv.)
Psalm 34:4–5, 6–7, 16–17, 18–19

The LORD saves the crushed in spirit.

The LORD saves the crushed in spirit.

I sought the LORD, and he answered me,
   and delivered me from all my fears.
Look to him, and be radiant;
   so your faces shall never be ashamed.

The LORD saves the crushed in spirit.

READING

James 2:14–19a, 24, 26

A reading from the Letter of James.

What good is it, my brothers and sisters, if you say you have faith but do not have works? Can faith save you? If a brother or sister is naked and lacks daily food, and one of you says to them, "Go in peace; keep warm and eat your fill," and yet you do not supply their bodily needs, what is the good of that? So faith by itself, if it has no works, is dead. But someone will say, "You have faith and I have works." Show me your faith apart from your works, and I by my works will show you my faith. You believe that God is one; you do well. You see that a person is justified by works and not by faith alone. For just as the body without the spirit is dead, so faith without works is also dead.

The Word of the Lord.

◆ All observe silence.

FOR SILENT REFLECTION

Think about this silently in your heart. How will you show your faith by what you do?

CLOSING PRAYER

Let us pray to God for our needs and the needs of others: our family, neighborhood, and the world. For each need we say, "Lord, hear our prayer."

◆ All may add their own prayers here.

Let us pray: **Our Father . . . Amen.**

Again, O God,
we hear of your command to help others,
especially those who are in need.
May we be generous and respond to them
as best as we can.
We ask this through our Lord, Jesus Christ.

Amen.

✛ All make the Sign of the Cross.

OPENING

We hear about the Beatitudes in today's Gospel. The word *beatitude* means "to be blessed." Jesus is teaching his disciples a way of living that will deepen their relationship with God. The words *poor in spirit* and *meek* mean to be humble, not self-centered or boastful. *Righteousness* means to want what is fair and just. *Merciful* means to be kind and forgiving. Today we celebrate the Solemnity of St. Joseph, a righteous man who was the husband of Mary and raised Jesus.

✝ All make the Sign of the Cross.

In the name of the Father, and of the Son, and of the Holy Spirit. Amen.

PSALM

(For a longer psalm, see page xiv.)
Psalm 34:4–5, 6–7, 16–17, 18–19

The LORD saves the crushed in spirit.

The LORD saves the crushed in spirit.

I sought the LORD, and he answered me,
  and delivered me from all my fears.
Look to him, and be radiant;
  so your faces shall never be ashamed.

The LORD saves the crushed in spirit.

◆ All stand and sing **Praise to you, Lord Jesus Christ** . . .

GOSPEL

Matthew 5:2–9

A reading from the holy Gospel according to Matthew.

Jesus began to speak to his disciples, and taught them, saying: "Blessed are the poor in spirit, for theirs is the kingdom of heaven.

Blessed are those who mourn, for they will be comforted. Blessed are the meek, for they will inherit the earth. Blessed are those who hunger and thirst for righteousness, for they will be filled. Blessed are the merciful, for they will receive mercy. Blessed are the pure in heart, for they will see God. Blessed are the peacemakers, for they will be called children of God."

The Gospel of the Lord.

◆ All sit and observe silence.

FOR SILENT REFLECTION

Think about this silently in your heart. Which of the Beatitudes can you act upon today? How?

CLOSING PRAYER

Let us pray to God for our needs and the needs of others: our family, neighborhood, and the world. For each need we say, "Lord, hear our prayer."

◆ All may add their own prayers here.

Let us pray: **Our Father . . . Amen.**

O God, during this holy season
help us to come closer to you.
Help us to fast from those things
that separate us from your love,
to give generously to others,
and to pray always.
We ask this in Christ's name.

Amen.

✝ All make the Sign of the Cross.

PRAYER SERVICE
SOLEMNITY OF ST. JOSEPH

Prepare six leaders for this service. The third leader will need a Bible for the passage from Matthew. Take time to help the third leader practice the readings. You may wish to sing "You Are the Light of the World," "Blest Are They," or "We Are Called," as opening or closing songs. If the group will sing, prepare someone to lead.

FIRST LEADER:

Today we remember St. Joseph, the husband of Mary and the foster father of Jesus here on earth. At several key times in his life, St. Joseph listened and followed special messengers that God directed to this humble carpenter. St. Joseph's faith led him to marry his fiancée, even though she became pregnant in a divinely inspired way. He courageously took them to Egypt to escape Herod's wrath. And St. Joseph raised Jesus as his own son, guiding his growth.

✚ All make the Sign of the Cross.

In the name of the Father, and of the Son, and of the Holy Spirit. Amen.

Let us remember St. Joseph as we begin by singing the opening song.

SONG LEADER:

◆ Gesture for all to stand, and lead the first few verses of the song.

SECOND LEADER:

Let us pray:
Almighty Father,
may we look to St. Joseph as our guide
as he responded to your call to be
a devoted husband and father.

We pray with him to your Son Jesus,
our Lord and Savior,
in union with the Holy Spirit.

Amen.

◆ Remain standing and sing **Praise to you,
Lord Jesus Christ** . . .

THIRD LEADER: Matthew 2:13–15
A reading from the holy Gospel according
to Matthew.

◆ Read the Gospel passage from the Bible.

The Gospel of the Lord.

◆ All remain standing and observe silence.

FOURTH LEADER:
Let us bring our hopes and needs to God as
we pray, Lord, hear our prayer.

For the courage to live our faith
through word and action
as St. Joseph did throughout his days,
we pray to the Lord.

For all who are struggling with
tough decisions in life,
may they look to St. Joseph as
a brave friend,
we pray to the Lord.

For all married couples,
may they continue to be an example
of the love and devotion that
St. Joseph and Mary shared,
we pray to the Lord.

For all fathers
and those who nurture others.
Help us to respect and protect life
from conception until natural death,
we pray to the Lord.

May we have the conviction
to lead the way, as St. Joseph did
to hope and the promise
of new life through Jesus Christ,
we pray to the Lord.

FIFTH LEADER:
Let us pray as Jesus taught us:

Our Father . . . Amen.

◆ Pause, and then say:

Let us offer one another the sign of
Christ's peace.

◆ All offer one another a sign of peace.

SIXTH LEADER:
Let us pray:
Heavenly Father,
your servant St. Joseph
was a man of great faith.
He listened to you in prayer
and to angels whom you sent
in dreams.
He is a symbol for courage
in following God's will.
May we look to him
in times of trouble or doubt.
We ask this through Christ our Lord.

ALL: Amen.

✝ All make the Sign of the Cross.

PRAYER FOR
FRIDAY, MARCH 20, 2020

OPENING

Today's Gospel reading is the parable of the true vine. Many of the stories or parables that Jesus told are metaphors. It sounds like the story is about one thing, but Jesus is really talking about something else. Jesus' parables teach us about the nature of God. The word *abide* means "to stay" or "remain."

✛ All make the Sign of the Cross.

In the name of the Father, and of the Son, and of the Holy Spirit. Amen.

PSALM

(For a longer psalm, see page xiv.)
Psalm 34:4–5, 6–7, 16–17, 18–19

The LORD saves the crushed in spirit.

The LORD saves the crushed in spirit.

I sought the LORD, and he answered me,
    and delivered me from all my fears.
Look to him, and be radiant;
    so your faces shall never be ashamed.

The LORD saves the crushed in spirit.

◆ All stand and sing **Praise to you, Lord Jesus Christ . . .**

GOSPEL

John 15:1–6a, 7

A reading from the holy Gospel according to John.

Jesus said, "I am the true vine, and my Father is the vinegrower. He removes every branch in me that bears no fruit. Every branch that bears fruit he prunes to make it bear more fruit. You have already been cleansed by the word that I have spoken to you. Abide in me as I abide in you. Just as the branch cannot bear fruit by itself unless it abides in the vine, neither can you unless you abide in me. I am the vine, you are the branches. Those who abide in me and I in them bear much fruit, because apart from me you can do nothing. Whoever does not abide in me is thrown away like a branch and withers. If you abide in me, and my words abide in you, ask for whatever you wish, and it will be done for you."

The Gospel of the Lord.

◆ All sit and observe silence.

FOR SILENT REFLECTION

Think about this silently in your heart. We are like leaves on the vine. What helps us to stay attached to the vine that is Jesus?

CLOSING PRAYER

Let us pray to God for our needs and the needs of others: our family, neighborhood, and the world. For each need we say, "Lord, hear our prayer."

◆ All may add their own prayers here.

Let us pray: **Our Father . . . Amen.**

Gracious God,
show us your mercy and forgive us
when we do not bear good fruit.
We thank you for the gift of your Son,
the True Vine,
and by your grace we abide in him,
in whose name we pray.

Amen.

✛ All make the Sign of the Cross.

OPENING

On this fourth Sunday of Lent, Jesus teaches that sickness is not a result of sin. This was a common belief in his time. Jesus heals the blind man and gives him his sight. We are also called to be healers in our world.

✚ All make the Sign of the Cross.

In the name of the Father, and of the Son, and of the Holy Spirit. Amen.

PSALM

(For a longer psalm, see page xiv.)
Psalm 34:4–5, 6–7, 16–17, 18–19

The LORD saves the crushed in spirit.

The LORD saves the crushed in spirit.

I sought the LORD, and he answered me,
  and delivered me from all my fears.
Look to him, and be radiant;
  so your faces shall never be ashamed.

The LORD saves the crushed in spirit.

◆ All stand and sing **Praise to you, Lord Jesus Christ . . .**

GOSPEL

John 9:1–7

A reading from the holy Gospel according to John.

As he walked along, he saw a man blind from birth. His disciples asked him, "Rabbi, who sinned, this man or his parents, that he was born blind?" Jesus answered, "Neither this man nor his parents sinned; he was born blind so that God's works might be revealed in him. We must work the works of him who sent me while it is day; night is coming when no one can work. As long as I am in the world, I am the light of the world." When he had said this, he spat on the ground and made mud with the saliva and spread the mud on the man's eyes, saying to him, "Go, wash in the pool of Siloam" (which means Sent). Then he went and washed and came back able to see.

The Gospel of the Lord.

◆ All sit and observe silence.

FOR SILENT REFLECTION

Think about this silently in your heart. How can you be a person who heals those who are hurting in some way?

CLOSING PRAYER

Let us pray to God for our needs and the needs of others: our family, neighborhood, and the world. For each need we say, "Lord, hear our prayer."

◆ All may add their own prayers here.

Let us pray: **Our Father . . . Amen.**

Good and gracious God,
may we follow Jesus.
May we be a light that shows
your goodness.
May we be a healing presence
to those who are suffering.
We ask this in Christ's name.

Amen.

✚ All make the Sign of the Cross.

PRAYER FOR
MONDAY, MARCH 23, 2020

OPENING

This week we will look at the ways Jesus is present in our lives. Today's reading says Jesus is our "advocate"; that is, someone who supports and defends us. Even though we fail to be our best selves at times, Jesus will always stay with us and help us get back on track. Remember that we are called to be like Jesus in our actions.

✛ All make the Sign of the Cross.

In the name of the Father, and of the Son, and of the Holy Spirit. Amen.

PSALM

(For a longer psalm, see page xiv.)
Psalm 34:4–5, 6–7, 16–17, 18–19

The LORD saves the crushed in spirit.

The LORD saves the crushed in spirit.

I sought the LORD, and he answered me,
 and delivered me from all my fears.
Look to him, and be radiant;
 so your faces shall never be ashamed.

The LORD saves the crushed in spirit.

READING

1 John 1:5; 2:1–5

A reading from the First Letter of John.

This is the message we have heard from Jesus and proclaim to you, that God is light and in him there is no darkness at all. My little children, I am writing these things to you so that you may not sin. But if anyone does sin, we have an advocate with the Father, Jesus Christ the righteous; and he is the atoning sacrifice for our sins, and not for ours only but also for the sins of the whole world. Now by this we may be sure that we know him, if we obey his commandments. Whoever says, "I have come to know him," but does not obey his commandments, is a liar, and in such a person the truth does not exist; but whoever obeys his word, truly in this person the love of God has reached perfection. By this we may be sure that we are in him.

The Word of the Lord.

◆ All observe silence.

FOR SILENT REFLECTION

Think about this silently in your heart. Who needs your support, encouragement, or defense this week?

CLOSING PRAYER

Let us pray to God for our needs and the needs of others: our family, neighborhood, and the world. For each need we say, "Lord, hear our prayer."

◆ All may add their own prayers here.

Let us pray: **Our Father . . . Amen.**

O God,
as we continue on our Lenten journey,
we pray that we may be faithful
to your commands.
By our fasting, prayer, and almsgiving,
may we be bearers of Christ's light.
We ask this in the name of your Son,
Jesus Christ our Lord.

Amen.

✛ All make the Sign of the Cross.

OPENING

Jesus taught people who were often excluded. Jesus' disciples were shocked that he taught the Samaritan woman as if she were a disciple too. Jesus wants all people to know God better. God's love is for everyone, not just for those who are like us.

✦ All make the Sign of the Cross.

In the name of the Father, and of the Son, and of the Holy Spirit. Amen.

PSALM

(For a longer psalm, see page xiv.)
Psalm 34:4–5, 6–7, 16–17, 18–19

The LORD saves the crushed in spirit.

The LORD saves the crushed in spirit.

I sought the LORD, and he answered me,
and delivered me from all my fears.
Look to him, and be radiant;
so your faces shall never be ashamed.

The LORD saves the crushed in spirit.

◆ All stand and sing **Praise to you, Lord Jesus Christ . . .**

GOSPEL

John 4:7, 9ab, 10–12a, 13–14

A reading from the holy Gospel according to John.

A Samaritan woman came to draw water, and Jesus said to her, "Give me a drink." The Samaritan woman said to him, "How is it that you, a Jew, ask a drink of me, a woman of Samaria?" Jesus answered her, "If you knew the gift of God, and who it is that is saying to you, 'Give me a drink,' you would have asked him, and he would have given you living water."

The woman said to him, "Sir, you have no bucket, and the well is deep. Where do you get that living water? Are you greater than our ancestor Jacob, who gave us the well?" Jesus said to her, "Everyone who drinks of this water will be thirsty again, but those who drink of the water that I will give them will never be thirsty. The water that I will give will become in them a spring of water gushing up to eternal life."

The Gospel of the Lord.

◆ All sit and observe silence.

FOR SILENT REFLECTION

Think about this silently in your heart. What would you ask Jesus if you met him at the well like the Samaritan woman did?

CLOSING PRAYER

Let us pray to God for our needs and the needs of others: our family, neighborhood, and the world. For each need we say, "Lord, hear our prayer."

◆ All may add their own prayers here.

Let us pray: **Our Father . . . Amen.**

Generous and loving God,
Jesus showed us that your love is
for all people in all times.
We thank you and praise you.
We pray to you in Christ Jesus' name.

Amen.

✦ All make the Sign of the Cross.

PRAYER FOR
WEDNESDAY, MARCH 25, 2020

OPENING

Today we celebrate the Solemnity of the Annunciation of the Lord, when the angel Gabriel came to Mary and asked her to be the mother of the Savior. In this we see how God prepared for his Son, Jesus, to be born into the world.

✚ All make the Sign of the Cross.

In the name of the Father, and of the Son, and of the Holy Spirit. Amen.

PSALM

(For a longer psalm, see page xiv.)
Psalm 34:4–5, 6–7, 16–17, 18–19

The Lord saves the crushed in spirit.

The Lord saves the crushed in spirit.

I sought the Lord, and he answered me,
    and delivered me from all my fears.
Look to him, and be radiant;
    so your faces shall never be ashamed.

The Lord saves the crushed in spirit.

◆ All stand and sing **Praise to you, Lord Jesus Christ** . . .

GOSPEL

Luke 1:26–33

A reading of the holy Gospel according to Luke.

In the sixth month the angel Gabriel was sent by God to a town in Galilee called Nazareth, to a virgin engaged to a man whose name was Joseph, of the house of David. The virgin's name was Mary. And he came to her and said, "Greetings, favored one! The Lord is with you." But she was much perplexed by his words and pondered what sort of greeting this might be. The angel said to her, "Do not be afraid, Mary, for you have found favor with God. And now you will conceive in your womb and bear a son, and you will call him Jesus. He will be great, and will be called the Son of the Most High, and the Lord God will give to him the throne of his ancestor David. He will reign over the house of Jacob forever, and of his kingdom there will be no end."

The Gospel of the Lord.

◆ All sit and observe silence.

FOR SILENT REFLECTION

Think about this silently in your heart. The angel Gabriel told Mary not to be afraid. Can you find strength in those words when you have to be courageous?

CLOSING PRAYER

Let us pray to God for our needs and the needs of others: our family, neighborhood, and the world. For each need we say, "Lord, hear our prayer."

◆ All may add their own prayers here.

Let us pray: **Our Father . . . Amen.**

Most holy God, because you loved the world you sent your Son Jesus to become one of us.
We thank you for Mother Mary,
who is a model for us.
May we trust in you
and always try to do your will.
We ask this in Christ's name.

Amen.

✚ All make the Sign of the Cross.

OPENING

Jesus has been our advocate, our teacher, and our healer. Jesus also assures us that death is not the end for us. Our Church teaches that Jesus will raise us to new life in heaven when we die. We see the power of his work with Lazarus.

✦ All make the Sign of the Cross.

In the name of the Father, and of the Son, and of the Holy Spirit. Amen.

PSALM

(For a longer psalm, see page xiv.)
Psalm 34:4–5, 6–7, 16–17, 18–19

The LORD saves the crushed in spirit.

The LORD saves the crushed in spirit.

I sought the LORD, and he answered me,
   and delivered me from all my fears.
Look to him, and be radiant;
   so your faces shall never be ashamed.

The LORD saves the crushed in spirit.

◆ All stand and sing **Praise to you, Lord Jesus Christ** . . .

GOSPEL

John 11:21, 33–34a, 38b–39a, 41–44

A reading from the holy Gospel according to John.

Martha said to Jesus, "Lord, if you had been here, my brother would not have died." When Jesus saw her weeping, and the Jews who came with her also weeping, he was greatly disturbed in spirit and deeply moved. He said, "Where have you laid him?" It was a cave, and a stone was lying against it. Jesus said, "Take away the stone." So they took away the stone.

And Jesus looked upward and said, "Father, I thank you for having heard me. I knew that you always hear me, but I have said this for the sake of the crowd standing here, so that they may believe that you sent me." When he had said this, he cried with a loud voice, "Lazarus, come out!" The dead man came out, his hands and feet bound with strips of cloth, and his face wrapped in a cloth. Jesus said to them, "Unbind him, and let him go."

The Gospel of the Lord.

◆ All sit and observe silence.

FOR SILENT REFLECTION

Think about this silently in your heart. How can you participate in giving people "new life"? By being more helpful and kind? By being a better friend?

CLOSING PRAYER

Let us pray to God for our needs and the needs of others: our family, neighborhood, and the world. For each need we say, "Lord, hear our prayer."

◆ All may add their own prayers here.

Let us pray: **Our Father . . . Amen.**

Heavenly Father,
by raising Lazarus
Jesus revealed your power over death.
You desire that we have life here on earth and someday with you in heaven.
For this we give you thanks and praise.
Through Christ our Lord.

Amen.

✦ All make the Sign of the Cross.

PRAYER FOR
FRIDAY, MARCH 27, 2020

OPENING

St. Paul gives good suggestions for specific ways we can carry on Jesus' work at home and in school. He encourages us to be imitators of Christ and to act as the beloved children we are.

✚ All make the Sign of the Cross.

In the name of the Father, and of the Son, and of the Holy Spirit. Amen.

PSALM

(For a longer psalm, see page xiv.)
Psalm 34:4–5, 6–7, 16–17, 18–19

The LORD saves the crushed in spirit.

The LORD saves the crushed in spirit.

I sought the LORD, and he answered me,
 and delivered me from all my fears.
Look to him, and be radiant;
 so your faces shall never be ashamed.

The LORD saves the crushed in spirit.

READING

Ephesians 4:25b–29, 32; 5:1–2

A reading from the Letter of Paul to the Ephesians [ee-FEE-zhuhnz].

Let all of us speak the truth to our neighbors, for we are members of one another. Be angry but do not sin; do not let the sun go down on your anger, and do not make room for the devil. Thieves must give up stealing; rather let them labor and work honestly with their own hands, so as to have something to share with the needy. Let no evil talk come out of your mouths, but only what is useful for building up, as there is need, so that your words may give grace to those who hear. And be kind to one another, tenderhearted, forgiving one another, as God in Christ has forgiven you. Therefore be imitators of God, as beloved children, and live in love, as Christ loved us and gave himself up for us, a fragrant offering and sacrifice to God.

The Word of the Lord.

◆ All observe silence.

FOR SILENT REFLECTION

Think about this silently in your heart. How can you imitate Jesus?

CLOSING PRAYER

Let us pray to God for our needs and the needs of others: our family, neighborhood, and the world. For each need we say, "Lord, hear our prayer."

◆ All may add their own prayers here.

Let us pray: **Our Father . . . Amen.**

O God,
you desire that we live in peace
with one another.
You sent Jesus to show us the way.
May we imitate him by forgiving others and being kind, loving, and forgiving.
We ask this in Christ's name.

Amen.

✚ All make the Sign of the Cross.

OPENING

Jesus' reputation grew with each miracle that he performed. People believed in him and started to follow him. As he attracted larger and larger crowds of people, the religious leaders began to see him as a threat.

✝ All make the Sign of the Cross.

In the name of the Father, and of the Son, and of the Holy Spirit. Amen.

PSALM

(For a longer psalm, see page xiv.)
Psalm 34:4–5, 6–7, 16–17, 18–19

The LORD saves the crushed in spirit.

The LORD saves the crushed in spirit.

I sought the LORD, and he answered me,
    and delivered me from all my fears.
Look to him, and be radiant;
    so your faces shall never be ashamed.

The LORD saves the crushed in spirit.

◆ All stand and sing **Praise to you, Lord Jesus Christ . . .**

GOSPEL

John 11:21–22, 25ab, 26b–27b, 34, 39a, 43–45

A reading from the holy Gospel according to John.

Martha said to Jesus, "Lord, if you had been here, my brother would not have died. But even now I know that God will give you whatever you ask of him." Jesus said to her, "I am the resurrection and the life. Do you believe this?" She said to him, "Yes, Lord, I believe that you are the Messiah, the Son of God." Jesus said, "Where have you laid him?" They said to him, "Lord, come and see." Jesus said, "Take away the stone." When he had said this, he cried with a loud voice, "Lazarus, come out!" The dead man came out, his hands and feet bound with strips of cloth, and his face wrapped in a cloth. Jesus said to them, "Unbind him, and let him go." Many of the Jews therefore, who had come with Mary and had seen what Jesus did, believed in him.

The Gospel of the Lord.

◆ All sit and observe silence.

FOR SILENT REFLECTION

Think about this silently in your heart. What problem or concern would you like to ask Jesus to help you with today?

CLOSING PRAYER

Let us pray to God for our needs and the needs of others: our family, neighborhood, and the world. For each need we say, "Lord, hear our prayer."

◆ All may add their own prayers here.

Let us pray: **Our Father . . . Amen.**

Good and loving God,
hear us call to you
when we are suffering.
Grant us your comfort and strength.
We ask this in Christ's name.

Amen.

✝ All make the Sign of the Cross.

PRAYER FOR
MONDAY, MARCH 30, 2020

OPENING

The stories we hear this week tell what happened to Jesus before he was arrested. Jesus rode a donkey into the city of Jerusalem and the people honored him. Many people hoped for a king to fight Rome, but Jesus was a different kind of king.

✛ All make the Sign of the Cross.

In the name of the Father, and of the Son, and of the Holy Spirit. Amen.

PSALM

(For a longer psalm, see page xiv.)
Psalm 34:4–5, 6–7, 16–17, 18–19

The LORD saves the crushed in spirit.

The LORD saves the crushed in spirit.

I sought the LORD, and he answered me,
    and delivered me from all my fears.
Look to him, and be radiant;
    so your faces shall never be ashamed.

The LORD saves the crushed in spirit.

◆ All stand and sing **Praise to you, Lord Jesus Christ . . .**

GOSPEL

Matthew 21:1ac–2, 6–11

A reading from the holy Gospel according to Matthew.

When they had come near Jerusalem, Jesus sent two disciples, saying to them, "Go into the village ahead of you, and immediately you will find a donkey tied, and a colt with her; untie them and bring them to me." The disciples went and did as Jesus had directed them; they brought the donkey and the colt, and put their cloaks on them, and he sat on them. A very large crowd spread their cloaks on the road, and others cut branches from the trees and spread them on the road. The crowds that went ahead of him and that followed were shouting, "Hosanna to the Son of David! Blessed is the one who comes in the name of the Lord! Hosanna in the highest heaven!" When he entered Jerusalem, the whole city was in turmoil, asking, "Who is this?" The crowds were saying, "This is the prophet Jesus from Nazareth in Galilee."

The Gospel of the Lord.

◆ All sit and observe silence.

FOR SILENT REFLECTION

Think about this silently in your heart. Jesus Christ came to teach us to change the world, not through force, but through love.

CLOSING PRAYER

Let us pray to God for our needs and the needs of others: our family, neighborhood, and the world. For each need we say, "Lord, hear our prayer."

◆ All may add their own prayers here.

Let us pray: **Our Father . . . Amen.**

O God,
as we near the end of Lent,
may we learn from
and be true to Jesus' teachings.
May we remember his great sacrifice for us.
We ask this through Christ our Lord.

Amen.

✛ All make the Sign of the Cross.

OPENING

The reading today continues the story of Jesus the week before he died. We hear about about one of the disciples, Judas, who was willing to betray Jesus.

✢ All make the Sign of the Cross.

In the name of the Father, and of the Son, and of the Holy Spirit. Amen.

PSALM

(For a longer psalm, see page xiv.)
Psalm 34:4–5, 6–7, 16–17, 18–19

The Lord saves the crushed in spirit.

The Lord saves the crushed in spirit.

I sought the Lord, and he answered me,
 and delivered me from all my fears.
Look to him, and be radiant;
 so your faces shall never be ashamed.

The Lord saves the crushed in spirit.

◆ All stand and sing **Praise to you, Lord Jesus Christ . . .**

GOSPEL

Matthew 26:1b–5, 14–16

A reading from the holy Gospel according to Matthew.

Jesus said to his disciples, "You know that after two days the Passover is coming, and the Son of Man will be handed over to be crucified." Then the chief priests and the elders of the people gathered in the palace of the high priest, who was called Caiaphas [KAY-uh-fuhs], and they conspired to arrest Jesus by stealth and kill him. But they said, "Not during the festival, or there may be a riot among the people." Then one of the twelve, who was called Judas Iscariot [ih-SKAYR-ee-uht], went to the chief priests and said, "What will you give me if I betray him to you?" They paid him thirty pieces of silver. And from that moment he began to look for an opportunity to betray him.

The Gospel of the Lord.

◆ All sit and observe silence.

FOR SILENT REFLECTION

Think about this silently in your heart. Judas was not a good friend. How can you be a better friend? Have you ever betrayed someone? Did you ask for forgiveness? Have you been betrayed? Can you forgive the person who betrayed you?

CLOSING PRAYER

Let us pray to God for our needs and the needs of others: our family, neighborhood, and the world. For each need we say, "Lord, hear our prayer."

◆ All may add their own prayers here.

Let us pray: **Our Father . . . Amen.**

Holy God,
Jesus knew what was to come,
and yet he remained faithful to his mission.
May we be faithful to you
and your commands,
even when it is difficult.
We ask this through Christ our Lord.

Amen.

✢ All make the Sign of the Cross.

PRAYER FOR
WEDNESDAY, APRIL 1, 2020

OPENING

Passover is the Jewish feast that commemorates Israel's deliverance from bondage in Egypt. In Jesus' time, thousands of people came to Jerusalem to celebrate the feast with their families. As observant Jews, Jesus and his disciples, also came to Jerusalem for Passover.

✤ All make the Sign of the Cross.

In the name of the Father, and of the Son, and of the Holy Spirit. Amen.

PSALM
(For a longer psalm, see page xiv.)
Psalm 34:4–5, 6–7, 16–17, 18–19

The LORD saves the crushed in spirit.

The LORD saves the crushed in spirit.

I sought the LORD, and he answered me,
  and delivered me from all my fears.
Look to him, and be radiant;
  so your faces shall never be ashamed.

The LORD saves the crushed in spirit.

◆ All stand and sing **Praise to you, Lord Jesus Christ . . .**

GOSPEL
Matthew 26:17a, 19–25

A reading from the holy Gospel according to Matthew.

On the first day of Unleavened Bread the disciples did as Jesus had directed them, and they prepared the Passover meal. When it was evening, he took his place with the twelve; and while they were eating, he said, "Truly I tell you, one of you will betray me." And they became greatly distressed and began to say to him one after another, "Surely not I, Lord?"

He answered, "The one who has dipped his hand into the bowl with me will betray me. The Son of Man goes as it is written of him, but woe to that one by whom the Son of Man is betrayed! It would have been better for that one not to have been born." Judas, who betrayed him, said, "Surely not I, Rabbi?" He replied, "You have said so."

The Gospel of the Lord.

◆ All sit and observe silence.

FOR SILENT REFLECTION

Think about this silently in your heart. To betray means to be disloyal. How do you think Jesus felt about Judas?

CLOSING PRAYER

Let us pray to God for our needs and the needs of others: our family, neighborhood, and the world. For each need we say, "Lord, hear our prayer."

◆ All may add their own prayers here.

Let us pray: **Our Father . . . Amen.**

We give you thanks, O God, for Jesus.
He showed us how to love you
and one another.
Help us to follow his example.
Through Christ our Lord.

Amen.

✤ All make the Sign of the Cross.

OPENING

When the priest says the words of consecration over the bread and wine at Mass, it is called the Memorial. He is remembering Jesus' words and actions at the Last Supper. The words that Jesus spoke at the Last Supper are repeated in hundreds of languages all over the world where Christians celebrate the Mass. Today we remember St. Francis of Paola, who gave spiritual guidance to kings of France in the 1400s.

✦ All make the Sign of the Cross.

In the name of the Father, and of the Son, and of the Holy Spirit. Amen.

PSALM

(For a longer psalm, see page xiv.)
Psalm 34:4–5, 6–7, 16–17, 18–19

The LORD saves the crushed in spirit.

The LORD saves the crushed in spirit.

I sought the LORD, and he answered me,
and delivered me from all my fears.
Look to him, and be radiant;
so your faces shall never be ashamed.

The LORD saves the crushed in spirit.

◆ All stand and sing **Praise to you, Lord Jesus Christ** . . .

GOSPEL

Matthew 26:26–30

A reading from the holy Gospel according to Matthew.

While they were eating, Jesus took a loaf of bread, and after blessing it he broke it, gave it to the disciples, and said, "Take, eat; this is my body." Then he took a cup, and after giving thanks he gave it to them, saying, "Drink from it, all of you; for this is my blood of the covenant, which is poured out for many for the forgiveness of sins. I tell you, I will never again drink of this fruit of the vine until that day when I drink it new with you in my Father's kingdom." When they had sung the hymn, they went out to the Mount of Olives.

The Gospel of the Lord.

◆ All sit and observe silence.

FOR SILENT REFLECTION

Think about this silently in your heart. Jesus Christ is with us always, and especially at the celebration of the Holy Mass.

CLOSING PRAYER

Let us pray to God for our needs and the needs of others: our family, neighborhood, and the world. For each need we say, "Lord, hear our prayer."

◆ All may add their own prayers here.

Let us pray: **Our Father . . . Amen.**

O God,
may we always appreciate this great gift
of the Holy Eucharist.
May we never forget how much you love us.
We give you thanks and praise
for the gift of your Son Jesus,
in whose name we pray.

Amen.

✦ All make the Sign of the Cross.

PRAYER FOR
FRIDAY, APRIL 3, 2020

OPENING

The Gospel today tells about Judas who betrayed Jesus for money. He probably didn't think Jesus would be put to death. We know from later Scripture passages that Judas felt sorry for what he did.

✛ All make the Sign of the Cross.

In the name of the Father, and of the Son, and of the Holy Spirit. Amen.

PSALM

(For a longer psalm, see page xiv.)
Psalm 34:4–5, 6–7, 16–17, 18–19

The LORD saves the crushed in spirit.

The LORD saves the crushed in spirit.

I sought the LORD, and he answered me,
    and delivered me from all my fears.
Look to him, and be radiant;
    so your faces shall never be ashamed.

The LORD saves the crushed in spirit.

◆ All stand and sing **Praise to you, Lord Jesus Christ . . .**

GOSPEL

Matthew 26:36, 47b–49, 50b, 55b–56a

A reading from the holy Gospel according to Matthew.

After the Passover meal, Jesus went with them to a place called Gethsemane; and he said to his disciples, "Sit here while I go over there and pray." Judas, one of the twelve, arrived; with him was a large crowd with swords and clubs, from the chief priests and the elders of the people. Now the betrayer had given them a sign, saying, "The one I will kiss is the man; arrest him." At once he came up to Jesus and said, "Greetings, Rabbi!" and kissed him.

Then they came and laid hands on Jesus and arrested him. Jesus said, "Have you come out with swords and clubs to arrest me as though I were a bandit? Day after day I sat in the temple teaching, and you did not arrest me. But all this has taken place, so that the scriptures of the prophets may be fulfilled."

The Gospel of the Lord.

◆ All sit and observe silence.

FOR SILENT REFLECTION

Think about this silently in your heart. Judas did something that he later felt sorry for. God will always forgive if we are sorry and ask for forgiveness.

CLOSING PRAYER

Let us pray to God for our needs and the needs of others: our family, neighborhood, and the world. For each need we say, "Lord, hear our prayer."

◆ All may add their own prayers here.

Let us pray: **Our Father . . . Amen.**

Loving and forgiving God,
help us to be truly sorry for ways that we have offended you
or hurt one another.
May we look to Jesus
as our supreme example.
We pray in his name.

Amen.

✛ All make the Sign of the Cross.

PRAYER FOR THE WEEK

WITH A READING FROM THE GOSPEL FOR **SUNDAY, APRIL 5, 2020**

OPENING

Today is Palm Sunday and begins Holy Week, a very important week in the Church. We will remember Jesus' Last Supper with his disciples, and his passion and death.

✚ All make the Sign of the Cross.

In the name of the Father, and of the Son, and of the Holy Spirit. Amen.

PSALM

(For a longer psalm, see page xiv.)
Psalm 34:4–5, 6–7, 16–17, 18–19

The LORD saves the crushed in spirit.

The LORD saves the crushed in spirit.

I sought the LORD, and he answered me,
  and delivered me from all my fears.
Look to him, and be radiant;
  so your faces shall never be ashamed.

The LORD saves the crushed in spirit.

◆ All stand and sing **Praise to you, Lord Jesus Christ . . .**

GOSPEL

Matthew 21:1ac–2, 6–11

A reading from the holy Gospel according to Matthew.

When they had come near Jerusalem, Jesus sent two disciples, saying to them, "Go into the village ahead of you, and immediately you will find a donkey tied, and a colt with her; untie them and bring them to me. The disciples went and did as Jesus had directed them; they brought the donkey and the colt, and put their cloaks on them, and he sat on them. A very large crowd spread their cloaks on the road, and others cut branches from the trees and spread them on the road. The crowds that went ahead of him and that followed were shouting, "Hosanna to the Son of David! Blessed is the one who comes in the name of the Lord! Hosanna in the highest heaven!" When he entered Jerusalem, the whole city was in turmoil, asking, "Who is this?" The crowds were saying, "This is the prophet Jesus from Nazareth in Galilee."

The Gospel of the Lord.

◆ All sit and observe silence.

FOR SILENT REFLECTION

Think about this silently in your hearts. How can we welcome Jesus in our hearts today?

CLOSING PRAYER

Let us pray to God for our needs and the needs of others: our family, neighborhood, and the world. For each need we say, "Lord, hear our prayer."

◆ All may add their own prayers here.

Let us pray: **Our Father . . . Amen.**

O God,
we sing our Hosannas of praise:
Jesus is our beloved teacher.
Jesus is our Lord and savior.
May we follow his way of love.
We pray this in Christ Jesus' name.

Amen.

✚ All make the Sign of the Cross.

PRAYER FOR
MONDAY, APRIL 6, 2020

OPENING

Jesus criticized the religious leaders of his time for serving themselves rather than caring for the people. When Jesus' popularity began growing quickly, those leaders felt so threatened that they got people to lie about Jesus so that they could accuse him of a crime.

✝ All make the Sign of the Cross.

In the name of the Father, and of the Son, and of the Holy Spirit. Amen.

PSALM

(For a longer psalm, see page xiv.)
Psalm 34:4–5, 6–7, 16–17, 18–19

The LORD saves the crushed in spirit.

The LORD saves the crushed in spirit.

I sought the LORD, and he answered me,
and delivered me from all my fears.
Look to him, and be radiant;
so your faces shall never be ashamed.

The LORD saves the crushed in spirit.

◆ All stand and sing **Praise to you, Lord Jesus Christ** . . .

GOSPEL

Matthew 26:57, 59–62b, 63–64a, 65c–66

A reading from the holy Gospel according to Matthew.

Those who had arrested Jesus took him to Caiaphas the high priest, in whose house the scribes and the elders had gathered. The chief priests and the whole council were looking for false testimony against Jesus so that they might put him to death, but they found none, though many false witnesses came forward. At last two came forward and said, "This fellow said, 'I am able to destroy the temple of God and to build it in three days.'" The high priest stood up and said, "Have you no answer?" But Jesus was silent. Then the high priest said to him, "I put you under oath before the living God, tell us if you are the Messiah, the Son of God." Jesus said to him, "You have said so." Then the high priest said, "You have now heard his blasphemy. What is your verdict?" They answered, "He deserves death."

The Gospel of the Lord.

◆ All sit and observe silence.

FOR SILENT REFLECTION

Think about this silently in your heart. When angry, do you ever accuse people of things they didn't say or do?

CLOSING PRAYER

Let us pray to God for our needs and the needs of others: our family, neighborhood, and the world. For each need we say, "Lord, hear our prayer."

◆ All may add their own prayers here.

Let us pray: **Our Father . . . Amen.**

God of mercy,
give us the courage to always speak the truth.
May our words be helpful and supportive.
May our actions be honest and kind.
We ask this in Christ's name.

Amen.

✝ All make the Sign of the Cross.

OPENING

Pilate was the Roman governor in Jerusalem. Pilate didn't think Jesus had done anything to deserve death, but he was afraid for his own job. If there was a riot because people were angry, the Roman emperor would remove him. Pilate could have helped Jesus but he didn't.

✝ All make the Sign of the Cross.

In the name of the Father, and of the Son, and of the Holy Spirit. Amen.

PSALM

(For a longer psalm, see page xiv.)
Psalm 34:4–5, 6–7, 16–17, 18–19

The LORD saves the crushed in spirit.

The LORD saves the crushed in spirit.

I sought the LORD, and he answered me,
   and delivered me from all my fears.
Look to him, and be radiant;
   so your faces shall never be ashamed.

The LORD saves the crushed in spirit.

◆ All stand and sing **Praise to you, Lord Jesus Christ . . .**

GOSPEL

Matthew 27:2, 15–17, 21c–22, 24c, 26

A reading from the holy Gospel according to Matthew.

The chief priests and elders bound Jesus, led him away, and handed him over to Pilate the governor. Now at the festival the governor was accustomed to release a prisoner for the crowd, anyone whom they wanted. At that time they had a notorious prisoner, called Jesus Barabbas. So after they had gathered, Pilate said to them, "Whom do you want me to release for you, Jesus Barabbas or Jesus who is called the Messiah?" And they said, "Barabbas." Pilate said to them, "Then what should I do with Jesus who is called the Messiah?" All of them said, "Let him be crucified!" Pilate took some water and washed his hands before the crowd, saying, "I am innocent of this man's blood." So he released Barabbas for them; and after flogging Jesus, he handed him over to be crucified.

The Gospel of the Lord.

◆ All sit and observe silence.

FOR SILENT REFLECTION

Think about this silently in your heart. Pray to have courage to defend people when they are being treated unjustly.

CLOSING PRAYER

Let us pray to God for our needs and the needs of others: our family, neighborhood, and the world. For each need we say, "Lord, hear our prayer."

◆ All may add their own prayers here.

Let us pray: **Our Father . . . Amen.**

Holy and loving God,
Jesus bore his trials with dignity
and with faith in you.
May we be constant in our faith,
even when it is difficult.
We ask this in Christ's name.

Amen.

✝ All make the Sign of the Cross.

PRAYER FOR
WEDNESDAY, APRIL 8, 2020

OPENING

In the ancient world, crucifixion was a death sentence of shame and disgrace. It was usually reserved for slaves, criminals of the worst sort from the lowest levels of society, military deserters, and especially traitors. It is almost impossible to imagine what Jesus' disciples and friends must have felt to see him being treated so cruelly.

✚ All make the Sign of the Cross.

In the name of the Father, and of the Son, and of the Holy Spirit. Amen.

PSALM

(For a longer psalm, see page xiv.)
Psalm 34:4–5, 6–7, 16–17, 18–19

The LORD saves the crushed in spirit.

The LORD saves the crushed in spirit.

I sought the LORD, and he answered me,
　　and delivered me from all my fears.
Look to him, and be radiant;
　　so your faces shall never be ashamed.

The LORD saves the crushed in spirit.

◆ All stand and sing **Praise to you, Lord Jesus Christ . . .**

GOSPEL

Matthew 27:27–31

A reading from the holy Gospel according to Matthew.

Then the soldiers of the governor took Jesus into the governor's headquarters, and they gathered the whole cohort around him. They stripped him and put a scarlet robe on him, and after twisting some thorns into a crown, they put it on his head. They put a reed in his right hand and knelt before him and mocked him, saying, "Hail, King of the Jews!" They spat on him, and took the reed and struck him on the head. After mocking him, they stripped him of the robe and put his own clothes on him. Then they led him away to crucify him.

The Gospel of the Lord.

◆ All sit and observe silence.

FOR SILENT REFLECTION

Think about this silently in your heart. Is there someone who is sick or hurting that you would like to pray for today?

CLOSING PRAYER

Let us pray to God for our needs and the needs of others: our family, neighborhood, and the world. For each need we say, "Lord, hear our prayer."

◆ All may add their own prayers here.

Let us pray: **Our Father . . . Amen.**

Holy God,
we thank you for Jesus,
our king and our savior.
May we follow his example and be obedient to your will for us.
We pray in his name.

Amen.

✚ All make the Sign of the Cross.

Before you begin, find the reading (John 13:3–5) in your Bible, ask for a volunteer to read it, and help the reader to practice reading it a few times. You could begin with a simple song, such as "Jesus, Remember Me," or "Amen." (We don't sing "Alleluia" until the Easter Vigil.) An older child or adult reads the leader parts.

LEADER

Today is Holy Thursday, and this evening we will remember two important things that Jesus did for his disciples and for us. On this night of the Last Supper, Jesus offered himself in the form of bread and wine and said, "This is my Body. . . . This is my Blood. Do this in memory of me." Later, he washed the feet of his followers, teaching them by example how we must be a servant for all.

✠ All make the Sign of the Cross.

In the name of the Father, and of the Son, and of the Holy Spirit. Amen.

LEADER: Psalm 27:1, 4, 11, 13–14

Let us repeat the Psalm Response:
Teach me your way, O LORD.

ALL: Teach me your way, O LORD.

The LORD is my light and my salvation;
    whom shall I fear?
The LORD is the stronghold of my life;
    of whom shall I be afraid?

ALL: Teach me your way, O LORD.

One thing I asked of the LORD,
    that will I seek after:
to live in the house of the LORD
    all the days of my life,
to behold the beauty of the LORD,
    and to inquire in his temple.

ALL: Teach me your way, O LORD.

I believe that I shall see the goodness
    of the LORD
    in the land of the living.
Wait for the LORD;
    be strong, and let your heart take courage;
    wait for the LORD!

ALL: Teach me your way, O LORD.

◆ All stand and sing **Praise to you, Lord Jesus Christ** . . .

LEADER: John 13:3–5

A reading from the holy Gospel according to John.

◆ Read the Gospel passage from the Bible.

The Gospel of the Lord.

◆ All sit and observe silence.

FOR SILENT REFLECTION

Why did Jesus, the disciples' leader,
wish to be their servant?

LEADER:

Let us pray as Jesus taught us:

Our Father . . . Amen.

LEADER:

Almighty God,
we remember Jesus'
act of service of washing his friends' feet.
May we honor you with
our acts of love and service today and always.
We ask this through Christ our Lord.

ALL: Amen.

✠ All make the Sign of the Cross.

HOME PRAYER
GOOD FRIDAY

Before you begin, find the reading (John 18:33–37) in your Bible, ask for a volunteer to read it, and help the reader to practice it a few times. You could begin with a simple song, such as "Jesus, Remember Me," or "Amen." (We don't sing "Alleluia" until the Easter Vigil.) An older child or adult reads the leader parts.

LEADER:

Today we remember Jesus' anguish and Death on the Cross. It is a sad time we don't understand. But Good Friday is also a day that we recall the goodness of God's Son who chose to die so that he could save us from sin and death. This day gives us so much hope because of the promise of new life!

✛ All make the Sign of the Cross.

In the name of the Father, and of the Son, and of the Holy Spirit. Amen.

LEADER: Psalm 31:1, 2, 5a, 21

Let us repeat the Psalm Response:
Into your hand I commit my spirit.

ALL: Into your hand I commit my spirit.

In you, O LORD, I seek refuge;
  do not let me ever be put to shame;
  in your righteousness deliver me.
Incline your ear to me;
  rescue me speedily.
Be a rock of refuge for me,
  a strong fortress to save me.

ALL: Into your hand I commit my spirit.

Blessed be the LORD,
  for he has wondrously shown his steadfast
    love to me
  when I was beset as a city under siege.

ALL: Into your hand I commit my spirit.

◆ All stand and sing **Praise to you, Lord Jesus Christ . . .**

LEADER: John 18:33–37

A reading from the holy Gospel according to John.

◆ Read the Gospel passage from the Bible.

The Gospel of the Lord.

◆ All sit and observe silence.

LEADER:

As I reflect on Jesus' love for me, how can I thank him?

LEADER:

Let us pray as Jesus taught us:

Our Father . . . Amen.

LEADER:

Today we remember Jesus' great love. Help us to honor him with our lives. We ask this in the name of the Father, the Son, and the Holy Spirit.

ALL: Amen.

EASTER TIME

MONDAY, APRIL 13 — SUNDAY, MAY 31

EASTER TIME

THE MEANING OF EASTER

The heart of Easter lies in the word *covenant*. A covenant is an agreement or contract between two parties. The history of salvation is the story of God's covenant with his people—God's promise to provide and care for humankind and humankind's response to return God's love and follow God's teachings to care for one another and all creation. In the Old Testament, God made covenants with Noah, Abraham, and Moses. In the New Testament, Jesus is the new covenant: "Whoever believes in me will never be thirsty" (John 6:35). With the Resurrection, God promises that the covenant of love will extend to all peoples for all time.

The Prayer for the Week will reflect the Sunday Gospels but during the week we will again "walk through the Bible." Scripture stories tell us of people throughout history from King David, to the Israelites, to the people of Jesus' time, to Paul and the early Christians who believed that faith and trust in God helped them to live joyfully in spite of difficulties.

As we read the stories of Jesus' appearances to his disciples after the Resurrection, we can reflect on how Jesus is always present in our lives. We will read stories of St. Paul and the early Christians who carried Jesus' teachings to people in many lands. Easter Time ends with the wonderful celebration of Pentecost. After Jesus died, his disciples were filled with fear and confusion. Jesus promised that he would send the Spirit to strengthen them. On Pentecost, we celebrate the Spirit that strengthened the disciples. This same Spirit fills us with wisdom, knowledge, courage, and love. These gifts make our lives and the world a better place for all God's creation.

PREPARING TO CELEBRATE EASTER IN THE CLASSROOM

SACRED SPACE

The liturgical color for Easter Time is white, so your prayer table cloth will need to change once more. You may want to add to your prayer table a vase of fresh daisies or lilies and a small glass bowl with a little water in it. When you introduce the water to your students you may say, "Jesus said, 'Let anyone who is thirsty come to me, and let the one who believes in me drink'" (John 7:37b–38a). Have children process in single file to the prayer table, carrying and placing the white cloth, a small white pillar candle, the flowers, and the bowl of water. Make sure you dim the lights before you begin. Then after all the objects have been placed on the prayer table, light the white pillar and chant the following phrase and response three times:

LEADER: The Light of Christ!

ALL: Thanks be to God!

Perhaps one of your students, or someone they know, received the Sacrament of Baptism at the Holy Saturday celebration of the Easter Vigil. If so, while standing before the water, you could explain that the water of Baptism recalls the great flood that Noah had to pass through to reach God's promise of peace, the Red Sea that Moses and the Israelites had to pass through to reach freedom, and the death that Jesus had to pass through to reach the life of the Resurrection. When we pass through (are baptized with) the water in the baptismal font, we enter into that same new life of the resurrected Christ.

Easter Time ends with the Solemnity of Pentecost. When you celebrate Pentecost as a group, make sure you exchange your white prayer table cloth for a red one.

MOVEMENT AND GESTURE

Children love this expanded form of the Easter Procession. After you have changed the color of the prayer cloth to white, carried in the white pillar candle, placed the objects on the prayer table, and lit the candle, sing "The Light of Christ" on one note. When you are finished singing, read a Gospel account of the Resurrection (such as John 20:11–18). Sing Alleluia and then announce the following: "Jesus has risen from the dead; Jesus, the Light of the World, has destroyed death. The light of the Risen Christ will never go out, for he shares his light and life with each of us. Not only that, but his light can spread and grow. Jesus shares his new life with each of us." Then call each child by name, one at a time, inviting them to come forward. For each child, light a small votive candle from the large pillar. As you give it to the child, say, "The Risen Christ shares his light with (child's name)." The child will then put the votive candle on the prayer table and sit down. Don't rush. Wait until the child is seated before you call the next child's name. If you are worried about fire, allow each child to hold his or her votive holder briefly, then you can place the candle on the table beside the lit pillar. Make sure you light a votive candle for yourself. When all the small candles are lit, sit in silence with the children and enjoy the beauty of the light. End your celebration by singing all the Alleluias that you know!

FESTIVITY IN SCHOOL AND HOME

You might want to engage some of the older children in making an Easter candle like the one that stands beside the altar in church. Use a tall white pillar candle. The Easter, or Paschal, candle has three symbols: a central cross identifies it as the Christ candle, and its flame burns despite the death Christ endured. The letters alpha and omega, which begin and end the Greek alphabet, signify that God is the beginning and the ending of all things. The current year indicates that God is present not just at the beginning and the end of time, but throughout history and among those gathered here and now around the candle. You can stand this candle on a candle holder beside the table in your prayer corner at school or at home.

In this book you will find special prayer services that may be used in the classroom or with a larger group. There is the service for Easter, pages 256–257; for the Ascension, pages 296–297; and for Pentecost, pages 304–305. There is also a special prayer service to honor May as the month of Mary, pages 276–277. In May, you might add pictures of Mary and fresh spring flowers to your prayer table. Invite children who know the Rosary to say a decade as part of your daily prayer.

SACRED MUSIC

Here are some Easter songs that children love: "Jesus Christ Is Risen Today," "What Wondrous Love Is This," "Alleluia, Sing to Jesus," "Come Down, O Love Divine," and "O Sons and Daughters." For Pentecost you might enjoy singing "Come, Holy Ghost" or "Veni Sancte Spiritus," or "Spirit of the Living God."

PRAYERS FOR EASTER

The following prayer is a beautiful psalm from the Easter Vigil:

Psalm 42:1–2, 43:3–4

As a deer longs for flowing streams,
    so my soul longs for you, O God.
My soul thirsts for God
    for the living God.
When shall I come and behold
    the face of God?
O send out your light and your truth;
    let them lead me;
let them bring me to your holy hill
    and to your dwelling.
Then I will go to the altar of God
    to God my exceeding joy;
and I will praise you with the harp,
    O God, my God.

A NOTE TO CATECHISTS

You may wish to study the prayers of Baptism with your students. The prayer of Blessing the Waters of Baptism is particularly rich in symbolism. You can recall with the children baptisms they remember seeing as well as stories and pictures of their own baptisms. You can find the Baptismal Rite online or ask your parish priest for a copy.

GRACE BEFORE MEALS

EASTER TIME

LEADER:
Jesus Christ is risen! He is truly risen!

ALL: Alleluia! Alleluia!

✝ All make the Sign of the Cross.

In the name of the Father, and of the Son, and of the Holy Spirit. Amen.

LEADER:
God, our Creator,
we are thankful for the
air we breathe and the
nourishment you offer
in our every moment on earth.
We are grateful for the meal
we are about to share,
for its nutrients sustain us and
give us energy for
working and playing for the glory
of Christ our Savior.
We ask this in his name.

ALL: Amen.

✝ All make the Sign of the Cross.

In the name of the Father, and of the Son, and of the Holy Spirit. Amen.

PRAYER AT DAY'S END

EASTER TIME

LEADER:
All the ends of the earth have seen

ALL: the victory of our God.

✚ All make the Sign of the Cross.

> In the name of the Father, and of the Son, and of the Holy Spirit. Amen.

LEADER:
Heavenly Father,
we are grateful for
what we've learned today.
We thank you for our
teachers, assistants, coaches,
and friends who guide us
along our path.
Help us through the remainder of this day
as we are renewed by your Spirit
and the promise of an
eternal Easter.
We ask this through Christ our Lord.

ALL: Amen.

✚ All make the Sign of the Cross.

> In the name of the Father, and of the Son, and of the Holy Spirit. Amen.

PRAYER SERVICE
EASTER

Prepare seven leaders for this prayer service. The third and fourth leaders will need Bibles for the Scripture passages and may need help finding them and practicing. You may wish to begin by singing "Jesus Christ Is Risen Today" and end with "Alleluia, Sing to Jesus." If there will be singing, prepare a song leader.

FIRST LEADER:

The grace, peace, and light of the Risen Christ be with us all.

ALL: Amen.

FIRST LEADER:

Today we celebrate Easter, the holiest, most important *solemnity* [suh-LEM-nuh-tee] of the Church, when we remember the Resurrection of Jesus Christ. Jesus won a great victory over death! He rose from death to new life and he will never die again! We can follow him and we too can rise from the dead and live forever with him. Easter is so important to us that one day could never contain all our joy, so we celebrate Easter for fifty days!

SECOND LEADER:

✦ All make the Sign of the Cross.

> **In the name of the Father, and of the Son, and of the Holy Spirit. Amen.**

Let us pray:
Heavenly Father,
our hearts are filled with thankfulness
and praise
as we think about Jesus' great love for us,
the sacrifice he made,

and the never-ending life he lives and shares
with us now.
May we always thank you for the gift your
Son has given to us.
We ask this through the same Jesus Christ
our Lord.

ALL: Amen.

THIRD LEADER: Isaiah 42:10–12
A reading from the Book of the prophet Isaiah.

◆ Read the Scripture passage from the Bible.

The Word of the Lord.

◆ All observe silence. Then all stand and sing
Alleluia.

FOURTH LEADER: John 20:11–18
A reading from the holy Gospel according
to John.

◆ Read the Gospel passage from the Bible.

The Gospel of the Lord.

◆ All sit and observe silence.

FIFTH LEADER:
Let us stand and bring our hopes and needs
to God as we pray, "Lord, hear our prayer."

For all who live in fear or worry, may the
power of the Resurrection give them new
hope, we pray to the Lord.

For an end to hatred, divisions, and war,
we pray to the Lord.

For all who are unable to see the hand of
God at work in their lives, may God open
their eyes, we pray to the Lord.

For those who are sick and for those who
have died, we pray to the Lord.

SIXTH LEADER:
Let us pray as Jesus taught us.

ALL: Our Father . . . Amen.

◆ Pause, and then say the following.

Let us offer one another a sign of
Christ's peace.

◆ All offer one another a sign of peace.

SEVENTH LEADER:
Let us pray:
Lord God almighty,
in the Death and Resurrection of your Son,
Jesus Christ,
you have created a new heaven and
a new earth.
Bring the light and life of the Resurrection
into our hearts so that we too may be
renewed in holiness.
We ask this through our Lord Jesus Christ,
your Son, who lives and reigns with
you in the unity of the Holy Spirit,
one God, for ever and ever.

ALL: Amen.

✝ All make the Sign of the Cross.

OPENING

Christ's Resurrection was part of God's saving plan for us. The ancient Jewish people also believed in God's saving power. David wrote this song of thanksgiving when God saved him from being killed by King Saul.

✣ *All make the Sign of the Cross.*

In the name of the Father, and of the Son, and of the Holy Spirit. Amen.

PSALM

(For a longer psalm, see page xiv.)
Psalm 105:1–2, 3–4, 6–7

Let the hearts of those who seek
the LORD rejoice.

**Let the hearts of those who seek
the LORD rejoice.**

O give thanks to the LORD, call on his name,
   make known his deeds among the peoples.
Sing to him, sing praises to him;
   tell of all his wonderful works.

**Let the hearts of those who seek
the LORD rejoice.**

READING

2 Samuel 22:2–3abc, 4ab, 7, 29, 31–32, 47

A reading from the Second Book of Samuel.

David said: The LORD is my rock, my fortress, and my deliverer, my God, my rock, in whom I take refuge, my shield and the horn of my salvation, my stronghold and my refuge, my savior. I call upon the LORD, who is worthy to be praised. In my distress I called upon the LORD; to my God I called. From his temple he heard my voice, and my cry came to his ears. Indeed, you are my lamp, O LORD, the LORD lightens my darkness. This God—his way is perfect; the promise of the LORD proves true; he is a shield for all who take refuge in him. For who is God, but the LORD? And who is a rock, except our God? The LORD lives! Blessed be my rock, and exalted be my God, the rock of my salvation.

The Word of the Lord.

◆ *All observe silence.*

FOR SILENT REFLECTION

Think about this silently in your heart. What should we thank God for in our prayers this week?

CLOSING PRAYER

Let us pray to God for our needs and the needs of others: our family, neighborhood, and the world. For each need we say, "Lord, hear our prayer."

◆ *All may add their own prayers here.*

Let us pray: **Our Father . . . Amen.**

We rejoice and are glad, O God,
in this Easter season.
We know that like Jesus Christ,
we will rise to new life.
Help us to be faithful followers of Jesus
and to live as he showed us.
We ask this in Christ's name.

Amen.

✣ *All make the Sign of the Cross.*

OPENING

The prophet Isaiah reminds Israel that God has called them by name. Israel is precious and honored by God. That's how God feels about us too.

✝ All make the Sign of the Cross.

In the name of the Father, and of the Son, and of the Holy Spirit. Amen.

PSALM

(For a longer psalm, see page xiv.)
Psalm 105:1–2, 3–4, 6–7

Let the hearts of those who seek the LORD rejoice.

Let the hearts of those who seek the LORD rejoice.

O give thanks to the LORD, call on his name,
    make known his deeds among the peoples.
Sing to him, sing praises to him;
    tell of all his wonderful works.

Let the hearts of those who seek the LORD rejoice.

READING

Isaiah 43:1, 3a, 4–5a, 10ab, 11–12ac

A reading from the Book of the prophet Isaiah.

But now thus says the LORD, he who created you, O Jacob, God who formed you, O Israel: Do not fear, for I have redeemed you; I have called you by name, you are mine. For I am the LORD your God, the Holy One of Israel, your Savior. Because you are precious in my sight, and honored, and I love you, I give people in return for you, nations in exchange for your life. Do not fear, for I am with you. You are my witnesses, says the LORD, and my servant whom I have chosen, so that you may know and believe me and understand that I am he. I, I am the LORD, and besides me there is no savior. I declared and saved and proclaimed, and you are my witnesses, says the LORD.

The Word of the Lord.

◆ All observe silence.

FOR SILENT REFLECTION

Think about this silently in your heart. How can we be witnesses to our loving God today?

CLOSING PRAYER

Let us pray to God for our needs and the needs of others: our family, neighborhood, and the world. For each need we say, "Lord, hear our prayer."

◆ All may add their own prayers here.

Let us pray: **Our Father . . . Amen.**

We believe, O God,
in your promises.
You are the Lord our God.
Through your power,
Christ our Savior has risen.
We praise you!
Alleluia! Alleluia!

Amen.

✝ All make the Sign of the Cross.

PRAYER FOR
WEDNESDAY, APRIL 15, 2020

OPENING

Through Jesus, God makes God's salvation known not just to Jews but to everyone. Today's reading tells of the Samaritan woman's recognition of Jesus as the Savior.

✛ All make the Sign of the Cross.

In the name of the Father, and of the Son, and of the Holy Spirit. Amen.

PSALM

(For a longer psalm, see page xiv.)
Psalm 105:1–2, 3–4, 6–7

Let the hearts of those who seek
the LORD rejoice.

**Let the hearts of those who seek
the LORD rejoice.**

O give thanks to the LORD, call on his name,
   make known his deeds among the peoples.
Sing to him, sing praises to him;
   tell of all his wonderful works.

**Let the hearts of those who seek
the LORD rejoice.**

◆ All stand and sing **Alleluia.**

GOSPEL

John 4:25ab, 26, 28–30, 39a, 40–42ad

A reading from the holy Gospel according to John.

The woman said to Jesus, "I know that Messiah is coming" (who is called Christ). Jesus said to her, "I am he, the one who is speaking to you." Then the woman left her water jar and went back to the city. She said to the people, "Come and see a man who told me everything I have ever done! He cannot be the Messiah, can he?"

They left the city and were on their way to him. Many Samaritans from that city believed in him because of the woman's testimony. So when the Samaritans came to him, they asked him to stay with them; and he stayed there two days. And many more believed because of his word. They said to the woman, "We know that this is truly the Savior of the world."

The Gospel of the Lord.

◆ All sit and observe silence.

FOR SILENT REFLECTION

Think about this silently in your heart. Just as he knew the Samaritan woman, Jesus knows each of us.

CLOSING PRAYER

Let us pray to God for our needs and the needs of others: our family, neighborhood, and the world. For each need we say, "Lord, hear our prayer."

◆ All may add their own prayers here.

Let us pray: **Our Father . . . Amen.**

At Easter Time, let us rejoice.
Christ is risen!
Let the earth proclaim God's glory.
Christ is risen!
May our hearts be joyful in the Lord.
We pray through Christ our Lord.

Amen.

✛ All make the Sign of the Cross.

OPENING

In the Letter to Timothy we hear that we're never too young to train ourselves to be good and loving servants of God. All of us, no matter our age, can be witnesses of God's saving power.

✝ All make the Sign of the Cross.

In the name of the Father, and of the Son, and of the Holy Spirit. Amen.

PSALM

(For a longer psalm, see page xiv.)
Psalm 105:1–2, 3–4, 6–7

Let the hearts of those who seek
the LORD rejoice.

**Let the hearts of those who seek
the LORD rejoice.**

O give thanks to the LORD, call on his name,
   make known his deeds among the peoples.
Sing to him, sing praises to him;
   tell of all his wonderful works.

**Let the hearts of those who seek
the LORD rejoice.**

READING

1 Timothy 4:6, 7b–8, 10–12

A reading from the First Letter to Timothy.

If you put these instructions before the brothers and sisters, you will be a good servant of Christ Jesus, nourished on the words of the faith and of the sound teaching that you have followed. Train yourself in godliness, for, while physical training is of some value, godliness is valuable in every way, holding promise for both the present life and the life to come. For to this end we toil and struggle, because we have our hope set on the living God, who is the Savior of all people, especially of those who believe. These are the things you must insist on and teach. Let no one despise your youth, but set the believers an example in speech and conduct, in love, in faith, in purity.

The Word of the Lord.

◆ All observe silence.

FOR SILENT REFLECTION

Think about this silently in your heart. Do you believe that you can be a witness to God's power to save? How?

CLOSING PRAYER

Let us pray to God for our needs and the needs of others: our family, neighborhood, and the world. For each need we say, "Lord, hear our prayer."

◆ All may add their own prayers here.

Let us pray: **Our Father . . . Amen.**

Although we are young, O God,
you call us to holiness.
You call us to serve you by being kind,
truthful, and strong in our faith.
May our lives give you praise.
We ask this through our Lord and Savior,
Jesus Christ.

Amen.

✝ All make the Sign of the Cross.

PRAYER FOR
FRIDAY, APRIL 17, 2020

OPENING

It is God's love for us that saves us. In Jesus God revealed his great love for us. We, in turn, love God back by loving one another, and especially by caring for the poor and the oppressed.

✚ All make the Sign of the Cross.

In the name of the Father, and of the Son, and of the Holy Spirit. Amen.

PSALM

(For a longer psalm, see page xiv.)
Psalm 105:1–2, 3–4, 6–7

Let the hearts of those who seek
the Lord rejoice.

**Let the hearts of those who seek
the Lord rejoice.**

O give thanks to the Lord, call on his name,
    make known his deeds among the peoples.
Sing to him, sing praises to him;
    tell of all his wonderful works.

**Let the hearts of those who seek
the Lord rejoice.**

READING

1 John 4:7, 9, 11–14, 16bc

A reading from the First Letter of John.

Beloved, let us love one another, because love is from God; everyone who loves is born of God and knows God. God's love was revealed among us in this way: God sent his only Son into the world so that we might live through him. Beloved, since God loved us so much, we also ought to love one another. No one has ever seen God; if we love one another, God lives in us, and his love is perfected in us. By this we know that we abide in him and he in us, because he has given us of his Spirit. And we have seen and do testify that the Father has sent his Son as the Savior of the world. God is love, and those who abide in love abide in God, and God abides in them.

The Word of the Lord.

◆ All observe silence.

FOR SILENT REFLECTION

Think about this silently in your heart. Who teaches you the most about God's love?

CLOSING PRAYER

Let us pray to God for our needs and the needs of others: our family, neighborhood, and the world. For each need we say, "Lord, hear our prayer."

◆ All may add their own prayers here.

Let us pray: **Our Father . . . Amen.**

We rejoice and are glad, O God,
We give you thanks for the gift of Jesus,
our Savior.
Jesus showed us how to love you
and to love one another.
May we follow him always.
We ask in the name of our Risen Lord,
Jesus Christ.

Amen.

✚ All make the Sign of the Cross.

Imagine how the disciples felt after Jesus died. His arrest and death happened so quickly. They must have been terribly sad, confused, and afraid. Jesus appeared to them several times after his Resurrection, and each time he comforted them and told them not to worry.

✝ All make the Sign of the Cross.

In the name of the Father, and of the Son, and of the Holy Spirit. Amen.

PSALM

(For a longer psalm, see page xiv.)
Psalm 105:1–2, 3–4, 6–7

Let the hearts of those who seek the LORD rejoice.

Let the hearts of those who seek the LORD rejoice.

O give thanks to the LORD, call on his name,
    make known his deeds among the peoples.
Sing to him, sing praises to him;
    tell of all his wonderful works.

Let the hearts of those who seek the LORD rejoice.

◆ All stand and sing **Alleluia.**

GOSPEL

John 20:19–22

A reading from the holy Gospel according to John.

When it was evening on that day, the first day of the week, and the doors of the house where the disciples had met were locked for fear of the Jews, Jesus came and stood among them and said, "Peace be with you." After he said this, he showed them his hands and his side. Then the disciples rejoiced when they saw the Lord. Jesus said to them again, "Peace be with you. As the Father has sent me, so I send you." When he had said this, he breathed on them and said to them, "Receive the Holy Spirit."

The Gospel of the Lord.

◆ All sit and observe silence.

FOR SILENT REFLECTION

Think about this silently in your heart. Jesus sent his disciples out to do God's work. How do we do God's work?

CLOSING PRAYER

Let us pray to God for our needs and the needs of others: our family, neighborhood, and the world. For each need we say, "Lord, hear our prayer."

◆ All may add their own prayers here.

Let us pray: **Our Father . . . Amen.**

O God, grant us your peace.
Just as you sent your Son Jesus to bring peace,
so you send us to be peacemakers
in our classrooms, our families,
and our communities.
Help us to do your will with courage.
We ask this in the name of our Risen Lord,
Jesus Christ.

Amen.

✝ All make the Sign of the Cross.

PRAYER FOR
MONDAY, APRIL 20, 2020

OPENING

In accordance with burial tradition, women went to Jesus' burial place to put spices on the body. What they found greatly surprised them.

✛ All make the Sign of the Cross.

In the name of the Father, and of the Son, and of the Holy Spirit. Amen.

PSALM

(For a longer psalm, see page xiv.)
Psalm 105:1–2, 3–4, 6–7

Let the hearts of those who seek
the LORD rejoice.

**Let the hearts of those who seek
the LORD rejoice.**

O give thanks to the LORD, call on his name,
   make known his deeds among the peoples.
Sing to him, sing praises to him;
   tell of all his wonderful works.

**Let the hearts of those who seek
the LORD rejoice.**

◆ All stand and sing **Alleluia.**

GOSPEL

Matthew 28:1–6, 7b, 8

A reading from the holy Gospel according to Matthew.

After the sabbath, as the first day of the week was dawning, Mary Magdalene and the other Mary went to see the tomb. And suddenly there was a great earthquake; for an angel of the Lord, descending from heaven, came and rolled back the stone and sat on it. His appearance was like lightning, and his clothing white as snow. For fear of him the guards shook and became like dead men. But the angel said to the women, "Do not be afraid; I know that you are looking for Jesus who was crucified. He is not here; for he has been raised, as he said. Come, see the place where he lay. He has been raised from the dead and is going ahead of you to Galilee; there you will see him." So they left the tomb quickly with fear and great joy, and ran to tell his disciples.

The Gospel of the Lord.

◆ All sit and observe silence.

FOR SILENT REFLECTION

Think about this silently in your heart. Why is the Resurrection of Jesus Christ from the dead a joyful story?

CLOSING PRAYER

Let us pray to God for our needs and the needs of others: our family, neighborhood, and the world. For each need we say, "Lord, hear our prayer."

◆ All may add their own prayers here.

Let us pray: **Our Father . . . Amen.**

We continue to rejoice, O God.
Christ is risen! Alleluia!
May we be joyful in our faith
and share this joy with others.
We ask this in the name of our Risen Lord,
Jesus Christ.

Amen.

✛ All make the Sign of the Cross.

OPENING

This week we hear the stories of Christ's appearances to his disciples after his Resurrection. The two friends in today's story don't recognize him. Today we celebrate the feast of St. Anselm, a bishop and Doctor of the Church.

✝ All make the Sign of the Cross.

In the name of the Father, and of the Son, and of the Holy Spirit. Amen.

PSALM

(For a longer psalm, see page xiv.)
Psalm 105:1–2, 3–4, 6–7

Let the hearts of those who seek
the LORD rejoice.

**Let the hearts of those who seek
the LORD rejoice.**

O give thanks to the LORD, call on his name,
   make known his deeds among the peoples.
Sing to him, sing praises to him;
   tell of all his wonderful works.

**Let the hearts of those who seek
the LORD rejoice.**

◆ All stand and sing **Alleluia**.

GOSPEL   Luke 24:13ab, 15b, 16–17ab, 18b, 19ab, 20, 21b–23

A reading from the holy Gospel according to Luke.

On the day it was discovered that Jesus' body was no longer in the tomb, two disciples were going to a village called Emmaus. Jesus himself came near, but their eyes were kept from recognizing him. And he said to them, "What are you discussing with each other while you walk?" Cleopas answered him, "Are you the only stranger in Jerusalem who does not know the things that have taken place?" He asked them, "What things?" They replied, "The things about Jesus of Nazareth, and how our chief priests and leaders handed him over to be condemned to death and crucified him. It is now the third day since these things took place. Moreover, some women of our group astounded us. They were at the tomb early this morning, and when they did not find his body there, they came back and told us that they had indeed seen a vision of angels who said that he was alive."

The Gospel of the Lord.

◆ All sit and observe silence.

FOR SILENT REFLECTION

Think about this silently in your heart. Can we be so absorbed in our own concerns that we miss seeing the holiness in people around us?

CLOSING PRAYER

Let us pray to God for our needs and the needs of others: our family, neighborhood, and the world. For each need we say, "Lord, hear our prayer."

◆ All may add their own prayers here.

Let us pray: **Our Father . . . Amen.**

Loving God,
like Jesus' disciples, we do not always recognize the Lord's presence.
Help us to see Jesus in one another.
We ask this through our Risen Lord,
Jesus Christ.

Amen.

✝ All make the Sign of the Cross.

OPENING

The story of two disciples on the road to Emmaus continues. Although Jesus joined them, they did not recognize him. Then something very particular happened and they recognized him.

✝ All make the Sign of the Cross.

In the name of the Father, and of the Son, and of the Holy Spirit. Amen.

PSALM

(For a longer psalm, see page xiv.)
Psalm 105:1–2, 3–4, 6–7

Let the hearts of those who seek
the LORD rejoice.

**Let the hearts of those who seek
the LORD rejoice.**

O give thanks to the LORD, call on his name,
    make known his deeds among the peoples.
Sing to him, sing praises to him;
    tell of all his wonderful works.

**Let the hearts of those who seek
the LORD rejoice.**

◆ All stand and sing **Alleluia.**

GOSPEL

Luke 24:28–32ab, 33, 35

A reading from the holy Gospel according to Luke.

As they came near the village to which they were going, he walked ahead as if he were going on. But they urged him strongly, saying, "Stay with us, because it is almost evening and the day is now nearly over." So he went in to stay with them. When he was at the table with them, he took bread, blessed and broke it, and gave it to them. Then their eyes were opened, and they recognized him; and he vanished from their sight. They said to each other, "Were not our hearts burning within us while he was talking to us?" That same hour they got up and returned to Jerusalem; and they found the eleven and their companions gathered together. Then they told what had happened on the road, and how Jesus had been made known to them in the breaking of the bread.

The Gospel of the Lord.

◆ All sit and observe silence.

FOR SILENT REFLECTION

Think about this silently in your heart. Do you recognize and experience Christ's presence when you receive Holy Communion?

CLOSING PRAYER

Let us pray to God for our needs and the needs of others: our family, neighborhood, and the world. For each need we say, "Lord, hear our prayer."

◆ All may add their own prayers here.

Let us pray: **Our Father . . . Amen.**

Loving God,
Christ is present in the gift of the Eucharist.
May we receive him with joy
and thanksgiving.
We pray in his name.

Amen.

✝ All make the Sign of the Cross.

OPENING

After Jesus' Death, his disciples were afraid. But Jesus wanted them to continue his work. He gave them strength and courage. His appearances gave the disciples comfort, and they were encouraged to continue God's work.

✛ All make the Sign of the Cross.

In the name of the Father, and of the Son, and of the Holy Spirit. Amen.

PSALM

(For a longer psalm, see page xiv.)
Psalm 105:1–2, 3–4, 6–7

Let the hearts of those who seek the LORD rejoice.

Let the hearts of those who seek the LORD rejoice.

O give thanks to the LORD, call on his name,
   make known his deeds among the peoples.
Sing to him, sing praises to him;
   tell of all his wonderful works.

Let the hearts of those who seek the LORD rejoice.

◆ All stand and sing **Alleluia.**

GOSPEL

Luke 24:36–43

A reading from the holy Gospel according to Luke.

While the disciples were talking, Jesus himself stood among them and said to them, "Peace be with you." They were startled and terrified, and thought that they were seeing a ghost. He said to them, "Why are you frightened, and why do doubts arise in your hearts? Look at my hands and my feet; see that it is I myself.

Touch me and see; for a ghost does not have flesh and bones as you see that I have." And when he had said this, he showed them his hands and his feet. While in their joy they were disbelieving and still wondering, he said to them, "Have you anything here to eat?" They gave him a piece of broiled fish, and he took it and ate in their presence.

The Gospel of the Lord.

◆ All sit and observe silence.

FOR SILENT REFLECTION

Think about this silently in your heart. Do you sometimes feel the presence of someone you have loved who has died?

CLOSING PRAYER

Let us pray to God for our needs and the needs of others: our family, neighborhood, and the world. For each need we say, "Lord, hear our prayer."

◆ All may add their own prayers here.

Let us pray: **Our Father . . . Amen.**

O God of peace,
may we take to heart Christ's words of peace
and know that we need not be afraid.
We ask this in the name of our Risen Lord.

Amen.

✛ All make the Sign of the Cross.

PRAYER FOR
FRIDAY, APRIL 24, 2020

OPENING

After Jesus' death the Apostle Paul is responsible for spreading the teachings of Jesus to non-Jewish peoples. In today's reading, he is talking to people of Corinth [KOHR-ihnth], Greece.

✚ All make the Sign of the Cross.

In the name of the Father, and of the Son, and of the Holy Spirit. Amen.

PSALM

(For a longer psalm, see page xiv.)
Psalm 105:1–2, 3–4, 6–7

Let the hearts of those who seek
the LORD rejoice.

**Let the hearts of those who seek
the LORD rejoice.**

O give thanks to the LORD, call on his name,
    make known his deeds among the peoples.
Sing to him, sing praises to him;
    tell of all his wonderful works.

**Let the hearts of those who seek
the LORD rejoice.**

READING

1 Corinthians 15:1ab, 3b–8

A reading from the First Letter of Paul to the Corinthians [kohr-IN-thee-unz].

Now I would remind you, brothers and sisters, of the good news that I proclaimed to you: that Christ died for our sins in accordance with the scriptures, and that he was buried, and that he was raised on the third day in accordance with the scriptures, and that he appeared to Cephas [SEE-fuhs], then to the twelve. Then he appeared to more than five hundred brothers and sisters at one time, most of whom are still alive, though some have died. Then he appeared to James, then to all the apostles. Last of all, as to one untimely born, he appeared also to me.

The Word of the Lord.

◆ All observe silence.

FOR SILENT REFLECTION

Think about this silently in your heart. Paul calls the stories and teaching of Jesus "good news." How are they "good news" to us?

CLOSING PRAYER

Let us pray to God for our needs and the needs of others: our family, neighborhood, and the world. For each need we say, "Lord, hear our prayer."

◆ All may add their own prayers here.

Let us pray: **Our Father . . . Amen.**

Holy and loving God,
may we hear the good news of the Gospel.
Through Jesus' life, death, and resurrection,
he revealed your power.
He taught us to believe in you.
May we always be faithful to his teachings.
We pray in his name.

Amen.

✚ All make the Sign of the Cross.

PRAYER FOR THE WEEK

WITH A READING FROM THE GOSPEL FOR **SUNDAY, APRIL 26, 2020**

OPENING

In this third week of Easter Time, we continue to rejoice that Christ is risen. The two disciples in the Gospel were very sad until they recognized Jesus in the breaking of the bread.

✦ All make the Sign of the Cross.

In the name of the Father, and of the Son, and of the Holy Spirit. Amen.

PSALM

(For a longer psalm, see page xiv.)
Psalm 105:1–2, 3–4, 6–7

Let the hearts of those who seek
the LORD rejoice.

**Let the hearts of those who seek
the LORD rejoice.**

O give thanks to the LORD, call on his name,
   make known his deeds among the peoples.
Sing to him, sing praises to him;
   tell of all his wonderful works.

**Let the hearts of those who seek
the LORD rejoice.**

✦ All stand and sing **Alleluia.**

GOSPEL

Luke 24:13a, 15–16, 28–29ab, 30–31, 33–34

A reading from the holy Gospel according to Luke.

Now on that same day two of the disciples were going to a village called Emmaus. While they were talking and discussing, Jesus himself came near and went with them, but their eyes were kept from recognizing him. As they came near the village to which they were going, he walked ahead as if he were going on. But they urged him strongly, saying, "Stay with us." When he was at the table with them, he took bread, blessed and broke it, and gave it to them. Then their eyes were opened, and they recognized him; and he vanished from their sight. That same hour they got up and returned to Jerusalem; and they found the eleven and their companions gathered together. They were saying, "The Lord has risen indeed, and he has appeared to Simon!"

The Gospel of the Lord.

◆ All sit and observe silence.

FOR SILENT REFLECTION

Think about this silently in your heart. Where, besides at Mass, do we recognize the presence of Jesus?

CLOSING PRAYER

Let us pray to God for our needs and the needs of others: our family, neighborhood, and the world. For each need we say, "Lord, hear our prayer."

◆ All may add their own prayers here.

Let us pray: **Our Father . . . Amen.**

Holy God,
help us to recognize the presence of Jesus.
Help us to see him in one another.
Help us remember that what we do to others, we do to him.
We pray in Christ's name.

Amen.

✦ All make the Sign of the Cross.

PRAYER FOR
MONDAY, APRIL 27, 2020

OPENING

In our third week of Easter rejoicing we'll hear stories of the earliest Christians. They were called "Followers of the Way," and the "Way" was Jesus. They were baptized, and they participated in the Breaking of the Bread, what we call Mass.

✛ All make the Sign of the Cross.

In the name of the Father, and of the Son, and of the Holy Spirit. Amen.

PSALM

(For a longer psalm, see page xiv.)
Psalm 105:1–2, 3–4, 6–7

Let the hearts of those who seek
the LORD rejoice.

**Let the hearts of those who seek
the LORD rejoice.**

O give thanks to the LORD, call on his name,
    make known his deeds among the peoples.
Sing to him, sing praises to him;
    tell of all his wonderful works.

**Let the hearts of those who seek
the LORD rejoice.**

READING

Acts 2:14ac, 22b, 23a, 32, 37–38, 41

A reading from the Acts of the Apostles.

But Peter, raised his voice and addressed them, "Jesus of Nazareth, a man attested to you by God with deeds of power, wonders, and signs, this man, this Jesus God raised up, and of that all of us are witnesses." Now when they heard this, they were cut to the heart and said to Peter and to the other apostles, "Brothers, what should we do?" Peter said to them, "Repent, and be baptized every one of you in the name of Jesus Christ so that your sins may be forgiven; and you will receive the gift of the Holy Spirit." So those who welcomed his message were baptized, and that day about three thousand persons were added.

The Word of the Lord.

◆ All observe silence.

FOR SILENT REFLECTION

Think about this silently in your heart. Pray for the Holy Spirit to come to you.

CLOSING PRAYER

Let us pray to God for our needs and the needs of others: our family, neighborhood, and the world. For each need we say, "Lord, hear our prayer."

◆ All may add their own prayers here.

Let us pray: **Our Father . . . Amen.**

We thank you, loving God,
for the gift of Baptism.
In Baptism you call us
to our Christian dignity;
you call us to be your sons and daughters.
We pray that we may be faithful to this call.
We ask this in the name of our Risen Lord,
Jesus Christ.

Amen.

✛ All make the Sign of the Cross.

OPENING

Usually the first Christians were a small group in a town. They lived communally; that is, they shared all their food, money, clothes, and homes with one another. Religious communities still live that way. Today is the feast of St. Peter Chanel, a missionary priest who spread Christianity in the South Pacific region. We also remember St. Louis Grignion de Montfort, who preached extensively on God's mercy.

✚ All make the Sign of the Cross.

In the name of the Father, and of the Son, and of the Holy Spirit. Amen.

PSALM

(For a longer psalm, see page xiv.)
Psalm 105:1–2, 3–4, 6–7

Let the hearts of those who seek
the LORD rejoice.

**Let the hearts of those who seek
the LORD rejoice.**

O give thanks to the LORD, call on his name,
    make known his deeds among the peoples.
Sing to him, sing praises to him;
    tell of all his wonderful works.

**Let the hearts of those who seek
the LORD rejoice.**

READING

Acts 2:42–47

A reading from the Acts of the Apostles.

They devoted themselves to the apostles' teaching and fellowship, to the breaking of bread and the prayers. Awe came upon everyone, because many wonders and signs were being done by the apostles. All who believed were together and had all things in common; they would sell their possessions and goods and distribute the proceeds to all, as any had need. Day by day, as they spent much time together in the temple, they broke bread at home and ate their food with glad and generous hearts, praising God and having the goodwill of all the people. And day by day the Lord added to their number those who were being saved.

The Word of the Lord.

◆ All observe silence.

FOR SILENT REFLECTION

Think about this silently in your heart. These early Christians shared everything they had, perhaps even with strangers. What do you think made them do that?

CLOSING PRAYER

Let us pray to God for our needs and the needs of others: our family, neighborhood, and the world. For each need we say, "Lord, hear our prayer."

◆ All may add their own prayers here.

Let us pray: **Our Father . . . Amen.**

Generous and loving God,
we pray for the same spirit
that inspired the early Christians.
Help us to be generous
and loving to all we meet
and to share our love for you
as Sts. Peter and Louis did.
We ask this in the name of our Risen Lord,
Jesus Christ.

Amen.

✚ All make the Sign of the Cross.

PRAYER FOR
WEDNESDAY, APRIL 29, 2020

OPENING

We continue to hear about the extraordinary sharing done by the early believers in Jesus. Today we remember St. Catherine of Siena, a philosopher and theologian. She is a Doctor of the Church because of her important writings and her leadership.

✝ All make the Sign of the Cross.

In the name of the Father, and of the Son, and of the Holy Spirit. Amen.

PSALM

(For a longer psalm, see page xiv.)
Psalm 105:1–2, 3–4, 6–7

Let the hearts of those who seek the LORD rejoice.

Let the hearts of those who seek the LORD rejoice.

O give thanks to the LORD, call on his name,
  make known his deeds among the peoples.
Sing to him, sing praises to him;
  tell of all his wonderful works.

Let the hearts of those who seek the LORD rejoice.

READING

Acts 4:32–37

A reading from the Acts of the Apostles.

Now the whole group of those who believed were of one heart and soul, and no one claimed private ownership of any possessions, but everything they owned was held in common. With great power the apostles gave their testimony to the resurrection of the Lord Jesus, and great grace was upon them all. There was not a needy person among them, for as many as owned lands or houses sold them and brought the proceeds of what was sold. They laid it at the apostles' feet, and it was distributed to each as any had need. There was a Levite, a native of Cyprus, Joseph, to whom the apostles gave the name Barnabas (which means "son of encouragement"). He sold a field that belonged to him, then brought the money, and laid it at the apostles' feet.

The Word of the Lord.

◆ All observe silence.

FOR SILENT REFLECTION

Think about this silently in your heart. What does it mean to be "in need"? Are only poor people "in need"?

CLOSING PRAYER

Let us pray to God for our needs and the needs of others: our family, neighborhood, and the world. For each need we say, "Lord, hear our prayer."

◆ All may add their own prayers here.

Let us pray: **Our Father . . . Amen.**

Generous and loving God,
we see your Spirit at work
in the lives of the early Christians.
May we learn to share what we have
with others, especially those who are poor
or are in need.
We pray in the name of our Risen Lord,
Jesus Christ.

Amen.

✝ All make the Sign of the Cross.

OPENING

Jesus' disciples were not always received with a welcome. In some towns they were persecuted and punished for speaking about Jesus and his message.

✛ All make the Sign of the Cross.

In the name of the Father, and of the Son, and of the Holy Spirit. Amen.

PSALM

(For a longer psalm, see page xiv.)
Psalm 105:1–2, 3–4, 6–7

Let the hearts of those who seek
the LORD rejoice.

**Let the hearts of those who seek
the LORD rejoice.**

O give thanks to the LORD, call on his name,
    make known his deeds among the peoples.
Sing to him, sing praises to him;
    tell of all his wonderful works.

**Let the hearts of those who seek
the LORD rejoice.**

READING

Acts 5:17bd, 18, 27c–28a, 29a, 33b, 35ab, 38b, 39c-42

A reading from the Acts of the Apostles.

The high priest and all who were with him, being filled with jealousy, arrested the apostles and put them in the public prison. The high priest questioned them, saying, "We gave you strict orders not to teach in this name." But Peter and the apostles answered, "We must obey God rather than any human authority." They were enraged and wanted to kill them. Then Gamaliel said to them, "Fellow Israelites, I tell you, keep away from these men and let them alone." They were convinced by him, and when they had called in the apostles, they had them flogged. Then they ordered them not to speak in the name of Jesus, and let them go. As they left the council, the apostles rejoiced that they were considered worthy to suffer dishonor for the sake of the name. And every day in the temple and at home they did not cease to teach and proclaim Jesus as the Messiah.

The Word of the Lord.

◆ All observe silence.

FOR SILENT REFLECTION

Think about this silently in your heart. Pray to be strong and courageous in your faith.

CLOSING PRAYER

Let us pray to God for our needs and the needs of others: our family, neighborhood, and the world. For each need we say, "Lord, hear our prayer."

◆ All may add their own prayers here.

Let us pray: **Our Father . . . Amen.**

Holy God,
some people do not respect or love you.
But may we stay strong in our faith and be witnesses to your love for everyone.
We ask this in Christ's name.

Amen.

✛ All make the Sign of the Cross.

OPENING

Today the Church honors St. Joseph the Worker. All over the world, people celebrate the dignity of labor—taking pride in what we do. In our reading we hear how the early followers of Jesus were called "Christians," because they followed Jesus, the Christ.

✝ All make the Sign of the Cross.

In the name of the Father, and of the Son, and of the Holy Spirit. Amen.

PSALM

(For a longer psalm, see page xiv.)
Psalm 105:1–2, 3–4, 6–7

Let the hearts of those who seek
the LORD rejoice.

**Let the hearts of those who seek
the LORD rejoice.**

O give thanks to the LORD, call on his name,
make known his deeds among the peoples.
Sing to him, sing praises to him;
tell of all his wonderful works.

**Let the hearts of those who seek
the LORD rejoice.**

READING

Acts 11:20, 22–26

A reading from the Acts of the Apostles.

But among them were some men of Cyprus and Cyrene who, on coming to Antioch [AN-tee-ahk], spoke to the Hellenists also proclaiming the Lord Jesus. News of this came to the ears of the church in Jerusalem, and they sent Barnabas to Antioch. When he came and saw the grace of God, he rejoiced, and he exhorted them all to remain faithful to the Lord with steadfast devotion; for he was a good man, full of the Holy Spirit and of faith. And a great many people were brought to the Lord. Then Barnabas went to Tarsus to look for Saul, and when he had found him, he brought him to Antioch. So it was that for an entire year they met with the church and taught a great many people, and it was in Antioch that the disciples were first called "Christians."

The Word of the Lord.

◆ All observe silence.

FOR SILENT REFLECTION

Think about this silently in your heart. What does it mean to be a Christian?

CLOSING PRAYER

Let us pray to God for our needs and the needs of others: our family, neighborhood, and the world. For each need we say, "Lord, hear our prayer."

◆ All may add their own prayers here.

Let us pray: **Our Father . . . Amen.**

God, our Father in heaven,
may we respect the dignity of all who labor
and work to make this world a better place.
May all who work know the importance
and value of what they do.
We ask this through Christ our Risen Lord.

Amen.

✝ All make the Sign of the Cross.

PRAYER FOR THE WEEK

WITH A READING FROM THE GOSPEL FOR **SUNDAY, MAY 3, 2020**

OPENING

Jesus often told stories to make his point. Today's Gospel has two metaphors, or comparisons. Jesus calls himself the shepherd and the gate. Jesus wants us to trust him and follow his teachings, which will lead us to God.

✛ All make the Sign of the Cross.

In the name of the Father, and of the Son, and of the Holy Spirit. Amen.

PSALM

(For a longer psalm, see page xiv.)
Psalm 118:1–2, 4, 22–24, 25–27a

The stone that the builders rejected
  has become the chief cornerstone.

The stone that the builders rejected
  has become the chief cornerstone.

O give thanks to the LORD, for he is good;
  his steadfast love endures forever!
Let Israel say,
  "His steadfast love endures forever."
Let those who fear the LORD say,
  "His steadfast love endures forever."

The stone that the builders rejected
  has become the chief cornerstone.

◆ All stand and sing **Alleluia.**

GOSPEL

John 10:1–5, 7a, 9

A reading from the holy Gospel according to John.

Jesus said, "Very truly, I tell you, anyone who does not enter the sheepfold by the gate but climbs in by another way is a thief and a bandit. The one who enters by the gate is the shepherd of the sheep. The gatekeeper opens the gate for him, and the sheep hear his voice. He calls his own sheep by name and leads them out. When he has brought out all his own, he goes ahead of them, and the sheep follow him because they know his voice. They will not follow a stranger, but they will run from him because they do not know the voice of strangers." So again Jesus said to them, "I am the gate. Whoever enters by me will be saved, and will come in and go out and find pasture."

The Gospel of the Lord.

◆ All sit and observe silence.

FOR SILENT REFLECTION

Think about this silently in your heart. Who has been a gate for you? Who has shown you the way to follow Jesus?

CLOSING PRAYER

Let us pray to God for our needs and the needs of others: our family, neighborhood, and the world. For each need we say, "Lord, hear our prayer."

◆ All may add their own prayers here.

Let us pray: **Our Father . . . Amen.**

We pray, O God, that we may know
the voice of the Good Shepherd.
We pray that we will follow him and enter
through the gate that leads to life with you.
We ask this in the name of our Risen Lord.

Amen.

✛ All make the Sign of the Cross.

PRAYER SERVICE
TO HONOR MARY IN MAY

Add an image or statue of Mary, flowers, and candles to the sacred space. Prepare six leaders for this service. The third leader will need a Bible for the passages from Luke. Take time to help the lector practice the readings. You may wish to sing "Sing of Mary" as the opening song. If the group will sing, prepare someone to lead it.

FIRST LEADER:

Throughout the month of May, we remember Mary, the Mother of our Lord Jesus. She was a life-giving caregiver for our Savior, and she remains so for us today. She represents the fullness of holiness, for she was conceived without sin and was assumed into heaven because of her special role in our salvation. She serves as an example for all of us to say "yes" in practical ways to God's Spirit of goodness. Many Catholics turn to this beloved first disciple of Christ for inspiration and for prayer, particularly as the events of Jesus' life unfold in Scripture during the Church year.

SONG LEADER:

◆ Gesture for all to stand, and lead the first few verses of the song.

SECOND LEADER:

✝ All make the Sign of the Cross.

In the name of the Father, and of the Son, and of the Holy Spirit. Amen.

Let us pray:
Almighty Father,
we honor Mary as our Mother
because you chose her to be
the human vessel for
your Son Jesus,
who was both human and divine.

Help us to be open to
the same Spirit
who appeared to Mary,
guiding her throughout her
challenging life with
the Savior of our world.
We ask this through Christ our Lord.

Amen.

◆ Remain standing and sing **Alleluia.**

THIRD LEADER: Luke 1:26–38
A reading from the holy Gospel according
to Luke.

◆ Read the Gospel passage from the Bible.

The Gospel of the Lord.

◆ All sit and observe silence.

FOURTH LEADER:

◆ Gesture for all to stand.

Let us bring our hopes and needs to God as
we respond, "Lord, hear our prayer."
For all mothers
and those who nurture others
throughout life.
May they be open to
God's creative Spirit to bring
new life into the world,

we pray to the Lord . . .

For those facing difficult decisions.
May they look to Mary
for guidance
in following God's plan,

we pray to the Lord . . .

For all married couples.
May they remain devoted
to God, to each other,
and to their Sacrament of Marriage,

we pray to the Lord . . .

For the sick and the abandoned.
For those who have passed
to the other side of life.
May they feel the loving arms
of Mary with Jesus,

we pray to the Lord . . .

FIFTH LEADER:
Let us pray the Hail Mary:

ALL: Hail Mary, full of grace . . .

◆ Pause, and then say:

Let us offer one another a sign of
Christ's peace.

◆ All offer one another a sign of peace.

SIXTH LEADER:
Let us pray Mary's special prayer,
the *Magnificat*:
"My soul magnifies the Lord,
    and my spirit rejoices in God my Savior,
for he has looked with favor on the lowliness
        of his servant.
    Surely, from now on all generations will
        call me blessed;
for the Mighty One has done great things
        for me,
    and holy is his name."

✚ All make the Sign of the Cross.

**In the name of the Father, and of the Son,
and of the Holy Spirit. Amen.**

CHILDREN'S DAILY PRAYER 2019–2020, © 2019 Archdiocese of Chicago: Liturgy Training Publications. All rights reserved. Orders: 800-933-1800 or www.LTP.org.

PRAYER FOR
MONDAY, MAY 4, 2020

OPENING

This week we'll look at some of Jesus' titles in the Gospel of Matthew. A title often reveals something about the person's character or work. The title "Son of David" means Jesus was descended from King David as the Messiah was supposed to be.

✚ All make the Sign of the Cross.

In the name of the Father, and of the Son, and of the Holy Spirit. Amen.

PSALM

(For a longer psalm, see page xv.)
Psalm 118:1–2, 4, 22–24, 25–27a

The stone that the builders rejected
   has become the chief cornerstone.

**The stone that the builders rejected
   has become the chief cornerstone.**

O give thanks to the LORD, for he is good;
   his steadfast love endures forever!
Let Israel say,
   "His steadfast love endures forever."
Let those who fear the LORD say,
   "His steadfast love endures forever."

**The stone that the builders rejected
   has become the chief cornerstone.**

◆ All stand and sing **Alleluia.**

GOSPEL

Matthew 9:27–31

A reading from the holy Gospel according to Matthew.

As Jesus went on from there, two blind men followed him, crying loudly, "Have mercy on us, Son of David!" When he entered the house, the blind men came to him; and Jesus said to them,

"Do you believe that I am able to do this?" They said to him, "Yes, Lord." Then he touched their eyes and said, "According to your faith let it be done to you." And their eyes were opened. Then Jesus sternly ordered them, "See that no one knows of this." But they went away and spread the news about him throughout that district.

The Gospel of the Lord.

◆ All sit and observe silence.

FOR SILENT REFLECTION

Think about this silently in your heart. How do we spread the good news about Jesus?

CLOSING PRAYER

Let us pray to God for our needs and the needs of others: our family, neighborhood, and the world. For each need we say, "Lord, hear our prayer."

◆ All may add their own prayers here.

Let us pray: **Our Father . . . Amen.**

Loving God,
each of us has blind spots, places where we do not clearly see how you love us.
May we have the faith of the blind men
and trust in your healing power.
We ask this in the name of our Risen Lord, Jesus Christ.

Amen.

✚ All make the Sign of the Cross.

OPENING

Jesus called himself "Son of Man" eighty-one times in the Gospels! It literally means a "human being." Our Church teaches that Jesus is fully God and fully human.

✛ All make the Sign of the Cross.

In the name of the Father, and of the Son, and of the Holy Spirit. Amen.

PSALM

(For a longer psalm, see page xv.)
Psalm 118:1–2, 4, 22–24, 25–27a

The stone that the builders rejected
    has become the chief cornerstone.

**The stone that the builders rejected
    has become the chief cornerstone.**

O give thanks to the LORD, for he is good;
    his steadfast love endures forever!
Let Israel say,
    "His steadfast love endures forever."
Let those who fear the LORD say,
    "His steadfast love endures forever."

**The stone that the builders rejected
    has become the chief cornerstone.**

◆ All stand and sing **Alleluia.**

GOSPEL

Matthew 9:1–7

A reading from the holy Gospel according to Matthew.

After getting into a boat Jesus crossed the sea and came to his own town. And just then some people were carrying a paralyzed man lying on a bed. When Jesus saw their faith, he said to the paralytic, "Take heart, son; your sins are forgiven." Then some of the scribes said to themselves, "This man is blaspheming." But Jesus, perceiving their thoughts, said, "Why do you think evil in your hearts? For which is easier, to say, 'Your sins are forgiven,' or to say, 'Stand up and walk'? But so that you may know that the Son of Man has authority on earth to forgive sins"—he then said to the paralytic—"Stand up, take your bed and go to your home." And he stood up and went to his home.

The Gospel of the Lord.

◆ All sit and observe silence.

FOR SILENT REFLECTION

Think about this silently in your heart. Jesus often made people feel better. How can you make someone feel better today?

CLOSING PRAYER

Let us pray to God for our needs and the needs of others: our family, neighborhood, and the world. For each need we say, "Lord, hear our prayer."

◆ All may add their own prayers here.

Let us pray: **Our Father . . . Amen.**

Loving God,
your Son Jesus understood our human needs.
He healed those who were suffering
in body, mind, and soul.
Help us to turn to him in our need.
We ask this in his name.

Amen.

✛ All make the Sign of the Cross.

PRAYER FOR
WEDNESDAY, MAY 6, 2020

OPENING

In today's reading we hear that Jesus welcomes the children. He teaches that children have a special relationship to God and reveal something about God's Kingdom to us.

✝ All make the Sign of the Cross.

In the name of the Father, and of the Son, and of the Holy Spirit. Amen.

PSALM

(For a longer psalm, see page xv.)
Psalm 118:1–2, 4, 22–24, 25–27a

The stone that the builders rejected
   has become the chief cornerstone.

**The stone that the builders rejected
   has become the chief cornerstone.**

O give thanks to the LORD, for he is good;
   his steadfast love endures forever!
Let Israel say,
   "His steadfast love endures forever."
Let those who fear the LORD say,
   "His steadfast love endures forever."

**The stone that the builders rejected
   has become the chief cornerstone.**

♦ All stand and sing **Alleluia.**

GOSPEL

Matthew 19:13–17acd, 18–19

A reading from the holy Gospel according to Matthew.

Then little children were being brought to him in order that he might lay his hands on them and pray. The disciples spoke sternly to those who brought them; but Jesus said, "Let the little children come to me, and do not stop them; for it is to such as these that the kingdom of heaven belongs." And he laid his hands on them and went on his way. Then someone came to Jesus and said, "Teacher, what good deed must I do to have eternal life?" And Jesus said to him, "If you wish to enter into life, keep the commandments." He said to Jesus, "Which ones?" And Jesus said, "You shall not murder; You shall not commit adultery; You shall not steal; You shall not bear false witness; Honor your father and mother; also, You shall love your neighbor as yourself."

The Gospel of the Lord.

♦ All sit and observe silence.

FOR SILENT REFLECTION

Think about this silently in your heart. Why do you think Jesus wanted the little children to be brought to him?

CLOSING PRAYER

Let us pray to God for our needs and the needs of others: our family, neighborhood, and the world. For each need we say, "Lord, hear our prayer."

♦ All may add their own prayers here.

Let us pray: **Our Father . . . Amen.**

We pray that we might grow in our understanding of your Kingdom, O God. Help us to trust that although we are young, we can serve you by how we live our lives. We ask this in the name of our Risen Lord, Jesus Christ.

Amen.

✝ All make the Sign of the Cross.

OPENING

Jesus was sometimes called by the title, "Son of God." The men in today's reading recognized Jesus as God's Son.

✦ All make the Sign of the Cross.

In the name of the Father, and of the Son, and of the Holy Spirit. Amen.

PSALM

(For a longer psalm, see page xv.)
Psalm 118:1–2, 4, 22–24, 25–27a

The stone that the builders rejected
  has become the chief cornerstone.

**The stone that the builders rejected
  has become the chief cornerstone.**

O give thanks to the LORD, for he is good;
  his steadfast love endures forever!
Let Israel say,
  "His steadfast love endures forever."
Let those who fear the LORD say,
  "His steadfast love endures forever."

**The stone that the builders rejected
  has become the chief cornerstone.**

✦ All stand and sing **Alleluia.**

GOSPEL

Matthew 8:28–33

A reading from the holy Gospel according to Matthew.

When Jesus came to the other side, to the country of the Gadarenes [GAD-uh-reenz], two demoniacs [deh-MOH-nee-acks] coming out of the tombs met him. They were so fierce that no one could pass that way. Suddenly they shouted, "What have you to do with us, Son of God? Have you come here to torment us before the time?" Now a large herd of swine was feeding at some distance from them. The demons begged him, "If you cast us out, send us into the herd of swine." And he said to them, "Go!" So they came out and entered the swine; and suddenly, the whole herd rushed down the steep bank into the sea and perished in the water. The swineherds ran off, and on going into the town, they told the whole story about what had happened to the demoniacs.

The Gospel of the Lord.

✦ All sit and observe silence.

FOR SILENT REFLECTION

Think about this silently in your heart. Pray for an end to violence in our communities and our world.

CLOSING PRAYER

Let us pray to God for our needs and the needs of others: our family, neighborhood, and the world. For each need we say, "Lord, hear our prayer."

✦ All may add their own prayers here.

Let us pray: **Our Father . . . Amen.**

Loving God,
as Jesus cast out demons
from those who were suffering,
help us to do our part
to stop bullying and violence.
We pray in the name of Christ our Risen Lord.

Amen.

✦ All make the Sign of the Cross.

PRAYER FOR
FRIDAY, MAY 8, 2020

OPENING

Today we will hear an invitation from Jesus. Jesus wants the people to come to him, and he extends that same invitation to us.

✛ All make the Sign of the Cross.

In the name of the Father, and of the Son, and of the Holy Spirit. Amen.

PSALM

(For a longer psalm, see page xv.)
Psalm 118:1–2, 4, 22–24, 25–27a

The stone that the builders rejected
    has become the chief cornerstone.

**The stone that the builders rejected
        has become the chief cornerstone.**

O give thanks to the LORD, for he is good;
    his steadfast love endures forever!
Let Israel say,
    "His steadfast love endures forever."
Let those who fear the LORD say,
    "His steadfast love endures forever."

**The stone that the builders rejected
        has become the chief cornerstone.**

◆ All stand and sing **Alleluia**.

GOSPEL

Matthew 11:28–30

A reading from the holy Gospel according to Matthew.

"Come to me, all you that are weary and are carrying heavy burdens, and I will give you rest. Take my yoke upon you, and learn from me; for I am gentle and humble in heart, and you will find rest for your souls. For my yoke is easy, and my burden is light."

The Gospel of the Lord.

◆ All sit and observe silence.

FOR SILENT REFLECTION

Think about this silently in your heart. What is troubling you? Can you bring that to Jesus in prayer?

CLOSING PRAYER

Let us pray to God for our needs and the needs of others: our family, neighborhood, and the world. For each need we say, "Lord, hear our prayer."

◆ All may add their own prayers here.

Let us pray: **Our Father . . . Amen.**

Loving God,
Jesus understood that sometimes we are tired or sad or frustrated.
Help us to turn to you at those times,
and to trust that you will give us the strength we need.
We ask this in Christ Jesus' name.

Amen.

✛ All make the Sign of the Cross.

OPENING

The disciples' hearts were deeply troubled by Jesus' death. Jesus assured them that he had taught them all they needed to know. Jesus tells us that he is the way, the truth, and the life. Through him, we will know God the Father.

✚ All make the Sign of the Cross.

In the name of the Father, and of the Son, and of the Holy Spirit. Amen.

PSALM

(For a longer psalm, see page xv.)
Psalm 118:1–2, 4, 22–24, 25–27a

The stone that the builders rejected
    has become the chief cornerstone.

**The stone that the builders rejected
        has become the chief cornerstone.**

O give thanks to the LORD, for he is good;
    his steadfast love endures forever!
Let Israel say,
    "His steadfast love endures forever."
Let those who fear the LORD say,
    "His steadfast love endures forever."

**The stone that the builders rejected
        has become the chief cornerstone.**

◆ All stand and sing **Alleluia.**

GOSPEL

John 14:1a, 3, 5–7a, 11–12

A reading from the holy Gospel according to John.

Jesus said to his disciples, "Do not let your hearts be troubled. If I go and prepare a place for you, I will come again and will take you to myself, so that where I am, there you may be also." Thomas said to him, "Lord, we do not know where you are going. How can we know the way?" Jesus said to him, "I am the way, and the truth, and the life. No one comes to the Father except through me. If you know me, you will know my Father also. Believe me that I am in the Father and the Father is in me; but if you do not, then believe me because of the works themselves. Very truly, I tell you, the one who believes in me will also do the works that I do and, in fact, will do greater works than these, because I am going to the Father."

The Gospel of the Lord.

◆ All sit and observe silence.

FOR SILENT REFLECTION

Think about this silently in your heart. How can you show someone you love them today?

CLOSING PRAYER

Let us pray to God for our needs and the needs of others: our family, neighborhood, and the world. For each need we say, "Lord, hear our prayer."

◆ All may add their own prayers here.

Let us pray: **Our Father . . . Amen.**

Holy God,
Jesus loves us so much that he showed us the way to you.
We believe that he is the way, the truth, and the life we need.
Help us to follow him.
We ask this in his name.

Amen.

✚ All make the Sign of the Cross.

PRAYER FOR
MONDAY, MAY 11, 2020

OPENING

In today's Gospel reading we hear Jesus call himself the Good Shepherd. As the Good Shepherd, Jesus knows his sheep and he protects them from harm. Jesus uses these images to communicate how he cares for each of us.

✛ All make the Sign of the Cross.

In the name of the Father, and of the Son, and of the Holy Spirit. Amen.

PSALM

(For a longer psalm, see page xv.)
Psalm 118:1–2, 4, 22–24, 25–27a

The stone that the builders rejected
   has become the chief cornerstone.

**The stone that the builders rejected
    has become the chief cornerstone.**

O give thanks to the LORD, for he is good;
   his steadfast love endures forever!
Let Israel say,
   "His steadfast love endures forever."
Let those who fear the LORD say,
   "His steadfast love endures forever."

**The stone that the builders rejected
    has become the chief cornerstone.**

◆ All stand and sing **Alleluia.**

GOSPEL

John 10:9–15a

A reading from the holy Gospel according to John.

Jesus said, "I am the gate. Whoever enters by me will be saved, and will come in and go out and find pasture. The thief comes only to steal and kill and destroy. I came that they may have life, and have it abundantly. I am the good shepherd. The good shepherd lays down his life for the sheep. The hired hand, who is not the shepherd and does not own the sheep, sees the wolf coming and leaves the sheep and runs away—and the wolf snatches them and scatters them. The hired hand runs away because a hired hand does not care for the sheep. I am the good shepherd. I know my own and my own know me, just as the Father knows me and I know the Father."

The Gospel of the Lord.

◆ All sit and observe silence.

FOR SILENT REFLECTION

Think about this silently in your heart. We know that Jesus is trustworthy. How do you experience his love and protection?

CLOSING PRAYER

Let us pray to God for our needs and the needs of others: our family, neighborhood, and the world. For each need we say, "Lord, hear our prayer."

◆ All may add their own prayers here.

Let us pray: **Our Father . . . Amen.**

We thank you and praise you, God,
for Jesus, our Good Shepherd.
As a shepherd cares for the sheep,
Jesus cares for us and knows what we need.
We pray in the name of Christ our Lord.

Amen.

✛ All make the Sign of the Cross.

OPENING

Jesus wants all people to live happy and healthy lives. He tells us how to make that happen. The word *love* is mentioned six times in today's reading. The word *abide* means "to stay" or "remain."

✛ All make the Sign of the Cross.

In the name of the Father, and of the Son, and of the Holy Spirit. Amen.

PSALM

(For a longer psalm, see page xv.)
Psalm 118:1–2, 4, 2–24, 25–27a

The stone that the builders rejected
has become the chief cornerstone.

**The stone that the builders rejected
has become the chief cornerstone.**

O give thanks to the LORD, for he is good;
his steadfast love endures forever!
Let Israel say,
"His steadfast love endures forever."
Let those who fear the LORD say,
"His steadfast love endures forever."

**The stone that the builders rejected
has become the chief cornerstone.**

◆ All stand and sing **Alleluia.**

GOSPEL

John 15:9–12

A reading from the holy Gospel according to John.

Jesus said, "As the Father has loved me, so I have loved you; abide in my love. If you keep my commandments, you will abide in my love, just as I have kept my Father's commandments and abide in his love. I have said these things to you so that my joy may be in you, and that your joy may be complete. This is my commandment, that you love one another as I have loved you."

The Gospel of the Lord.

◆ All sit and observe silence.

FOR SILENT REFLECTION

Think about this silently in your heart. Whom can you tell that you love them today?

CLOSING PRAYER

Let us pray to God for our needs and the needs of others: our family, neighborhood, and the world. For each need we say, "Lord, hear our prayer."

◆ All may add their own prayers here.

Let us pray: **Our Father . . . Amen.**

We rejoice and are glad, O God.
We long to remain in your love
and to keep your commandments.
Please give us the grace we need.
We ask this in the name of our Risen Lord,
Jesus Christ.

Amen.

✛ All make the Sign of the Cross.

PRAYER FOR
WEDNESDAY, MAY 13, 2020

OPENING

The four Gospels tell the stories of the life of Jesus. The stories in these four Gospels are a wonderful gift to us because they tell us how to live. Jesus taught us and showed us the way. Today we honor Mary, Our Lady of Fatima. In 1917, the Blessed Mother appeared to three children and urged them to pray for sinners and to pray the Rosary.

✛ All make the Sign of the Cross.

In the name of the Father, and of the Son, and of the Holy Spirit. Amen.

PSALM
(For a longer psalm, see page xv.)
Psalm 118:1–2, 4, 22–24, 25–27a

The stone that the builders rejected
  has become the chief cornerstone.

**The stone that the builders rejected
  has become the chief cornerstone.**

O give thanks to the LORD, for he is good;
  his steadfast love endures forever!
Let Israel say,
  "His steadfast love endures forever."
Let those who fear the LORD say,
  "His steadfast love endures forever."

**The stone that the builders rejected
  has become the chief cornerstone.**

◆ All stand and sing **Alleluia.**

GOSPEL
John 14:6–7a, 8–9ab, 10bc–11

A reading from the holy Gospel according to John.

Jesus said to him, "I am the way, and the truth, and the life. No one comes to the Father except through me. If you know me, you will know my Father also." Philip said to him, "Lord, show us the Father, and we will be satisfied." Jesus said to him, "Have I been with you all this time, Philip, and you still do not know me? Whoever has seen me has seen the Father. The words that I say to you I do not speak on my own; but the Father who dwells in me does his works. Believe me that I am in the Father and the Father is in me; but if you do not, then believe me because of the words themselves."

The Gospel of the Lord.

◆ All sit and observe silence.

FOR SILENT REFLECTION

Think about this silently in your heart. What do we know about God the Father from Jesus' life and teachings?

CLOSING PRAYER

Let us pray to God for our needs and the needs of others: our family, neighborhood, and the world. For each need we say, "Lord, hear our prayer."

◆ All may add their own prayers here.

Let us pray: **Our Father . . . Amen.**

We continue to praise and thank you,
O God, for the gift of your Son, Jesus.
He revealed your love for us
and for all that you have created.
Help us believe and follow him.
We ask this in his name.

Amen.

✛ All make the Sign of the Cross.

OPENING

Following Jesus is not always easy. But Jesus says that those who love him and keep his word will receive courage and peace through the Holy Spirit. Before the descent of the Holy Spirit at Pentecost, the Apostles chose St. Matthias to replace Judas as one of the Twelve. We celebrate St. Matthias' feast day today.

✝ All make the Sign of the Cross.

In the name of the Father, and of the Son, and of the Holy Spirit. Amen.

PSALM
(For a longer psalm, see page xv.)
Psalm 118:1–2, 4, 22–24, 25–27a–9

The stone that the builders rejected
  has become the chief cornerstone.

**The stone that the builders rejected
  has become the chief cornerstone.**

O give thanks to the LORD, for he is good;
  his steadfast love endures forever!
Let Israel say,
  "His steadfast love endures forever."
Let those who fear the LORD say,
  "His steadfast love endures forever."

**The stone that the builders rejected
  has become the chief cornerstone.**

◆ All stand and sing **Alleluia.**

GOSPEL
John 14:23–27

A reading from the holy Gospel according to John.

Jesus said, "Those who love me will keep my word, and my Father will love them, and we will come to them and make our home with them. Whoever does not love me does not keep my words; and the word that you hear is not mine, but is from the Father who sent me. I have said these things to you while I am still with you. But the Advocate, the Holy Spirit, whom the Father will send in my name, will teach you everything, and remind you of all that I have said to you. Peace I leave with you; my peace I give to you. I do not give to you as the world gives. Do not let your hearts be troubled, and do not let them be afraid."

The Gospel of the Lord.

◆ All sit and observe silence.

FOR SILENT REFLECTION

Think about this silently in your heart. Jesus helps us to not be afraid. Would you like to ask Jesus for courage today?

CLOSING PRAYER

Let us pray to God for our needs and the needs of others: our family, neighborhood, and the world. For each need we say, "Lord, hear our prayer."

◆ All may add their own prayers here.

Let us pray: **Our Father . . . Amen.**

God of peace,
once again we hear Jesus
wish his disciples peace.
We know that peace is your gift to us.
May we bring that peace to others.
We ask this in the name of our Risen Lord,
Jesus Christ.

Amen.

✝ All make the Sign of the Cross.

PRAYER FOR
FRIDAY, MAY 15, 2020

OPENING

Jesus says he came as light to the world so that people would not remain in darkness. Light helps us see things. Jesus helps us understand God and the meaning of our lives. Today we honor St. Isidore of Seville, who is the patron saint of farmers. He was devoted to God, attending daily Mass before working in the fields.

✚ All make the Sign of the Cross.

In the name of the Father, and of the Son, and of the Holy Spirit. Amen.

PSALM

(For a longer psalm, see page xv.)
Psalm 118:1–2, 4, 22–24, 25–27a

The stone that the builders rejected
    has become the chief cornerstone.

**The stone that the builders rejected
        has become the chief cornerstone.**

O give thanks to the Lord, for he is good;
    his steadfast love endures forever!
Let Israel say,
    "His steadfast love endures forever."
Let those who fear the Lord say,
    "His steadfast love endures forever."

**The stone that the builders rejected
        has become the chief cornerstone.**

◆ All stand and sing **Alleluia.**

GOSPEL

John 12:44–46, 49–50

A reading from the holy Gospel according to John.

Then Jesus cried aloud: "Whoever believes in me believes not in me but in him who sent me. And whoever sees me sees him who sent me.

I have come as light into the world, so that everyone who believes in me should not remain in the darkness. For I have not spoken on my own, but the Father who sent me has himself given me a commandment about what to say and what to speak. And I know that his commandment is eternal life. What I speak, therefore, I speak just as the Father has told me."

The Gospel of the Lord.

◆ All sit and observe silence.

FOR SILENT REFLECTION

Think about his silently in your heart. Jesus is the Light of the World. What are some other positive qualities of light?

CLOSING PRAYER

Let us pray to God for our needs and the needs of others: our family, neighborhood, and the world. For each need we say, "Lord, hear our prayer."

◆ All may add their own prayers here.

Let us pray: **Our Father . . . Amen.**

Holy God, our Father,
help us to listen to Jesus,
the Light of the World.
Help us to be like St. Isidore
and increase our devotion to you.
We ask this in the name of our Risen Lord,
Jesus Christ.

Amen.

✚ All make the Sign of the Cross.

PRAYER FOR THE WEEK

OPENING

We continue to celebrate Christ's Resurrection. God loves us and we too will live with God after our physical death. God's Holy Spirit reminds us of that love and how we should respond to it.

✝ All make the Sign of the Cross.

In the name of the Father, and of the Son, and of the Holy Spirit. Amen.

PSALM

(For a longer psalm, see page xv.)
Psalm 118:1–2, 4, 22–24, 25–27a

The stone that the builders rejected
   has become the chief cornerstone.

**The stone that the builders rejected
   has become the chief cornerstone.**

O give thanks to the LORD, for he is good;
   his steadfast love endures forever!
Let Israel say,
   "His steadfast love endures forever."
Let those who fear the LORD say,
   "His steadfast love endures forever."

**The stone that the builders rejected
   has become the chief cornerstone.**

◆ All stand and sing **Alleluia.**

GOSPEL

John 14:15–17ac, 18–21

A reading from the holy Gospel according to John.

Jesus said, "If you love me, you will keep my commandments. And I will ask the Father, and he will give you another Advocate, to be with you forever. This is the Spirit of truth. You know the Spirit, because he abides with you, and he will be in you. I will not leave you orphaned; I am coming to you. In a little while the world will no longer see me, but you will see me; because I live, you also will live. On that day you will know that I am in my Father, and you in me, and I in you. They who have my commandments and keep them are those who love me; and those who love me will be loved by my Father, and I will love them and reveal myself to them."

The Gospel of the Lord.

◆ All sit and observe silence.

FOR SILENT REFLECTION

Think about this silently in your heart. How do you show your love for God when you keep the commandments?

CLOSING PRAYER

Let us pray to God for our needs and the needs of others: our family, neighborhood, and the world. For each need we say, "Lord, hear our prayer."

◆ All may add their own prayers here.

Let us pray: **Our Father . . . Amen.**

Most holy God,
your Son Jesus cared for the disciples
and for us so much that he promised to send
the Holy Spirit.
Help us to show our thanks and our love by
keeping your commands.
We ask this in his name.

Amen.

✝ All make the Sign of the Cross.

PRAYER FOR
MONDAY, MAY 18, 2020

OPENING

Stephen, the first deacon of the Church, invited others to follow Jesus. He was persecuted by Saul, who later was converted to Christianity and whom we know as St. Paul.

✝ All make the Sign of the Cross.

In the name of the Father, and of the Son, and of the Holy Spirit. Amen.

PSALM

(For a longer psalm, see page xv.)
Psalm 118:1–2, 4, 22–24, 25–27a

The stone that the builders rejected
  has become the chief cornerstone.

**The stone that the builders rejected
    has become the chief cornerstone.**

O give thanks to the LORD, for he is good;
  his steadfast love endures forever!
Let Israel say,
  "His steadfast love endures forever."
Let those who fear the LORD say,
  "His steadfast love endures forever."

**The stone that the builders rejected
    has become the chief cornerstone.**

READING

Acts 6:8–9ac, 10–11, 13; 7:54, 58–59, 60c; 8:1a

A reading from the Acts of the Apostles.

Stephen, full of grace and power, did great wonders and signs among the people. Then some of those who belonged to the synagogue of the Freedmen stood up and argued with Stephen. But they could not withstand the wisdom and the Spirit with which he spoke. Then they secretly instigated some men to say, "We have heard him speak blasphemous words against Moses and God." They set up false witnesses who said, "This man never stops saying things against this holy place and the law." When the Council heard these things, they became enraged and ground their teeth at Stephen. Then they dragged him out of the city and began to stone him; and the witnesses laid their coats at the feet of a young man named Saul. While they were stoning Stephen, he prayed, "Lord Jesus, receive my spirit." When he had said this, he died. And Saul approved of their killing him.

The Word of the Lord.

◆ All observe silence.

FOR SILENT REFLECTION

Think about this silently in your heart. Do we ever stone; that is, really hurt someone with our words or actions?

CLOSING PRAYER

Let us pray to God for our needs and the needs of others: our family, neighborhood, and the world. For each need we say, "Lord, hear our prayer."

◆ All may add their own prayers here.

Let us pray: **Our Father . . . Amen.**

God of truth and justice,
we pray that we may follow Jesus
as St. Stephen did.
Even when it was hard,
he was faithful to your word.
Help us to overcome challenges
and to be true to you.
We ask this in Christ's name.

Amen.

✝ All make the Sign of the Cross.

OPENING

We continue the story of Saul. In spite of Saul's persecution, the Apostles kept telling people about Jesus. Today we hear about the Apostle Philip and how he helped to spread Christ's Good News.

✛ All make the Sign of the Cross.

In the name of the Father, and of the Son, and of the Holy Spirit. Amen.

PSALM

(For a longer psalm, see page xv.)
Psalm 118:1–2, 4, 22–24, 25–27a

The stone that the builders rejected
   has become the chief cornerstone.

**The stone that the builders rejected
     has become the chief cornerstone.**

O give thanks to the LORD, for he is good;
   his steadfast love endures forever!
Let Israel say,
   "His steadfast love endures forever."
Let those who fear the LORD say,
   "His steadfast love endures forever."

**The stone that the builders rejected
     has become the chief cornerstone.**

READING

Acts 8:1b–8

A reading from the Acts of the Apostles.

That day a severe persecution began against the church in Jerusalem, and all except the apostles were scattered throughout the countryside of Judea and Samaria. Devout men buried Stephen and made loud lamentation over him. But Saul was ravaging the church by entering house after house; dragging off both men and women, he committed them to prison.

Now those who were scattered went from place to place, proclaiming the word. Philip went down to the city of Samaria and proclaimed the Messiah to them. The crowds with one accord listened eagerly to what was said by Philip, hearing and seeing the signs that he did, for unclean spirits, crying with loud shrieks, came out of many who were possessed; and many others who were paralyzed or lame were cured. So there was great joy in that city.

The Word of the Lord.

◆ All observe silence.

FOR SILENT REFLECTION

Think about this silently in your heart. Pray for those who are persecuted for their faith.

CLOSING PRAYER

Let us pray to God for our needs and the needs of others: our family, neighborhood, and the world. For each need we say, "Lord, hear our prayer."

◆ All may add their own prayers here.

Let us pray: **Our Father . . . Amen.**

O God,
we know that even today people are persecuted and suffer because of their faith.
Please help all people to be respectful of others.
We ask this in the name of our Lord, Jesus Christ.

Amen.

✛ All make the Sign of the Cross.

PRAYER FOR
WEDNESDAY, MAY 20, 2020

OPENING

St. Paul believed in Jesus completely after his experience with the Risen Christ and became a great Christian teacher and writer. This was a conversion experience; that is, it changed Paul and he acted differently.

✛ All make the Sign of the Cross.

In the name of the Father, and of the Son, and of the Holy Spirit. Amen.

PSALM

(For a longer psalm, see page xv.)
Psalm 118:1–2, 4, 22–24, 25–27a

The stone that the builders rejected
  has become the chief cornerstone.

**The stone that the builders rejected
   has become the chief cornerstone.**

O give thanks to the Lord, for he is good;
  his steadfast love endures forever!
Let Israel say,
  "His steadfast love endures forever."
Let those who fear the Lord say,
  "His steadfast love endures forever."

**The stone that the builders rejected
   has become the chief cornerstone.**

READING

Acts 9:1, 2bc, 3–6, 8–9

A reading from the Acts of the Apostles.

Meanwhile Saul, still breathing threats and murder against the disciples of the Lord, went to the high priest, so that if he found any who belonged to the Way, men or women, he might bring them bound to Jerusalem. Now as he was going along and approaching Damascus, suddenly a light from heaven flashed around him. He fell to the ground and heard a voice saying to him, "Saul, Saul, why do you persecute me?" He asked, "Who are you, Lord?" The reply came, "I am Jesus, whom you are persecuting. But get up and enter the city, and you will be told what you are to do." Saul got up from the ground, and though his eyes were open, he could see nothing; so they led him by the hand and brought him into Damascus. For three days he was without sight, and neither ate nor drank.

The Word of the Lord.

◆ All observe silence.

FOR SILENT REFLECTION

Think about this silently in your heart. Who or what has helped convert you; that is, helped you change to be a better person?

CLOSING PRAYER

Let us pray to God for our needs and the needs of others: our family, neighborhood, and the world. For each need we say, "Lord, hear our prayer."

◆ All may add their own prayers here.

Let us pray: **Our Father . . . Amen.**

In the conversion of Saul, O Lord Jesus,
we see the power of your grace.
Help us to remember that no one is beyond your care or your healing power.
May St. Paul be an example for us
of how to honor you,
who live and reign with the Father in the unity of the Holy Spirit, one God,
for ever and ever.

Amen.

✛ All make the Sign of the Cross.

OPENING

Jesus sends Ananias [a-nuh-NĪ-uhs] to heal Saul/Paul's blindness. This Scripture hints that Paul will not have an easy time following Jesus.

✚ All make the Sign of the Cross.

In the name of the Father, and of the Son, and of the Holy Spirit. Amen.

PSALM

(For a longer psalm, see page xv.)
Psalm 118:1–2, 4, 22–24, 25a–27a

The stone that the builders rejected
  has become the chief cornerstone.

**The stone that the builders rejected
    has become the chief cornerstone.**

O give thanks to the LORD, for he is good;
  his steadfast love endures forever!
Let Israel say,
  "His steadfast love endures forever."
Let those who fear the LORD say,
  "His steadfast love endures forever."

**The stone that the builders rejected
    has become the chief cornerstone.**

READING

Acts 9:10a, 11–12, 16–18a

A reading from the Acts of the Apostles.

Now there was a disciple in Damascus named Ananias [a-nuh-NĪ-uhs]. The Lord said to him, "Get up and go to the street called Straight, and at the house of Judas look for a man of Tarsus named Saul. At this moment he is praying, and he has seen in a vision a man named Ananias come in and lay his hands on him so that he might regain his sight. I myself will show him how much he must suffer for the sake of my name." So Ananias went and entered the house. He laid his hands on Saul and said, "Brother Saul, the Lord Jesus, who appeared to you on your way here, has sent me so that you may regain your sight and be filled with the Holy Spirit." And immediately something like scales fell from his eyes, and his sight was restored.

The Word of the Lord.

◆ All observe silence.

FOR SILENT REFLECTION

Think about this silently in your heart. Are we "blind" to the goodness of any of our classmates or someone in our family?

CLOSING PRAYER

Let us pray to God for our needs and the needs of others: our family, neighborhood, and the world. For each need we say, "Lord, hear our prayer."

◆ All may add their own prayers here.

Let us pray: **Our Father . . . Amen.**

Holy God,
just as you helped St. Paul
to see the truth of your Word,
help us to recognize the truth of the Gospel.
Help us to be open
to the power of your Spirit.
We ask this in Christ's name.

Amen.

✚ All make the Sign of the Cross.

PRAYER FOR
FRIDAY, MAY 22, 2020

OPENING

Saul was a very good speaker and convinced many people that Jesus was the Messiah. But, sometimes, speaking the truth makes people angry when it challenges what they believe.

✛ All make the Sign of the Cross.

> **In the name of the Father, and of the Son, and of the Holy Spirit. Amen.**

PSALM

(For a longer psalm, see page xv.)
Psalm 118:1–2, 4, 22–24, 25–27a

The stone that the builders rejected
   has become the chief cornerstone.

The stone that the builders rejected
     has become the chief cornerstone.

O give thanks to the LORD, for he is good;
   his steadfast love endures forever!
Let Israel say,
   "His steadfast love endures forever."
Let those who fear the LORD say,
   "His steadfast love endures forever."

The stone that the builders rejected
     has become the chief cornerstone.

READING

Acts 9:18c–21ab, 22–23, 24b–25

A reading from the Acts of the Apostles.

Then Saul got up and was baptized, and after taking some food, he regained his strength. For several days he was with the disciples in Damascus, and immediately he began to proclaim Jesus in the synagogues, saying, "He is the Son of God." All who heard him were amazed and said, "Is not this the man who made havoc in Jerusalem among those who invoked this name?" Saul became increasingly more powerful and confounded the Jews who lived in Damascus by proving that Jesus was the Messiah. After some time had passed, the Jews plotted to kill him. They were watching the gates day and night so that they might kill him; but his disciples took him by night and let him down through an opening in the wall, lowering him in a basket.

The Word of the Lord.

◆ All observe silence.

FOR SILENT REFLECTION

Think about this silently in your heart. What do I need to speak the truth about in school or at home?

CLOSING PRAYER

Let us pray to God for our needs and the needs of others: our family, neighborhood, and the world. For each need we say, "Lord, hear our prayer."

◆ All may add their own prayers here.

Let us pray: **Our Father . . . Amen.**

God of truth and justice,
sometimes it is not easy to speak your truth.
Send your Spirit to help us speak and hear the truth.
We ask this in the name of our Risen Lord, Jesus Christ.

Amen.

✛ All make the Sign of the Cross.

PRAYER FOR THE WEEK

WITH A READING FROM THE GOSPEL FOR **SUNDAY, MAY 24, 2020**

OPENING

Today we celebrate the Solemnity of the Ascension of the Lord. Before he went back to the Father, Jesus commissioned the disciples to carry on his work. He assures them, and us, that he will be with us always.

✚ All make the Sign of the Cross.

In the name of the Father, and of the Son, and of the Holy Spirit. Amen.

PSALM

(For a longer psalm, see page xv.)
Psalm 118:1–2, 4, 22–24, 25–27a.

The stone that the builders rejected
  has become the chief cornerstone.

**The stone that the builders rejected
  has become the chief cornerstone.**

O give thanks to the LORD, for he is good;
  his steadfast love endures forever!
Let Israel say,
  "His steadfast love endures forever."
Let those who fear the LORD say,
  "His steadfast love endures forever."

**The stone that the builders rejected
  has become the chief cornerstone.**

◆ All stand and sing **Alleluia.**

GOSPEL

Matthew 28:16–20

A reading from the holy Gospel according to Matthew.

Now the eleven disciples went to Galilee, to the mountain to which Jesus had directed them. When they saw him, they worshiped him; but some doubted. And Jesus came and said to them, "All authority in heaven and on earth has been given to me. Go therefore and make disciples of all nations, baptizing them in the name of the Father and of the Son and of the Holy Spirit, and teaching them to obey everything that I have commanded you. And remember, I am with you always, to the end of the age."

The Gospel of the Lord.

◆ All sit and observe silence.

FOR SILENT REFLECTION

Think about this silently in your heart. In what ways is Jesus with you? Does this change anything for you?

CLOSING PRAYER

Let us pray to God for our needs and the needs of others: our family, neighborhood, and the world. For each need we say, "Lord, hear our prayer."

◆ All may add their own prayers here.

Let us pray: **Our Father . . . Amen.**

How good, O Lord,
is the message of your Son, Jesus.
Although he reigns with you in heaven,
he is also with us, until the end of time.
Help us to know his presence with us.
We ask this in his name.

Amen.

✚ All make the Sign of the Cross.

PRAYER SERVICE
ASCENSION

Prepare six leaders and a song leader for this service. The second and third leaders will need Bibles to read the Scripture passages and may need help finding and practicing them. You may wish to begin by singing "All Will Be Well" and end with "Sing Out, Earth and Skies." Help the song leader prepare to lead the singing.

SONG LEADER:
Please stand and join in singing our opening song.

FIRST LEADER:
So if you have been raised with Christ, seek the things that are above, where Christ is, seated at the right hand of God.

ALL: Amen.

FIRST LEADER:
Today we celebrate the Solemnity of the Ascension of the Lord. We are joyful on this fortieth day of Easter because Jesus Christ returned to his Father in heaven, and he promised that we could experience his Presence in Spirit forever.

✝ All make the Sign of the Cross.

In the name of the Father, and of the Son, and of the Holy Spirit. Amen.

Let us pray:
Almighty God,
you fulfilled your promise
of sending a Savior
to redeem the world.
Now he sits at your right hand
and your Spirit guides us
with holy Presence.
Help us to listen and act according to
your will

so that we can enter into
your Kingdom too.
We ask this through Christ our Lord.

ALL: Amen.

◆ Gesture for all to sit.

SECOND LEADER: Colossians 3:2–4

A reading from the Letter of Paul to the
Colossians.

◆ Read the Scripture passage from the Bible.

The Word of the Lord.

◆ All observe silence.

THIRD LEADER: Acts 1:6–11

A reading from the Acts of the Apostles.

◆ Read the Scripture passage from the Bible.

The Word of the Lord.

◆ All observe silence.

FOURTH LEADER:

Let us stand and bring our hopes and needs
to God as we pray, "Lord, hear our prayer."

For our brothers and sisters around the world
who do not know Christ.
May they experience
our Risen Lord in eternity,

we pray to the Lord . . .

For our parents and family members
who care for us.
May we remain grateful for their
acts of sacrificial love
that are a reflection of
God's abundant love for us,

we pray to the Lord . . .

For the teachers, school assistants,
and coaches who
guide us in our school activities.
May they continue to
teach us about God
through their
kindness and generosity,

we pray to the Lord . . .

For those who suffer from
illness, hunger, or political strife.
For those who have died,

we pray to the Lord . . .

FIFTH LEADER:

Let us pray the prayer that Jesus taught us:
Our Father . . . Amen.

◆ Pause and then say the following:

Let us offer one another a sign of Christ's
peace.

◆ All offer one another a sign of peace.

SIXTH LEADER:

Let us pray:
Lord our God,
your immense love for us
shines for all to see
in the glory of your Resurrection
and in your return to God.
We praise you for your Spirit
of truth and light
and the promise of your
return again.
We ask this through Christ our Lord.

ALL: Amen.

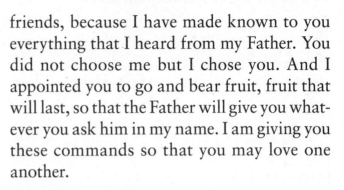

OPENING

In today's reading, we hear the message that Jesus gives to his followers. He calls them his friends.

✛ All make the Sign of the Cross.

In the name of the Father, and of the Son, and of the Holy Spirit. Amen.

PSALM

(For a longer psalm, see page xv.)
Psalm 118:1–2, 4, 22–24, 25–27a

The stone that the builders rejected
	has become the chief cornerstone.

**The stone that the builders rejected
	has become the chief cornerstone.**

O give thanks to the Lord, for he is good;
  his steadfast love endures forever!
Let Israel say,
  "His steadfast love endures forever."
Let those who fear the Lord say,
  "His steadfast love endures forever."

**The stone that the builders rejected
	has become the chief cornerstone.**

◆ All stand and sing **Alleluia.**

GOSPEL

John 15:12–17

A reading of the holy Gospel according to John.

"This is my commandment, that you love one another as I have loved you. No one has greater love than this, to lay down one's life for one's friends. You are my friends if you do what I command you. I do not call you servants any longer, because the servant does not know what the master is doing; but I have called you friends, because I have made known to you everything that I heard from my Father. You did not choose me but I chose you. And I appointed you to go and bear fruit, fruit that will last, so that the Father will give you whatever you ask him in my name. I am giving you these commands so that you may love one another.

The Gospel of the Lord.

◆ All sit and observe silence.

FOR SILENT REFLECTION

Think about this silently in your heart. Do you think of Jesus as your friend? What kind of friend is he?

CLOSING PRAYER

Let us pray to God for our needs and the needs of others: our family, neighborhood, and the world. For each need we say, "Lord, hear our prayer."

◆ All may add their own prayers here.

Let us pray: **Our Father . . . Amen.**

Your love for us is so great, O God!
We are connected to you through Jesus.
May we remember that Jesus chose us to be his friends.
Help us to understand what this means for our lives.
We ask this in the name of your Son, Jesus Christ, our Risen Lord.

Amen.

✛ All make the Sign of the Cross.

OPENING

In today's reading Jesus tells us that we will have what we need. He reminds us that God knows our needs, and so we should not worry. St. Philip Neri, whose feast we celebrate today, believed that people needed the Eucharist and encouraged them to receive Holy Communion frequently.

✚ All make the Sign of the Cross.

In the name of the Father, and of the Son, and of the Holy Spirit. Amen.

PSALM

(For a longer psalm, see page xv.)
Psalm 118:1–2, 4, 22–24, 25–27a

The stone that the builders rejected
    has become the chief cornerstone.

**The stone that the builders rejected
    has become the chief cornerstone.**

O give thanks to the LORD, for he is good;
  his steadfast love endures forever!
Let Israel say,
  "His steadfast love endures forever."
Let those who fear the LORD say,
  "His steadfast love endures forever."

**The stone that the builders rejected
    has become the chief cornerstone.**

◆ All stand and sing **Alleluia.**

GOSPEL

Matthew 6:25abce, 26, 28abd–30c, 32b

A reading from the holy Gospel according to Matthew.

Jesus said, "Therefore I tell you, do not worry about your life, what you will eat or what you will drink, what you will wear. Look at the birds of the air; they neither sow nor reap nor gather into barns, and yet your heavenly Father feeds them. Are you not of more value than they? And why do you worry about clothing? Consider the lilies of the field; they neither toil nor spin, yet I tell you, even Solomon in all his glory was not clothed like one of these. But if God so clothes the grass of the field, which is alive today and tomorrow is thrown into the oven, will he not much more clothe you? And indeed your heavenly Father knows that you need all these things."

The Gospel of the Lord.

◆ All sit and observe silence.

FOR SILENT REFLECTION

Think about this silently in your heart. What do you need? Trust in God and bring that need to him in prayer.

CLOSING PRAYER

Let us pray to God for our needs and the needs of others: our family, neighborhood, and the world. For each need we say, "Lord, hear our prayer."

◆ All may add their own prayers here.

Let us pray: **Our Father . . . Amen.**

Heavenly Father,
we know that you love us and you want us to trust in your care.
Thank you for everything you provide to us.
Through Christ our Lord.

Amen.

✚ All make the Sign of the Cross.

PRAYER FOR
WEDNESDAY, MAY 27, 2020

OPENING

Today we hear how Jesus provided for the needs of the people who came to listen to him. In Jesus' actions we see how generous and loving God is.

✚ All make the Sign of the Cross.

In the name of the Father, and of the Son, and of the Holy Spirit. Amen.

PSALM

(For a longer psalm, see page xv.)
Psalm 118:1–2, 4, 22–24, 25–27a

The stone that the builders rejected
    has become the chief cornerstone.

**The stone that the builders rejected
    has become the chief cornerstone.**

O give thanks to the LORD, for he is good;
  his steadfast love endures forever!
Let Israel say,
  "His steadfast love endures forever."
Let those who fear the LORD say,
  "His steadfast love endures forever."

**The stone that the builders rejected
    has become the chief cornerstone.**

◆ All stand and sing **Alleluia.**

GOSPEL

Luke 9:12–13a, 14–17

A reading from the holy Gospel according to Luke.

The day was drawing to a close, and the twelve came to Jesus and said, "Send the crowd away, so that they may go to the surrounding villages and countryside, to lodge and get provisions; for we are here in a deserted place." But Jesus said to them, "You give them something to eat." They said, "We have no more than five loaves and two fish." For there were about five thousand men. And he said to his disciples, "Make them sit down in groups of about fifty each." They did so and made them all sit down. And taking the five loaves and the two fish, he looked up to heaven, and blessed and broke them, and gave them to the disciples to set before the crowd. And all ate and were filled. What was left over was gathered up, twelve baskets of broken pieces.

The Gospel of the Lord.

◆ All sit and observe silence.

FOR SILENT REFLECTION

Think about this silently in your heart. What message do you hear in today's Gospel reading?

CLOSING PRAYER

Let us pray to God for our needs and the needs of others: our family, neighborhood, and the world. For each need we say, "Lord, hear our prayer."

◆ All may add their own prayers here.

Let us pray: **Our Father . . . Amen.**

Generous and gracious God,
help us to trust in your abundant love.
Help us to give what we can to others
and to trust that you will provide for us.
We ask this in the name of Jesus Christ our Risen Lord.

Amen.

✚ All make the Sign of the Cross.

OPENING

In today's reading, St. Paul reminds us that the commandments help us to live together in community. They are a guide, and when we follow them we are able to live with peace. *Adultery* means "to have sexual relations with someone other than your husband or wife." To covet means "to want something that belongs to another person."

✦ All make the Sign of the Cross.

In the name of the Father, and of the Son, and of the Holy Spirit. Amen.

PSALM

(For a longer psalm, see page xv.)
Psalm 118:1–2, 4, 22–24, 25–27a

The stone that the builders rejected
  has become the chief cornerstone.

The stone that the builders rejected
  has become the chief cornerstone.

O give thanks to the LORD, for he is good;
  his steadfast love endures forever!
Let Israel say,
  "His steadfast love endures forever."
Let those who fear the LORD say,
  "His steadfast love endures forever."

The stone that the builders rejected
  has become the chief cornerstone.

READING

Romans 12:9–10; 13:8–10

A reading from the Letter of Paul to the Romans.

Let love be genuine; hate what is evil, hold fast to what is good; love one another with mutual affection; outdo one another in showing honor.

Owe no one anything, except to love one another; for the one who loves another has fulfilled the law. The commandments, "You shall not commit adultery; You shall not murder; You shall not steal; You shall not covet"; and any other commandment, are summed up in this word, "Love your neighbor as yourself." Love does no wrong to a neighbor; therefore, love is the fulfilling of the law.

The Gospel of the Lord.

◆ All observe silence.

FOR SILENT REFLECTION

Think about this silently in your heart. Why do you think that love is the basis of all of the commandments?

CLOSING PRAYER

Let us pray to God for our needs and the needs of others: our family, neighborhood, and the world. For each need we say, "Lord, hear our prayer."

◆ All may add their own prayers here.

Let us pray: **Our Father . . . Amen.**

God of love,
thank you for giving us the commandments
that help us to live in peace and in community.
May we learn to love one another.
We ask this in Christ's name.

Amen.

✦ All make the Sign of the Cross.

OPENING

On Sunday we will celebrate the Solemnity of Pentecost. Before Jesus ascended into heaven, he told his disciples that he would send the Holy Spirit to guide and strengthen them to carry on his mission. This promise comforted the disciples and gave them hope.

✚ All make the Sign of the Cross.

In the name of the Father, and of the Son, and of the Holy Spirit. Amen.

PSALM
(For a longer psalm, see page xv.)
Psalm 118:1–2, 4, 22–24, 25–27a

The stone that the builders rejected
    has become the chief cornerstone.

**The stone that the builders rejected
    has become the chief cornerstone.**

O give thanks to the LORD, for he is good;
  his steadfast love endures forever!
Let Israel say,
  "His steadfast love endures forever."
Let those who fear the LORD say,
  "His steadfast love endures forever."

**The stone that the builders rejected
    has become the chief cornerstone.**

◆ All stand and sing **Alleluia.**

GOSPEL
John 15:26ab, 26d–27; 16:12–15a

A reading from the holy Gospel according to John.

Jesus said to his disciples, "When the Advocate comes, whom I will send to you from the Father, he will testify on my behalf. You also are to testify because you have been with me from the beginning. I still have many things to say to you, but you cannot bear them now. When the Spirit of truth comes, he will guide you into all the truth; for he will not speak on his own, but will speak whatever he hears, and he will declare to you the things that are to come. He will glorify me, because he will take what is mine and delcare it to you. All that the Father has is mine."

The Gospel of the Lord.

◆ All sit and observe silence.

FOR SILENT REFLECTION

Think about this silently in your heart. To testify means "to give evidence" or "bear witness." How do you testify to your faith in Jesus?

CLOSING PRAYER

Let us pray to God for our needs and the needs of others: our family, neighborhood, and the world. For each need we say, "Lord, hear our prayer."

◆ All may add their own prayers here.

Let us pray: **Our Father . . . Amen.**

Holy Spirit,
walk with us each day
and remind us to testify our love for Jesus
by our kindness and fairness to others.
We ask this through Christ our Lord.

Amen.

✚ All make the Sign of the Cross.

PRAYER FOR THE WEEK

OPENING

On this day of Pentecost (fifty days after Easter), we celebrate the birth of the Church. We hear of how Jesus appeared to the Apostles who were fearful and gathered together in an upper room. He assured them with a greeting of peace. Then he breathed the Holy Spirit upon them and sent them out into the world to do his work.

✦ All make the Sign of the Cross.

In the name of the Father, and of the Son, and of the Holy Spirit. Amen.

PSALM

(For a longer psalm, see page xv.)
Psalm 118:1–2, 4, 22–24, 25–27a

The stone that the builders rejected
    has become the chief cornerstone.

**The stone that the builders rejected
    has become the chief cornerstone.**

O give thanks to the LORD, for he is good;
  his steadfast love endures forever!
Let Israel say,
  "His steadfast love endures forever."
Let those who fear the LORD say,
  "His steadfast love endures forever."

**The stone that the builders rejected
    has become the chief cornerstone.**

◆ All stand and sing **Alleluia.**

GOSPEL

John 20:19–23

A reading from the holy Gospel according to John.

When it was evening on that day, the first day of the week, and the doors of the house where the disciples had met were locked for fear of the Jews, Jesus came and stood among them and said, "Peace be with you." After he said this, he showed them his hands and his side. Then the disciples rejoiced when they saw the Lord. Jesus said to them again, "Peace be with you. As the Father has sent me, so I send you." When he had said this, he breathed on them and said to them, "Receive the Holy Spirit. If you forgive the sins of any, they are forgiven them; if you retain the sins of any, they are retained."

The Gospel of the Lord.

◆ All sit and observe silence.

FOR SILENT REFLECTION

Think about his silently in your heart. The Holy Spirit empowers us to do God's work in the world also. How do you do God's work?

CLOSING PRAYER

Let us pray to God for our needs and the needs of others: our family, neighborhood, and the world. For each need we say, "Lord, hear our prayer."

◆ All may add their own prayers here.

Let us pray: **Our Father . . . Amen.**

We thank you, O God,
for sending your Holy Spirit.
We pray that the Spirit will fill our hearts with love and joy,
as well as the courage to tell others about you.
We ask this in Christ's name.

Amen.

✦ All make the Sign of the Cross.

PRAYER SERVICE
PENTECOST

Prepare a simple environment with a table covered with a red cloth. Leave a Bible and candle off to the side until the entrance procession. If possible, ring wind chimes during the procession. "Come, Holy Ghost," may be sung. Prepare the three leaders, the reader, and the three processors. The processors get in place: chimer, candle bearer, and lector with Bible. As the song begins they move slowly to the table in a solemn manner with chimes ringing gently. At the table the chimer moves to the side, the candle bearer places the candle, and the lector places the Bible. Then the chimes are silenced and the processors move away. When the song ends:

✛ All make the Sign of the Cross.

FIRST LEADER:

> **In the name of the Father and of the Son and of the Holy Spirit. Amen.**

ALL: Amen.

FIRST LEADER:

God came to us in the Person of Jesus
 to let us know
 how much we are loved and forgiven.
Jesus promised the disciples that when he
 ascended into heaven
 they would not be left alone.
God the Holy Spirit would be with them
 always.
That promise was for us, too.

Let us pray:
We call on you, Holy Spirit,
 to give us wisdom in everything we do
 and courage to always do the right thing.
 We ask for the gift of wonder and awe
 so we will always know the beauty of
 God's world.
 We ask this through Christ our Lord.

CHILDREN'S DAILY PRAYER 2019–2020, © 2019 Archdiocese of Chicago: Liturgy Training Publications. All rights reserved. Orders: 800-933-1800 or www.LTP.org.

◆ Gesture for all to sit.

LECTOR: Acts 1:8–9; 2:1–4
A reading from the Acts of the Apostles.

◆ Read the passage from the Bible.

The Word of the Lord.

FOR SILENT REFLECTION

FIRST LEADER:
What gifts of the Holy Spirit do we see in
our friends?

◆ All observe silence.

SECOND LEADER:

Let us stand. (pause)

◆ All stand.
We say together, "Come, Holy Spirit, come!"

ALL: Come, Holy Spirit, come!

SECOND LEADER:
Come, Holy Spirit, come!
And from your celestial home
  Shed a ray of light divine!
Come, Father of the poor!
Come, source of all our store!
We say together:

ALL: Come . . .

Heal our wounds, our strength renew;
On our dryness pour your dew;
  Wash the stains of guilt away:
Bend the stubborn heart and will;
Melt the frozen, warm the chill;
  Guide the steps that go astray.

We say together:

ALL: Come . . .
On the faithful, who adore
And confess you, evermore
  In your sevenfold gift descend;
Give them virtue's sure reward;
Give them your salvation, Lord;
  Give them joys that never end. Amen.
We say together:

ALL: Come . . .

THIRD LEADER:

Let us pray:
Holy Spirit, strengthen us with your many
    good gifts.
Help us become more and more
    a part of the Holy Trinity's life of love.
We ask this through Jesus Christ our Lord.

ALL: Amen.

✦ All make the Sign of the Cross.

THIRD LEADER:

      **In the name of the Father and of the
      Son and of the Holy Spirit. Amen.**

Let us offer one another a sign of
Christ's peace.

◆ All exchange a sign of peace.

HOME PRAYER
PENTECOST

Pentecost Sunday concludes our celebration of the Easter season. Just as we celebrated Easter in our homes, so we, as a family, can also mark this important feast at home. A parent or older child can lead the prayer and another read the Scripture. If possible, light a red candle or place the Bible on a red tablecloth. If you are familiar with a song that celebrates the Holy Spirit, be sure to sing it.

LEADER:

Today we celebrate Pentecost and give thanks for the gifts of the Holy Spirit. Jesus sent the Holy Spirit to be with us and to guide us.

And so we pray:
We call on you, Holy Spirit,
to give us wisdom to know what is right
and the courage to follow God's will.

✚ All make the Sign of the Cross.

> **In the name of the Father, and of the Son, and of the Holy Spirit. Amen.**

READER: Acts 2:1–4

A reading from the Acts of the Apostles.

◆ Read the passage from the Bible.

The Word of the Lord.

FOR SILENT REFLECTION

Give thanks for the gifts of the Holy Spirit and ask the Holy Spirit to give you what you need to follow Jesus.

◆ All observe some silence.

LEADER:

Come, Holy Spirit,
  fill the hearts of your faithful.
And kindle in them the fire of your love.

Send forth your Spirit
  and they shall be created.
And you will renew the face of the earth.

ALL: Amen.

✚ All make the Sign of the Cross.

> **In the name of the Father and of the Son and of the Holy Spirit. Amen.**

ORDINARY TIME SUMMER

MONDAY, JUNE 1 — FRIDAY, JUNE 26

SUMMER **ORDINARY TIME**

THE MEANING OF ORDINARY TIME

We just celebrated the great feasts of Easter and Pentecost and now move back to Ordinary Time—the ordered time when each week has a number. The Prayers for the Week will reflect the Sunday Gospels but during the week we will again "walk through the Bible."

On Pentecost, the Spirit descended upon Jesus' disciples, strengthening them with wisdom and courage. Passages from the Acts of the Apostles and the letters of St. Paul tell stories of the travels of Jesus' disciples to spread his teachings to love God and to love one another.

We will read several stories of Jesus' miracles. Jesus used two languages in his preaching: one was words, particularly the parables, and another was signs, particularly the miracles. Miracles consist of an observable action. But with Jesus' touch or presence something very unusual and unexpected happens: a stormy sea is calmed; hundreds of people are fed from just a few fish and a few loaves of bread; water becomes wine. Like the parables, the miracle stories contain more than what appears to us at first glance. As "signs," they carry a deeper meaning about the Kingdom of God—a time when there will be no suffering, hunger or death. The miracles are an announcement of hope—they are points of light that help us "see" what the Kingdom of God is like.

As we end this school year with the Twelfth Week in Ordinary Time, our focus is mission. The Scripture passages tell us that Jesus told his disciples to go out and proclaim the Kingdom of God and they did. As we prepare for summer vacation, it is a good time to remind ourselves that we are Christ's disciples and our mission is also to proclaim God's love through our words and our actions.

During these weeks of Ordinary Time, we celebrate the Solemnities of the Most Holy Trinity and the Most Sacred Heart of Jesus. A solemnity is a very high celebration in the Church calendar.

PREPARING TO CELEBRATE ORDINARY TIME IN THE CLASSROOM

This will be your last time changing the prayer tablecloth this year. Even if you haven't had a procession each time the cloth changes, try to have one now. As the school year winds down, it is good to bring the students' focus squarely on the prayer life of your classroom community. You may wish to invite the students to choose something to carry in the procession that helped their spiritual growth this year. Clear an area near the prayer table, spread it with a green cloth, and let the children place their objects there. As a final project, ask them to write a short essay or poem about the significance of the object they chose. Suggest that they illustrate their work. Invite them to share their writings aloud during one of your final prayer times together. (Some students might feel uncomfortable sharing private thoughts in front of a group. Don't force them to participate in this aspect of your celebration.) You might even consider collecting all the papers into a booklet, which you can photocopy for each student to keep as a memento of the year.

SACRED SPACE

Bring your potted plant back to the prayer table. You may want to discuss how it might be different from how it looked when you first placed it on the prayer table. Some plants, such as spider plants, send out shoots with new plants on them. If your spider plant is sufficiently mature, you may even have enough "spider babies" to clip and give to each of your students in a paper cup with a little soil in it. Or you may like to keep the table adorned with fresh flowers from a spring garden. Children love to bring flowers from their parents' or grandparents' gardens.

SACRED MUSIC

If you have been singing with your students all year, they will probably be quite comfortable with at least one or two of their favorite hymns. Consider scheduling a visit to one of the other classrooms to offer a small concert or sing-along (an older classroom could visit a younger grade; smaller children could sing for the "big kids"). If your students are particularly confident, you may even suggest that they volunteer to sing for an all-school Mass or end-of-the-year prayer service. If you invite parents to the class for one of your final sessions, don't be shy about including them in your prayer. And by all means, sing for them! Some songs that work well in this season are "Christ for the World We Sing," "Lord, I Want to Be a Christian," and "Spirit of the Living God."

MOVEMENT AND GESTURE

Children love to sing this song by David Haas and add movement.

PRAYER FOR PEACE

"Peace before us, peace behind us, peace under our feet. Peace within us, peace over us, let all around us be peace."

(You can repeat many times, changing out the word "Peace" for "Love," "Light," and "Christ.")

Movement: peace before us (extend arms in front body), peace behind us (extend arms behind body), peace under our feet (bend down and extend arms toward feet), peace within us (stand up and fold hands over heart), peace over us (extend arms over head and open them), let all around us be peace (extend arms in a semicircle in front of body). Repeat movement with each stanza.

PRAYERS FOR ORDINARY TIME

There are only a few precious places in the Gospel where we have the chance to listen to Jesus as he prays to his Father in heaven. In these moments, we can see clearly what it is Jesus wants for the world. The following prayer, taken from the Gospel according to John, shows how much Jesus wants us to abide in his love and to live with each other in the love and peace shared by the Father, Son, and Holy Spirit.

"As you, Father, are in me and I am in you, may my followers also be in us, so that the world may believe that you have sent me. The glory that you have given me I have given them, so that they may be one, as we are one, I in them and you in me, that they may become completely one, so that the world may know that you have sent me and have loved them even as you have loved me" (John 17:21b–23).

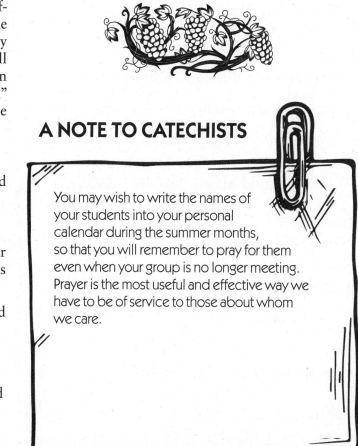

A NOTE TO CATECHISTS

You may wish to write the names of your students into your personal calendar during the summer months, so that you will remember to pray for them even when your group is no longer meeting. Prayer is the most useful and effective way we have to be of service to those about whom we care.

GRACE BEFORE MEALS

ORDINARY TIME • SUMMER

LEADER:
O give thanks to the Lord, for he is good;

ALL: for his steadfast love endures forever.

✝ All make the Sign of the Cross.

In the name of the Father, and of the Son, and of the Holy Spirit. Amen.

LEADER:
God of abundance,
your grace fills the hearts of
all those who call you Lord,
and even those who may not
know you yet.
Thank you for the gift of this meal
and the nourishment it will provide.
We are grateful for this time to
share it with each other.
May we work together to fill the plates
of those in our community and around the
world who may experience
extreme hunger or thirst today.
We ask this through Christ our Lord.

ALL: Amen.

✝ All make the Sign of the Cross.

In the name of the Father, and of the Son, and of the Holy Spirit. Amen.

PRAYER AT DAY'S END

ORDINARY TIME • SUMMER

LEADER:

See what love the Father has given us,

ALL: that we should be called children of God.

✚ All make the Sign of the Cross.

In the name of the Father, and of the Son, and of the Holy Spirit. Amen.

LEADER:

Almighty Father,
you created us in your image
of goodness and light.
Grant that we may offer you
all that we are in thanksgiving,
here at the end of our school day,
and this night, when we close our eyes
for restful sleep.
May the peace of Christ remain with us
now and forever.
We ask this in Christ's name.

ALL: Amen.

✚ All make the Sign of the Cross.

In the name of the Father, and of the Son, and of the Holy Spirit. Amen.

PRAYER FOR
MONDAY, JUNE 1, 2020

OPENING

On Pentecost, the disciples of Jesus received the power of the Spirit, which empowered them to go out and preach the Gospel of Jesus Christ.

✝ All make the Sign of the Cross.

In the name of the Father, and of the Son, and of the Holy Spirit. Amen.

PSALM

(For a longer psalm, see page xv.)
Psalm 85:8–9, 10–11, 12–13

The LORD speaks of peace to his people.

The LORD speaks of peace to his people.

Let me hear what God the LORD will speak,
    for he will speak peace to his people,
      to his faithful, to those who turn to him in
        their hearts.
Surely his salvation is at hand for those who
      fear him,
    that his glory may dwell in our land.

The LORD speaks of peace to his people.

READING

Acts 2:1–8, 11b–12

A reading from the Acts of the Apostles.

When the day of Pentecost had come, they were all together in one place. And suddenly from heaven there came a sound like the rush of a violent wind, and it filled the entire house where they were sitting. Divided tongues, as of fire, appeared among them, and a tongue rested on each of them. All of them were filled with the Holy Spirit and began to speak in other languages, as the Spirit gave them ability. Now there were devout Jews from every nation under heaven living in Jerusalem. And at this sound the crowd gathered and was bewildered, because each one heard them speaking in the native language of each. Amazed and astonished, they asked, "Are not all these who are speaking Galileans? And how is it that we hear, each of us, in our own native language? In our own languages we hear them speaking about God's deeds of power." All were amazed and perplexed, saying to one another, "What does this mean?"

The Word of the Lord.

✝ All observe silence.

FOR SILENT REFLECTION

Think about this silently in your heart. Ask the Holy Spirit to help you do something that feels hard or impossible to do.

CLOSING PRAYER

Let us pray to God for our needs and the needs of others: our family, neighborhood, and the world. For each need we say, "Lord, hear our prayer."

✝ All may add their own prayers here.

Let us pray: **Our Father . . . Amen.**

O God, we pray for the gift of understanding.
May the Holy Spirit open our hearts
to all people,
especially those who are different from us.
We ask this through Christ our Lord.

Amen.

✝ All make the Sign of the Cross.

OPENING

Today's reading is from a letter that St. Paul wrote to early Christians. He tells them of the wonderful qualities we experience when we follow Jesus' commandment to love one another. St. Paul calls these qualities the "fruit of the Spirit." Today we also remember two martyrs, Sts. Marcellinus and Peter. While imprisoned, they converted a jailer and his family to become believers in Christ.

✚ All make the Sign of the Cross.

In the name of the Father, and of the Son, and of the Holy Spirit. Amen.

PSALM

(For a longer psalm, see page xv.)
Psalm 85:8–9, 10–11, 12–13

The LORD speaks of peace to his people.

The LORD speaks of peace to his people.

Let me hear what God the LORD will speak,
for he will speak peace to his people,
to his faithful, to those who turn to him in their hearts.
Surely his salvation is at hand for those who fear him,
that his glory may dwell in our land.

The LORD speaks of peace to his people.

READING

Galatians 5:13–14, 22–23a, 25–26

A reading from the Letter of Paul to the Galatians [guh-LAY-shuhnz].

For you were called to freedom, brothers and sisters; only do not use your freedom as an opportunity for self-indulgence, but through love become slaves to one another. For the whole law is summed up in a single command-ment, "You shall love your neighbor as your-self." The fruit of the Spirit is love, joy, peace, patience, kindness, generosity, faithfulness, gentleness, and self-control. If we live by the Spirit, let us also be guided by the Spirit. Let us not become conceited, competing against one another, envying one another.

The Word of the Lord.

✚ All observe silence.

FOR SILENT REFLECTION

Think about this silently in your heart. Pray that you give and receive love, joy, peace, kindness, generosity, and faithfulness today.

CLOSING PRAYER

Let us pray to God for our needs and the needs of others: our family, neighborhood, and the world. For each need we say, "Lord, hear our prayer."

✚ All may add their own prayers here.

Let us pray: **Our Father . . . Amen.**

Loving God,
help us to open our hearts
and receive the gifts of the Spirit
so that we might love one another
as Jesus taught us.
We ask this through Christ our Lord.

Amen.

✚ All make the Sign of the Cross.

OPENING

St. Paul wrote many letters to the early Christian communities. He wanted to help them understand how Jesus revealed God's love and unites us to God through his Holy Spirit. Today we remember the Ugandan saints, Charles Lwanga and his Companions, who died for their faith.

✚ All make the Sign of the Cross.

In the name of the Father, and of the Son, and of the Holy Spirit. Amen.

PSALM

(For a longer psalm, see page xv.)
Psalm 85:8–9, 10–11, 12–13

The LORD speaks of peace to his people.

The LORD speaks of peace to his people.

Let me hear what God the LORD will speak,
for he will speak peace to his people,
to his faithful, to those who turn to him in
their hearts.
Surely his salvation is at hand for those who
fear him,
that his glory may dwell in our land.

The LORD speaks of peace to his people.

READING

Romans 8:28, 31b; 34–35a; 38–39

A reading from the Letter of Paul to the Romans.

We know that all things work together for good for those who love God, who are called according according to his purpose. If God is for us, who is against us? Who is to condemn? It is Christ Jesus, who died, yes, who was raised, who is at the right hand of God, who intercedes for us. Who will separate us from the love of Christ? I am convinced that neither death, nor life, nor angels, nor rulers, nor things present, nor things to come, nor powers, nor height, nor depth, nor anything else in all creation, will be able to separate us from the love of God in Christ Jesus our Lord.

The Word of the Lord.

◆ All observe silence.

FOR SILENT REFLECTION

Think about this silently in your heart. How do you understand St. Paul's words that all things will work together for the good, if we love God?

CLOSING PRAYER

Let us pray to God for our needs and the needs of others: our family, neighborhood, and the world. For each need we say, "Lord, hear our prayer."

◆ All may add their own prayers here.

Let us pray: **Our Father . . . Amen.**

Holy God,
strengthen our faith.
Let us never be separated from you.
We pray in the name of our Lord,
Jesus Christ.

Amen.

✚ All make the Sign of the Cross.

OPENING

Christianity began roughly two thousand years ago, shortly after the death, Resurrection, and Ascension of Christ. Early Christian services consisted mainly of preaching and performing Baptisms. They celebrated the Lord's Supper each time they gathered together. But soon early Christians were being persecuted by the Romans. St. Paul wrote letters to these early Christians assuring them that the Spirit was with them, to strengthen, heal, and protect them.

✢ All make the Sign of the Cross.

In the name of the Father, and of the Son, and of the Holy Spirit. Amen.

PSALM

(For a longer psalm, see page xv.)
Psalm 85:8–9, 10–11, 12–13

The LORD speaks of peace to his people.

The LORD speaks of peace to his people.

Let me hear what God the LORD will speak,
    for he will speak peace to his people,
        to his faithful, to those who turn to him in
            their hearts.
Surely his salvation is at hand for those who
        fear him,
    that his glory may dwell in our land.

The LORD speaks of peace to his people.

READING

Romans 8:26–27

A reading from the Letter of Paul to the Romans.

The Spirit of Jesus Christ helps us in our weakness; for we do not know how to pray as we ought, but that very Spirit intercedes with sighs too deep for words. And God, who searches the heart, knows what is the mind of the Spirit, because the Spirit intercedes for the saints according to the will of God.

The Word of the Lord.

✢ All observe silence.

FOR SILENT REFLECTION

Think about this silently in your heart. The Spirit is always present to help us also. Is there something you would like to ask for help with?

CLOSING PRAYER

Let us pray to God for our needs and the needs of others: our family, neighborhood, and the world. For each need we say, "Lord, hear our prayer."

✢ All may add their own prayers here.

Let us pray: **Our Father . . . Amen.**

Loving God,
we trust that you know what is in our hearts.
Help us to turn to you, even when we are
confused or do not know how to pray.

Amen.

✢ All make the Sign of the Cross.

PRAYER FOR
FRIDAY, JUNE 5, 2020

OPENING

Today we remember St. Boniface, who devoted his life to the conversion of the Germanic peoples. In today's reading, the disciples Peter and John continue Jesus' work, compassionately caring for the poor and the sick. The man in this story was a beggar, shunned because he was crippled, and therefore considered unclean.

✛ All make the Sign of the Cross.

In the name of the Father, and of the Son, and of the Holy Spirit. Amen.

PSALM

(For a longer psalm, see page xv.)
Psalm 85:8–9, 10–11, 12–13

The LORD speaks of peace to his people.

The LORD speaks of peace to his people.

Let me hear what God the LORD will speak,
 for he will speak peace to his people,
  to his faithful, to those who turn to him in
   their hearts.
Surely his salvation is at hand for those who
   fear him,
 that his glory may dwell in our land.

The LORD speaks of peace to his people.

READING

Acts 3:1–2a, 3–8, 10b

A reading from the Acts of the Apostles.

One day Peter and John were going up to the temple at the hour of prayer, at three o'clock in the afternoon. And a man lame from birth was being carried in. When he saw Peter and John about to go into the temple, he asked them for alms. Peter looked intently at him, as did John, and said, "Look at us." And he fixed his attention on them, expecting to receive something from them. But Peter said, "I have no silver or gold, but what I have I give you; in the name of Jesus Christ of Nazareth, stand up and walk." And he took him by the right hand and raised him up; and immediately his feet and ankles were made strong. Jumping up, the man stood and began to walk, and he entered the temple with them, walking and leaping and praising God; and all the people were filled with wonder and amazement at what had happened to him.

The Word of the Lord.

✛ All observe silence.

FOR SILENT REFLECTION

Think about this silently in your heart. Often it is a simple act of kindness that can make a difference to someone who feels left out.

CLOSING PRAYER

Let us pray to God for our needs and the needs of others: our family, neighborhood, and the world. For each need we say, "Lord, hear our prayer."

✛ All may add their own prayers here.

Let us pray: **Our Father . . . Amen.**

Loving God,
we are grateful for the many ways
that you show your love.
Like the man who was healed,
may we give you praise and glory.
We ask this in the name of Jesus Christ,
our Lord.

Amen.

✛ All make the Sign of the Cross.

PRAYER FOR THE WEEK

WITH A READING FROM THE GOSPEL FOR **SUNDAY, JUNE 7, 2020**

OPENING

Today is Holy Trinity Sunday, when we celebrate the power and relationship of God the Father, Jesus the Son, and the Holy Spirit. The Gospel tells how much God loved humanity that he sent his only Son to save us.

✚ All make the Sign of the Cross.

In the name of the Father, and of the Son, and of the Holy Spirit. Amen.

PSALM

(For a longer psalm, see page xv.)
Psalm 85:8–9, 10–11, 12–13

The LORD speaks of peace to his people.

The LORD speaks of peace to his people.

Let me hear what God the LORD will speak,
    for he will speak peace to his people,
    to his faithful, to those who turn to him in
        their hearts.
Surely his salvation is at hand for those who
        fear him,
    that his glory may dwell in our land.

The LORD speaks of peace to his people.

◆ All stand and sing **Alleluia.**

GOSPEL

John 3:16–18

A reading from the holy Gospel according to John.

For God so loved the world that he gave his only Son, so that everyone who believes in him may not perish but may have eternal life. Indeed, God did not send the Son into the world to condemn the world, but in order that the world might be saved through him. Those who believe in him are not condemned; but those who do not believe are condemned already, because they have not believed in the name of the only Son of God.

The Gospel of the Lord.

✚ All sit and observe silence.

FOR SILENT REFLECTION

Think about this silently in your heart. God is Love. What does that mean to you?

CLOSING PRAYER

Let us pray to God for our needs and the needs of others: our family, neighborhood, and the world. For each need we say, "Lord, hear our prayer."

✚ All may add their own prayers here.

Let us pray: **Our Father . . . Amen.**

Teach us to love, O God, as you love.
Help us to recognize the needs of others.
Help us to respond with care and kindness.
We ask this in Christ's name.

Amen.

✚ All make the Sign of the Cross.

OPENING

This week the readings focus on Jesus' miracles. Miracles were unexpected actions that gave people what they needed, like calming fear in today's reading. Miracles showed that Jesus had special powers, and they were always a response to human needs.

✚ All make the Sign of the Cross.

In the name of the Father, and of the Son, and of the Holy Spirit. Amen.

PSALM

(For a longer psalm, see page xv.)
Psalm 85:8–9, 10–11, 12–13

The LORD speaks of peace to his people.

The LORD speaks of peace to his people.

Let me hear what God the LORD will speak,
  for he will speak peace to his people,
    to his faithful, to those who turn to him in
      their hearts.
Surely his salvation is at hand for those who
      fear him,
  that his glory may dwell in our land.

The LORD speaks of peace to his people.

◆ All stand and sing **Alleluia.**

GOSPEL

Matthew 8:23–27

A reading from the holy Gospel according to Matthew.

And when he got into the boat, his disciples followed him. A windstorm arose on the sea, so great that the boat was being swamped by the waves; but he was asleep. And they went and woke him up, saying, "Lord, save us! We are perishing!" And he said to them, "Why are you afraid, you of little faith?" Then he got up and rebuked the winds and the sea; and there was a dead calm. They were amazed, saying, "What sort of man is this, that even the winds and the sea obey him?"

The Gospel of the Lord.

✚ All sit and observe silence.

FOR SILENT REFLECTION

Think about this silently in your heart. It felt miraculous when Jesus calmed the disciples' fear. Could you comfort someone who is afraid?

CLOSING PRAYER

Let us pray to God for our needs and the needs of others: our family, neighborhood, and the world. For each need we say, "Lord, hear our prayer."

✚ All may add their own prayers here.

Let us pray: **Our Father . . . Amen.**

Holy and gracious God,
your power is so great.
Through you, people's fears are calmed;
the sick are healed; the blind see.
We thank you for your goodness.
We pray in Christ's name.

Amen.

✚ All make the Sign of the Cross.

OPENING

In today's miracle story, Jesus is saying to Peter, "You too can do amazing things, if you trust in me." If we have faith in Jesus, he can help us through difficult times.

✢ All make the Sign of the Cross.

In the name of the Father, and of the Son, and of the Holy Spirit. Amen.

PSALM

(For a longer psalm, see page xv.)
Psalm 85:8–9, 10–11, 12–13

The LORD speaks of peace to his people.

The LORD speaks of peace to his people.

Let me hear what God the LORD will speak,
   for he will speak peace to his people,
      to his faithful, to those who turn to him in
         their hearts.
Surely his salvation is at hand for those who
      fear him,
   that his glory may dwell in our land.

The LORD speaks of peace to his people.

◆ All stand and sing **Alleluia.**

GOSPEL

Matthew 14:25b–26ab, 27–32

A reading from the holy Gospel according to Matthew.

Jesus came walking toward the disciples on the sea. But when the disciples saw him walking on the sea, they were terrified, saying, "It is a ghost!" Immediately Jesus spoke to them and said, "Take heart, it is I; do not be afraid." Peter answered him, "Lord, if it is you, command me to come to you on the water." He said, "Come." So Peter got out of the boat, started walking on the water, and came toward Jesus. But when he noticed the strong wind, he became frightened, and beginning to sink, he cried out, "Lord, save me!" Jesus immediately reached out his hand and caught him, saying, "You of little faith, why did you doubt?" When they got into the boat, the wind ceased.

The Gospel of the Lord.

✢ All sit and observe silence.

FOR SILENT REFLECTION

Think about this silently in your heart. If you act kindly to someone that people make fun of, would that feel miraculous to that person?

CLOSING PRAYER

Let us pray to God for our needs and the needs of others: our family, neighborhood, and the world. For each need we say, "Lord, hear our prayer."

✢ All may add their own prayers here.

Let us pray: **Our Father . . . Amen.**

Holy God,
give us a strong faith.
Help us to do what is right,
even when it is hard.
We ask this in Christ's name.

Amen.

✢ All make the Sign of the Cross.

PRAYER FOR
WEDNESDAY, JUNE 10, 2020

OPENING

The miracle story today is a familiar one. With just a few fish and a few loaves of bread, Jesus feeds a huge crowd of people. Jesus is always compassionate and hospitable. "Do not send them away hungry for they might faint," he says. We have to ask ourselves if we care for those who are hungry the way Jesus did.

✦ All make the Sign of the Cross.

In the name of the Father, and of the Son, and of the Holy Spirit. Amen.

PSALM

(For a longer psalm, see page xv.)
Psalm 85:8–9, 10–11, 12–13

The LORD speaks of peace to his people.

The LORD speaks of peace to his people.

Let me hear what God the LORD will speak,
  for he will speak peace to his people,
  to his faithful, to those who turn to him in
    their hearts.
Surely his salvation is at hand for those who
    fear him,
  that his glory may dwell in our land.

The LORD speaks of peace to his people.

◆ All stand and sing **Alleluia.**

GOSPEL

Matthew 15:32–37a

A reading from the holy Gospel according to Matthew.

Jesus called his disciples to him and said, "I have compassion for the crowd, because they have been with me now for three days and have nothing to eat; and I do not want to send them away hungry, for they might faint on the way." The disciples said to him, "Where are we to get enough bread in the desert to feed so great a crowd?" Jesus asked them, "How many loaves have you?" They said, "Seven, and a few small fish." Then ordering the crowd to sit down on the ground, he took the seven loaves and the fish; and after giving thanks he broke them and gave them to the disciples, and the disciples gave them to the crowds. And all of them ate and were filled.

The Gospel of the Lord.

✦ All sit and observe silence.

FOR SILENT REFLECTION

Think about this silently in your heart. How can you be more aware of helping feed people who are hungry?

CLOSING PRAYER

Let us pray to God for our needs and the needs of others: our family, neighborhood, and the world. For each need we say, "Lord, hear our prayer."

✦ All may add their own prayers here.

Let us pray: **Our Father . . . Amen.**

Generous God,
when Jesus knew the people were hungry,
he fed them.
Help us to respond to the needs of the poor
and hungry as best as we can, as he did.
We ask this in his name.

Amen.

✦ All make the Sign of the Cross.

OPENING

In today's miracle story, we see the relationship between Jesus and his mother. Mary knew that Jesus could do things that others couldn't do. Jesus respected his mother so much that he was willing to do as she asked, even though he did not want to.

✠ All make the Sign of the Cross.

In the name of the Father, and of the Son, and of the Holy Spirit. Amen.

PSALM

(For a longer psalm, see page xv.)
Psalm 85:8–9, 10–11, 12–13

The LORD speaks of peace to his people.

The LORD speaks of peace to his people.

Let me hear what God the LORD will speak,
　for he will speak peace to his people,
　to his faithful, to those who turn to him in
　　their hearts.
Surely his salvation is at hand for those who
　　fear him,
　that his glory may dwell in our land.

The LORD speaks of peace to his people.

◆ All stand and sing **Alleluia.**

GOSPEL

John 2:1b, 2–6ac, 7a, 8bc, 9ad, 10ad

A reading from the holy Gospel according to John.

There was a wedding in Cana of Galilee. Jesus and his disciples had been invited to the wedding. When the wine gave out, the mother of Jesus said to him, "They have no wine." And Jesus said to her, "Woman, what concern is that to you and to me? My hour has not yet come." His mother said to the servants, "Do whatever he tells you." Now standing there were six stone water jars, each holding twenty or thirty gallons. Jesus said to them, "Fill the jars with water. Draw some out, and take it to the chief steward." When the steward tasted the water, he called the bridegroom and said to him, "You have kept the good wine until now."

The Gospel of the Lord.

✠ All sit and observe silence.

FOR SILENT REFLECTION

Think about this silently in your heart. Are you willing to do what your mother asks even when you don't want to?

CLOSING PRAYER

Let us pray to God for our needs and the needs of others: our family, neighborhood, and the world. For each need we say, "Lord, hear our prayer."

✠ All may add their own prayers here.

Let us pray: **Our Father . . . Amen.**

God, our Father,
we thank you for our parents.
May we honor and respect them.
May we do our part to make our families happy and peaceful.
We ask this through Christ our Lord.

Amen.

✠ All make the Sign of the Cross.

PRAYER FOR
FRIDAY, JUNE 12, 2020

OPENING

Jesus surprises the fishermen in today's miracle story by telling them they will become fishers of men. Jesus is calling them to follow him, and he calls us as well.

✤ All make the Sign of the Cross.

In the name of the Father, and of the Son, and of the Holy Spirit. Amen.

PSALM

(For a longer psalm, see page xv.)
Psalm 85:8–9, 10–11, 12–13

The LORD speaks of peace to his people.

The LORD speaks of peace to his people.

Let me hear what God the LORD will speak,
   for he will speak peace to his people,
      to his faithful, to those who turn to him in
         their hearts.
Surely his salvation is at hand for those who
      fear him,
   that his glory may dwell in our land.

The LORD speaks of peace to his people.

◆ All stand and sing **Alleluia.**

GOSPEL

Luke 5:4b–5, 6b, 8a, 10b–11

A reading from the holy Gospel according to Luke.

Jesus said to Simon, "Put out into the deep water and let down your nets for a catch." Simon answered, "Master, we have worked all night long but have caught nothing. Yet if you say so, I will let down the nets." They caught so many fish that their nets were beginning to break. When Simon Peter saw this, he fell down at Jesus' knees. For he and all who were with him were amazed at the catch of fish that they had taken. Then Jesus said to Simon, "Do not be afraid; from now on you will be catching people." When they had brought their boats to shore, they left everything and followed him.

The Gospel of the Lord.

✤ All sit and observe silence.

FOR SILENT REFLECTION

Think about this silently in your heart. What does it mean to be a fisher of people for Jesus?

CLOSING PRAYER

Let us pray to God for our needs and the needs of others: our family, neighborhood, and the world. For each need we say, "Lord, hear our prayer."

✤ All may add their own prayers here.

Let us pray: **Our Father . . . Amen.**

Loving God,
we are called to be Jesus' disciples.
We are called to follow his example
and his teachings.
May we open our hearts and ears to his call.
We ask this through Jesus Christ, our Lord.

Amen.

✤ All make the Sign of the Cross.

PRAYER FOR THE WEEK

WITH A READING FROM THE GOSPEL FOR **SUNDAY, JUNE 14, 2020**

OPENING

Today we celebrate the Solemnity of the Most Holy Body and Blood of Christ. When we come to Holy Communion, we receive Jesus Christ. When we leave church, we carry Christ into the world.

✜ All make the Sign of the Cross.

In the name of the Father, and of the Son, and of the Holy Spirit. Amen.

PSALM

(For a longer psalm, see page xv.)
Psalm 85:8–9, 10–11, 12–13

The LORD speaks of peace to his people.

The LORD speaks of peace to his people.

Let me hear what God the LORD will speak,
    for he will speak peace to his people,
    to his faithful, to those who turn to him in
        their hearts.
Surely his salvation is at hand for those who
        fear him,
    that his glory may dwell in our land.

The LORD speaks of peace to his people.

◆ All stand and sing **Alleluia.**

GOSPEL

John 6:51–58

A reading from the holy Gospel according to John.

Jesus said to the Jews, "I am the living bread that came down from heaven. Whoever eats of this bread will live forever; and the bread that I will give for the life of the world is my flesh." The Jews then disputed among themselves, saying, "How can this man give us his flesh to eat?" So Jesus said to them, "Very truly, I tell you, unless you eat the flesh of the Son of Man and drink his blood, you have no life in you. Those who eat my flesh and drink my blood have eternal life, and I will raise them up on the last day; for my flesh is true food and my blood is true drink. Those who eat my flesh and drink my blood abide in me, and I in them. Just as the living Father sent me, and I live because of the Father, so whoever eats me will live because of me. This is the bread that came down from heaven, not like that which your ancestors ate, and they died. But the one who eats this bread will live forever."

The Gospel of the Lord.

✜ All sit and observe silence.

FOR SILENT REFLECTION

Think about this silently in your heart. Each time we partake of the Body and Blood of Christ, we allow Christ to fill and transform every part of our lives.

CLOSING PRAYER

Let us pray to God for our needs and the needs of others: our family, neighborhood, and the world. For each need we say, "Lord, hear our prayer."

✜ All may add their own prayers here.

Let us pray: **Our Father . . . Amen.**

We pray, O God,
that the gift of the Body and Blood of Christ
will strengthen us to do your will.
We pray in the name of Jesus Christ, our Lord.

Amen.

✜ All make the Sign of the Cross.

PRAYER FOR
MONDAY, JUNE 15, 2020

OPENING

The theme of this week's readings is God sending people into the world to carry out his plan. Moses was one of the greatest leaders of the Hebrew people. He led them out of slavery in Egypt to the Promised Land. This victory is celebrated each year at the great Jewish feast of Passover. But Moses was just an ordinary man when God asked him to do great things.

✛ All make the Sign of the Cross.

> **In the name of the Father, and of the Son, and of the Holy Spirit. Amen.**

PSALM

(For a longer psalm, see page xv.)
Psalm 85:8–9, 10–11, 12–13

The Lord speaks of peace to his people.

The Lord speaks of peace to his people.

Let me hear what God the Lord will speak,
  for he will speak peace to his people,
    to his faithful, to those who turn to him in
      their hearts.
Surely his salvation is at hand for those who
      fear him,
  that his glory may dwell in our land.

The Lord speaks of peace to his people.

READING

Exodus 3:7ab, 8a, 10–12a, 13–14

A reading from the Book of Exodus.

Then the Lord said, "I have observed the misery of my people who are in Egypt; and I have come down to deliver them from the Egyptians. So come, I will send you to Pharaoh to bring my people, the Israelites, out of Egypt." But Moses said to God, "Who am I that I should go to Pharaoh, and bring the Israelites out of Egypt?" He said, "I will be with you." But Moses said to God, "If I come to the Israelites and say to them, 'The God of your ancestors has sent me to you,' and they ask me, 'What is his name?' what shall I say to them?" God said to Moses, "I AM WHO I AM." He said further, "Thus you shall say to the Israelites, 'I AM has sent me to you.'"

The Word of the Lord.

✛ All observe silence.

FOR SILENT REFLECTION

Think about this silently in your heart. Moses didn't think he could do what God asked. What did God tell Moses?

CLOSING PRAYER

Let us pray to God for our needs and the needs of others: our family, neighborhood, and the world. For each need we say, "Lord, hear our prayer."

✛ All may add their own prayers here.

Let us pray: **Our Father . . . Amen.**

God of all creation,
throughout history you have called people
to freedom from slavery.
Through our faith in you, may we be free
from the slavery of sin.
We ask this in the name of our Savior,
Jesus Christ.

Amen.

✛ All make the Sign of the Cross.

OPENING

Many people followed John the Baptist and thought he might be the Messiah. But John knew he had been sent by God to announce Jesus as the Messiah.

✦ All make the Sign of the Cross.

In the name of the Father, and of the Son, and of the Holy Spirit. Amen.

PSALM

(For a longer psalm, see page xv.)
Psalm 85:8–9, 10–11, 12–13

The LORD speaks of peace to his people.

The LORD speaks of peace to his people.

Let me hear what God the LORD will speak,
for he will speak peace to his people,
to his faithful, to those who turn to him in
their hearts.
Surely his salvation is at hand for those who
fear him,
that his glory may dwell in our land.

The LORD speaks of peace to his people.

◆ All stand and sing **Alleluia.**

GOSPEL

John 3:22–23a, 26–27a, 28–30

A reading from the holy Gospel according to John.

After this Jesus and his disciples went into the Judean countryside, and he spent some time there with them and baptized. John also was baptizing at Aenon [EE-nuhn] near Salim [SAY-lim] because water was abundant there. John's disciples came to him and said to him, "Rabbi, the one who was with you across the Jordan, to whom you testified, here he is baptizing, and all are going to him." John answered, "You yourselves are my witnesses that I said, 'I am not the Messiah, but I have been sent ahead of him.' He who has the bride is the bridegroom. The friend of the bridegroom, who stands and hears him, rejoices greatly at the bridegroom's voice. For this reason my joy has been fulfilled. He must increase, but I must decrease."

The Gospel of the Lord.

✦ All sit and observe silence.

FOR SILENT REFLECTION

Think about his silently in your heart. Telling people about Jesus filled John with joy. How does Jesus fill you with joy?

CLOSING PRAYER

Let us pray to God for our needs and the needs of others: our family, neighborhood, and the world. For each need we say, "Lord, hear our prayer."

✦ All may add their own prayers here.

Let us pray: **Our Father . . . Amen.**

Good and gracious God,
we give you thanks and praise.
We thank you for the gift of Baptism,
in which we are called to be your children.
May we live our Baptismal calling each day.
We ask this in Christ's name.

Amen.

✦ All make the Sign of the Cross.

PRAYER FOR
WEDNESDAY, JUNE 17, 2020

OPENING

Today's Gospel shows us how the disciples continued Jesus' ministry of healing and caring for others. The disciples knew that their faith was a gift that was greater than silver or gold.

✚ All make the Sign of the Cross.

In the name of the Father, and of the Son, and of the Holy Spirit. Amen.

PSALM

(For a longer psalm, see page xv.)
Psalm 85:8–9, 10–11, 12–13

The LORD speaks of peace to his people.

The LORD speaks of peace to his people.

Let me hear what God the LORD will speak,
    for he will speak peace to his people,
    to his faithful, to those who turn to him in
        their hearts.
Surely his salvation is at hand for those who
        fear him,
    that his glory may dwell in our land.

The LORD speaks of peace to his people.

READING

Acts 3:1–4ab, 6bc, 7b, 8ac

A reading from the Acts of the Apostles.

One day Peter and John were going up to the temple at the hour of prayer, at three o'clock in the afternoon. And a man lame from birth was being carried in. People would lay him daily at the gate of the temple called the Beautiful Gate so that he could ask for alms from those entering the temple. When he saw Peter and John about to go into the temple, he asked them for alms. Peter looked intently at him, as did John, and said, "I have no silver or gold, but what I have I give you; in the name of Jesus Christ of Nazareth, stand up and walk." And immediately his feet and ankles were made strong. Jumping up, he entered the temple with them, walking and leaping and praising God.

The Word of the Lord.

✚ All observe silence.

FOR SILENT REFLECTION

Think about this silently in your heart. God calls us to care for people in many ways. How do you care for people?

CLOSING PRAYER

Let us pray to God for our needs and the needs of others: our family, neighborhood, and the world. For each need we say, "Lord, hear our prayer."

✚ All may add their own prayers here.

Let us pray: **Our Father . . . Amen.**

God our Father,
because they had faith in you and in Jesus,
the disciples were able to do great things.
We ask that we may be faithful in our prayer
and generous in our actions.
Through Christ our Lord.

Amen.

✚ All make the Sign of the Cross.

OPENING

In today's reading from the Acts of the Apostles, we hear the names of Jesus' other disciples. They helped to spread the Good News to many lands.

✛ All make the Sign of the Cross.

In the name of the Father, and of the Son, and of the Holy Spirit. Amen.

PSALM

(For a longer psalm, see page xv.)
Psalm 85:8–9, 10–11, 12–13

The LORD speaks of peace to his people.

The LORD speaks of peace to his people.

Let me hear what God the LORD will speak,
    for he will speak peace to his people,
    to his faithful, to those who turn to him in
        their hearts.
Surely his salvation is at hand for those who
        fear him,
    that his glory may dwell in our land.

The LORD speaks of peace to his people.

READING

Acts 13:1–5

A reading from the Acts of the Apostles.

Now in the church at Antioch [AN-tee-ahk] there were prophets and teachers: Barnabas, Simeon who was called Niger [NĪ-guhr], Lucius of Cyrene [sī-REEN], Manaen [MAN-ee-uhn] a member of the court of Herod the ruler, and Saul. While they were worshiping the Lord and fasting, the Holy Spirit said, "Set apart for me Barnabas and Saul for the work to which I have called them." Then after fasting and praying they laid their hands on them and sent them off. So, being sent out by the Holy Spirit, they went down to Seleucia; and from there they sailed to Cyprus. When they arrived at Salamis [SAL-uh-mihs], they proclaimed the word of God in the synagogues of the Jews. And they had John also to assist them.

The Word of the Lord.

✛ All observe silence.

FOR SILENT REFLECTION

Think about this silently in your heart. Barnabas and Saul had the support and encouragement of many people. Who supports and encourages you?

CLOSING PRAYER

Let us pray to God for our needs and the needs of others: our family, neighborhood, and the world. For each need we say, "Lord, hear our prayer."

✛ All may add their own prayers here.

Let us pray: **Our Father . . . Amen.**

Almighty God,
you call people all over the world
to hear the Good News.
Help us continue the work of the early
Christians and spread your Word.
We ask this in Christ's name.

Amen.

✛ All make the Sign of the Cross.

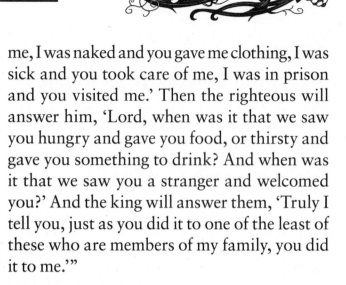

OPENING

Today the Church honors the Most Sacred Heart of Jesus. Jesus has a great love for all people, especially those in need. In today's reading, Jesus compassionately called attention to the needs of the poor and challenged people who had money to look after them, saying, "In the face of the poor, you see God."

✦ All make the Sign of the Cross.

In the name of the Father, and of the Son, and of the Holy Spirit. Amen.

PSALM

(For a longer psalm, see page xv.)
Psalm 85:8–9, 10–11, 12–13

The LORD speaks of peace to his people.

The LORD speaks of peace to his people.

Let me hear what God the LORD will speak,
    for he will speak peace to his people,
        to his faithful, to those who turn to him in
            their hearts.
Surely his salvation is at hand for those who
        fear him,
    that his glory may dwell in our land.

The LORD speaks of peace to his people.

◆ All stand and sing **Alleluia.**

GOSPEL

Matthew 25:34ab, 35–38a, 40

A reading from the holy Gospel according to Matthew.

Jesus said, "Then the king will say to those at his right hand, 'Come, you that are blessed by my Father; for I was hungry and you gave me food, I was thirsty and you gave me something to drink, I was a stranger and you welcomed me, I was naked and you gave me clothing, I was sick and you took care of me, I was in prison and you visited me.' Then the righteous will answer him, 'Lord, when was it that we saw you hungry and gave you food, or thirsty and gave you something to drink? And when was it that we saw you a stranger and welcomed you?' And the king will answer them, 'Truly I tell you, just as you did it to one of the least of these who are members of my family, you did it to me.'"

The Gospel of the Lord.

✦ All sit and observe silence.

FOR SILENT REFLECTION

Think about his silently in your heart. How can you help people who have less than you do?

CLOSING PRAYER

Let us pray to God for our needs and the needs of others: our family, neighborhood, and the world. For each need we say, "Lord, hear our prayer."

✦ All may add their own prayers here.

Let us pray: **Our Father . . . Amen.**

Jesus' word is clear:
how we care for others
is how we care for him.
May we see Jesus in all we meet, especially those who are poor, hungry, in prison, or different from us.
We pray in Christ's name.

Amen.

✦ All make the Sign of the Cross.

PRAYER FOR THE WEEK

WITH A READING FROM THE GOSPEL FOR **SUNDAY, JUNE 21, 2020**

OPENING

Today's Gospel is a powerful reminder of God's love and care for each person and for all that God has created. Nothing is too small or too insignficant in God's eyes.

✚ All make the Sign of the Cross.

In the name of the Father, and of the Son, and of the Holy Spirit. Amen.

PSALM

(For a longer psalm, see page xv.)
Psalm 85:8–9, 10–11, 12–13

The LORD speaks of peace to his people.

The LORD speaks of peace to his people.

Let me hear what God the LORD will speak,
　for he will speak peace to his people,
　　to his faithful, to those who turn to him in
　　　their hearts.
Surely his salvation is at hand for those who
　　　fear him,
　that his glory may dwell in our land.

The LORD speaks of peace to his people.

◆ All stand and sing **Alleluia.**

GOSPEL

Matthew 10:26–30

A reading from the holy Gospel according to Matthew.

So have no fear of them; for nothing is covered up that will not be uncovered, and nothing secret that will not become known. What I say to you in the dark, tell in the light; what you hear whispered, proclaim from the housetops. Do not fear those who kill the body but cannot kill the soul; rather fear him who can destroy both soul and body in hell. Are not two spar-rows sold for a penny? Yet not one of them will fall to the ground apart from your Father. And even the hairs of your head are all counted.

The Gospel of the Lord.

◆ All sit and observe silence.

FOR SILENT REFLECTION

Think about this silently in your heart. What does it mean that even the "hairs of your head are all counted"? What does that say about how much God cares for you?

CLOSING PRAYER

Let us pray to God for our needs and the needs of others: our family, neighborhood, and the world. For each need we say, "Lord, hear our prayer."

◆ All may add their own prayers here.

Let us pray: **Our Father . . . Amen.**

O God,
how great and loving you are!
May all creation sing your praise!
May all creation rejoice in you!
We pray in the name of your Son,
Jesus Christ, our Lord.

Amen.

✚ All make the Sign of the Cross.

329

OPENING

In the Gospel for today, Jesus again refers to himself as the good shepherd. The people who heard Jesus speaking would have understood what it meant for a shepherd to care for his sheep. Jesus surprises them by saying that he cares not only for his flock but also for the sheep that are not a part of his fold.

✚ *All make the Sign of the Cross.*

In the name of the Father, and of the Son, and of the Holy Spirit. Amen.

PSALM

(For a longer psalm, see page xv.)
Psalm 85:8–9, 10–11, 12–13

The LORD speaks of peace to his people.

The LORD speaks of peace to his people.

Let me hear what God the LORD will speak,
   for he will speak peace to his people,
     to his faithful, to those who turn to him in
       their hearts.
Surely his salvation is at hand for those who
     fear him,
   that his glory may dwell in our land.

The LORD speaks of peace to his people.

♦ *All stand and sing* **Alleluia.**

GOSPEL

John 10:14–16

A reading from the holy Gospel according to John.

Jesus said to them, "I am the good shepherd. I know my own and my own know me, just as the Father knows me and I know the Father. And I lay down my life for the sheep. I have other sheep that do not belong to this fold. I must bring them also, and they will listen to my voice. So there will be one flock, one shepherd."

The Gospel of the Lord.

♦ *All sit and observe silence.*

FOR SILENT REFLECTION

Think about this silently in your heart. Who might be the "other sheep" that Jesus wants to bring into his sheepfold?

CLOSING PRAYER

Let us pray to God for our needs and the needs of others: our family, neighborhood, and the world. For each need we say, "Lord, hear our prayer."

♦ *All may add their own prayers here.*

Let us pray: **Our Father . . . Amen.**

Help us to know Jesus, our Good Shepherd,
O God.
May we follow his voice and listen to him.
We pray that one day we will be united
as one flock under one shepherd.
We pray in the name of our Good Shepherd,
Jesus Christ.

Amen.

✚ *All make the Sign of the Cross.*

OPENING

Today we hear from the First Letter of St. John. Once again we are reminded that God knows what is in our hearts. We are are also reminded that we show what is in our hearts more by our actions than by our words.

✦ All make the Sign of the Cross.

In the name of the Father, and of the Son, and of the Holy Spirit. Amen.

PSALM

(For a longer psalm, see page xv.)
Psalm 85:8–9, 10–11, 12–13

The LORD speaks of peace to his people.

The LORD speaks of peace to his people.

Let me hear what God the LORD will speak,
for he will speak peace to his people,
to his faithful, to those who turn to him in their hearts.
Surely his salvation is at hand for those who fear him,
that his glory may dwell in our land.

The LORD speaks of peace to his people.

READING

1 John 3:18–22

A reading from the First Letter of St. John.

Little children, let us love, not in word or speech, but in truth and action. And by this we will know that we are from the truth and will reassure our hearts before him whenever our hearts condemn us; for God is greater than our hearts, and he knows everything. Beloved, if our hearts do not condemn us, we have boldness before God; and we receive from him whatever we ask, because we obey his commandments and do what pleases him.

The Word of the Lord.

✦ All observe silence.

FOR SILENT REFLECTION

Think about this silently in your heart. In what ways do actions speak louder than words?

CLOSING PRAYER

Let us pray to God for our needs and the needs of others: our family, neighborhood, and the world. For each need we say, "Lord, hear our prayer."

✦ All may add their own prayers here.

Let us pray: **Our Father . . . Amen.**

Loving God,
so often we hear of your great love.
Help us to love you in return
and to show this love by what we do.
We pray this in Christ's name.

Amen.

✦ All make the Sign of the Cross.

PRAYER FOR
WEDNESDAY, JUNE 24, 2020

OPENING

Today we celebrate the Nativity (the birth) of John the Baptist. In Hebrew the name *John* means that "God has shown favor." John's mother, Elizabeth, and his father, Zechariah, knew that God had looked favorably on them in giving them a son. John the Baptist is Jesus' cousin, and he helped to prepare people to hear Jesus' message.

✚ All make the Sign of the Cross.

In the name of the Father, and of the Son, and of the Holy Spirit. Amen.

PSALM
(For a longer psalm, see page xv.)
Psalm 85:8–9, 10–11, 12–13

The LORD speaks of peace to his people.

The LORD speaks of peace to his people.

Let me hear what God the LORD will speak,
   for he will speak peace to his people,
      to his faithful, to those who turn to him in
         their hearts.
Surely his salvation is at hand for those who
      fear him,
   that his glory may dwell in our land.

The LORD speaks of peace to his people.

◆ All stand and sing **Alleluia.**

GOSPEL
Luke 1:57–63

A reading from the holy Gospel according to Luke.

Now the time came for Elizabeth to give birth, and she bore a son. Her neighbors and relatives heard that the Lord had shown his great mercy to her, and they rejoiced with her. On the eighth day they came to circumcise the child, and they were going to name him Zechariah after his father. But his mother said, "No, he is to be called John." They said to her, "None of your relatives has this name." Then they began motioning to his father to find out what name he wanted to give him. He asked for a writing tablet and wrote, "His name is John." And all of them were amazed.

The Gospel of the Lord.

◆ All sit and observe silence.

FOR SILENT REFLECTION

Think about this silently in your heart. Names are chosen for their meaning or because some names are traditionally handed down in families. What does your name signify?

CLOSING PRAYER

Let us pray to God for our needs and the needs of others: our family, neighborhood, and the world. For each need we say, "Lord, hear our prayer."

◆ All may add their own prayers here.

Let us pray: **Our Father . . . Amen.**

Holy God,
John the Baptist called people
to listen to Jesus.
May we follow his example
in our own time and place.
We ask this through Christ our Lord.

Amen.

✚ All make the Sign of the Cross.

OPENING

Today we hear from one of the letters St. Paul wrote to the early Christian community of the Philippians [fih-LIP-ee-uhnz]. St. Paul expresses his great appreciation for them and promises to pray for them always. As we end the school year, we can remember to pray for one another during our summer vacation.

✝ *All make the Sign of the Cross.*

In the name of the Father, and of the Son, and of the Holy Spirit. Amen.

PSALM

(For a longer psalm, see page xv.)
Psalm 85:8–9, 10–11, 12–13

The LORD speaks of peace to his people.

The LORD speaks of peace to his people.

Let me hear what God the LORD will speak,
   for he will speak peace to his people,
   to his faithful, to those who turn to him in
      their hearts.
Surely his salvation is at hand for those who
      fear him,
   that his glory may dwell in our land.

The LORD speaks of peace to his people.

READING

Philippians 1:3–6

A reading from the Letter of Paul to the Philippians.

I thank my God every time I remember you, constantly praying with joy in every one of my prayers for all of you, because of your sharing in the gospel from the first day until now. I am confident of this, that the one who began a good work among you will bring it to completion by the day of Jesus Christ.

The Word of the Lord.

◆ *All observe silence.*

FOR SILENT REFLECTION

Think about this silently in your heart. Who helped you during this school year? Give thanks for them in prayer.

CLOSING PRAYER

Let us pray to God for our needs and the needs of others: our family, neighborhood, and the world. For each need we say, "Lord, hear our prayer."

◆ *All may add their own prayers here.*

Let us pray: **Our Father . . . Amen.**

Most loving God,
we thank you for the time we have shared together this year.
Help us to be safe during the summer months.
Let us remember to pray for one another.
We ask this through Christ our Lord.

Amen.

✝ *All make the Sign of the Cross.*

PRAYER FOR
FRIDAY, JUNE 26, 2020

OPENING

As we conclude our school year, we hear the Gospel parable of the mustard seed. Jesus compares the Kingdom of God to a tiny mustard seed, which can grow into a large shrub. This parable explains the strength of God's power.

✝ All make the Sign of the Cross.

In the name of the Father, and of the Son, and of the Holy Spirit. Amen.

PSALM

(For a longer psalm, see page xv.)
Psalm 85:8–9, 10–11, 12–13

The Lord speaks of peace to his people.

The Lord speaks of peace to his people.

Let me hear what God the Lord will speak,
  for he will speak peace to his people,
    to his faithful, to those who turn to him in
      their hearts.
Surely his salvation is at hand for those who
    fear him,
  that his glory may dwell in our land.

The Lord speaks of peace to his people.

◆ All stand and sing **Alleluia.**

GOSPEL

Mark 4:30–32

A reading from the holy Gospel according to Mark.

Jesus also said, "With what can we compare the kingdom of God, or what parable will we use for it? It is like a mustard seed, which, when sown upon the ground is the smallest of all the seeds on earth; yet when it is sown it grows up and becomes the greatest of all shrubs, and puts forth large branches so that the birds of the air can make nests in its shade."

The Gospel of the Lord.

◆ All sit and observe silence.

FOR SILENT REFLECTION

Think about this silently in your heart. What does this parable tell you about the Kingdom of God?

CLOSING PRAYER

Let us pray to God for our needs and the needs of others: our family, neighborhood, and the world. For each need we say, "Lord, hear our prayer."

◆ All may add their own prayers here.

Let us pray: **Our Father . . . Amen.**

Almighty and holy God,
we thank you for all of the ways
that Jesus reveals your Kingdom.
Help us to remember
that we are not too young
or too small to do our part to bring about
your Kingdom on earth.
We ask this in the name of Christ our Lord.

Amen.

✝ All make the Sign of the Cross.

✝ All make the Sign of the Cross.

ALL: In the name of the Father, and of the Son, and of the Holy Spirit. Amen.

LEADER:
Loving God,
you created all the people of the world,
and you know each of us by name.
We thank you for N., who today
    celebrates his/her birthday.
Bless him/her with your love and friendship
that he/she may grow in wisdom, knowledge,
    and grace.
May he/she love his/her family always
and be faithful to his/her friends.

Grant this through Christ our Lord.

ALL: Amen.

LEADER:
Let us bow our heads and pray for N.

◆ All observe silence.

LEADER:
May God, in whose presence our ancestors
walked, bless you.

ALL: Amen.

LEADER:
May God, who has been your shepherd
from birth until now, keep you.

ALL: Amen.

LEADER:
May God, who saves you from all harm, give
you peace.

ALL: Amen.

✝ All make the Sign of the Cross.

**In the name of the Father, and of the
Son, and of the Holy Spirit. Amen.**

PRAYER SERVICE
LAST DAY OF SCHOOL

Prepare eight leaders for this service. The fourth leader will need a Bible for the Scripture passage and may need help practicing the reading. You may wish to begin by singing "In the Lord I'll Be Ever Thankful" and end with "Send Forth Your Spirit, O Lord." If the group will sing, prepare a song leader.

FIRST LEADER:

Our school year is drawing to a close, and we can see in ourselves so much growth! With each passing day, God worked through each person to make a new creation. Together, let us thank our Creator for the many blessed memories we've shared in our time together.

SECOND LEADER:

✚ All make the sign of the Cross.

In the name of the Father, and of the Son, and of the Holy Spirit. Amen.

Let us pray:
God of all creation,
we are blessed to be with one another
in this time and place.
We are excited to start our break,
yet we may feel sad as we
think about friends
we may not see for a while.
In these times of change,
help us to stay
connected with you, Lord,
for you desire happiness and peace
for all your brothers and sisters.
We ask this through Jesus Christ our Lord.

ALL: Amen.

THIRD LEADER: Psalm 119:1–3, 10–11, 41–42, 89–90, 105

Let us repeat the Psalm Response: Your word is a lamp to my feet and a light to my path.

ALL: Your word is a lamp to my feet and a light to my path.

Happy are those whose way is blameless,
    who walk in the law of the LORD.
Happy are those who keep his decrees,
    who seek him with their whole heart,
who also do no wrong,
    but walk in his ways.

ALL: Your word is a lamp to my feet and a light to my path.

With my whole heart I seek you;
    do not let me stray from your
        commandments.
I treasure your word in my heart,
    so that I may not sin against you.

ALL: Your word is a lamp to my feet and a light to my path.

Let your steadfast love come to me, O LORD,
    your salvation according to your promise.
Then I shall have an answer for those who
        taunt me,
    for I trust in your word.

ALL: Your word is a lamp to my feet and a light to my path.

The LORD exists forever;
    your word is firmly fixed in heaven.
Your faithfulness endures to all generations;
    you have established the earth, and it
        stands fast.

ALL: Your word is a lamp to my feet and a light to my path.

FOURTH LEADER: Romans 12:9–18

A reading from the Letter of Paul to the Romans.

✝ Read the Scripture passage from the Bible.

The Word of the Lord.

✝ All observe silence.

FIFTH LEADER:

Let us bring our hopes and needs to God as we
pray, "Lord, hear our prayer."
For our teachers, administrators,
volunteers, coaches, and school staff
who worked hard to produce our
quality learning time together,

we pray to the Lord . . .

For our parents, grandparents,
and family members who helped us
with homework and other tasks
throughout the year,

we pray to the Lord . . .

For the friends we've made
and those on the horizon,
may they reflect the warmth and compassion
that Jesus feels for us,

we pray to the Lord . . .

For those who are dealing with sickness,
job loss, or other difficulties in life,
for those who have gone before us
to the other side of life,
may they experience the peace of Christ,

we pray to the Lord . . .

SIXTH LEADER:

Lord Jesus,
your gentle Spirit has
nudged and guided us
these past several months.
May we continue to seek your wisdom
as we daily pray to you,
ever mindful of
how much you care for us.
We ask this in your name.

Amen.

SEVENTH LEADER:

Let us offer to one another a sign of
Christ's peace:

✝ All offer one another a sign of peace.

EIGHTH LEADER:

Let us pray:
Creator God,
you are Lord of all things,
and you are always with us.
May we embrace
all our new experiences
in our break from school.
Help us to listen to you,
source of all truth,
and go forth to
new adventures,
cherishing the love that
we've shared this year.

ALL: Amen.

✝ All make the Sign of the Cross.

PRAYER SERVICE
FOR SAD DAYS

The following prayer can be used when there is a sad or tragic event in the school community. This may be an illness or death of a student, faculty, or staff member, or a parent of a student. It may also be used at a time of a local or national crisis when the school gathers to pray. For this prayer, an adult should take the part of the leader as it is important to offer a few words that describe the particular need or concern.

✝ All make the Sign of the Cross.

ALL: In the name of the Father, and of the Son, and of the Holy Spirit. Amen.

LEADER:
We gather today to pray for [name the person or concern].
We trust, O God, that you hear us.
We trust that you understand the suffering and pain of your people.
We trust that you are with all those in need.
Let us listen to the Word of God.

READER: Matthew 11:28–30
A reading from the holy Gospel according to Matthew.

"Come to me, all you that are weary and are carrying heavy burdens, and I will give you rest. Take my yoke upon you, and learn from me; for I am gentle and humble in heart, and you will find rest for your souls. For my yoke is easy, and my burden is light."

LEADER:
Let us take a few moments to pray in our hearts for [name the person or concern].

LEADER:
Let us pray:
God of all,
help us to remember that your son Jesus suffered, died, and rose so that we might know of your great love.

He invites us to bring our cares and concerns to you in prayer, and so we ask you to be with [name the persons]. Give them courage and peace.

We ask you also to be with us during this time of difficulty. Help us to trust that you are always with us.

◆ [If appropriate, invite spontaneous prayers from those gathered.]

LEADER:
Assured of your great love, we pray:
Our Father . . . Amen.

◆ Pause and say:

As we conclude our prayer, let us offer one another the sign of Christ's peace.

◆ All offer one another a sign of peace.

LEADER:
May God the Creator bless us:

✝ All make the Sign of the Cross.

In the name of the Father, and of the Son, and of the Holy Spirit. Amen.

CHILDREN'S DAILY PRAYER 2019–2020, © 2019 Archdiocese of Chicago: Liturgy Training Publications. All rights reserved. Orders: 800-933-1800 or www.LTP.org.

PSALMS AND CANTICLES

PSALM 23

This psalm is appropriate during all liturgical seasons. It may be prayed in times of difficulty or stress, when comfort is needed, or to meditate on Christ's presence in the sacraments.

The LORD is my shepherd, I shall not want.
   He makes me lie down in green pastures;
he leads me beside still waters;
   he restores my soul.
He leads me in right paths
   for his name's sake.

Even though I walk through the darkest valley,
   I fear no evil;
for you are with me;
   your rod and your staff—
   they comfort me.

You prepare a table before me
   in the presence of my enemies;
you anoint my head with oil;
   my cup overflows.
Surely goodness and mercy shall follow me
   all the days of my life,
and I shall dwell in the house of the LORD
   my whole life long.

PSALM 27

Psalm 27:1, 4–5, 7–9, 13–14

*Use this psalm during times of darkness, anxiety, or uncertainty.
This psalm is also an affirmation of God's goodness at any
moment in life.*

The LORD is my light and my salvation;
   whom shall I fear?
The LORD is the stronghold of my life;
   of whom shall I be afraid?

One thing I asked of the LORD,
   that will I seek after:
to live in the house of the LORD
   all the days of my life,
to behold the beauty of the LORD,
   and to inquire in his temple.

For he will hide me in his shelter
   in the day of trouble;
he will conceal me under the cover of his tent;
   he will set me high on a rock.

Hear, O LORD, when I cry aloud,
   be gracious to me and answer me!
"Come," my heart says, "seek his face!"
   Your face, LORD, do I seek.
   Do not hide your face from me.

I believe that I shall see the goodness of the LORD
   in the land of the living.
Wait for the LORD;
   be strong, and let your heart take courage;
   wait for the LORD!

PSALM 34

Psalm 34:1–8

This psalm of trust in God's power may be prayed by anyone seeking to wonder and rejoice in Christ's presence in the Eucharist. It is especially appropriate for those preparing to celebrate First Communion.

I will bless the LORD at all times;
   his praise shall continually be in my mouth.
My soul makes its boast in the LORD;
   let the humble hear and be glad.
O magnify the LORD with me,
   and let us exalt his name together.

I sought the LORD, and he answered me,
   and delivered me from all my fears.
Look to him, and be radiant;
   so your faces shall never be ashamed.
This poor soul cried, and was heard by the LORD,
   and was saved from every trouble.
The angel of the LORD encamps
   around those who fear him, and delivers them.
O taste and see that the LORD is good;
   happy are those who take refuge in him.

PSALM 46

Psalm 46:1–5

This psalm may be used during times of suffering, confusion, or fear. Its offer of comfort and renewal will give cause for hope in any extremity.

God is our refuge and strength,
    a very present help in trouble.
Therefore we will not fear, though the earth should change,
    though the mountains shake in the heart of the sea;
though its waters roar and foam,
    though the mountains tremble with its tumult.

There is a river whose streams make glad the city of God,
    the holy habitation of the Most High.
God is in the midst of the city; it shall not be moved;
    God will help it when the morning dawns.

PSALM 51

Psalm 51:1–2, 6, 10, 12, 15

*This is a penitential psalm that is especially appropriate during
a communal celebration of the Sacrament of Reconciliation.
It can also be incorporated into any Lenten prayer service.*

Have mercy on me, O God,
   according to your steadfast love;
according to your abundant mercy
   blot out my transgressions.
Wash me thoroughly from my iniquity,
   and cleanse me from my sin.

You desire truth in the inward being;
   therefore teach me wisdom in my secret heart.

Create in me a clean heart, O God,
   and put a new and right spirit within me.
Restore to me the joy of your salvation,
   and sustain in me a willing spirit.

O LORD, open my lips,
   and my mouth will declare your praise.

PSALM 100

This is a joyful psalm of thanksgiving that helps orient the heart to God.

Make a joyful noise to the LORD, all the earth.
  Worship the LORD with gladness;
  come into his presence with singing.
Know that the LORD is God.
  It is he that made us, and we are his;
  we are his people, and the sheep of his pasture.
Enter his gates with thanksgiving,
  and his courts with praise.
  Give thanks to him, bless his name.
For the LORD is good;
  his steadfast love endures forever,
  and his faithfulness to all generations.

PSALM 103

Psalm 103:1–5, 19–22

This is a deeply meditative psalm of grateful acknowledgment of God's gifts and God's mercy.

Bless the LORD, O my soul,
  and all that is within me,
  bless his holy name.
Bless the LORD, O my soul,
  and do not forget all his benefits—
who forgives all your iniquity,
  who heals all your diseases,
who redeems your life from the Pit,
  who crowns you with steadfast love and mercy,
who satisfies you with good as long as you live
  so that your youth is renewed like the eagle's.

The LORD has established his throne in the heavens,
  and his kingdom rules over all.
Bless the LORD, O you his angels,
  you mighty ones who do his bidding,
  obedient to his spoken word.
Bless the LORD, all his works,
  in all places of his dominion.
Bless the LORD, O my soul.

PSALM 148

Psalm 148:1-4; 7-13

This is a psalm praising God for the glory of creation. It is a good prayer to use especially during the weeks in which the Scripture readings focus on creation of the earth.

Praise the LORD!
Praise the LORD from the heavens; praise him in the heights!
Praise him, all his angels; praise him all his host!

Praise him, sun and moon; praise him, all you shining stars!
Praise him, you highest heavens, and your waters below the heavens!

Praise the LORD from the earth,
    you sea monsters and all deeps,
fire and hail, snow and frost, stormy wind fulfilling his command!

Mountains and all hills, fruit trees and all cedars!
Wild animals and all cattle, creeping things and flying birds!

Kings of the earth and all peoples,
    Princes and all rulers of the earth1
Young men and women alike, old and young together.

Let them praise the name of the LORD,
    For his name alone is exalted;
His glory is above earth and heaven.

PSALMS

PSALM 150

Psalm 150

This psalm praises God, suggesting that we use all sorts of musical instruments to offer our praise. It is a song of great joy and rejoicing.

Praise the LORD!
Praise God in his sanctuary; praise him in his mighty firmament!
Praise him for his mighty deeds; praise him
    according to his surpassing greatness!

Praise him with trumpet sound; praise him with lute and harp!
Praise him with tambourine and dance;
    praise him with strings and pipe!
    Praise him with clanging cymbals;
        Praise him with loud clashing cymbals!
    Let everything that breathes praise the LORD!
    Praise the LORD!

THE *MAGNIFICAT* OF MARY

Luke 1:46–55

Mary prayed with these words when she visited her relative, Elizabeth, after Elizabeth declared, "Blessed are you among women and blessed is the fruit of your womb!" For centuries, this beautiful song of praise and trust has been the Church's evening prayer.

And Mary said,
"My soul magnifies the Lord,
   and my spirit rejoices in God my Savior,
for he has looked with favor on the lowliness of his servant.
   Surely, from now on all generations will call me blessed;
for the Mighty One has done great things for me,
   and holy is his name.
His mercy is for those who fear him
   from generation to generation.
He has shown strength with his arm;
   he has scattered the proud in the thoughts of their hearts.
He has brought down the powerful from their thrones,
   and lifted up the lowly;
he has filled the hungry with good things,
   and sent the rich away empty.
He has helped his servant Israel,
   in remembrance of his mercy,
according to the promise he made to our ancestors,
   to Abraham and to his descendants forever."

CANTICLES

THE *BENEDICTUS* OF ZECHARIAH

Luke 1:68–79

Zechariah had been struck mute during the pregnancy of his wife, Elizabeth. After their baby was born, on the day when they gave him his name, Zechariah's voice was restored and he spoke these prophetic words over his child, John the Baptist. His prophecy is part of the Church's traditional morning prayer.

"Blessed be the Lord God of Israel,
    for he has looked favorably on his people and redeemed them.
He has raised up a mighty savior for us
    in the house of his servant David,
as he spoke through the mouth of his holy prophets from of old,
        that we would be saved from our enemies and from the hand
            of all who hate us.
Thus he has shown the mercy promised to our ancestors,
    and has remembered his holy covenant,
the oath that he swore to our ancestor Abraham,
    to grant us that we, being rescued from the hands
        of our enemies,
might serve him without fear, in holiness and righteousness,
    before him all our days.
And you, child, will be called the prophet of the Most High;
    for you will go before the Lord to prepare his ways,
to give knowledge of salvation to his people
    by the forgiveness of their sins.
By the tender mercy of our God,
    the dawn from on high will break upon us,
to give light to those who sit in darkness and in the shadow
        of death,
    to guide our feet into the way of peace."

THE CANTICLE OF SIMEON

Luke 2:29–32

The canticle, or song, of Simeon is often called the Nunc Dimittis, from the first lines of the song. This is the prayer that Simeon offered when he recognized the infant Jesus as the Messiah. Simeon was an old man, and for many years he had prayed for the Messiah to come. It is a wonderful prayer that is said each evening in Compline, the evening prayer of the Church. It is especially fitting to pray the Canticle of Simeon at the time of the Feast of the Presentation of the Lord on February 2.

"Master, now you are dismissing your servant in peace,
   according to your word;
for my eyes have seen your salvation,
   which you have prepared in the presence
   of all peoples,
a light for revelation to the Gentiles
   and for glory to your people Israel."

RESOURCES FOR PRAYING WITH CHILDREN

In addition to *Children's Daily Prayer*, teachers, principals, and catechists may find these LTP resources to be helpful in their work of developing prayer services and preparing children for Mass and reception of the sacraments.

PREPARING MASSES WITH CHILDREN: 15 EASY STEPS

A resource to assist teachers and catechists in preparing children to participate fully in the Mass.

FROM MASS TO MISSION

A small guide that explains the significance of the Mass for living a Christian life. There is a guide for children and a guide for teens; each has a leader's guide to accompany the book.

THE YEAR OF GRACE LITURGICAL CALENDAR

This annual circular calendar displays the liturgical year. It highlights the color for each liturgical season and provides a visual guide to the major feasts and saints' days throughout the year. Each year, the calendar has beautiful art to illustrate a particular theme or liturgical focus.

CHILDREN'S LITURGY OF THE WORD

An annual publication that offers a guide to help prepare a Liturgy of the Word for children on Sundays and Holydays of Obligation.

BLESSINGS AND PRAYERS THROUGH THE YEAR: A RESOURCE FOR SCHOOL AND PARISH

This is an illustrated collection of prayers and blessings and prayer services, which includes two CD-ROMS of music with vocal instruction and musical accompaniment to facilitate singing.

COMPANION TO THE CALENDAR: A GUIDE TO THE SAINTS, SEASONS, AND HOLIDAYS OF THE YEAR.

An invaluable resource for learning more about the particular saint or feast of the day. This book could be used to help children learn more about their patron saint or saints of special interest.

SCHOOL YEAR, CHURCH YEAR: CUSTOMS AND DECORATIONS FOR THE CLASSROOM

Teachers and catechists who wish to create an environment in the classroom that reflects the liturgical season will find many creative and doable ideas in this book.